# The Drugs Offences Handbook

# The Drugs Offences Handbook

**Tim Moloney QC**
Doughty Street Chambers

**Steven Bird**
Director, Birds Solicitors

**Tom Stevens**
Barrister, Doughty Street Chambers

**Paul Mason**
Barrister, Doughty Street Chambers

**Abigail Bright**
Barrister, Doughty Street Chambers

**Harriet Johnson**
Barrister, Doughty Street Chambers

Bloomsbury Professional

**Bloomsbury Professional**

An imprint of Bloomsbury Publishing Plc

Bloomsbury Professional Ltd
41–43 Boltro Road
Haywards Heath
RH16 1BJ
UK

Bloomsbury Publishing Plc
50 Bedford Square
London
WC1B 3DP
UK

**www.bloomsbury.com**

**BLOOMSBURY and the Diana logo are trademarks of**

**Bloomsbury Publishing Plc**

© Bloomsbury Professional Ltd 2018

**British Library Cataloguing-in-Publication Data**

A catalogue record for this book is available from the British Library.

| ISBN: | PB | 978 1 78043 663 0 |
|---|---|---|
| | Epub | 978 1 78043 664 7 |
| | Epdf | 978 1 78451 160 9 |

Typeset by Phoenix Photosetting, Chatham, Kent
Printed and bound by CPI Group (UK) Ltd, Croydon, CR0 4YY

To find out more about our authors and books visit www.bloomsburyprofessional.com. Here you will find extracts, author information, details of forthcoming events and the option to sign up for our newsletters

# Preface

The aim of this book is to offer a focused guide on drugs offences, sentencing and confiscation. Since our initial proposal for the book, the *Psychoactive Substances Act 2016* has come into force. We have included the relevant provisions for the offences themselves and also matters arising for sentencing and subsequent confiscation.

We have divided the book into three main areas. The first deals with drugs offences. Chapter 1 sets out the issues concerning the manufacture and cultivation of drugs. Chapter 2 focuses upon drug importation offences. Chapters 3, 4, 5 and 6 deal with offences of possession and supply. The liability of occupiers of premises in drugs cases is considered in Chapter 7. The first section of the book concludes in Chapter 8, which discusses difficulties around conspiracy in supply cases, and trans-jurisdictional issues.

The second part of the book is concerned with investigative and evidential issues. Chapter 9 addresses police powers of search and seizure in drugs cases. Chapter 10 deals with the use of forensic and covert evidence and the role of experts.

We conclude in the third section of the book with two chapters on post-conviction matters. In Chapter 11 sentencing for drugs offences are set out, including recent cases on so-called 'cuckoo-ing'. Finally, Chapter 12 deals with the often complex matters surrounding confiscation.

The authors would like to thank all those at Bloomsbury Professional. In particular, Kiran Goss for her expertise, guidance and seemingly never-ending patience with us in getting the book to print.

*Tim Moloney QC*
*Steven Bird*
*Tom Stevens*
*Paul Mason*
*Abigail Bright*
*Harriet Johnson*

# Contents

*Preface*                                                                      *v*

*Table of statutes*                                                            *xv*

*Table of statutory instruments*                                              *xxi*

*Table of EC and International Materials*                                    *xxiii*

*Table of cases*                                                              *xxv*

**1   MANUFACTURE AND CULTIVATION**                                            **1**

Introduction                                                                    1

Medicinal Uses Of Controlled Drugs                                              4

The Meanings Of 'Product' And 'Preparation'                                     5

Cultivation                                                                      8

Defences Available, In Principle, To Accused Persons Involved In
     Manufacture Or Cultivation                                                 9

Use Of Extradition Proceedings As A Means Of Law Enforcement                   12

Summary Of Key Points                                                           13

**2   IMPORTATION**                                                            **15**

The Offences                                                                    15

How The Offence Is Charged                                                      17

Procedure And Sentence                                                          18

Elements Of The Offence                                                         20

     Section 170(1) and 170(2)                                                  20

     The Actus Reus                                                             21

     The Mens Rea                                                               25

Admissibility Issues In Importation Cases                                       27

The Psychoactive Substances Act 2016                                           29

Summary Of Key Points                                                          31

**3   POSSESSION: UNLAWFUL POSSESSION, CONTROL
     AND KNOWLEDGE**                                                           **33**

Introduction                                                                    33

Unlawful Possession                                                             34

     Section 5 of the MDA 1971                                                  34

The Ingredients Of The Offence                                                 35

Custody And/Or Control: The Physical Element Of Possession                     36

Knowledge: The Mental Element Of Possession 40
*Warner* and Possession 41
*Mcnamara*: Simplifying The Law Of Possession 43
Imputing An Intention To Possess 44
*R v Lambert* 46
Mistake As To The Drug Possessed 47
Possession And Memory 47
The Relevance Of Quantity To Possession 48
Where Drugs Have Been Consumed 50
Summary Of Key Points 51

**4    POSSESSION: PROHIBITED DRUGS AND DEFENCES    53**
Proving The Drug Is Prohibited 53
The Legislative Provisions: Section 2 And Schedule 2 53
Temporary Class Drugs Orders 54
The Provisions Of Section 2a And 2b 55
Possession Of A Temporary Class Drug Is Not An Offence 55
The Burden Of Proof: Forensic Analysis 57
Cases Involving Cocaine 58
Forensic Evidence Is Not Always Required 59
Admissions 60
Defences 62
Section 5(4): Lawful Intention 62
Section 28: Lack Of Knowledge 63
The Parameters Of Section 28 (2)–(3) 64
Section 28 And The Burden Of Proof 66
'To Prove': Not A Legal Burden But An Evidential Burden 68
Self–induced Intoxication And The Objective Limb Of A
    Section 28 Defence 70
Section 28 Does Not Apply To Those Charged With
    Conspiracy 71
Lawful Possession 71
Section 7 of the MDA 1971 71
Self-Treatment 72
The Failed Defence Of Medical Necessity 73
Section 10 Of The Misuse Of Drugs Act 1971 76
The Misuse Of Drugs Regulations 76

The Psychoactive Substances Act 2016                                         77
   The Meaning Of Psychoactive Substance                      78
   The Offences In Brief Overview                              78
   Simple Possession Is Not An Offence                         81
   Exemptions                                                  82
Summary Of Key Points                                                        83

**5   SUPPLY AND BEING CONCERNED IN SUPPLY   85**

The Offences                                                                 85
A Brief Overview                                                             86
The Meaning Of Supply                                                        87
   A Physical Transfer Of Control Is Required                  87
   Issuing a Prescription is not an Act of Supply              88
The Supply Must Be To The Benefit Of/For The Purposes Of
   The Recipient                                               89
The Transfer Of Drugs To A Custodian Or Courier Is Not An
   Act Of Supply                                               91
A Custodian Who Returns Drugs Is Guilty Of Supplying Them                    92
The Decision In *Maginnis*                                                   94
Involuntary Possession And Intent To Supply                                  96
Territorial Restrictions On The Provisions Of The Misuse Of
   Drugs Act                                                   97
Supplying Includes Distributing                                              99
   Being in Joint Possession is no Defence                     99
The Case Of *Harris*: Administering Is Not Supplying                        101
Making An Offer To Supply                                                    102
   Scenario 1                                                 103
   Scenario 2                                                 103
   Scenario 3                                                 104
An Offer To Supply Remains Until It Is Either Resiled From
   Or Has Been Completed                                      107
An Offer Of Consumption Is An Offer To Supply                               108
Being Concerned In The Supply/Offer To Supply Drugs                         109
A Broad Construction                                                        110
   The *Hughes* Definition                                    110
Is Proof Of An Actual Supply Of Controlled Drugs Required To
   Be Found Guilty Of Being Concerned In It?                   112
Supply To 'Another'                                                         114
Summary Of Key Points                                                       115

**6    POSSESSION WITH INTENT TO SUPPLY**                      **117**

The Offence                                                      117

Overview                                                         117

An Intention To Supply Does Not Require An Intention To Make
  Financial Gain                                                 118

An Intention To Supply A Different Drug To The One Charged
  Affords No Defence                                             119

An Intention To Supply Need Not Be An Intention To Supply
  Immediately                                                    120

Section 5(3) And Possessing Drugs Not Ready For Harvest          121

Motive Is Irrelevant                                             123

Proving Intention                                                124

The Quantity Of Drugs Possessed                                  124

Expert Evidence On Consumption Patterns                          125

The Admissibility Of Evidence Of An Extravagant Lifestyle/
  Possession of Money                                            128

  Directing the Jury                                             131

Where A Guilty Plea To Possession Is Offered                     132

Aggravated Supply                                                133

Lawful Supply                                                    135

Summary Of Key Points                                            136


**7    OCCUPIERS OF PREMISES**                                   **137**

Overview                                                         137

Being The Occupier Or Concerned In The Management Of
  The Premises                                                   137

Permitting Premises To Be Used For Drug Offending                138

Liability Pursuant To Section 8 Of The 1971 Act                 139

What Constitutes Premises, In Section 8?                         141

  Knowledge                                                      141

Investigatory Powers; Entry, Search And Seizure                 141

Enlarged Investigatory Powers: The Psychoactive Substances
  Act 2016                                                       143

Prohibition Orders: The 2016 Act                                 146

Anti-Social Behaviour (Interim) Orders                           147

Summary Of Key Points                                            147


**8    CONSPIRACY AND CROSS-JURISDICTIONAL
       OFFENCES**                                                **149**

Introduction                                                     149

The Indictment                                                   150

| | |
|---|---|
| What Is An Agreement? | 152 |
| Qualified Agreements | 154 |
| Parties To The Agreement | 155 |
| Criminal Conduct | 157 |
| Mens Rea Of Conspiracy | 160 |
| Impossibility | 163 |
| Proving Agreement | 164 |
| Acquittal of the Co-Conspirator | 165 |
| Jurisdiction | 166 |
| Co-Conspirator Based Abroad | 166 |
| Domestic Conspiracies to Commit an Offence Abroad | 167 |
| Conspiracy Formed Abroad to Commit an Offence in England and Wales | 167 |
| Conspiracy Formed Abroad to Commit an Offence Abroad | 169 |
| Summary Of Key Points | 169 |

**9    SEARCH AND SEIZURE — 171**

| | |
|---|---|
| Powers Of Search And Seizure | 171 |
| Obstruction Of Searches | 175 |
| Return Of Seized Property | 176 |
| Forfeiture And Destruction Of Seized Property | 179 |
| Summary Of Key Points | 180 |

**10   FORENSIC AND COVERT EVIDENCE — 183**

| | |
|---|---|
| Expert Forensic Evidence | 183 |
| Forensic Analysis Of Drugs And Drug Traces | 184 |
| Covert Evidence | 188 |
| Impact Of Non-Compliance | 190 |
| Admissibilty Of Covert Evidence | 192 |
| Covert Policing And Agents Provocateurs | 193 |
| Summary Of Key Points | 195 |

**11   SENTENCING FOR DRUGS OFFENCES — 197**

| | |
|---|---|
| The Sentence Guidelines | 197 |
| Applying The Guidelines | 198 |
| Culpability | 199 |
| Harm | 199 |
| Conspiracy Offences | 200 |

Importation                                                      201
Supplying Or Offering To Supply A Drug                           205
    Class A Drugs                            205
    Class B or Class C drugs                 208
    Prevalence of Supply                     209
    Cuckoo-ing                               210
Production And/Or Cultivation                                    212
Permitting Premises To Be Used For Consumption Of A Drug         216
Possession Of A Controlled Drug                                  216
Sentences For Servicemen And Women                               217
Psychoactive Substances Act 2016                                 218
Ancillary Orders                                                 219
    Confiscation                             219
    Forfeiture                               219
Summary Of Key Points                                            221

**12   RESTRAINT AND CONFISCATION**      **223**

Introduction                                                    223
Restraint Orders                                                224
Confiscation Proceedings                                        228
    Instigation of confiscation proceedings  228
    Procedure                                230
    Provision of Information by Defendant: section 18   230
    Prosecutor's Statement of Information: section 16   231
    Defendant's response to Statement of Information: section 17   232
The Determinations To Be Made By The Court                      233
    Criminal Lifestyle                       233
    Criminal conduct                         235
    Benefit                                  237
    Couriers and custodians                  239
    The Corporate veil                       240
    Joint benefit                            241
    Value                                    241
    Assumptions as to benefit                242
    Recoverable Amount                       243
    Available Amount                         245
    Determination of Extent of Defendant's Interest in Property   246
    Legal aid contributions from Capital     248

Making The Order                                           249
   Time to pay                                            250
   Interest on unpaid sums                                 251
   Period in default                                      251
Variation Of An Order                                       252
   Application by the defendant                            252
   Applications by the prosecution                         253
Enforcement                                                 253
Public Funding For Confiscation Proceedings                 254
Summary Of Key Points                                       255

**Appendix A    Extracts from MDA 1971**                    **257**

**Appendix B    Extracts from PSA 2016**                    **289**

**Appendix C    Extracts from PACE 1984**                   **305**

**Appendix D    Drug Offences Definitive Guideline**        **333**

*Index*                                                     *367*

# Table of statutes

PARA

Anti-Social Behaviour Act
2003 .............................. 7.5–7.54

Channel Tunnel Act 1987.......... 2.8
Child Abduction Act 1984
s 1....................................... 8.39, 8.84
Children and Young Persons Act
1993
s 1......................................... 7.46
Computer Misuse Act 1990 ...... 7.46
Coroners and Justice Act 2009
s 72.................................. 8.87–8.88
Criminal Attempts Act 1981 ..... 8.73
s 1(1)..................................... 2.59
Criminal Justice Act 1988
s 93C(2)................................ 8.9
Criminal Justice (International
Co-operation) Act 1990
s 12.................................... 12.62
(1)(a) .............................. 1.13
(3).................................... 1.14
19...................................... 12.62
23(1).................................. 9.7
(4).................................... 9.7
Sch 2.................................. 12.62
Criminal Justice Act 1993
Part 1 (ss 1–6) ...................... 8.95
Criminal Justice (Terrorism and
Conspiracy) Act 1998.... 8.87–8.88
Criminal Justice Act 2003 ........ 2.64
s 98....................................... 2.61
101 ..................................... 2.61
(1)(d)............................... 2.62
(3).................................... 2.63
258(2B)............................ 12.157
282(2)................................ 2.16
Criminal Justice and Police Act
2001 ................................... 9.1
Part 2 (ss 50–70) .................. 9.1, 9.6
s 50(1)................................... 9.6
(2)....................................... 9.6
Criminal Justice and Public
Order Act 1994
s 36 ................... 10.15–10.17 10.45

PARA

Criminal Law Act 1977.......... 8.1–8.2,
8.100
s 1 ............................ 8.4, 8.17, 8.40,
8.53–8.56,
8.91, 8.96
(1)................................ 8.9, 8.11,
8.29, 8.87–8.89
(a) ........................... 8.50–8.51
(b)............................ 8.72–8.76
1A ................................ 8.87–8.89,
8.100
2(2).............................. 8.31–8.32
3(1).................................... 8.97
4(2).................................... 8.5
5(8).............................. 8.79–8.80
(9).............................. 8.79–8.80
s 8(2).................................... 8.37
Customs and Excise Act 1952
s 304 ............................ 2.10–2.11
Customs and Excise Manage-
ment Act 1979...................
... 1.15–1.17, 2.4, 2.10–2.11
s 3....................................... 2.8
(2)....................................... 2.14
5......................................... 2.77
(2)....................................... 2.28
(3)....................................... 2.28
(6)....................................... 2.28
50 ............................... 2.5, 2.79
68 ....................................... 2.5
70(4).................................... 2.15
(5).................................... 2.13
146(A) ................................ 2.12
154(2).......................... 2.39–2.40
170 ......................... 2.5–2.7, 2.17,
2.21, 2.27, 2.37,
2.47–2.49, 2.56,
2.59–2.60,
2.67–2.68, 2.79
(1) .................. 2.22, 2.24, 2.26
(b)......................... 2.6–2.7,
2.57–2.58
(2) ......................... 2.23–2.26,
2.37, 2.41, 2.79

PARA

Customs and Excise Management Act 1979 – *contd*
s 170(2)(b)............................ 2.43
(4) ............................ 2.15, 2.79
Sch 1.................................... 2.15
(1)(b) ........................... 2.15
(2) ............................... 2.16
2.................................... 2.21

Dangerous Drugs Act 1965
s 2 ...................................... 2.3
3.......................................... 2.3
5 ................................. 7.8–7.10
10........................................ 2.3
Drug Trafficking Act 1994.... 12.1–12.3
s 49(2) ................................. 8.9
65(1) ................................. 9.7
Sch 1
para 4 ............................. 9.7
Drug Trafficking Offences Act
1986 ............................. 12.1–12.2
Drugs (Prevention of Misuse)
Act 1964.......................... 3.6
s 1 ........................................ 3.41
(1)............................... 3.85, 6.81
5.......................................... 2.3
Drugs Act 2005
s 2.................................. 6.39, 6.42

Human Rights Act 1998
s 6 .............................. 10.28, 10.45

Insolvency Act 1986
s 386 .................................... 12.119
Sch 6.................................... 12.119

Judgments Act 1838
s 17 ...................................... 12.152

Magistrates Court Act 1980
s 85 ...................................... 12.165
Magistrates Courts Act 1980
s 76...................................... 7.26
Medicines Act 1968 ............. 1.19–1.20
Misuse of Drugs Act 1971... 1.20, 1.44,
1.55, 1.58, 3.6,
3.41, 3.79,
4.12–4.13, 4.48, 7.40
s 2(1)................................ 4.31, 4.34

PARA

Misuse of Drugs Act 1971 – *contd*
s 2(1)(a) ................................. 4.2
(2).................................... 4.11
2A .................................... 4.8
(2)-(3) ......................... 4.8
(4)(a)-(b)...................... 4.9
B........................................ 4.8
3 ............................... 2.1–2.4,
2.10–2.11, 2.79
(1)................................ 2.1
(b)................................ 5.70
(2)................................ 2.1, 2.3
4 ............................... 1.2, 1.4, 5.6,
5.41, 5.43, 5.98,
5.110, 9.39
(1)................................ 1.2–1.3, 1.6,
1.68, 4.100, 5.5,
5.49, 5.125, 6.1,
6.89, 7.18
(a)................................ 1.2
(b)...................... 1.2, 5.1, 5.100
(2)................................ 1.3, 1.68,
4.57, 4.95, 12.62
(a)................... 1.50–1.51, 8.48
(b)................................ 1.3, 6.25,
8.48, 8.52
(3)...................... 4.57, 4.95, 5.3,
5.122–5.126, 5.143,
6.81, 6.87, 12.62
(a)................... 5.3, 5.26–5.33,
5.77, 5.93, 5.96–5.97,
5.112, 5.117,
5.137, 6.5
(b)................................ 5.3, 5.115,
5.126–5.129,
5.130, 5.132,
5.137–5.138,
5.140–5.141
(c)................................ 5.3, 5.115,
5.118–5.121,
5.130–5.131
4A .................................... 4.128,
6.81–6.88, 6.91
(3) ......................... 6.82–6.83
(5) ................................ 6.83
(6) ......................... 6.84–6.85
(7) ................................ 6.85
(8) ................................ 6.86
5 ................................. 3.7, 3.89

PARA

**Misuse of Drugs Act 1971** – *contd*

s 5(1)...................... 3.7–3.8, 3.12,
3.80, 4.1, 4.20,
4.22, 4.28, 4.49,
4.55, 4.100, 4.104
(2).......................... 1.26, 3.7, 3.9,
3.80, 4.1, 4.20,
4.28, 4.51, 4.75, 4.95
(3)............................ 4.95, 5.4, 5.6,
5.16–5.18, 5.41, 5.43,
5.45–5.48, 5.61–5.63,
5.70, 5.117, 5.143,
6.1–6.5, 6.8, 6.11,
6.15–6.16, 6.20,
6.26–6.31, 6.35,
6.38–6.41, 6.76,
6.91, 12.62
(4).............................. 3.10, 3.65,
4.49–4.55, 4.151
(a)............................ 4.52–4.54
(b).............................. 4.54–4.55
(4A).............................. 6.39, 6.42
(4B).............................. 6.39, 6.42
(4C).............................. 6.39, 6.42
6...................................... 1.40–1.41
(1).............................. 1.40–1.41,
1.47–1.49, 4.100
(2)................................. 1.43, 4.57
7...................... 1.2, 1.4–1.5, 1.40,
1.42, 1.68, 3.7–3.8,
4.97–4.106, 4.121–4.123,
5.1, 6.89, 6.91
(1)(b).............................. 4.100
(2).................................... 4.101
(3)....................................... 1.6,
4.102–4.106, 4.151
(a)................................. 1.68
(b).............................. 1.68
(4).................................... 4.111
(10).................................... 1.5
7A ...................................... 1.2,
1.4–1.5, 1.68
8............................... 7.2, 7.4, 7.7,
7.12–7.14,
7.17–7.24, 7.54, 12.62
(d)....................................... 7.5
9...................................... 4.57, 4.95
10............................ 4.121–4.123
(1)................................... 4.21

PARA

**Misuse of Drugs Act 1971** – *contd*

s 10(2)................................... 4.121
(a) ............................... 7.29
11 ....................................... 7.29
18(2).................................... 2.3
20 ....................................... 12.62
23 ........................... 9.7, 9.17,
9.26, 9.32, 9.41
(2)(a) ............... 9.15, 9.24–9.25
(3)................................... 9.7
(4).......................... 9.22, 9.41
(a) ............................... 9.25
23A ............................. 4.14, 9.8
27 ...................... 9.36, 9.38, 9.40,
11.101, 11.103–11.106,
11.110, 11.112
(1)...................... 9.36, 11.101
(2)................................. 11.101
(3)................................. 11.102
28 ...................... 1.3, 1.40, 1.43,
3.7, 3.10, 3.67, 4.49,
4.57–4.58, 4.61–4.79,
4.83–4.84, 4.89, 4.91,
4.95, 4.138, 4.151,
5.4, 6.1, 6.17
(2)...................... 4.59, 4.69,
4.72, 4.85, 4.89
(3)...................... 4.71, 4.85,
5.92, 5.105
(a) ............................... 3.67,
4.57–4.60, 4.71
(b)(i) ...................... 3.65, 4.71,
4.89, 4.92
(ii) ............................. 4.60
37 ................................ 1.12, 5.74
(1)...................... 1.9, 1.11, 4.4,
4.136, 5.9, 5.71
(a) ............................... 1.13
(3)...................... 3.11, 3.15, 3.89,
4.142, 5.78
Sch 2...................... 1.23, 1.30, 3.89,
4.2–4.3, 4.6, 4.16,
4.19, 4.21, 4.151
Part 1 ...................... 1.25, 4.3
para 1-4...................... 1.23, 1.29
5 .................... 1.23–1.25, 1.28
Part 2 .......................... 4.3
Part 3 .......................... 4.3
Part 4 .......................... 4.4

PARA

**Misuse of Drugs Act 1971** – *contd*
Sch 5
  para 2 .......................... 2.3

**Police (Property) Act 1897**
s 1 ...................... 9.29, 9.35, 9.41
**Police Act 1997** ......................... 10.31
  Part 3 (ss 91–108) ......... 10.18, 10.45
**Police and Criminal Evidence Act 1984**
  Part 1 (ss 1–7) .............. 9.1–9.2, 9.41
  s 1 ............................ 9.2, 9.41
  2 ...................... 9.17–9.18, 9.41
  Part 2 (ss 8–23) ...................... 9.1, 9.5
  s 8 ...................................... 9.5
  16(5) ................................. 9.14
  17 .......................... 7.25–7.27
  17–18 ................................ 9.5
  19–22 ................................ 9.5
  19(4) ................................. 9.35
  20(1) ................................. 9.35
  22 .......................... 9.28, 9.31,
                          9.34–9.35, 9.41
  (2) ................................. 9.35
  32 ...................................... 7.27
  76 ............................ 10.31, 10.45
  78 .................. 9.16, 10.31, 10.45
**Police Reform and Social Responsibility Act 2011**
  s 151 ..................... 2.2, 3.7, 4.6, 9.7
  Sch 17 ................................. 2.2, 4.6
    paras 1 and 6 ..................... 3.7
       1 and 15 ................... 9.7
**Policing and Crime Act 2009**
  Part 4 (ss 34–50) ..................... 7.46
  s 111 ................................. 9.7
  112(2) ................................ 9.7
  Sch 8
    Part 12 ............................ 9.7
    13 ................................. 6.42
**Powers of Criminal Courts (Sentencing) Act 2000**
  s 43(1) ................................. 11.100
  110 ........................... 2.20, 11.32
**Proceeds of Crime Act 2002** ..... 2.21,
                          4.12, 7.46, 9.38,
                          11.96, 12.1–12.6
  s 6(2)–(3) ............................. 12.34
  (4) ................................. 12.41

PARA

**Proceeds of Crime Act 2002** – *contd*
  s 6(5)(b) ............................... 12.41
  7 ........................................ 12.115
  (2) ................................. 12.41
  9(1) ................................. 12.118
  (2) ................................. 12.119
  10 .................. 12.51, 12.76–12.77,
                          12.99–12.100
  10A ..................................... 12.124
  11(1) ................................. 12.146
  (2)–(3) ............................. 12.147
  (5) ................................. 12.149
  (6) ................................. 12.148
  (8) ................................. 12.150
  12 ...................................... 12.152
  14(4) ................................. 12.39
  (5) ................................. 12.39
  (6) ................................. 12.39
  (8) ................................. 12.40
  16 .................... 12.43, 12.49–12.53
  (3) ................................. 12.50
  (4) ................................. 12.51
  (5) ................................. 12.52
  (6A) ................................. 12.53
  17 .................... 12.43, 12.55–12.59
  (1) ................................. 12.55
  (2) ................................. 12.56
  (3) ................................. 12.57
  (6) ................................. 12.58
  18 .................... 12.42, 12.44–12.48
  (1)–(3) ............................. 12.44
  (4) ................................. 12.45
  (6) ................................. 12.46
  (9) ................................. 12.47
  21 ...................................... 12.162
  22 ........................... 12.144, 12.162
  23 ...................................... 12.159
  35 ...................................... 12.165
  (2A) ................................. 12.153
  (3)(b) ............................. 12.165
  40 ...................................... 12.7
  (2) ................................. 12.8
  (3) ................................. 12.9
  (4) ................................. 12.11
  (5) ................................. 12.13
  (6) ................................. 12.14
  (7) ................................. 12.10
  (8) ................................. 12.15
  41 ...................................... 12.6

PARA

**Proceeds of Crime Act 2002** – *contd*
s 41(2) ................................... 12.17
(2A)-(2B) ...................... 12.21
(3) ................................. 12.18
(5) ................................. 12.20
75(1) ................................. 12.61
(2)(b) ............................. 12.65
(2)(c) ............................. 12.65
(3) ................................. 12.68
(4) ................................. 12.69
76 .............................. 12.79–12.82
(1) ................................. 12.71
(4) ................................. 12.78
(7) ................................. 12.78
77 ................................. 12.120
78 ................................. 12.120
81 ................................. 12.122
457 ................................. 9.7
Sch 2 ................. 12.61, 12.63–12.64
para 1 ...................... 9.36, 12.62
(b) .......................... 6.2
10 ............................. 9.36
Sch 12 ................................. 9.7

**Psychoactive Substances Act
2016** ............... 2.79, 4.124–4.126,
7.15, 7.17,
7.40–7.42, 7.47, 12.174
s 2 ......................................... 7.39
(1)(a) ............................. 4.129
(2) ................................. 4.130
(3) ................................. 4.131
3(1) ................................. 4.149
4 ........................................ 4.127,
4.133–4.134, 12.62
4-9 ................................. 4.150
4(1)(a) ............................. 4.134
(b) ............................. 4.134
(c) ............................. 4.134
5 ..................... 4.127, 4.135–4.140,
4.143, 11.97, 12.62
(1)(a) ............................. 4.138
(c) ............................. 4.138
(d) ............................. 4.138
2) ............................. 4.139–4.140
6 ............................... 4.128, 11.97
(10) ............................. 4.148
7 ......................................... 4.127,
4.141–4.144, 12.62
(1)(a) ............................. 4.141

PARA

**Psychoactive Substances Act
2016** – *contd*
s 7(1)(b) ............................... 4.143
8 ......................... 2.71–2.72, 4.127
(1)(a)-(d) .................... 2.73–2.75
(3) ................................. 2.76
(4) ................................. 2.77
9 ................... 4.146, 11.98, 12.62
10(1)(d) ............................. 4.127
(2)(d) ............................. 4.147
11 ................................. 7.48
12 ................................. 11.95
12-35 ......................... 7.43, 7.54
12(1) ................................. 7.49
17(1) ................................. 7.48
36 ................................. 7.33
36-48 ................. 7.32–7.33, 7.54
37 ................................. 7.16
38 ................................. 7.16
41-48 ................................. 7.54
42(2) ......................... 7.34–7.35
56 ................................. 7.44
59(2)(a) ............................. 4.133
(b) ............................. 4.136
(3) ................................. 4.142
Sch 1 ......................... 4.149, 7.39
2 ......................... 4.150–4.151
para 1A ............................. 12.62

**Regulation of Investigatory
Powers Act 2000** ....... 10.27, 10.31
Part 2 (ss 26-48) ........... 10.18–10.20,
10.45
s 26(2) ................................. 10.19
(3)-(5) ............................. 10.19
(8) ......................... 10.25, 10.45
28 ......................... 10.26, 10.45
29 ......................... 10.26, 10.45
48 ................................. 10.23

**Serious Crime Act 2007** ....... 7.45–7.46
Sch 1 ................................. 2.21
**Serious Crime Act 2015**
Sch 4
para 19 ............................. 12.41
**Sexual Offences Act 2003** ......... 7.46
**Street Offences Act 1959** .......... 7.46
**Suicide Act 1961**
s 2 ......................................... 1.53

|  | PARA |  | PARA |
|---|---|---|---|
| Terrorism Act 2006 | 7.46 | Tobacco Products Duty Act 1979 |  |
| Therapeutic Substances Act 1925 | 1.19 | s 1 | 4.149 |

# Table of statutory instruments

PARA

Channel Tunnel (Customs and
Excise) Order 1990, 1990/2167
art 5(1)................................. 2.9
(6)................................. 2.9
Controlled Drugs (Drug
Precursors) (Community
External Trade) Regulations
2008, 2008/296 .......... 1.16–1.17
reg 7(1) ................................ 1.15
Controlled Drugs (Drug Pre-
cursors) (Intra-Community
Trade) Regulations 2008,
2008/295
reg 8 ..................................... 9.9
Criminal Procedure Rules ........ 8.6
Drugs Offences: Definitive
Guideline, February 2012
(Sentencing Council)... 11.1–11.8,
11.13, 11.25, 11.28,
11.31–11.35, 11.37,
11.39–11.41, 11.47–11.50,
11.63–11.72, 11.83–11.94, 11.112
Human Medicines Regulations
2012, 2012/1916................ 4.149
Misuse of Drugs Act 1971
(Temporary Class Drug)
(No 2) Order 2015,
2015/1396......................... 4.15
Misuse of Drugs Act 1971
(Temporary Class Drug)
(No 3) Order 2015,
2015/1929.................... 4.15, 4.19
Misuse of Drugs Act 1971
(Temporary Class Drug)
Order 2012, 2012/980 ....... 4.15
Misuse of Drugs Act 1971
(Temporary Class Drug)
Order 2013, 2013/1294 ..... 4.15
Misuse of Drugs Act 1971
(Temporary Class Drug)
Order 2015, 2015/102 ....... 4.15
Misuse of Drugs Act 1971
(Temporary Class Drug)
Order 2016, 2016/1126 ... 4.15, 4.18

PARA

Misuse of Drugs (Supply to
Addicts) (Amendment)
Regulations 2012, 2012/
2394 ................................. 6.90
Misuse of Drugs (Safe Custody)
(Amendment) (England,
Wales and Scotland) Regu-
lations 2014, 2014/1275..... 6.90
Misuse of Drugs (Designation)
Order 2001, 2001/3997 ..... 4.111
Misuse of Drugs Regulations
1973, 1972/797
reg 4(1) ............................... 4.22
8 ..................................... 4.104
10................................... 4.104
Sch 1.............................. 4.22–4.23
Misuse of Drugs (Safe Custody)
Regulations 1973, 1973/798: 6.90
Misuse of Drugs (Supply to
Addicts) Regulations 1997,
1997/1001 ......................... 6.90
Misuse of Drugs Regulations
2001, 2001/399 ............ 1.42, 6.90
Misuse of Drugs (Amendment)
Regulations 2017, 2017/
631 ................................... 6.90
Psychoactive Substances Act 2016
(Commencement) Regu-
lations 2016, 2016/553........ 7.47
Regulation of Investigatory
Powers (Extension of
Authorisation Provisions:
Legal Consultation) Order
2010, 2010/461 ....... 10.20, 10.22
Regulation of Investigatory
Powers (Covert Human
Intelligence Sources: Code
of Practice) Order 2014,
2014/3119......................... 10.28
Regulation of Investigatory
Powers (Covert Surveillance
and Property Interference:
Code of Practice) Order
2014, SI 2014/3103 ........... 10.28

# Table of EC and International Materials

PARA

EUROPEAN

Council Regulation (EC)
111.2005 on rules for
monitoring trade in drug
precursors
Annex ...................... 1.16–1.17, 9.9
Council Regulation (EC)
273.2004 on drug precursors
art 3 ..................................... 9.9
European Convention on
Human Rights 1950
art 3 .............................. 1.56, 4.85,
4.115–4.116

PARA

European Convention on
Human Rights 1950 – *contd*
art 6 .............................. 4.83, 4.151,
12.107–12.108
(1) ...................... 12.107, 12.168
8 ...................................... 4.110
9 ............................. 4.118, 4.120
Protocol 1
art 1 ................................. 12.27

INTERNATIONAL

BERMUDA
Misuse of Drugs Act 1972 ......... 5.68

# Table of cases

PARA

## A

Attorney General for the Cayman Islands v Roberts [2002] UKPC 18 ....... 4.33–4.34
Attorney General's Reference No.1 of 1981 [1982] QB 848 .......................... 2.41
Attorney General's Reference No.1 of 1998 (1999) 163 JP 390 .................. 2.43–2.44
Attorney General's Reference No.2 of 2004 [2005] 1 WLR 3642 ....... 1.45–1.53, 1.57
Attorney General's Reference No.34 of 2011 [2012] 1 Cr App R (S) 288 ....... 11.43
Attorney General's Reference Nos.15-17 of 2012 [2012] EWCA Crim 1414 ..... 11.8, 11.27, 11.36
Attorney General's Reference Nos.15-17 of 2013 [2013] 1 Cr App R 52 ........ 11.24

## B

B (A) Minor v DPP [2000] 2 AC 428 ................................................................. 3.63
Bird v Adams [1972] Crim LR 174 .............................................................. 4.42–4.43
Black v DPP [1995] COD 381 ........................................................................ 9.10
Bonner v DPP [2004] EWHC 2415 ............................................................. 9.19–9.20

## C

Cassel v The Queen [2016] UKPC 19 ............................................................ 8.35
Chief Constable of Mersyside v Owens [2012] EWHC 1515 (Admin) ........... 9.31
Complaint of Surveillance, Re a [2014] 2 All ER 576 ................................... 10.24
CPS v Piper [2011] EWHC 3570 Admin ............................................. 12.130–12.135
Criminal Practice Directions 2015 [2015] EWCA Crim 1567 ........................ 10.3

## D

DPP v Brooks [1974] 2 WLR 899 .................................................................... 3.1
DPP v Goodchild [1978] 2 All ER 161 ........................................................... 4.5
DPP v Meaden [2003] EWHC 3005 ............................................................... 9.21
DPP v Nock [1978] AC 979 ...................................................................... 8.74–8.75
DPP v P (1991) 93 Cr App R 267 ................................................................... 6.68

## F

Fisher v Bell [1961] 1 QB 394 ........................................................................ 5.116
Foster v Attard (1986) 83 Cr App R 214 ........................................................ 9.14
French v DPP [1997] COD 174 .................................................................. 9.13, 9.27

## G

Ghani v Jones [1970] 1 QB 693 ..................................................................... 9.30
Gough v Chief Constable of the West Midlands Police, *The Times*, 4 March 2004 ....................................................................................................... 9.34
Gwilliam v DPP [2010] EWHC 3312 ............................................... 4.37–4.38, 10.1

## H

Haggard v Mason [1976] 1 WLR 187 ............................. 5.94–5.97, 11.108
Hambleton v Callinan and Others [1968] 3 WLR 235 ..................... 3.84–3.86, 3.88

PARA

Harris (Kevin Arthur) v Cox (Joseph) [1996] 1 Cr App R 369 ........................ 1.12
Hodder v DPP; Matthews v DPP [1990] Crim LR 26 ............................. 1.25–1.29
Holmes v Chief Constable of Merseyside [1976] Crim LR 125................. 5.73–5.75
Howarth v Commissioner of Police of the Metropolis [2012] ACD 41 ........... 9.3

**J**

Jeffrey v Black [1978] QB 490 ...................................................................... 9.16
Josephs (Ivan Dick) and Christie (Ransford) v The Queen (1977) 65 Cr App R
    253 ........................................................................................................... 7.12

**K**

Keane v Gallagher [1980] SLT 144................................................. 3.80–3.82
Kerr v HM Advocate (1986) JC 41 ................................................... 5.132

**L**

Lloyd v Bow Street Magistrates' Court [2003] EWHC 2294 Admin ............... 12.168
Lockhart v Hardie [1994] SCCR 722 ................................................ 6.6, 6.19–6.22
Lockyer v Gibb [1967] 2 QB 243 ................................................. 3.37–3.38

**M**

McCarthy v Chief Constable of Northern Ireland [2016] NICA 36 ................ 9.31
McKenzie v Skeen (1983) SLT 121 ..................................................... 4.74
MacNeil v HM Advocate (1986) JC 146 .............................................. 2.42
Mellor v Monahan [1961] Crim LR 175 ............................................. 5.116
Michaels v Highbury Corner Magistrates' Court [2009] EWHC 2928
    (Admin) .................................................................................................. 9.18
Mogford v The Queen, 1970, Glamorgan Assizes, unreported ..................... 7.8–7.10
Mulcahy v R (1868) LR 3 HL 306 ................................................. 8.77
Murray v United Kingdom (1996) 22 EHRR 29 ............................................. 10.17

**O**

Olah v Hungary, 27 April 2016, unreported, QBD (Admin) .......................... 3.86

**P**

Partridge v Crittenden [1968] 1 WLR 1204 ..................................... 5.116
Prest v Petrodel Resources Ltd [2013] 2 AC 415, SC ................................ 12.92

**R**

R v Absolam (1989) 88 Cr App R 332 ..................................................... 9.16
R v Adcock [2016] EWCA Crim 1272 ..................................................... 11.46
R v Ahmad [2014] UKSC 36 ........................................................ 12.95–12.96
R v Ajayi and Others [2017] EWCA Crim 1011 ................................. 11.59–11.63
R v Akinsete [2012] EWCA Crim 2377 ........................................... 5.133–5.139
R v Allpress [2009] EWCA Crim 8 ................................. 12.84–12.85, 12.87
R v Altham [2006] Cr App R 8, CA ........................... 1.55–1.56, 1.59, 4.113–4.116
R v Anderson [1986] AC 27 ................................................. 8.53–8.57, 8.67
R v AP; R v U Ltd [2008] 1 Cr App R 39, CA ............................................. 12.27
R v Ardalan [1972] 1 WLR 463 ................................................. 2.36, 2.50

R  v Ashdown  (Robert  James);  Howard  (Leonard  Edward);  Howard  (Judith
    Mary); Stuart (Michael Adrian) (1974) 59 Cr App R 193, CA .................    7.11
R  v Ashton-Rickardt [ 1978] 1 All ER 173..............................................    4.74–4.79
R  v Askew [1987] Crim LR 584 ..............................................................    11.108
R  v Aziz [2012] Crim LR 801.................................................................    1.61
R  v B [2008] EWCA Crim 1374..............................................................    12.29
R  v Bagnall [2012] EWCA Crim 677 ......................................................    12.76–12.77
R  v Bailey & Smith [1993] 3 All ER 513 .................................................    10.35
R  v Bajwa [2012] 1 WLR 601 .................................................................    2.27
R  v Baker, [2009] EWCA Crim 535..........................................................    5.127–5.129
R  v Bala [2016] EWCA Crim 560 ...........................................................    8.32
R  v Balogun [1997] Crim LR 500.............................................................    2.70
R  v Bamford [2013] 1 Cr App R 4...........................................................    11.73–11.77
R  v Batt [1994] Crim L R 592.....................................    6.59–6.63, 6.65, 6.67
R  v Bayliss [2013] EWCA Crim 1067 .......................................................    11.46
R  v Beard [1975] Crim LR 92 ..................................................    9.37, 11.103
R  v Bell [2011] EWCA Crim 6.................................................................    2.36
R  v Black 2009 EWCA Crim 754..............................................................    11.26
R  v Blake (1979) 68 Cr App R 1..............................................    5.118–5.121
R  v Bland (1987) 151 JP 857.............................3.27, 3.31, 3.33–3.34
R  v Boardman (1975) AC 421 .................................................................    2.64
R  v Bondzie [2016] EWCA Crim 552 ....................    11.52–11.56, 11.112
R  v Bonython (1984) 38 SASR 45 ...........................................    6.55–6.56
R  v Boothe (1987) 9 Cr App R 8.............................................................    11.108
R  v Boughton-Fox [2014] EWCA Crim 227 ...........................................    12.4
R  v Bourne (1952) 36 Cr App R 125.........................................................    5.23
R  v Boyake [2012] EWCA Crim 838.............................    11.8–11.9, 11.28, 11.30
R  v Boyesen [1982] AC 768 ....................................    3.3, 3.12, 3.61, 3.75
R  v Boyle Transport (Northern Ireland) Ltd [2016] 2 Cr App R (S) 11, CA....    12.92
R  v Briggs-Price [2009] UKHL 19............................................    12.73–12.74
R  v Brissac 4 East, 164...........................................................................    8.77
R  v Bristol [2007] EWCA Crim 3214........................................................    9.17
R  v Bryan, 8 November 1984, unreported .....................................    6.45–6.47, 6.51
R  v Buchan [1964] 1 WLR 365................................................................    10.34
R  v Buckley & Lane (1979) 69 Cr App R 371 ................................    5.74–5.80, 5.83
R  v Buckman [1997] 1 Cr App R (S) 325 .......................................................    12.128
R  v Bussell [1972] 1 WLR 64...................................................................    3.73
R  v Byrne [2003] EWCA Crim 1073.......................................    10.42–10.43
R  v Caippara (1988) 87 Cr App R 316.........................................    2.36, 2.42
R  v Carey [1990] 20 NSWLR 292...............................................    5.13, 5.58
R  v Carver [1978] QB 472.........................................................    3.79, 3.81
R  v Cavendish [1961] 1 WLR 1083...............................................    3.14, 3.22
R  v Chalkley & Jeffries [1998] 2 Cr App R 79.........................................    10.37
R  v Chandler [2002] EWCA Crim 3167 .................................................    10.41
R  v Chatwood & Others [1980] 70 Cr App R 39.........................    4.42–4.43
R  v Chief Constable of Lancashire, ex p. Parker 97 Cr.App R 90 ....................    9.35
R  v Clark [2011] EWCA Crim 15 ............................................................    12.88
R  v Clough 2009 EWCA Crim 1669..........................................................    11.26
R  v Cogan [1976] QB 217 .......................................................................    5.23

PARA

R v Compton [2002] EWCA Crim 2835 .............................................. 10.12, 10.16
R v Conway and Burkes [1994] Crim LR 826 .............................. 3.27, 3.31–3.33
R v Cooke [1986] AC 909 ....................................................................... 8.12
R v Coughlan, 12 May 1997, unreported...................................................... 2.36
R v Courtie [1984] AC 463...................................................................... 2.56
R (on the application of Wright) v Crown Prosecution Service [2015] EWHC
    628 (Admin)...................................................................................... 10.2
R v Cuncliffe [1986] Crim LR 547 ....................................................... 1.33–1.35
R v Cuthbertson [1981] AC 470...................................... 9.39, 11.103–11.105
R v D [2009] EWCA Crim 584..................................................... 8.3, 8.24
R v Da Silva [2006] EWCA Crim 1654 ...................................................... 4.134
R v Dang [2014] EWCA Crim 348...................................................... 8.44–8.52
R v Delaney (1989) 88 Cr App R 388................................................ 9.16
R v Delgado [1984] 1 WLR 89 ........................................................ 5.16–5.18
R v Demsey (1986) 82 Cr App R 291 ................... 5.26–5.34, 5.48–5.50
R v Denslow [1998] Crim LR 566...................................................... 5.80–5.84
R v Descombre [2013] 2 Cr App R 51 ............................................. 11.78–11.82
R v Dhillon [2000] Crim LR 760 .................................................. 5.111–5.116
R v Djahit [1999] 2 Cr App R 142.................................................... 11.2
R v Dlugosz & Ors [2013] EWCA Crim 2..................................................... 10.4
R v Drew, 2000, unreported....................................................... 8.13–8.16
R v Dunbar [1981] 1 WLR 1536................................................. 4.103–4.106
R v Duncanson [2016] EWCA Crim 1537...................................... 11.56
R v Dyer [2014] 2 Cr App R 11....................................................... 11.2, 11.42
R v Edwards [1991] Crim LR 45 ............................................... 8.57
R v Edwards [2001] 9 Archbold News.......................................... 6.48–6.51, 6.54
R v Faruqe and Anwar 2015 EWCA Crim 179 .......................................... 11.8
R v Finch (1993) 14 Cr App R 226.............................................. 6.32–6.33
R v Fleur [2004] EWCA Crim 2372 ........................................... 10.13
R v Flynn [2016] EWCA Crim 201 ............................... 12.140–12.142
R v Forde (1985) 81 Cr App R 19............................................... 9.23
R v Fowles [2005] EWCA Crim 97 ............................................... 12.86
R v Gale [2011] 1 WLR 2760 .................................................. 12.75
R v Garjo [1985] EWCA Crim 1169 ........................................ 9.23–9.24
R v Gill [1993] 97 Cr App R 215........................................... 5.106–5.107
R v Glynn Edwards [2005] 2 Cr App R 29................................. 2.29
R v Goddard [2012] EWCA Crim 1756.................................... 8.70–8.71
R v Goodard [1992] Crim LR 588.................................. 5.98–5.100, 5.106
R (AlFawwaz) v Governor of Brixton Prison [2002] 1 AC 556...................... 8.94
R v Grant [1996] 1 Cr App R 73 ........................................ 6.71
R v Green [1976] QB 985.......................................... 2.34–2.37
R v Greenfield (1984) 78 Cr App R 179 ........................................ 5.45–5.48
R v Greensmith [1983] 1 WLR 1124........................................ 4.33
R v Griffin [2009] Cr App R (S) 587.................................... 12.145
R v Griffiths (1966) 1 QB 589.................................... 8.20–8.21
R v GS [2005] EWCA Crim 887 ........................................ 10.27
R v Happe [2011] 1 Cr App R 14................................ 11.43
R v Hardy [2003] 1 Cr App R 30, CA.................................... 10.25
R v Harmes & Crane [2006] EWCA Crim 928.......................... 10.29, 10.40

  PARA

R v Harris (Janet Marjorie) [1968] 1 WLR 769 ........................................ 5.85–5.87
R v Healey [2013] 1 Cr App R 33................................................................ 11.4, 11.82
R v Hennessey (1979) 68 Cr App R 419 ........................................................ 2.55
R v Hill (1993) 96 Cr App R 456.................................................................. 4.39–4.40
R v Hodges [2003] 2 Cr App R 15................................................................ 6.51–6.55
R v Hollinshead (1985) 80 Cr App R 285 .................................................... 8.40, 8.45
R v Hughes (1985) 81 Cr App R 344..................... 5.117, 5.122–5.126, 5.130–5.131
R v Hunt [1987] AC 352............................................... 4.2, 4.22, 4.24–4.27
R v Hussain [1969] 2 QB 567 .................................................. 2.54–2.55, 2.58
R v Hussain [2002] EWCA Crim 6............................................................... 8.9–8.11
R v Hussain (Shabbir) [2010] EWCA Crim 970 ...................................... 5.36–5.42, 5.65
R v Ibrahima [2005] EWCA Crim 1436 ............................ 6.7, 6.9–6.14, 6.44, 6.57
R v ICR Haulage Ltd [1944] KB 551............................................................. 8.35
R v Ilomuanya (2005) EWCA Crim 58......................................................... 2.70
R v Islam [2009] UKHL 30........................................................................... 12.98
R v Jackson [2000] 1 Cr App R 97 ............................................................... 8.13–8.14
R v Jakeman (1983) 76 Cr App R 223........................................................... 2.31, 2.46
R v Jaramillo [2013] 1 Cr App R 110 ........................................................... 11.27
R v Johncock [2016] EWCA Crim 2218........................................................ 11.56
R v Jones [2010] EWCA Crim 915 ............................................................... 10.44
R v Kahn (1983) 76 Cr App R 29 ................................................................. 11.109
R v Kahn [2011] EWCA Crim 2049.............................................................. 11.26
R v Kenning [2008] EWCA Crim 1534................................... 8.41, 8.45, 8.48–8.49
R v Khalid [2017] EWCA Crim 592.............................................................. 11.56
R v Khan (Sultan) [1997] AC 558................................................................. 10.31
R v Khan [2013] EWCA Crim 2230.............................................................. 10.30
R v Khan and others [2013] EWCA Crim 800............................... 11.14–11.20
R v King [1978] Crim LR 228....................................................................... 5.119
R v Lambert [2002] 2 AC 545 ............................................. 3.63–3.65, 4.83–4.88
R v Lazarus [2004] EWCA Crim 2297.......................................................... 12.86
R v Leeson [2000] 1 Cr App R 233................................. 3.67, 4.46–4.47, 6.15–6.18
R v Lewis [1988] 87 Cr App R 270................................................ 3.56–3.58, 3.62
R v Littleford [1978] Crim LR 48................................................................. 9.11–9.12
R v Llewellyn (1985) 7 Cr App R 225........................................... 11.107–11.108
R v Longman & Cribben [1981] 72 Cr App 121 ............................. 8.38, 8.81, 8.83
R v Longman [1988] 1 WLR 619.................................................................. 9.14
R v Looseley [2001] UKHL 53 ........................................... 10.31, 10.39, 10.42
R v Lovelock [1997] Crim LR 821 ............................................................... 6.72–6.73
R v Lunnon [2004] EWCA Crim 1125.......................................................... 12.86
R v McGowan [1990] Crim LR 399 .............................................................. 4.96
R v McIntosh [2011] EWCA Crim 1501 ....................................................... 12.115
R v McNamara & McNamara [1998] Crim LR 278................... 3.34, 3.50–3.53, 3.59
R v McNamara [1988] 87 Cr App R 246 ....................................... 3.4, 3.12, 6.16
R v Maginnis [1987] AC 303...................................... 5.10, 5.13, 5.31, 5.34,
                                                                5.42, 5.50–5.59, 5.61
R v Malik [2000] 2 Cr App R 8 ................................................................... 6.71
R v Manning [1999] QB 980 ....................................................................... 8.94
R v Marriott (Charles Percival) [1971] 1 WLR 187...................................... 3.83
R v Martin & Brimecome [2014] EWCA Crim 1940 ................. 5.133, 5.140–5.141

PARA

R v Martin (Dwain Ashley) [2014] EWCA Crim 1940 .................................. 5.124
R v Martindale [1996] 1 WLR 1042.......................................................... 3.71–3.72
R v Mashaollahi [2001] 1 Cr App R 6 ........................................................ 11.31
R v May [2008] UKHL 28 ............................................ 12.80–12.82, 12.84, 12.94
R v McDonnell [1966] 1 QB 233................................................................. 8.36
R v Mealey (1974) 60 Cr App R 59 ............................................................ 10.38
R v Mehta [2012] EWCA Crim 2824 ......................................................... 8.18
R v Melim [2014] EWCA Crim 1915........................................................... 11.46
R v Meyrick and Ribuffi (1930) 21 Cr App R 94....................................... 8.24, 8.86
R v Mills [1963] 2 WLR 137...................................................................... 5.14–5.15
R (on the application of Nicklinson) v Ministry of Justice; R. (on the application
    of Lamb) v Ministry of Justice; R (on the application of AM) v DPP [2015]
    AC 657............................................................................................ 1.53
R v Mitchell [1992] Crim LR 723 ............................................... 5.88, 5.101–5.106
R v Moon [2004] EWCA Crim 2872 .................................................. 10.32, 10.43
R v Moore [1979] Crim LR 789.................................................... 5.117–5.119
R v Morgan [1977] Crim LR 488 ............................................... 9.38, 11.108
R v Morgan [2009] 1 Cr App R (S) 60........................................................ 12.37
R v Morris [1995] 2 Cr App R 69................................................................ 6.67–6.70
R v Murphy [2002] EWCA Crim 1768 ....................................................... 4.52
R v Neale and others [1984] 3 All ER 156 ...................... 2.24–2.26, 2.37–2.39, 2.50
R v Nguyen (Khin Quoc) [2010] EWCA Crim 2658................................... 5.116
R v Panayi [1989] 1 WLR 187 ................................................................. 2.48–2.49
R v Panton [2001] EWCA Crim 611 ........................................................ 5.59–5.62
R v Parnell (1881) 14 Cox 508.................................................................. 8.86
R v Patel, 7 August 1991, unreported........................................................ 8.68
R v Pearce [1996] Crim LR 442 ............................................ 9.40, 11.110–11.111
R v Pearce [2001] EWCA Crim 2834 ........................................................ 8.32
R v Peaston [1979] 69 Cr App R 203 ....................................................... 3.20–3.21
R v Peters (1995) 2 Cr App R 77 ............................................................. 2.66–2.68
R v Pitts and Others [2014] EWCA Crim 1615 ........................................ 11.20
R v Plunkett (Daniel) & Plunkett (James) [2013] 2 Cr App R 2, CA.............. 10.23
R v Prior [2004] EWCA Crim 1147 ......................................... 5.108–5.110
R v Quale and Others [2005] EWCA Crim 1415................................. 4.108–4.115
R v Reed [1982] Crim LR 819................................................................... 8.27–8.28
R v Reid [2013] EWCA Crim 1844 .......................................................... 8.23, 8.25
R v Ribeyre (1982) 4 Cr App R 165 ......................................................... 11.108
R v Roberts (1987) 78 Cr App R 41 ...................................... 8.38, 8.82–8.83
R v Roberts [1997] 1 Cr App R 217........................................................... 10.36
R v Roberts [1998] 1 Cr App R 441........................................................... 8.7
R v Rosenberg [2006] EWCA Crim 6........................................................ 10.33
R v Saik [2006] UKHL 18 ....................................................................... 8.29
R v Sale [2013] EWCA Crim 1306 .......................................................... 12.90
R v Sanchez-Canadas [2013] 1 Cr App R 114 ........................................... 11.44
R v Sanghera and Others 2016 EWCA Crim 94 ....................................... 11.26
R v Sansom (1991) 2 QB 130.................................................................... 8.94
R v Seager and Blatch [2009] EWCA Crim 1303....................................... 12.90
R v Searle [1971] Crim LR 592 ............................................................... 3.28–3.29
R v Shabir [2008] EWCA 1809................................................................. 12.37

PARA

R v Sherry [1993] Crim LR 536 .............................................................. 8.39, 8.84
R v Shillam [2013] EWCA Crim 160 ...................................................... 8.19
R v Shivpuri (1987) AC 1 ...................................................................... 2.57–2.59
R v Simms (1987) 9 Cr App R (S) 8 ....................................................... 11.108
R v Siracusa (1990) 90 Cr App R 340 ............................................. 2.55, 8.64–8.68
R v Sivaramen [2009] 1 Cr App R (S) 80 ............................................... 12.84
R v Smith [1973] QB 924 ...................................................................... 2.32–2.33
R v Smith [2004] EWCA Crim 631 ......................................................... 8.93–8.94
R v Stevens [1981] Crim LR 568 ............................................................ 1.29–1–32
R v Strong and Berry [1989] 86(10) LSG 41 ........................................... 3.30
R v Suski [2016] EWCA Crim 24 ............................................................ 8.32
R v Szrajber 15 Cr App R (S) 821, CA ................................................... 12.153
R v Taaffe [1983] 2 All ER 625 CA ........................................................ 2.53–2.54
R v Taaffe [1984] AC 539 HL ................................................................. 2.52, 2.54
R v Talebi [2013] 2 Cr App R 49 ........................................................... 11.31
R v Taylor [1986] Crim LR 680 ............................................................. 5.19–5.21
R v Taylor [2001] EWCA Crim 2263 ...................................................... 4.117–4.120
R v Testouri [2003] EWCA Crim 3735 ................................................... 8.38
R v Turner [2013] EWCA Crim 642 ....................................................... 10.21
R v Walker [1987] Crim LR 565 ............................................................. 1.36–1.39
R v Wall [1974] 1 WLR 930 ................................................................... 2.30–2.32
R v Warner [1969] 2 AC 256 ........................................ 3.12, 3.36, 3.41–3.45,
                                                  3.47–3.51, 3.53–3.54, 3.63, 4.48
R v Watts and Stack (1980) 70 Cr App R 187 .......................................... 2.40
R v Waya [2012] UKSC 51 ...................................................................... 12.41
R v Whitehead [1982] QB 1272 .............................................................. 2.10–2.11
R v Whittington [2009] EWCA Crim 1641 ....................... 12.113–12.114, 12.117
R v Willis, 29 January 1979, unreported ................................................. 2.68–2.69
R v Worsell [1970] 1 WLR 111 ............................................................... 3.77
R v Wright [1976] 62 Cr App R 169 ........................................................ 3.47
R v Wright [1994] Crim LR 55 ............................................................... 6.63–6.68
R v Wright [2011] 2 Cr App R 15 ........................................................... 6.24–6.31
R v X [1994] Crim L 827 ....................................................................... 6.35–6.36
R v Yeardley [2000] 2 Cr App R 141 ...................................................... 6.76–7.80
R v Young [1984] 1 WLR 654 ................................................................. 4.92–4.94
RE v United Kingdom 63 EHRR 2 .......................................................... 10.22

**S**

S (Restraint Order), Re [2005] 1 WLR 1338, CA ................................... 12.26
Salmon v HM Advocate 1999 JC 67 ................................................ 4.61–4.71, 4.73
Salomon v A. Salomon & Co. Ltd [1897] AC 22, HL ............................... 12.92
Scopelight Ltd v Chief Constable of Northumbria [2010] 1 Cr App R 19 ....... 9.33
Seymour v The Queen [2007] UKPC 59 ................................................. 5.67–5.69
Smith v HM Advocate [2008] HCJAC 7 ................................................. 10.14
Somchai Liangsiriprasert v Government of the United States of America [1991]
    1 AC 225 ..................................................................... 8.92, 8.94, 8.99

**T**

Tansley v Painter [1969] Crim LR 139 ................................................... 3.26

PARA

Tao (Ben Nien) v The Queen [1977] QB 141 .......................................... 7.4–7.7, 7.10

**W**

Warner v Metropolitan Police Commissioner [1969] 2 AC 256 .................... 3.5, 6.16
Webb v Chief Constable of Merseyside Police [2000] QB 427 ........................ 9.32
Webber v CPS [2006] EWHC 2893 (Fam) ....................................................... 12.136

**Y**

Yip ChieuChung v The Queen [1995] 1 AC 111 ....................................... 8.58–8.63

# 1   Manufacture and Cultivation

Abigail Bright

## Introduction

### 1.1

The manufacture and cultivation of controlled drugs in the UK runs parallel to the regulation of medicinal products. Manufacture and cultivation of controlled drugs should not be confused with, and is discrete to, such medicinal and – generally stated – pharmaceutical, regulation.

### 1.2

*Section 4* of the *Misuse of Drugs Act 1971* (*MDA 1971*) stipulates what is the basis for the statutory restriction on production and supply of controlled drugs. What amounts to 'production' is key to grasping the legal prohibition on the manufacture and cultivation of controlled drugs. *Section 4(1)* of the *MDA 1971* specifies:

> 'Subject to any regulations under section 7 of this Act [or any provision made in a temporary class drug order by virtue of section 7A] for the time being in force, it shall not be lawful for a person—
>
> (a)   to produce a controlled drug; or
>
> (b)   to supply or offer to supply a controlled drug to another.'

### 1.3

*Section 4(2)* of the *MDA 1971* clarifies that liability arising from production of a controlled drug, in contravention of *s 4(1)*, is subject to *s 28* of the *MDA 1971*. *Section 4(2)(b)* thereby makes clear that it is an offence for a person [emphasis added] 'to be concerned in the production of such a drug in contravention of that subsection by another.'

### 1.4

Exposure to the risk of criminal liability conferred by *s 4* of the *MDA 1971* is to be read jointly and together with *ss 7* and *7A* of the Act. *Section 7* ('Authorisation of activities otherwise unlawful under foregoing provisions') specifies the power of the Secretary of State to make such other provisions

1

(whether the Secretary of State elects to state prohibitions or elects to confer permissions) as the Secretary of State thinks fit.

**1.5**

*Section 7A* ('Temporary class drug orders: power to make further provision') is to similar purpose: it reserves to the Secretary of State power to make orders within the statutory scheme of the *MDA 1971*. *Sections* 7 and *7A* together do the heavy-lifting of statutory construction of limitations on liability for being involved in the manufacture and cultivation of a controlled drug: *s 7(10)* specifies that 'reference to "controlled drugs" does not include a reference to temporary class drugs'.

**1.6**

What 'temporary class drugs' are itemised in *s 7A*? *Section 7(3)* makes clear that the Secretary of State is to exercise any such legislating with an express intention foremost in mind. *Section 7(3)* provides:

'Subject to subsection (4) below, the Secretary of State shall so exercise his power to make regulations under subsection (1) above as to secure—

(a)   that it is not unlawful under section 4(1) of this Act for a doctor, dentist, veterinary practitioner or veterinary surgeon, acting in his capacity as such, to prescribe, administer, manufacture, compound or supply a controlled drug, or for a pharmacist or a person lawfully conducting a retail pharmacy business, acting in either case in his capacity as such, to manufacture, compound or supply a controlled drug; and

(b)   that it is not unlawful under section 5(1) of this Act for a doctor, dentist, veterinary practitioner, veterinary surgeon, pharmacist or person lawfully conducting a retail pharmacy business to have a controlled drug in his possession for the purpose of acting in his capacity as such.'

**1.7**

The meanings of 'manufacture' and 'cultivation', unsurprisingly, have been construed by the courts consistent with an approach of purposive interpretation. The context specific to this is the presumptive prohibition on, and operative deterrence of, involvement in controlled drugs. The courts readily resort to the mischief rule of statutory construction of criminal liability when interpreting what meanings should be accorded, for the purpose of recognising individual liability, to statutory definitions.

**1.8**

The policy of the law – the prohibition on manufacture and cultivation of controlled drugs and, consequentially, deterrence – underpins all legislation and judicial adjudication on point of manufacture and cultivation of controlled drugs. This is consistent with the overriding imperatives of government and policing initiatives, both national and international, aimed at eradicating the circulation of controlled drugs.

**1.9**

What is the proper interpretation of *s 37(1)* of the *MDA 1971* regarding production of cannabis? Does production mean no more than mere cultivation? The short point is that production does indeed have a deliberately wider meaning than mere cultivation.

**1.10**

There is express prohibition of involvement in (handling and coming into possession of) substances that are useful for the manufacture of controlled drugs: for example, as a base or otherwise as a constituent of manufacture. This is separate to prohibitions in primary UK domestic legislation on the manufacture and cultivation of controlled drugs.

**1.11**

*Section 37(1)* of the *MDA 1971* provides that production of a controlled drug means production of it in the very widest meaning of 'production': production by manufacture, production by cultivation, or, indeed, production by any other method. 'Any other method' is to be understood with sufficient comprehension so as to include the preparation of cannabis plants whereby those parts of the plants are discarded which were always intended to be discarded because not usable, whilst those parts which are usable are not discarded.

**1.12**

Stripping of cannabis plants after harvest of those plants amounts to 'production' of a controlled drug, contrary to liability contemplated by *s 37* of *MDA 1971*: *Harris (Kevin Arthur) and Cox (Joseph)* [1996] 1 Cr App R 369, CA, Collins J, Leggatt LJ, Judge Capstick QC. The approach in *Harris* and *Cox* continues to hold good, having been cited with approval in much more recent decisions.

**1.13**

For the purposes of the *MDA 1971*, 'production' is at the heart of what is really intended when reference is made to the manufacture and cultivation of controlled drugs. Within 'production' are concepts such as 'preparation'. *The Criminal Justice (International Co-operation) Act 1990 (CJA 1990)* mirrors and closely tracks this approach of the *MDA 1971*. In *s 12* subs (1)(a) of the *CJA 1990*, the term 'manufacture' is to be contrasted with the broader term 'production', consistently with 'production' appearing in subs (1) of the *CJA 1990*.

**1.14**

Accordingly, subs (3) of the *CJA 1990* should be read such that 'production' is equated with the meaning given to the same word in the *Misuse of Drugs Act 1971*. Consideration is given, below, to how cultivation of a controlled drug is probably not a process of manufacture.

**1.15**

Specific provision in law is made for the control of substances useful for the manufacture of drugs. In this regard, the *Customs and Excise Management Act 1979* (*CEMA 1979*) falls to be read together with reg 7(1) of the Controlled Drugs (Drug Precursors) (Community External Trade) Regulations 2008 (SI 2008/296).

**1.16**

The mischief at which *CEMA 1979* in combination with the 2008 Regulations is aimed is what is termed 'certain drug precursors'. The 2008 Regulations specify that 'certain drug precursors' are a specified substance useful for the manufacture of controlled drugs. 'Certain drug precursors' are listed in Category 1 of the Annex to Council Regulation (EC) No. 111/2005. The 2008 Regulations require operators concerned in the export of a drug precursor to have a valid export authorisation.

**1.17**

*CEMA 1979* together with the 2008 Regulations specify which scheduled substances [scheduled for the purpose of Category 1 of the Annex to Council Regulation (EC) No. 111/2005] shall be 'deemed' to be imported into the UK contrary to a restriction, presently, unless otherwise stated, in force, where any such importation is without the requisite authorisation.

# Medicinal uses of controlled drugs

**1.18**

An overview of the manufacture and cultivation of controlled drugs would be incomplete without at least having an eye to the regulatory landscape that applies to legal governance of medicinal products.

**1.19**

Medicinal products have been regulated in the UK since the coming into force of the *Therapeutic Substances Act 1925*. Greater regulatory control of the creation and circulation of medicinal products was secured with enactment of the *Medicines Act 1968*. The 1968 Act itself dovetails with the raft of regulatory systems driven by European legislation, finding effect in English law via direct and indirect legal implementation.

**1.20**

There is common use and interpretation of terms as between the *MDA 1971* and the *Medicines Act 1968*. In the UK, every aspect of the design, testing, promotion and marketing of medicines and medicinal products, including medical devices such as prosthetic components, is now closely regulated.

**1.21**

In the UK, the Medicines and Healthcare Products Regulatory Agency (the MHRA) is the designated and competent authority for assessing whether manufacturers and their medical devices meet the relevant legislative requirements. The MHRA is an executive agency of the Department of Health: it regulates medicines, medical devices and blood components for transfusion in the UK.

**1.22**

The relevant regulatory authority, will only allow a product to be put (and, thereafter, maintained) on the market if it is satisfied that the product meets appropriate standards of safety, efficacy and quality. Those standards are reviewed and revised at such intervals as the Secretary of State thinks fit. Those standards are published.

## The meanings of 'product' and 'preparation'

**1.23**

Fungus containing psilocin or an ester of psilocin (popularly known as 'magic mushrooms') is now listed in Sch 2 of the *MDA 1971*. Prior to that listing, Sch 2 (Pt I, para 5) of the *MDA 1971* featured, and still features, the word 'product'. It reads 'Any preparation or other product containing a substance or product for the time being specified in any of paragraphs 1 to 4 above'. Inclusion in Sch 2 of a description of material constituting 'magic mushrooms' has rendered academic, in practice, the need for consideration to be given by earlier courts of this question: What does the word 'product' mean?

**1.24**

The approach of those earlier courts in giving this question consideration remains valuable precisely because the principles there proposed continue to hold good. This earlier learning of the courts still governs the principled approach to concepts critical to manufacture and cultivation: the meanings of 'preparation' and 'product'. The short point is that the word 'preparation', in the context of para 5 of Pt I, has no technical or scientific or pharmaceutical meaning.

**1.25**

In *Hodder v Director of Public Prosecutions; Matthews v Director of Public Prosecutions* (unreported) [1990] Crim LR 26, the Divisional Court held that, where a person picked, packaged and froze a quantity of so-called 'magic mushrooms', that person was in possession of a 'product' within the statutory meaning of para 5 [of Sch 2 (Pt 1) of *MDA 1971*].

**1.26**

It was not disputed that the mushrooms contained a Class A drug within *MDA 1971*, Sch 2 (Pt 1). Hodder and Matthews, the convicted accused, appealed by way of case stated against convictions of possession of a drug ('magic mushrooms'), offences contrary to *s 5(2)* of *MDA 1971*.

**1.27**

The appellants submitted that the act of freezing of the mushrooms was not, itself, alone, an act of preparation. Instead, the two submitted, that act was an act of preservation. The act and process of freezing did not of itself render the mushrooms usable as a drug. The underlying conduct was having picked mushrooms, having then separated them into packages and then freezing them. The admitted intention was that the mushrooms would be used for hallucination.

**1.28**

A Divisional Court of the Queen's Bench Division dismissed the appeals against conviction of the two, Hodder and Matthews. 'Prepare', the Court held, meant 'to bring into a usable condition'. The mushrooms would have had to be defrosted before use. Regardless, the Court considered that the mushrooms as picked, packaged and frozen were a 'product' within the permissible meaning of para 5. The convictions were upheld as not incorrect – and safe.

**1.29**

The Divisional Court in *Hodder and Matthews* had considered the case of *R v Stevens* (unreported) [1981] Crim LR 568. *Stevens* was a case decided a decade earlier by the Court of Appeal, Criminal Division. Stevens appealed against conviction for having had in his possession powdered mushrooms which contained a derivative of a Class A controlled drug within *MDA 1971*, Sch 2, Pt 1, para 1

**1.30**

Stevens' defence at trial, and the basis for his appeal, was that he had had no hand in preparation. He submitted that the sun had dried out the mushrooms, naturally. He had been charged with, and convicted by a jury of, possessing a 'preparation' containing the drug. 'Preparation', within the meaning of Sch 2 of *MDA 1971*, the Court held, was intended to have its ordinary and natural meaning.

### 1.31

No gloss was to be added to, or put on, that natural, everyday meaning. The expression 'preparation' not a technical term; nor was it a legal one. It had no scientific or pharmaceutical meaning. The jury at Stevens' trial had been directed correctly when the trial judge had so observed.

### 1.32

The jury had been entitled to find, consistently with Stevens' defence, that the mushrooms had deliberately been placed in the sun in order that they would dry out. That act alone, without more, could constitute 'preparation'. Stevens had intentionally lent himself to a natural process, the result of which was that the mushrooms in his possession were in some material way prepared such that they could be used. Stevens had engineered that the mushrooms would be put into a usable condition. Before the drying out process had been completed, the mushrooms could not have been used.

### 1.33

'Preparation' was again considered by the Court of Appeal, Criminal Division, in *R v Cuncliffe* [1986] Crim LR 547. Cuncliffe appealed against conviction of possession of a Class A controlled drug. His appeal was dismissed. The Court held that the dried mushrooms in Cuncliffe's possession were a 'preparation' containing a substance or product, as specified in the *MDA 1971*.

### 1.34

The Court of Appeal in *Cuncliffe* cited the earlier case of *Stevens*. The Court observed that the governing principle, which still holds good, is that preparation needs no more than that the mushrooms had (a) ceased being in their natural growing state and (b) in some way 'altered by the hand of man' (c) such that that alteration put them into a condition in which they could be used.

### 1.35

The Court held that there was, properly, a triable issue in respect of whether Cuncliffe had lent himself to 'preparation'. The jury was entitled to conclude (as presumably it had concluded, as a prior condition of its verdict adverse to Cunliffe) that what Cuncliffe had done was to pick a collection of psilocybin mushrooms and made that collection subject to a process of drying. That act involved, the jury was permitted to find, and did find, an act of 'preparation'.

**1.36**

*R v Walker* [1987] (unreported) Crim LR 565 was decided a year after Cuncliffe. In *Walker*, the Court of Appeal rejected the submission of the Crown that the act of merely picking magic mushrooms amounted to 'preparation'. This approach was consistent with that of the earlier decisions. The Court left the point open.

**1.37**

The appellant Walker's conviction of possession of a preparation containing psilocybin was quashed. The Court did so because it accepted that there had been a material omission by the trial judge in his direction of the jury. That omission went to the heart of the safety of the conviction.

**1.38**

The trial judge had failed to direct the jury that it was a legal element of the offence that it must be proved that a change to the condition of the mushrooms had deliberately been brought about. The jury should have been so directed. The failure to so direct is what made the conviction unsafe.

**1.39**

In principle, it follows that, had that direction in law been given, a jury would have been entitled to convict Walker – if it had thought it fair to do so in all the particular circumstances of the immediate case.

# Cultivation

**1.40**

Cultivation of cannabis is invariably where the classic battleground is drawn in respect of criminal liability. *Section 6* of *MDA 1971* proscribes cultivation of the cannabis plant. *Section 6* does so in the terms of a blanket prohibition:

'(1)   Subject to any regulations under s 7 of this Act for the time being in force, it shall not be lawful for a person to cultivate any plant of the genus Cannabis.

(2)   Subject to s 28 of this Act, it is an offence to cultivate any such plant in contravention of subsection (1) above.'

**1.41**

The regulations made express in *s 6(1)* of *MDA 1971* permit that the Secretary of State may, as he thinks fit, bring into effect authorisation in law of activities otherwise unlawful under the foregoing provisions of *MDA 1971, s 6*.

**1.42**

Those regulations are by arrangement of a statutory instrument, the Misuse of Drugs Regulations 2001/3998. *Section 7* envisages a number of factual scenarios, which the Secretary of State may (but certainly need not) authorise and so statutorily exempt from criminal liability. Until and unless the Secretary of State does give the requisite authorisation, the regulations exist as a permissive power in law on which the Secretary of State may, and may not, think fit to act.

**1.43**

*Section 6(2)* of *MDA 1971* concerns *s 28* of the same Act. *Section 28* contemplates proof of lack of knowledge that a substance or product in question was a controlled drug – and lack of reason to suspect the same. In certain proscribed circumstances, proof of lack of knowledge (accepted by a jury) may amount to a defence in proceedings for certain offences.

## Defences available, in principle, to accused persons involved in manufacture or cultivation

**1.44**

What defences in law are, in principle, available to acts of manufacture or cultivation of controlled drugs? Is a defence of necessity available? If it is not, are there circumstances in which *MDA 1971* (and, now, the 2016 Act) can operate contrary to Convention rights and fundamental principles?

**1.45**

Medical necessity is not available where reliance is placed on possession, manufacture or cultivation being excused by the alleviation of pain.[1] *AG Ref No. 2 of 2004* remains good law and was foremost a set of conjoined appeals concerning unauthorised instances of possession of a controlled drug, cannabis.

**1.46**

The submissions framed by the several conjoined appellants were such that the central issue of unauthorised possession played out on appeal by way of a root and branch focus on possession, cultivation, importation, and supply of cannabis – acts all done for putative purpose of alleviating pain and suffering.

**1.47**

The first appellant was charged with cultivating cannabis. He had pleaded guilty to an offence contrary to s 6(1) of *MDA 1971*, a judge having ruled that the

---

1   Re Att-Gen's Reference (No. 2 of 2004) [2005] 1 WLR 3642

defence of necessity was not available to him at trial. His positive defence case had been that he grew cannabis out of necessity: he grew it and he used it to alleviate his severe pain and so to help him sleep.

## 1.48

The Court dismissed the first appellant's appeal against conviction upon his confession. The Court observed that what it called 'necessitous' medical use of cannabis was in conflict with the purpose and effect of the clear legislative scheme. On the evidence in the particular case, in all the circumstances, there was no basis for concluding that the scheme conflicted with the Convention; in any event, for the defence of necessity of circumstances to be available, in principle, there had to be circumstances independent of the assertions of the accused, capable of objective scrutiny by judge and jury.

## 1.49

That latter test was not satisfied by pain not directly associated with immediate danger of physical injury. Necessity in the context of a defence proposed to manufacture and cultivation of controlled drugs was required, in law, to be founded on facts involving avoidance of risk of harm to the person. Mere prevention or alleviation of pain and suffering, without more, was insufficient to found a proposed defence of necessity.

## 1.50

The second appellant was convicted by a jury of the offence of production of cannabis, contrary to s 4(2)(a) of *MDA 1971*. The appellant had called evidence in his defence at trial that he was in chronic pain; that he took cannabis because the drugs prescribed for him could not be tolerated by him or were inadequate to relieve his pain.

## 1.51

The judge directed the jury that the defence of necessity was only available if the appellant believed that he would imminently and inevitably suffer serious injury. No explanation had been given by the judge to the jury on point of what might constitute serious injury. The appellant's conviction was upheld. He had not faced a risk of serious physical or psychological injury as a result of natural pain suffered by him. Had he resorted to alternative medicines, rather than taken cannabis, on a regular basis, he would not have risked serious physical or psychological injury.

## 1.52

A common approach taken by the Court to all appellants was that no one appellant could rely on the defence of necessity. In the appeal concerning the Attorney General's reference, the trial judge had wrongly left the defence of necessity to the jury. No such defence could be founded – save in exceptional circumstances where the context is ongoing trials for medical research purposes. No subsequent decision has criticised or undermined the approach and outcome in *Quayle* and others.

**1.53**

Against that, in a relatively recent case, decided in June 2014, *R (on the application of Nicklinson) v Ministry of Justice*; *R. (on the application of Lamb) v Ministry of Justice*; *R (on the application of AM) v DPP* [2015] AC 657, on point of the *Suicide Act 1961, s 2*, the Supreme Court declined to order the Director of Public Prosecutions to amend her policy on prosecuting cases of alleged assisted suicide. Quayle was, there, cited in skeleton submissions by the parties but was not referred to by the Supreme Court.

**1.54**

Where evidence so permits, on a strictly factual and case-specific basis, are there circumstances in which the State itself was, in some significant way, implicated in exacerbation of a pre-existing medical condition?

**1.55**

This very question was considered in *R v Altham* [2006] 2 Cr App R 8, CA. That Court held that, where the sufferer of a medical condition had chosen to use cannabis to alleviate his pain, there was no reason or corresponding duty on the criminal courts to read *MDA 1971* as if it were subject to a defence of medical necessity.

**1.56**

The Act is not subject to such a caveat. Such a course is not necessary in order to ensure compatibility with art 3 of the European Convention on Human Rights – the general and absolute prohibition on State sponsorship of inhuman or degrading treatment. In any event, on the facts in *Altham*, the Court observed, there was no basis to find that the State had been involved in exacerbation of a pre-existing medical condition. *Altham* can be read so far as to establish that the State is not required to take steps to alleviate the condition.

**1.57**

Consistently with the observations of the Court in *Quayle,* any other or different approach would be in conflict with, and subversive of, the purpose and effect of the legislative scheme. The legislative scheme amounts to a general prohibition on the use of, and involvement in, controlled drugs.

**1.58**

Exceptions to that general prohibition are circumscribed and plainly stated in the statute. The courts are clearly reluctant to admit of exceptional cases save, as may conceivably occur, in a case where the State itself has been shown to have exacerbated an existing medical condition.

**1.59**

Such exacerbation would require evidence tantamount to connivance by the State in an individual having suffered to the extent and degree of the critical test envisaged in art 3 of the Convention. Such a case is hard, properly viewed, to conceive. The Court in *Altham* did not linger on the point of what circumstances, in principle, it considered would satisfy this requirement of State-based exacerbation.

**1.60**

It is unlikely that mere acquiescence of the State in an accused person's pain and suffering would satisfy the courts – for example, due to several cancelled hospital appointments where these were cancelled by a State agency or department, such as the National Health Service.

**1.61**

Observance of religious or cultural practices is no defence as a bar to prosecution and conviction. If a religious group, even a recognised and well-established one, adopts as part of its rituals a deliberately unlawful act, the fact of religious ceremony is no justification in law.[2]

## Use of extradition proceedings as a means of law enforcement

**1.62**

Vital to the policing of manufacture and cultivation of controlled drugs is that there exists international legal cooperation and mutual legal assistance between friendly States. International-level cooperation between executive agencies of national governments is essential in the investigation and prosecution of the manufacture and supply of proscribed substances.

**1.63**

Extradition is but one means available to law enforcement officers and prosecutors to give effect to orders of national courts. In March 2014, UK prosecutors applied for, and obtained, a European Arrest Warrant (EAW) for the arrest and extradition of Martin Hickman, to be extradited from Spain, where he was living, to the UK, where he was required to serve a term of

---

2   *R v Aziz* (unreported) [2012] Crim LR 801.

imprisonment of ten years for his non-payment of a confiscation order made by the Crown Court sitting at Southwark in April 2012.

**1.64**

A confiscation order was made for £14,407,850.28. A portion of that amount was paid. At the time of the issue and execution of the arrest warrant for Mr Hickman's extradition, the confiscation order stood at £13,940,391.44, plus interest. Service in prison of the default sentence does not expunge the debt by way of the confiscation order.

**1.65**

Mr Hickman was arrested in Spain in early July 2014; he was extradited to the UK on 13 August of the same year. He was taken immediately to prison to begin his sentence, passed in his absence, for having defaulted on payment of a confiscation order. Mr Hickman had been convicted, in March 2009, after a prosecution brought by the Department for Work and Pensions, for his involvement in the illegal sale and supply of medicinal products. Mr Hickman had pleaded guilty to several counts on an indictment for trial specifying offences entailing the sale of unlicensed medicines via the internet.

**1.66**

The Medicines and Healthcare Products Regulatory Agency (MHRA) had started a criminal investigation into Mr Hickman on suspicion of unlawful trading of unlicensed and counterfeit medicines via the internet. Mr Hickman was subsequently charged. Upon the criminal convictions having been recorded, the Crown Prosecution Service commenced confiscation proceedings at Southwark Crown Court.

**1.67**

The criminal benefit figure for which the Crown contended was £15.3 million. The losers of that sum were the Department for Work and Pensions and the Department of Health. Extradition proceedings were used to execute the failure to pay the sum owing on the confiscation order.

## Summary of key points

**1.68**

- 'Production' is key to the legal prohibition on manufacture and cultivation of controlled drugs.

- *Section 4(1)* of *MDA 1971* specifies what meaning Parliament intended to confer on the statutory language: 'produce a controlled drug'.

- *Section 4(2)* of *MDA 1971* clarifies that production of a controlled drug, contrary to *s 4(1)* of the Act, is subject to *s 28* of the Act. *Section 4(2) (b)* clarifies that it is an offence for a person 'to be concerned in the production of such a drug'.

- *Sections 7* and *7A* of *MDA 1971* permit the Secretary of State, as the Secretary of State thinks fit, to make orders within the statutory scheme of the Act. Those orders may exclude or permit of liability (of categories of persons and/or categories of conduct) for involvement in controlled drugs, within the statutory scheme.

- *Section 7(3)(a)* and *(b)* of *MDA 1971* specify that any such modification of the 1971 statutory scheme by the Secretary of State must be purposive insofar as certain categories of persons must be excluded from exposure to criminal liability.

- Medicinal products have been, and are, regulated in the UK pursuant to a different and separate statutory regime than that governing controlled drugs (*MDA 1971*). Regulation of medicinal and pharmaceutical substances and products should not be conflated with the legal prohibition on involvement in controlled drugs.

- Reported cases arising from the appellate jurisdiction of the criminal courts have considered and observed on how 'production', 'cultivation, 'manufacture' and 'preparation' should be defined for the purpose of recognising criminal liability.

- Very limited, wholly fact-specific and highly case-sensitive defences are, in principle, open to persons accused of involvement in manufacture or cultivation of controlled drugs. The real limitations of those defences are emphasised.

- Extradition is a means by which law enforcement officers and prosecutors can reach to an accused or convicted person in the context of manufacture and cultivation of controlled drugs – and illegal sale of unlicensed medicines.

# 2    Importation

Paul Mason

## The offences

### 2.1

Restrictions on the importation and exportation of drugs are set out in *s 3* of the *Misuse of Drugs Act 1971 (MDA 1971).* The provision reads as follows:

'3.—(1) Subject to subsection (2) below—

the importation of a controlled drug; and

a.    the exportation of a controlled drug, are hereby prohibited.

(2)    Subsection (1) above does not apply—

a.    to the importation or exportation of a controlled drug which is for the time being excepted from paragraph (a) or, as the case may be, paragraph (b) of subsection (1) above by regulations under s 7 of this Act or by provision made in a temporary class drug order by virtue of s 7A; or

b.    to the importation or exportation of a controlled drug under and in accordance with the terms of a licence issued by the Secretary of State and in compliance with any conditions attached thereto.'

### 2.2

*Section 3* was amended by *s 151* and *Sch 17* to the *Police Reform and Social Responsibility Act 2011 (PRSRA 2011).* Schedule 17 to the *PRSRA 2011* introduced temporary class drug orders and thus *s 3* of the *MDA 1971* was amended to apply the restrictions of importation and exportation to a temporary class drug.

### 2.3

The exception set out in *s 3(2)* of the *MDA 1971* also apply to licences granted under two further statutes. These are *s 5* of the *Drugs (Prevention of Misuse) Act 1964* and *ss 2, 3* and *10* of the *Dangerous Drugs Act 1965.* Licences granted under these provisions have the same effect as if granted under *s 3(2)* of the *1971 Act.*[1] Under *s 18(2)* of the *MDA 1971,* it is an offence to contravene the conditions of a licence issued under *s 3.*

---

1    *Para 2 of Sch 5 to the MDA 1971.*

## 2.4

*Section 3* does not create the offence of importation or exportation. It sets out the prohibition on such activity. The offence arises either from the improper importation or exportation of goods; or the fraudulent evasion of the prohibition itself. These offences are contained in the *Customs and Excise Management Act 1979 (CEMA 1979)*.

## 2.5

*CEMA 1979* remains the principal legislation under which Customs and Excise use their powers. It creates two sets of offences for improper importation of goods (*s 50*) and the exportation of goods (*s 68*). However, *s 170* is the much more broadly drafted and it is that provision under which drug importation offences are most commonly charged.

## 2.6

*Section 170* of *CEMA 1979* states as follows:

'170 Penalty for fraudulent evasion of duty, etc.

  i.   Without prejudice to any other provision of the Customs and Excise Acts 1979, if any person—

  knowingly acquires possession of any of the following goods, that is to say—

[ … ]

  (iii)  goods with respect to the importation or exportation of which any prohibition or restriction is for the time being in force under or by virtue of any enactment; or

  is in any way knowingly concerned in carrying, removing, depositing, harbouring, keeping or concealing or in any manner dealing with any such goods, and does so with intent to defraud Her Majesty of any duty payable on the goods or to evade any such prohibition or restriction with respect to the goods he shall be guilty of an offence under this s and may be arrested.

(2)  Without prejudice to any other provision of the Customs and Excise Acts 1979, if any person is, in relation to any goods, in any way knowingly concerned in any fraudulent evasion or attempt at evasion—

[ … ]

of any prohibition or restriction for the time being in force with respect to the goods under or by virtue of any enactment;

[ … ]

he shall be guilty of an offence under this section and may be arrested.'

**2.7**

As noted above, *s 170* is widely drawn. As well as creating the offences of importation and exportation of prohibited goods, it also includes actions beyond that, as set out in *s 170(1)(b)*.

**2.8**

The improper importation or exportation of goods by pipeline is dealt with by *s 3* of *CEMA 1979*. It provides that any prohibition on importation and exportation of goods applies to pipelines also.

**2.9**

Where the Channel Tunnel has been used for importation or exportation of drugs, the provisions of the *Channel Tunnel Act 1987* may be engaged.[2]

## How the offence is charged

**2.10**

The relationship between the *MDA 1971* and *CEMA 1979* was addressed by the Court of Appeal in *R v Whitehead* [1982] QB 1272. The Appellant had been convicted of, amongst other things, conspiracy to evade the prohibition on the importation of drugs. At trial, the offence had been charged under *s 3* of the *MDA 1971* and the prosecution had made it clear that they relied on *s 3* as creating the offence. The defence had sought to quash the indictment at trial, arguing that the offence was not created by *s 3*, but by *s 304* of the *Customs and Excise Act 1952 (1952 Act)*.[3] The application to quash was refused by the trial judge.

**2.11**

The question for the Court of Appeal was whether the underlying offence was provided by *s 3* of the *MDA 1971*, or by *s 304* of the *1952 Act*. The Court found that the offence of prohibition was created by a combination of both statutes. Although it would be correct to charge the offence under either, that did not mean that it 'arises under one to the exclusion of the other'.[4]

---

2  See Channel Tunnel (Customs and Excise) Order 1990 (SI 1990/2167), Art 5(1) and 5(6).
3  This was the equivalent provision to *s 170* of *CEMA 1979*, as noted above. A prosecution under *s 304* of the 1952 Act required an order of the Customs and Excise Commissioners, which had not been obtained by the prosecution.
4  at 1281H.

# Procedure and sentence[5]

### 2.12

The offence is triable either way. On indictment, proceedings may commence up to 20 years from the date the offence was committed. In summary proceedings the period is up to three years (*s 146A*).

### 2.13

*Section 170(5)* prevents there being any duplication of questions of double jeopardy. It states that:

'(5)   In any case where a person would, apart from this subsection, be guilty of—

 a.   an offence under this section in connection with a prohibition or restriction; and

 b.   a corresponding offence under the enactment or other instrument imposing the prohibition or restriction, being an offence for which a fine or other penalty is expressly provided by that enactment or other instrument, he shall not be guilty of the offence mentioned in paragraph (a) of this subsection.'

### 2.14

*Section 3(2)* of *CEMA 1979* sets out that on indictment, the maximum penalty is any amount, and/or imprisonment up to a maximum of seven years. On summary conviction, it is a penalty of £20,000 or of three times the value of the goods, whichever is the greater, and/or imprisonment not exceeding six months.

### 2.15

However, in drugs cases, *s 170(4)* provides that penalties may be enhanced. These are set out in *Sch I* to *CEMA 1979*. For Class A drugs offences, convicted on indictment the penalty is of any amount, or to imprisonment for life or both. Where the drugs are Class B or are a temporary class drug, the penalty can be of any amount, or to imprisonment for a term not exceeding 14 years, or to both (*Sch I (1)(b)*).

### 2.16

*Schedule I (2)* sets out a similar enhancement where the offence involves Class C drugs. The penalty on summary conviction is a penalty of three times the value of the goods or level 5 on the standard scale, whichever is the greater, or

---

5   See also Ch 11.

imprisonment for a term not exceeding 3 [12][6] months, or to both. A conviction on indictment, attracts a penalty of any amount, or to imprisonment for a term not exceeding 14 years, or to both.

### 2.17

Drug importation offences under *s 170* are dealt with in the Sentencing Guideline for Drugs Offences ('the Guideline').[7] Like other drugs offences, the Guideline is divided into harm and culpability categories for Class A, B and C drugs.

### 2.18

For the importation of Class A drugs, these range from a starting point of three years six months imprisonment for an offender considered to be in a lesser role with relatively small amounts in Category 3 (for example, 150g of heroin); to 16 years' custody for a leading role in importing 5kg or more of heroin. The Guideline also notes that 'where the operation is on the most serious and commercial scale, involving a quantity of drugs significantly higher than category 1, sentences of 20 years and above may be appropriate, depending on the role of the offender'.[8]

### 2.19

As with other sentencing guidelines, there are a number of non-exhaustive factors relating to the offence and offender, which may result in upward or downward adjustment from the starting point.

### 2.20

For class A drugs, *s 110* of the *Powers of Criminal Courts (Sentencing) Act 2000* (*PCCSA 2000*) applies. A court should impose a minimum sentence of at least seven years custody for a third, class A drugs trafficking offence. The Act does provide for an exception where the court determines that there are particular circumstances that relate to any of the offences or to the offender; and would make it unjust to do so in all the circumstances.[9]

### 2.21

A drugs offence under *s 170* is a 'lifestyle offence' for the purpose of the *Proceeds of Crime Act 2002* (*Sch 2* to *CEMA 1979*). It is also a 'serious offence' within *Sch 1* to the *Serious Crime Act 2007*.[10]

---

6   The increase to 12 months will occur when *s 282(2)* of the *Criminal Justice Act 2003* is in force.
7   Sentencing Council, *Drugs Offences – Definitive Guideline* (24 January 2012) pp.3-8.
8   Guideline, p. 4.
9   *PCCSA 2010, s 110 (2)*.
10  See Ch 12.

## Elements of the offence

**2.22**

For a drugs importation offence under *s 170(1)*, the prosecution must prove two things. First that the accused knowingly acquired possession of the drugs or that they were 'knowingly concerned' in carrying, removing, depositing, harbouring, keeping or concealing, 'or in any other manner dealing' with the drugs. Secondly, that the drugs were subject to a prohibition or restriction on importation or exportation that is in force.

**2.23**

For an offence under *s 170(2)*, the prosecution must prove two things also. First, that there has been a fraudulent evasion or attempt at evasion of any prohibition on the importation or exportation of drugs. Secondly, that the accused was knowingly concerned in that fraudulent evasion.

## *Section 170(1) and 170(2)*

**2.24**

The relationship between the two subsections was discussed in *R v Neale and others* [1984] 3 All ER 156. Mr Neale was convicted with others of being knowingly concerned in the fraudulent evasion of the prohibition on the importation of cannabis resin contrary to *s 170(2)* of *CEMA 1979*.

**2.25**

In appealing the conviction, one question for the Court of Appeal was whether *s 170(2)* applied only to cases where a defendant was part of or connected with the actual smuggling; or whether it also covered the situation where the defendant had come into possession of the goods but had not taken part in the actual smuggling.

**2.26**

It was suggested in *Neale* that it was difficult to see what would fall within *s 170(2)* that would not be covered by *s 170(1)*. However, Griffiths LJ suggested that:

'... subsection (2) has consistently appeared in a similar form in a succession of Customs and Excise Acts as the final and sweeping up provision ... We are satisfied that it was inserted by the draftsman with the intention of casting his net as widely as words enabled him —note his language, "in any person" and "in any way"'.[11]

---

11  At p.288.

## *The Actus Reus*

**2.27**

'Evasion' in *s 170* has been defined by the Court of Appeal as:

' … avoiding doing something which a person is under an obligation to do. A person can only avoid doing something if he knows that he is obliged to do it. The person will "evade" the obligation if he deliberately so organises affairs that he is able to avoid doing what he knows he has to do.'[12]

**2.28**

The time period for evasion has been interpreted much more widely than that for importation. *Section 5(2)* of *CEMA 1979*, defines the timing of importation and exportation as follows:[13]

'[ … ]

(a)  where the goods are brought by sea, the time when the ship carrying them comes within the limits of a port;

(b)  where the goods are brought by air, the time when the aircraft carrying them lands in the United Kingdom or the time when the goods are unloaded in the United Kingdom, whichever is the earlier;

(c)  where the goods are brought by land, the time when the goods are brought across the boundary into Northern Ireland.'

**2.29**

The timing of importation is finite and not continuous.[14] In contrast, a person may be liable for acts committed before or after the importation itself.

**2.30**

In *R v Wall* [1974] 1 WLR 930, the defendant had helped to load cannabis resin onto a van in Afghanistan, which was later driven by others to the UK. It was held that even if the defendant's acts had been restricted to acts done abroad in order to further the fraudulent evasion of a restriction on importation into this country, he had been knowingly concerned in the importation of the drug into the UK.

---

12  *R v Bajwa* [2012] 1 WLR 601, at para 91.
13  There are two exceptions. The first is under *s 5(3)* concerning goods brought by sea of which entry is not required under Reg 5 of the Customs Controls on Importation of Goods Regulation 1991; and secondly *s 5(6)* concerning goods imported by pipeline.
14  *R v Glynn Edwards* [2005] 2 Cr App R 29.

## 2.31

*Wall* was applied in *R v Jakeman* (1983) 76 Cr App R 223, where the defendant had agreed to bring cannabis from Accra, Ghana to London. After a change of heart, she left the suitcases at a stopover in Paris. It was held that the defendant's guilty mind at Accra had led to the luggage ending up in London. Her alleged repentance did not absolve her of criminal responsibility. She had brought about the importation deliberately and with criminal intent.

## 2.32

In *R v Smith* [1973] QB 924 also applying *Wall,* the Court of Appeal dismissed an appeal against conviction where cannabis had been sent from Kenya to Bermuda via London. The defendant had argued that, as he had done nothing to facilitate the transaction of the cannabis from the staging post in London to Bermuda, he was not party to the importation.

## 2.33

The Court found that it was quite unnecessary for the Crown to have to prove that the defendant had done anything to further the transaction. It held that 'goods deliberately introduced into the United Kingdom are nonetheless imported because the intention is to pass them through this country to another terminus'.[15]

## 2.34

Equally, liability extends to actions after the importation. In *R v Green* [1976] QB 985, customs authorities replaced cannabis they had found in a crate with peat. The crate was then delivered to a garage in London rented by the defendant. Subsequently, he was convicted of being knowingly concerned in the fraudulent evasion of the prohibition on the importation of cannabis.

## 2.35

On appeal, the Court found that the importation of cannabis was a continuing offence, it did not end when the cannabis was seized by the authorities. The renting of the garage, knowing it was to be used to store cannabis was an act concerned in the evasion of the prohibition.[16]

## 2.36

Provided the goods are prohibited and the acquisition is done knowingly and with intent to evade prohibition, the offence can be committed at any time after importation.[17]

---

15  per Edmund Davies LJ, p.936B–C.
16  At p.993E.
17  *R v Ardalan* [1972] 1 WLR 463. See also *R v Caippara* [1988] 87 Cr App R 316, *R v Bell* [2011] EWCA Crim 6 and *R v Coughlan* 12 May 1997, unreported.

**2.37**

The court's interpretation of this window of liability – the continuous nature of the offence under *s 170* of *CEMA 1979* – is well illustrated in *Neale*. In that case, customs officers found six hundredweight of cannabis resin at the defendant's farmhouse in Wales. There was no evidence as to where or how it had been imported. The defendant was convicted under *s 170(2)* of *CEMA 1979*.

**2.38**

On appeal, and in dealing with the question of liability arising after the importation, Griffiths LJ cited, with approval the trial judge's summing up to the jury. It is worth citing in full:

'Let me give you a very simple example. A boat arrives in a port in this country and it has on board cannabis resin. One of the sailors, one of the crew, actually carries that cannabis resin ashore. He hands it over to another man who is waiting, who loads it into a van. The van is driven off to some place where the drug is unloaded and is stored away in some building and there you have someone who helps in that unloading-perhaps the owner of the building in which it is stored. Maybe, at a later stage, it is transported to yet another building and is stored there and it may be (I am taking an entirely hypothetical case) that behind all this operation, controlling it and supervising it, is some organising person. Now you see, of all those men – the sailor, the van driver, the store keeper, the organizer – strictly speaking, only the sailor has imported the drug into this country. He is the only person who has carried it into this country, and that is what importation means, but he and each of those other persons-the van driver, the store keeper and the organizer – have all taken a part in evading the prohibition on the importation of that drug and taken their part in getting round it, in setting at nought the ban which the law imposes on the importation of the drug. I hope you see why "the evasion of the prohibition on the importation" is a much wider expression than simply "importation".'

**2.39**

The prosecution must prove importation. This may seem obvious, but the wording of *s 154(2)* of *CEMA 1979* appears to suggest the burden lies with the defendant. It states that:

'154 Proof of certain other matters

(2)    Where in any proceedings relating to customs or excise any question arises as to the place from which any goods have been brought or as to whether or not—

[ ... ]

> (f) any goods are or were subject to any prohibition of or restriction on their importation or exportation, then [ … ] the burden of proof shall lie upon the other party to the proceedings.'

## 2.40

It had argued by the prosecution in *R v Watts and Stack*, (1980) 70 Cr App R 187 that *s 154(2)* places the burden of proving that there had been no importation on the defendant. The Court of Appeal held that the onus to prove importation rested with the prosecution, it stated that 'the onus on the Crown to prove that intent must involve establishing a link or nexus between the actus reus of the offence and some prohibited importation'.[18]

## 2.41

'Fraudulent evasion' in *s 170(2)* requires the prosecution to prove dishonest conduct deliberately intended to evade the prohibition or restriction with respect to the goods. There was no necessity for the prosecution to prove that acts of deceit had been practised on a customs officer in his presence.[19]

## 2.42

'Concerned' has not been given any particular definition by the courts, beyond its ordinary natural meaning.[20] It requires some role to played, beyond simply being kept informed.[21] Put simply, importation must result as a consequence of, at least in part, the defendant's actions.

## 2.43

A defendant can be knowingly concerned in the fraudulent evasion without taking any actual steps to bring about the importation. In *Attorney General's Reference (No. 1 of 1998)* (1999) 163 JP 390, the defendant agreed to look after a parcel which was due to arrive from The Netherlands. He knew that it might contain drugs. The parcel duly arrived and subsequently, the defendant was convicted under *s 170(2)(b)* of *CEMA 1979*.

## 2.44

Dismissing the appeal against conviction, the Court of Appeal found that the defendant had been prepared to assist in the fraudulent evasion if certain circumstances arose and he had committed the offence. Further, it found that if the uncertainty over whether the importation would actually take place allowed a defendant to escape liability, the effect of *s 170(2)(b)* would be weakened as it was not unusual for such an enterprise to be subject to uncertainty.

---

18 per Bridge LJ at p.192.
19 *Attorney-General's Reference (No. 1 of 1981)* [1982] QB 848.
20 *Caiparra.*
21 *MacNeil v HM Advocate* (1986) JC 146.

# The Mens Rea

## 2.45

To establish the offence under *s 170(2)*, the prosecution must prove two things. First, that the defendant knew the goods being imported were prohibited or restricted. Secondly, that his conduct was designed to evade, fraudulently that prohibition or restriction.

## 2.46

Assessing the timing of the defendant's guilty mind is important. It is the defendant's state of mind at the time they are concerned with the bringing about of the importation that matters, rather than their state of mind at the exact moment of the importation itself.[22]

## 2.47

An offence under *s 170* requires specific intent. That is, to be knowingly concerned in the fraudulent evasion of a prohibition. It follows of course that recklessness is not enough.

## 2.48

In *R v Panayi* [1989] 1 WLR 187, customs officers boarded the defendants' yacht, which was within UK territorial waters. They found 690 kilogrammes of cannabis resin on board. The defendants had alleged that they were transporting the drugs from Spain to Holland and that they were only in UK waters because of navigational errors they had made.

## 2.49

The Court of Appeal found that the specific intent required for *s 170* required the prosecution to establish that, at the time of the offence, the accused intended dishonestly to evade the prohibition and import the drugs by entering UK territorial waters, and knew that they had in fact entered those waters. It was not sufficient, as the trial judge had wrongly directed, that the defendants were aware of the risk of entering into territorial waters and nonetheless went on to take that risk.

## 2.50

Importation offences under *s 170* are a continuous act, as *Neale* and *Ardalan* note. However, in practical terms, the further removed a person is from the importation itself, the more difficult it will be for the prosecution to establish the requisite mens rea.

---

22 *Jakeman.*

## 2.51

The prosecution is not required to prove that the defendant knew the exact nature of the prohibited or restricted goods. However, if the defendant is importing goods which they believe are not subject to restriction or prohibition, then they cannot be found guilty. They are to be judged on the facts as they believe them to be.

## 2.52

In *R v Taaffe* [1984] AC 539, the defendant was charged under *s 170(2)* with having been knowingly concerned in the fraudulent evasion of the prohibition on the importation of cannabis resin. The defendant admitted that he had been asked to import packages from The Netherlands into the UK. The packages contained cannabis, but the defendant mistakenly thought he was importing money. Currency was not subject to prohibition, but the defendant thought it was.

## 2.53

The House of Lords agreed with the earlier decision in the Court of Appeal[23] that the defendant was to be judged on the facts as he believed them to be. Had the material been currency and not cannabis, he would not have been convicted. Lord Scarman reiterating that point, stated that:

> ' ... the principle that a man must be judged upon the facts as he believes them to be is an accepted principle of the criminal law when the state of a man's mind and his knowledge are ingredients of the offence with which he is charged.'[24]

## 2.54

However, the House of Lords distinguished the facts in *Taaffe* from two earlier cases. In *R v Hussain* [1969] 2 QB 567, the Court of Appeal held that knowledge that the goods were prohibited and that he was involved in an operation to evade that prohibition was enough. The fact that the defendant was unaware that the packages in fact contained cannabis had no bearing on matters.

## 2.55

*Hussain* was applied in *R v Hennessey* (1979) 68 Cr App R 419. In *Hennessey*, the defendant mistakenly believed he was importing pornography, concealed in his car. The packages in fact contained 28.14kg of cannabis resin. The Court, in dismissing the defendant's appeal against conviction found that it did not matter what the goods were, as long as the defendant knew that he was bringing into the UK goods which he should not bring in.[25]

---

23 [1983] 2 All ER 625.
24 p.546 H.
25 See also *R v Syracusa* (1989) 90 Cr App R 340.

**2.56**

Specific knowledge of the goods imported becomes more complex in a drugs context. As noted above,[26] the class of drug is an important determinative factor in assessing the maximum penalty of an offence under *s 170* of *CEMA 1979*. Does this mean *s 170* comprises three offences relating to Class A, B and C drugs respectively?[27] If it does, then each of these offences would require the prosecution to prove that the defendant had knowledge of the class of drug they were importing.

**2.57**

This question was put before the House of Lords in *R v Shivpuri* (1987) AC 1. The defendant had been convicted under *s 170(1)(b)* of *CEMA 1979* of being knowingly concerned with and dealing in heroin. He had received a suitcase from India which he believed contained either heroin or cannabis. The suitcase was found to contain snuff.

**2.58**

In following *Hussain*, Lord Bridge noted that:

> 'Irrespective of the different penalties attached to offences in connection with the importation of different categories of prohibited goods, *Hussain* established that the only mens rea necessary for proof of any such offence was knowledge that the goods were subject to a prohibition on importation.'[28]

**2.59**

*Shivpuri* dealt also with the question of attempt. The Court found that where a person imports what he believes to be a controlled drug for the purposes of *s 170*, but the drug was in fact harmless, he may be convicted of an attempt to commit that offence, under *s 1(1)* of the *Criminal Attempts Act 1981*.

## Admissibility issues in importation cases

**2.60**

A common defence to *s 170* offences is that the drugs were planted on the defendant, or that the defendant was helping somebody else. In such cases, the prosecution will often seek to adduce evidence to demonstrate a link between the defendant and the drugs. This evidence may not have any direct relevance to the importation of drugs itself.

---

26 At 3.17–3.21.
27 For a parallel argument on sexual offences concerning the requisite factual ingredients of an offence based on its sentence guideline, see *R v Courtie* [1984] AC 463.
28 P.2D.

## 2.61

Such evidence will be considered bad character under *s 98* of the *Criminal Justice Act 2003* (*CJA 2003*). Bad character evidence is only admissible through one of the seven statutory gateways.[29]

## 2.62

The evidence sought to link a defendant to an importation offence will be admissible if it is considered 'relevant to an important matter in issue between the prosecution and the defendant'.[30] This will usually be knowledge that the defendant is concerned in the importation.

## 2.63

In assessing the admissibility of such evidence, the court must bear in mind also whether admitting it would have such an adverse effect on the fairness of the proceedings that the court ought not to admit it.[31]

## 2.64

Prior to the *CJA 2003*, evidence of previous misconduct was admissible to rebut a defence of innocent association. Such evidence remains admissible under the *CJA 2003* provisions. The principle consideration at common law is the probative force of the evidence sought to be admitted. In *R v Boardman* (1975) AC 421, Lord Hailsham noted that:

> '... a properly instructed jury, applying their minds to the facts, can come to the conclusion that they are satisfied so that they are sure that to treat the matter as pure coincidence by reason of the "nexus", "pattern", "system", "striking resemblances" or whatever phrase is used is "an affront to common sense" ... In this the ordinary rules of logic and common sense prevail.'[32]

## 2.65

Thus, in drug importation cases evidence of finding drugs in a defendant's home is relevant and admissible. This is because a jury is entitled to consider such a coincidence in light of the defence that has been raised.

## 2.66

In *R v Peters* (1995) 2 Cr App R 77, the defendant had been convicted of importing a Class B drug under *s 170*. He had denied that he had any connection

---

29 *CJA 2003, s 101.*
30 ibid, *s 101(1)(d).*
31 ibid, *s 101(3).*
32 At p.453H to 454A.

to drugs. At trial, the prosecution had adduced evidence from a search of his house, namely small quantities of cannabis and drug-related equipment.

**2.67**

In finding that the evidence had been admissible, the Court of Appeal said:

> '... when knowledge is in issue, which carries with it the implication that the defendant is the "innocent victim" of some other person who has concealed drugs in the defendant's luggage, or in his vehicle, then evidence showing that the defendant was connected with the kind of drugs inside the United Kingdom is relevant and admissible, subject to the court's power to exclude it on grounds of undue prejudice.'[33]

**2.68**

The Court of Appeal in *Peters* relied on its earlier judgment in *R v Willis*.[34] In that case, the defendant was convicted of importing heroin and opium. The drugs had been concealed in the covers of two photograph albums that the defendant said she had bought in Thailand. A search of the defendant's house found a spoon on which traces of heroin were found, and a box containing a folded piece of paper inside which were 18mg of heroin.

**2.69**

The defence had sought to have the evidence excluded. The trial judge had allowed it to go before the jury. The Court of Appeal considered that the jury had been entitled to consider whether the items found were a coincidence or destroyed her defence of no knowledge.

**2.70**

In *R v Ilomuanya* (2005) EWCA Crim 58, the court set out the central concerns in any assessment of the admissibility of such evidence. These were the relevance of the evidence and the need to consider each case on its facts. However, where the issue was involvement in a specific importation, such evidence has been held to have little or no probative force.[35]

## The Psychoactive Substances Act 2016

**2.71**

*Section 8* of the *Psychoactive Substances Act 2016 (PSA 2016)* creates two offences of importing or exporting psychoactive substances.

---

33 At p.5C-F.
34 29 January 1979, unreported.
35 *R v Balogun* [1997] Crim LR 500.

**2.72**

A person is guilty of the offence if they import or exports a psychoactive substance and the three mental elements are satisfied.

**2.73**

These are set out in *s 8(1)(a)–(d)*. They are that firstly, a person must intend to import or export the substance. Secondly, they must know or suspect, or ought to know or suspect, that the substance is a psychoactive substance. Thirdly, the defendant must either intend to consume the substance him or herself for its psychoactive effects, or must know, or be reckless as to whether, the substance is likely to be consumed by other individuals for its psychoactive effects.

**2.74**

These offences concern importation and exportation of psychoactive substances whether for personal use or for the purpose of supplying others.

**2.75**

The conduct element of these offences does not account for the situation where a person imports or exports a controlled drug wrongly believing it to be a psychoactive substance.

**2.76**

However, *s 8(3)* provides for that scenario, as follows:

'(3)   In a case where a person imports or exports a controlled drug suspecting it to be a psychoactive substance, the person is to be treated for the purposes of this section as if the person had imported or exported a psychoactive substance suspecting it to be such a substance.'

**2.77**

The definition of 'importation' of the purposes of the *PSA 2016* is that set out in *s 5* of *CEMA 1979*,[36] as noted above.[37]

**2.78**

Importation of a psychoactive substance carries a maximum sentence of seven years on indictment; and six months and/or an unlimited fine summarily.[38]

---

36  *PSA 2016, s 8(4)*.
37  See 3.28.
38  See Ch 11.

# Summary of key points

**2.79**

- Restrictions on the importation and exportation of drugs are set out in *s 3* of the *MDA 1971*.

- *Section 3* does not create the offence of importation or exportation. The offence arises either from the improper importation or exportation of goods; or the fraudulent evasion of the prohibition itself. These offences are contained in *CEMA 1979*.

- Although *s 50* of *CEMA 1979* deals with the improper importation of goods, it is *s 170* that is the provision under which drug importation offences are most commonly charged.

- The offence of prohibition is created by a combination of both *CEMA 1979* and the *MDA 1971*. Although it would be correct to charge the offence under either, that did not mean that it arises under one to the exclusion of the other.

- The offence is triable either way. On indictment, the maximum penalty is any amount, and/or imprisonment up to a maximum of seven years. On summary conviction, it is a penalty of £20,000 or of three times the value of the goods, whichever is the greater, and/or imprisonment not exceeding six months. However, in drugs cases, penalties may be enhanced under *s 170(4)* of *CEMA 1979*.

- For an importation offence under *s 170* of *CEMA 1979*, the prosecution must prove that the accused knowingly acquired possession of the drugs or that they were 'knowingly concerned' with the drugs; and that the drugs were subject to a prohibition or restriction on importation or exportation that is in force.

- For an offence under *s 170(2)*, the prosecution must prove that there has been a fraudulent evasion or attempt at evasion of any prohibition on the importation or exportation of drugs; and that the accused was knowingly concerned in that evasion.

- The time period for evasion has been interpreted much more widely than that for importation. The timing of importation is finite and not continuous, but a person may be liable for acts committed before or after the importation itself.

- 'Fraudulent evasion' in *s 170(2)* requires the prosecution to prove dishonest conduct deliberately intended to evade the prohibition or restriction with respect to the goods.

- It is the defendant's state of mind at the time they are concerned with the bringing about of the importation that matters, rather than their state of mind at the exact moment of the importation itself.

31

- An offence under *s 170* requires specific intent. Recklessness is not enough.

- The prosecution is not required to prove that the defendant knew the exact nature of the prohibited or restricted goods. However, if the defendant is importing goods that they believe are not subject to restriction or prohibition, then they cannot be found guilty.

- The evidence sought to link a defendant to an importation offence will be admissible as bad character evidence if it is considered 'relevant to an important matter in issue between the prosecution and the defendant'.

- The *PSA 2016* creates the offence of importing a psychoactive substance. The prosecution must prove an intent to import, knowledge or suspicion that the substance is a psychoactive substance; and that the defendant must either intend to consume the substance or know, or be reckless as to whether, the substance is likely to be consumed by other individuals for its psychoactive effects.

- Importation of a psychoactive substance carries a maximum sentence of seven years on indictment; and six months and/or an unlimited fine summarily.

# 3   Possession: Unlawful Possession, Control and Knowledge

Tom Stevens

## Introduction

### 3.1

In the case of *DPP v Brooks* [1974] 2 WLR 899, Lord Diplock stated:[1]

'... one has in one's possession whatever is, to one's own knowledge, physically in one's custody or under one's physical control. This is obviously what was intended to be prohibited in the case of dangerous drugs'.

### 3.2

This definition may give the impression that the law in relation to possession is conceptually straightforward, but in reality it is not. What constitutes possession under the provisions of the legislation designed to restrict the use and distribution of illicit drugs has been the source of considerable judicial debate.

### 3.3

As Lord Scarman noted in *R v Boyesen* [1982] A.C. 768:[2]

'Possession is a deceptively simple concept. It denotes a physical control or custody of a thing plus knowledge that you have it in your custody or control. you may possess a thing without knowing or comprehending its nature: but you do not possess it unless you know you have it'.

### 3.4

This chapter seeks to explore how the legal provisions relevant to drugs possession have been interpreted and explain what the currently recognised legal ingredients of possession are. In doing so it will become apparent that there are many qualifications and exceptions to the seemingly straightforward

---

1   At p.899.
2   At p.773.

definition of possession provided by Lord Diplock above, with many non-ideal forms of possession in need of consideration.[3]

### 3.5

As Lord Morris stated in the seminal case of *Warner v Metropolitan Police Commissioner* [1969] 2 A.C. 256, possession is 'an illusive concept at common law. It depends on the circumstances of the particular case, as well as the wording and intent, for instance, of the particular statute creating the offence.'[4]

## Unlawful possession

### Section 5 of the MDA 1971

#### 3.6

As of the 1 July 1973 the *Misuse of Drugs Act 1971* (*MDA 1971*) came wholly into force, replacing the earlier provisions of *The Drugs (Prevention of Misuse) Act of 1964*. It is described as, 'An Act to make new provision with respect to dangerous or otherwise harmful drugs and related matters, and for purposes connected therewith'.[5] This Act, subject to subsequent amendments, remains the primary piece of legislation governing the law in relation to the possession of controlled drugs.

#### 3.7

*Section 5* of the Act states as follows:[6]

'**5.**   (1) Subject to any regulations under section 7 of this Act for the time being in force, it shall not be lawful for a person to have a controlled drug in his possession.

(2)   Subject to section 28 of this Act and to subsection (4) below, it is an offence for a person to have a controlled drug in his possession in contravention of subsection (1) above.

(2A) Subsections (1) and (2) do not apply in relation to a temporary class drug.'

#### 3.8

It is self-evident that *s 5* restricts the possession of controlled drugs. The leading provision within the section is subs (1) which provides that, subject to relevant in force regulations allowing for the lawful possession of certain drugs by

---

3   See p. 250 of *R v McNamara* [1988] 87 Cr App R.
4   At p. 275.
5   See the Introductory Text to the *MDA 1971*.
6   This section is printed as amended by the *Police Reform and Social Responsibility Act 2011*, *s 151*, and Sch 17, paras 1 & 6.

certain persons acting in certain capacities (implemented by the Secretary of State pursuant to the provisions of *s* 7 of the Act), it shall not be lawful for a person to have a controlled drug in his possession.

**3.9**

The offences are created by subs (2), which explicitly provides that it is an offence for a person to have a controlled drug in his possession. The sentences that follow conviction for possession of a controlled drug are examined in detail in **Chapter 11**.

**3.10**

The Act also provides a person who is found to be in possession of a controlled drug with a number of defences. *Section 5(4)* contains a defence that proceeds on the assumption that the person knew or suspected that the thing which was in his possession was a controlled drug but took all reasonable steps to 'destroy' the drug in question or deliver it to someone who could take lawful custody of it. *Section 28* in very basic terms deals with the defences of lack of knowledge. Both of these defences are examined in **Chapter 4**.

**3.11**

The 1971 Act does not provide a definition of possession. The only legislative assistance that can be found is under the supplementary provisions of *s 37(3)* where it is stated: 'For the purposes of this Act the things which a person has in his possession shall be taken to include any thing subject to his control which is in the custody of another', allowing for the possibility of so called 'constructive' possession whereby an individual is deemed to have possession over a thing without having actual physical control of it.

## The ingredients of the offence

**3.12**

In order for an accused to be found guilty of possession of a controlled drug under the provisions of *s 5(1)* of the 1971 Act, the essential elements that the prosecution must prove are:

(a) that the accused is in control of or has custody of the item in question (the physical element);

(b) that the accused knew or could reasonably have known of the item in question (the mental element); and

(c) that the item in question is a controlled drug within the meaning of the 1971 Act.[7]

---

7   See *R v Warner* [1969] 2 AC 256; *R v Boyesen* [1982] AC 768, 773-774 and *R v McNamara* 87 Cr App R 246.

**3.13**

For ease of reference each of these three components of possession will be examined in turn, although it is acknowledged that there is regular overlap in the considerations involved in determining whether an accused has the requisite control/custody and accompanying knowledge of a drug within a number of given scenarios.

## Custody and/or control: the physical element of possession

**3.14**

The physical element of possession (the *corpus*) requires the prosecution to prove that the accused was in control of or had custody of the drug in question. As Lord Parker noted in *R v Cavendish* [1961] 1 WLR 1083:[8]

'It is quite clear, without referring to authority, that before a man can be found to have possession, actual or constructive, of goods, something more must be proved than that the goods have been found on his premises. It must be shown either, if he was absent, that on his return he became aware of them and exercised some control over them or… that the goods had come, albeit in his absence, at his invitation or by arrangement. It is also clear that a man cannot be convicted of receiving goods which have been taken delivery of by his servant unless there is evidence that he, the employer, had given the servant authority or instructions to take the goods.'

**3.15**

The concept of physical control is enlarged by the provisions of *s 37(3)* of the 1971 Act allowing for an individual to be considered in control of a drug even when not in physical possession of it.

**3.16**

In cases where a controlled drug is found on an accused person there may be little difficulty in establishing that they had the physical control and/or custody of the drug. For example, if it were in their pocket, or in a bag being carried by them. However, having control or custody of a drug is not limited to such straightforward scenarios.

**3.17**

A drug need not be found on one's person in order to be considered in control of it. For example, if I place a bag of cannabis inside a safety deposit

---

8   At p.1085.

box, lock it and retain the key, it is common sense that I would still have control of the cannabis. That is the case irrespective of how far I travelled away from the safety deposit box. Clearly control does not always equate to physical possession.

### 3.18

Similarly, if I arrange for a drug to be delivered to me, at the point that it is delivered the law deems that I am in control of it. That is the case, irrespective of whether I am aware of the time of delivery or present at the point of delivery to physically take hold of it.

### 3.19

Furthermore, someone else may take custody of it for me to collect at a later date. In such a situation I could still be deemed to be in control of the drug. The delivery of it was on my instruction, and logically that suggests a degree of control.

### 3.20

In *R v Peaston* [1979] 69 Cr App R 203, the appellant received a film capsule through the post in an envelope. It contained 7.7g of amphetamine hydrochloride, which was a Class B prohibited drug. The appellant was unaware of the envelope's arrival, but it was later shown to him by a police officer, who had retrieved it during a search of the appellant's property.

### 3.21

The appellant was charged with being in possession of a controlled drug contrary to *s 5 (1)* of the *MDA 1971*. The appellant pleaded guilty following a failed submission of no case to answer. He appealed on the ground that on the admitted facts he could not be said to be in 'possession' of the drug in question in that he was neither aware of when it was delivered nor did he take any physical control of it. His appeal was dismissed with the Court of Appeal finding that since the appellant had ordered the supplier to send the drug through the post to his address, he was properly to be regarded as in possession of the envelope containing it when it arrived through his letterbox.

### 3.22

Similarly, in *Cavendish*, the owner of a yard was said to be in possession of stolen oil delivered to the yard by his employee at a time when he was not present. It was held on appeal that there was evidence that made it more probable than not that the delivery of the oil was made by an arrangement with the defendant. Therefore, the judge was right in ruling that there was a case to go to the jury that the appellant had control over the delivered oil and was therefore in possession of it.

**3.23**

The requirement that an individual have control and or custody of a drug in order to be considered in possession of it is evident when considering scenarios involving individuals that know of the presence of drugs but exercise no form of control over them. In such scenarios the law is clear, mere knowledge of a drug is not enough to equate to possession.

**3.24**

The above principle is a matter of common sense. Should you or I be aware that our next door neighbour was in physical possession of a bag of crack cocaine it could not be said that we too were in possession of it simply because we had knowledge of it.

**3.25**

What if we were living with someone who kept drugs in a communal home, or we were found travelling alongside others in a vehicle containing drugs? Could our awareness and proximity to the drugs in question within scenarios such as these be equated to having a degree of joint control over them?

**3.26**

In *Tansley v Painter* [1969] Crim LR 139, the appellant was seen by police officers sitting in the passenger seat of a car in the company of another male. This other male was the owner of the car and was observed by the officers selling drugs from it. The appellant did not refute that he was aware that the other male was in possession of drugs, some of which were found within the car he was seen sitting in.

**3.27**

The Divisional Court quashed his conviction. In doing so they noted that mere knowledge of the drugs did not amount to having control over them, some additional degree of control was also required. Interestingly, given the particular facts of this case, the appellant could have been charged with aiding and abetting a drug offence but this would still require proof that he offered encouragement or assistance of some sort (either actively or passively) to his co-accused.[9]

**3.28**

Similarly, in *R v Searle* [1971] Crim LR 592, the appellant was found in a car with several other passengers. The car was searched and drugs were found. Given the prosecution were unable to attribute the possession of any particular drug to any particular defendant the case was brought on the basis of joint possession

---

9   See the cases of *R v Conway and Burkes* [1994] Crim LR 826 and *R v Bland* (1987) 151 JP 857.

by all the defendants of all the drugs. The judge's direction to the jury had simply equated knowledge with possession.

**3.29**

On appeal, the Court of Appeal again stressed that:[10]

'... mere knowledge of the presence of the forbidden article in the hands of a confederate was not enough. Where joint possession had to be established consider whether the drugs form a common pool from which all had the right to draw at will and whether there was a joint enterprise to consume drugs together because then possession of the drugs by one of them pursuant of that common intention might well be possession on the part of all of them.'

**3.30**

In the case of *R v Strong and Berry* [1989] 86(10) LSG 41 the appellant was accused of being in joint possession of a quantity of cannabis again found in a car. In this case the car actually belonged to the accused but it was also occupied by others. His appeal was allowed by the Court of Appeal, who found that for joint possession to be established in circumstances where the defendants did not have the drugs on their individual persons, each had to have the right to say what should be done with them. Again, the court asserted that knowledge of the presence of the drugs did not within itself prove control.

**3.31**

In cases involving more than one individual being aware of the presence of a particular drug, the issue of whether one can be said to be aiding and abetting the other may need to be considered. The law suggests that a degree of encouragement or assistance to the other in possession of the drugs is required. What constitutes encouragement or assistance will depend on the facts of each case. It is worth noting the cases of *R v Conway and Burkes* [1994] Crim LR 826 and *R v Bland* (1987) 151 JP 857.

**3.32**

In the former case of *Conway and Burkes*, the Court of Appeal allowed the appeal against conviction for possessing cannabis. The Court ruled that mere acquiescence was insufficient to establish possession and that there must at least be evidence of encouragement or something akin to this.

**3.33**

The Court in *Conway and Burkes* considered the case of *Bland*. In *Bland* the court ruled that simply living alongside someone, in the same room from which

---

10 At p.593.

they dealt drugs did not equate to either active or passive assistance of that drugs supply.

**3.34**

However, given the particular intimacy of the accused relationship with the supplier of the drugs in *Bland*, other cases have been keen to stress that the case should not be elevated as providing a guiding principle (*R v McNamara & McNamara* [1998] Crim LR 278).

**3.35**

As the above cases illustrate, possession amounts to having a degree of control or custody over a drug. However, this physical element of possession alone is not enough. A degree of knowledge of the item under one's control or custody is also required to be considered legally in possession of it.

## Knowledge: the mental element of possession

**3.36**

The comments of Lord Morris in *R v Warner* [1969] 2 AC 256 encapsulate what is now an established legal ingredient of possession in relation to controlled drugs. He said:[11]

> '... I think that the notion of having something in one's possession involves a mental element. It involves in the first place that you know that you have something in your possession. It does not, however, involve that you know precisely what it is that you have got'

**3.37**

There is an important distinction between mere physical custody of an object and having legal possession of it. The latter connotes that a degree of awareness is required of the object in one's custody and/or control. This is the so-called mental element, the *animus possidendi* (intention to possess). As Lord Parker CJ remarked in the case of *Lockyer v Gibb* [1967] 2 Q.B. 243, 'if something was slipped into your basket and you had not the vaguest notion it was there at all, you could not possibly be said to be in possession of it'.[12]

**3.38**

Lord Parker's conclusion is not difficult to understand. It ensures that those who are not remotely blameworthy for carrying drugs avoid conviction.

---

11 At p.286.
12 At p.248.

**3.39**

More difficult questions arise when the drug is concealed in a box or a bag, for example. These so-called 'container cases' have generated significant judicial debate on what the legal parameters of the mental element of possession are.

**3.40**

For example, what precisely must an accused be aware of in order to be in possession of a controlled drug? Is it enough that they are aware of the container that houses the drug but are mistaken to its content, or must the accused have knowledge that the container did in fact contain controlled drugs in order to be considered in possession of them?

**3.41**

The first House of Lords case to rule on the ingredients of possession, focusing particularly on the mental ingredients of the offence that the prosecution had to prove was *Warner.* This was a case heard under *s 1* of the now repealed *Drugs (Prevention of Misuse) Act 1963*. However, many of leading principles that can be extracted from it are still applicable when considering the provisions of the *MDA 1971* today.

## Warner *and Possession*

**3.42**

The brief facts of *Warner* are as follows. The appellant was tasked by another to collect some boxes. The appellant did so believing that the boxes would contain scent. Having collected the boxes and placed them in his van without checking to see what their contents were, he was stopped by the police. One of the boxes did contain scent, another, however, contained 20,000 amphetamine tablets.

**3.43**

He was subsequently charged with possession of controlled drugs. This charge was challenged on the basis that the appellant was unaware that the box in question contained controlled drugs and consequently he could not be said to be in legal possession of them.

**3.44**

In rejecting this legal proposition, Lord Morris stated as follows:[13]

'In my view, in order to establish possession the prosecution must prove that an accused was knowingly in control of something in circumstances

---

13  At p.289.

which showed that he was assenting to being in control of it: they need not prove that in fact he had actual knowledge of the nature of that which he had.'

## 3.45

He added further[14] that it was for the prosecution to prove:

'that the accused was knowingly in control of some article or thing or substance or package or container in circumstances which had enabled him to know or to discover… what it was that he had before assuming control of it'.

## 3.46

Consequently, having an opportunity to discover the nature of the item under one's control (what was inside the box in this case), whether or not an individual chooses to make use of that opportunity, is an important consideration when determining whether they can be said to be in possession of it.

## 3.47

In cases where no such opportunity is present, possession is unlikely to be made out. Such cases may involve fleeting moments of control. In *R v Wright* [1976] 62 Cr App R 169, the appellant was handed a tin can that contained cannabis. Very shortly after receiving it and before he has time to examine the content he is told to throw it away. He did so immediately. In providing the judgment of the court and applying the principles enunciated in *Warner*, MacKenna J stated that in such circumstances the appellant could not be said to be in possession of the cannabis that was later seized.

## 3.48

In *Warner* Lord Pearce warned against any additional requirement that an accused must know of the precise nature of the item he is in control of in order to be considered in possession of it. He remarked:

'I think that the term 'possession' is satisfied by a knowledge only of the existence of the thing itself and not its qualities, and that ignorance or mistake as to its qualities is not an excuse. This would comply with the general understanding of the word 'possess.' Though I reasonably believe the tablets which I possess to be aspirin, yet if they turn out to be heroin I am in possession of heroin tablets. This would be so I think even if I believed them to be sweets. It would be otherwise if I believed them to be something of a wholly different nature.'

---

14 At p.296.

**3.49**

The principles extracted from *Warner*, were that the prosecution was required to prove that the accused had some awareness of the 'thing' that he was in control of (in this case, the box itself). This would ensure those who unknowingly had drugs planted on them were not unjustly convicted. Conversely however, the majority view (with Lord Reid dissenting[15]) was that to require the prosecution to then prove that the accused was also aware of the precise substance he was in possession of (in this case, what was inside the box) would '*stultify the practical efficacy of the Act*'[16], and act as a barrier to successful prosecution. Accordingly, the majority rejected the proposition advanced by the appellant.

## *Mcnamara*: **simplifying the law of possession**

**3.50**

The case of *McNamara* provides a welcome simplification of the law in relation to drug possession as analysed in *Warner*. The facts of the case were analogous with *Warner* in that it involved an appellant who was carrying a container that when searched was found to contain controlled drugs (namely cannabis resin). As in *Warner* the appellant challenged his conviction for possession on the basis that he was not aware that the box he was carrying contained drugs as he believed it contained pornography – something of a wholly different nature.

**3.51**

In considering the various opinions expressed in *Warner*, now in the context of the 1971 Act, the Lord Chief Justice concluded that four key propositions emerged[17]. They are as follows:

(1)  A man does not have possession of something which has been put into his pocket or into his house without his knowledge: in other words something which is 'planted' on him.

(2)  A mere mistake as to the quality of a thing under the defendant's control is not enough to prevent him being in possession of it. For instance, if a man is in possession of heroin, believing it to be cannabis or believing it perhaps to be aspirin.

(3)  If the defendant believes that the thing is of a wholly different nature from that which in fact it is, then the result would be otherwise.

(4)  In the case of a container or a box, the defendant's possession of the box leads to the strong inference that he is in possession of the contents or

---

15  At p.279.
16  Lord Pearce's in *Warner* at p. 304.
17  At pp. 250–251.

whatsoever it is inside the box. But if the contents are quite different in kind from what he believed, he is not in possession of it.

**3.52**

Importantly, the court went on to note that the inference referred to in proposition four above, may be rebutted by the defendant, if *he* proves (or raises a real doubt in the matter) either:

(a) that he was a servant or bailee who had no right to open it and no reason to suspect that its contents were illicit or were drugs; or

(b) that although he was the owner he had no knowledge of (including a genuine mistake as to) its actual contents or of their illicit nature and that he received them innocently and also that he had had no reasonable opportunity since receiving the package of acquainting himself with its actual contents.'

## Imputing an intention to possess

**3.53**

One of the most controversial aspects of the law of possession to emerge out of *Warner*, as identified in *McNamara,* was the proposition that those taking possession of a container are inferred to have taken possession of its contents also, in circumstances where one could have discovered what was contained within it but failed to do so.

**3.54**

In such circumstances knowledge of what is inside the container, be it not actually known, may be 'imputed'[18]. There may be no overt injustice flowing from this proposition if confined to obvious container cases as in many instances the task of checking their content may not be particularly troublesome.

**3.55**

Difficulty and unfairness however arises when one interprets the term 'container' broadly. May for example a house be considered a container? If so, can knowledge of its contents, including a small quality of drugs secreted somewhere within it, be imputed in circumstances where a tenant has failed to search the house?

**3.56**

This appears to have been the rationale in the case of *R v Lewis* [1988] 87 Cr App R 270 where the accused, as the sole tenant of a house was found to be

---

18 A term used by Lord Wilberforce at p. 311 of his judgment in *Warner.*

guilty of possession of a small quantity of amphetamine sulphate and cannabis resin found by a police officer within his home.

### 3.57

In *Lewis*, the accused argued that as he had no knowledge of the said drugs and as there was nothing that put him on notice so as to conduct any sort of inquiry he could not be said to be in possession of them. He appealed his conviction on the basis that the trial judge had failed to direct the jury that actual knowledge of the item, which turned out to be controlled drugs was required to find him guilty of possession.

### 3.58

The Court of Appeal in dismissing the appeal held that the question the jury had to answer was whether on the facts of the case the appellant was proved to have or ought to have *imputed* to him the intention to possess or the knowledge that he did possess what was in fact a prohibited substance. It was not necessary for the jury to be directed that they had to be satisfied that the appellant had actual knowledge that he had the drugs in question under his control before they could convict. Accordingly, the judge was not guilty of any misdirection and correctly left the proper question to the jury.

### 3.59

It is difficult to reconcile this decision with the first legal proposition enunciated in *McNamara*[19], that being: 'first of all a man does not have possession of something which has been put into his pocket or into his house without his knowledge'.

### 3.60

Much will depend on the individual circumstances of a case, when deciding whether a defendant should have imputed to him an intention to possess that which is physically under their control.

### 3.61

As Lord Scarman emphasised in the case of *Boyesen,* a jury must consider 'the "modes or events" by which the custody commences and the legal incident in which it is held.' This involves examining matters such as, but not limited, to:

(1) The manner and circumstances in which the substance, or something which contains it, has been received by the accused;

(2) What knowledge or means of knowledge as to the presence of the substance, or as to the nature of what has been received, the accused had

---

19 At p. 248.

at the time of receipt or thereafter up to the moment when he is found with it; and

(3)    The accused legal relation to the substance or package, including his right of access to it.[20]

**3.62**

The case of *Lewis* serves to illustrate the difficulties often encountered when interpreting the law of possession. Despite McNamara's useful clarification of the law in relation to possession, the question of what is the mental element involved in cases of drug possession have been revisited on a number of occasions.

# R v Lambert

**3.63**

In the case of *R v Lambert* [2002] 2 A.C. 545 (another so called 'container case'), the question of what constituted the mental element of possession within the context of drugs offences was reopened. Those on behalf of the appellant sought to argue that in light of the House of Lord's ruling in the case of *B (A) Minor v DPP* [2000] 2 A.C. 428, the dissenting opinion of Lord Reid in the case of *Warner* should now be adopted so as to require the prosecution to prove that the accused specifically knew that he was in possession of a controlled drug.

**3.64**

The argument advanced by the appellant was unanimously rejected. Affirming the principles highlighted in McNamara, Lord Slynn of Haley, making reference to cases where drugs were found within a bag, stated:

'... the prosecution must prove that the accused had a bag with something in it in his custody or control; and that the something in the bag was a controlled drug. It is not necessary for the prosecution to prove that the accused knew that the thing was a controlled drug let alone a particular controlled drug.'

**3.65**

In reaching this view, their Lordships noted that were the prosecution required to prove that the accused knew that he was in possession of a controlled drug, the defence of lack of knowledge, afforded to an accused under the provisions of *s 28* would be otiose, and that more particularly, in reading the wording of

---

20  At p. 435 of *R v Boyesen* [1982] 75 Cr App R 51.

the defences found under *s 5(4)* and *s 28(3)(b)(i)* it was apparent that proving the accused knew or at least suspected that what he was in control of was a controlled drug was not an ingredient of the offence that the prosecution had to prove.

## Mistake as to the drug possessed

### 3.66

It is now established law that the prosecution need not prove that the accused knew he was in possession of a particular drug. So long as it is established that the drug possessed was a controlled drug, it is not a defence for the accused to state that he believed he was in possession of some other controlled drug which is not named in the charge.

### 3.67

In *Leeson* [2000] 1 Cr App R 233, the Court of Appeal made clear that a mistake as to the type of controlled drug possessed was not a defence to which the provisions of *s 28* of the 1971 Act could be applied (see *s 28(3)(a)*).

### 3.68

As Roch LJ. stated:[21]

> 'Parliament clearly intended that a person in possession of a controlled drug with intent to supply should not be able to say "I did not know it was cocaine. I thought it was another controlled drug".'

## Possession and memory

### 3.69

Where a defendant is found to be in possession of a controlled drug and asserts that he had forgotten he had the drug in his custody or under his control, can this constitute a defence to a charge of possession, based on a lack of knowledge of the drug possessed? The answer is, unequivocally no.

### 3.70

Providing the accused had been aware of possessing the drug initially, it matters not that he subsequently forgot about it. Possession, is not dependent upon the alleged possessor's powers of memory.

---

21 At p. 240.

**3.71**

Nor does possession come and go as memory revives or fails. As Lord Lane CJ sensibly remarked in the case of *R v Martindale* [1996] 1 WLR 1042 (at page 1044*): '*If it were to do so, a man with a poor memory would be acquitted, he with the good memory would be convicted.'

**3.72**

In *Martindale*, the appellant had in his pocket a wallet that was found to contain a small amount of cannabis resin (366 milligrams). His conviction for possession of a controlled drug was challenged on the basis that having been given the drug two years previously he had completely forgotten about it and accordingly the mental element required to prove possession was not made out.

**3.73**

This argument was regarded by Lord Lane CJ as '*fallacious*' as he drew from the remarks of Phillimore LJ in the earlier case of *R v Bussell* [1972] 1 WLR 64, in which Phillimore LJ stated:[22]

> ' .. this court thinks that it cannot be said that simply as a result of your mistaken belief or your failure to appreciate that you have got them, they thereby in some way passed out of your possession ... But if you have got it in your custody and you put it in some safe place, and then forget that you have got it, and discover a year or two later, when you happen to look in that particular receptacle that it is still there, it seems to this court idle to suggest that during those two years it has not been in your possession. It has been there under your hand and control. If it has not been in your possession, in whose possession has it been? Presumably it has not been in a state of limbo.'

## The relevance of quantity to possession

**3.74**

Cases concerning simply possession can often involve very small amounts of controlled drugs being found. Where amounts too large to be consistent with personal use are discovered a charge of possession with intent to supply may well be preferred. What however is the legal position when the amounts found are miniscule?

**3.75**

It has been argued that in cases where only traces of drugs are found, so infinitesimal in amount that they are incapable of being used, one cannot

---

22 At p. 67.

be said to in possession of them. However, as Lord Scarman outlined in the case of *R v Boyesen* [1982] AC 768, this suggested test of usability is incorrect in law.

### 3.76

The question to ask is not whether the quantity of the drug was usable but simply whether the defendant was in possession of the drug and that possession denoted a physical control or custody of a thing together with knowledge that one had it in one's control or custody.

### 3.77

The suggestion that that drugs needed to be found in a usable quantity in order to be able to be in possession of them appears to derive from *R v Worsell* [1970] 1 WLR 111, a case involving droplets of heroin being found in a tube.

### 3.78

In *Worsell*, the Court noted that the tube was, in reality empty and the appellant could therefore not be in possession of its contents. Whatever the tube contained, obviously it could not be used and it could not be sold.

### 3.79

This decision was followed by *R v Carver* [1978] QB 472, where it was held that if the quantity is so minute that it is not usable in any manner prohibited by the *MDA 1971*, then a conviction for being in possession of the minute quantity of the drug would not be justified.

### 3.80

This analysis was heavily criticised in *Keane v Gallagher* 1980 SLT 144, where the court noted that 'It is the possession of the controlled drug which is made punishable by s 5 (1) and (2), not its use or potential use. There is no ambiguity in the words used and no absurdity is produced.'[23]

### 3.81

In noting the difference in judicial opinion evidenced in the cases of *Gallagher* and *Carver*, Lord Scarman in *Boyesen* was persuaded by the reasoning in *Gallagher*, stating that:

> 'Quantity is, however, of importance in two respects when one has to determine whether or not an accused person has a controlled drug in his possession. First, is the quantity sufficient to enable a court to find as a matter of fact that it amounts to something? If it is visible, tangible,

---

23  At p.147.

and measurable, it is certainly something. The question is one of fact for the common sense of the tribunal …'.[24]

### 3.82

Interestingly, Lord Scarman then goes on to acknowledge that whilst one can be in legal possession of small traces of drugs, the amount found is likely to have a direct bearing on the likelihood of whether the accused was aware of the drug, which in turn has a direct bearing on whether he could be said to be in possession of it.

### 3.83

In *R v Marriott* (Charles Percival) [1971] 1 WLR 187, the court held that a person in possession of a penknife bearing only traces of a minute quantity of cannabis resin cannot be convicted of unauthorised possession of the drug unless he had reason to know at least that there was some foreign substance on the object.

## Where drugs have been consumed

### 3.84

Ordinarily, cases involving possession of drugs involve analysis of illicit drugs that have yet to be used by those said to possess them, but what is the position whereby someone is accused of being in possession of drugs that they have already consumed?

### 3.85

In *Hambleton v Callinan and Others* [1968] 3 WLR 235 it was held that where there was evidence that those accused had consumed a controlled drug it was impossible to say that the defendants were in possession of the said controlled drug within the meaning of *s 1(1)* of the *Drugs (Prevention of Misuse) Act of 1964*.

### 3.86

More specifically, Lord Parker CJ said:[25]

> ' … there may be cases where a man, as it were, consumes something, puts it in his mouth or swallows it, such as a diamond or a gold ring, in order to conceal it, when nevertheless he may well be in possession of it. I entirely agree but when, as here, something is literally consumed and changed in character, it seems to me impossible to say that a man is in possession of it within the meaning of this Act…'

---

24 At p.777.
25 At p.432.

**3.87**

Applying this analysis, the act of consumption itself does not afford someone an absolute defence to a possession charge. Whether the drugs consumed have 'changed in character' post consumption (by reason of ingestion) is clearly the determinative question. Consequently, those who swallow drugs wrapped in protective packaging to avoid ingestion (such as so called 'drugs mules'), are still said to be in possession of the drugs within their system.

**3.88**

It is also important to note, as Lord Parker CJ himself did, that in reality the question being posed in the case of *Hambleton* was academic, in that, evidence of the consumption of controlled drugs was capable of being considered prima facie evidence of prior possession[26]. Importantly, Lord Parker CJ found no reason in law why a charge of possession could not predate the time when the consumed drugs were first detected. Consequently, evidence of drug consumption can support a charge of possession under the provisions of *s 5* of the Act.

# Summary of key points

**3.89**

- *Section 5* of the *MDA 1971* prohibits the possession of controlled drugs (as listed in Sch 2 of the Act).

- To be in possession of a controlled drug the prosecution is required to prove that an accused is in control of or has custody of it (the physical element of the offence)

- A person need not be in actual physical possession of a controlled drug in order to possess it. *Section 37(3)* of the *MDA 1971* allows for 'constructive possession', whereby you are said to possess that which is subject to your control but which is in the custody of another.

- To be in possession of a controlled drug the prosecution is further required to prove that an accused had some knowledge of 'the thing' in their possession, this does not equate to knowledge of it's precise 'qualities' (the mental element of the offence)

- Knowledge of/an intention to possess a controlled drug may be imputed in circumstances where a defendant could reasonably have known about drugs found in their custody and/or control.

- Someone can be in joint possession of controlled drugs where they (along with others) have some right to say what can be done with them.

---

26 This principle was recently considered by the Administrative Court in the case of *Olah v Hungary* unreported; QBD (Admin); 27 April 2016.

- Being mistaken as to the quality/type of the drug in an accused custody and/or control is no defence to an offence of possession.

- Forgetting you are in possession of a controlled drug, of which you were initially aware, is no defence to an offence of possession.

- A controlled drug need not be found in a usable amount in order to be in possession of it.

# 4    Possession: Prohibited Drugs and Defences

Tom Stevens

## Proving the drug is prohibited

**4.1**

The essence of an offence contrary to the provisions of *s 5(1)–(2)* of the *Misuse of Drugs Act 1971* (*MDA 1971*) is having in one's possession a prohibited substance. In order to establish guilt, the prosecution must prove that the substance that the accused was allegedly in possession of is, in fact a prohibited substance. Failure to satisfy this third ingredient of the offence of possession will result in no offence being established.

## The legislative provisions: section 2 and Schedule 2

**4.2**

The expression 'controlled drug' is defined in *s 2(1)(a)* of the Act as 'any substance or product for the time being specified in Part I, II or III of Schedule 2 to this Act'.[1]

**4.3**

Schedule 2 of the Act groups controlled drugs into three categories. These are classified according to the degree and type of harm they are considered to cause to both the individual user and wider society. This is determined by the Advisory Council on the Misuse of Drugs (ACMD) who are tasked with advising the UK government on controlled drug categorisation. Part 1 of Sch 2 lists Class A drugs which are deemed to have the most harmful impact (this is reflected in the sentences for those found in possession of such, alone, or with an intention to supply them – as examined in **Chapter 11**). Part 2 lists Class B drugs and Pt 3 lists Class C drugs.

**4.4**

Each drug listed is identified according to a pharmaceutical description with further clarification as to the meanings of certain expressions used found within

---

1    See, eg, *R v Hunt* [1987] AC 352).

the interpretive provisions of Pt 4 of Sch 2, and more particularly in the case of 'cannabis', 'cannabis resin' and 'prepared opium' under the provisions of *s 37(1)* of the Act.

**4.5**

Furthermore, and as Lord Diplock acknowledged in the case of *DPP v Goodchild* [1978] 2 All ER 161, 67 Cr App Rep 56:

> 'Following upon the lists of controlled drugs specified by name in each of the three classes are additional paragraphs designed to incorporate in the class closely related chemical analogues of the listed drugs, such as stereoisomers, esters, ethers and salts. In addition there is a paragraph which incorporates within the relevant class 'any preparation or other product containing a substance or product for the time being specified in [the list of drugs] above.'[2]

# Temporary class drugs orders

**4.6**

In addition to the permanently controlled drugs as listed in Sch 2 of the *MDA 1971*, in light of new and emerging drug threats, most notably the recent proliferation of so called 'legal highs', since the 15 November 2011 the MDA has been amended[3] to enable the Secretary of State to place new psychoactive substances, which are causing sufficient concerns about their potential harm to users, under temporary control, by making such substances subject to a temporary class drug order (TCDO).

**4.7**

Parliamentary procedure to permanently control a drug under the provisions of the 1971 Act, following consideration of the advice provided by the ACMD, remains the preferred approach.[4] However, a TCDO may be considered where there is concern about a new drug's harmful impact in circumstances where a faster legislative response may be necessary to protect the public. The ACMD will then make a full assessment of a new drug's harm to consider whether a subsequent recommendation for permanent control as a Class A, B or C drug under the 1971 Act should be made.

---

2   At p. 581.
3   The amendment to the Misuse of Drugs 1971 was made by the *Police Reform and Social Responsibility Act 2011, s 151* and Sch 17.
4   See the Home Office's 'Temporary Class Drug – Factsheet' (first published 15 November 2011).

## The provisions of section 2A and 2B

**4.8**

The power to make a TCDO is found under the provisions of *s 2A, subss (2)* and *(3)* of the 1971 Act. The Home Secretary may make a temporary class drug order providing two conditions are satisfied. They are as follows:

(a) The drug(s) to be made subject to the proposed order must not already be controlled under the provisions of the Act; and

(b) The Secretary of State must have determined that the order should be made having consulted the Advisory Council on the Misuse of Drugs, or the Home Secretary has received a recommendation from the Advisory Council that the order should be made.[5]

**4.9**

Furthermore, the Secretary of State can only make a TCDO if, having considered advice from the ACMD:

(a) it appears that the substance or product under consideration is a drug that is being, or is likely to be, misused; and

(b) misuse is having, or is capable of having, harmful effects (as stipulated by the provisions of *s 2A(4)(a)–(b)* of the *MDA 1971*).

**4.10**

A TCDO will come into immediate effect. This remains so, subject to parliamentary agreement within 40 sitting days of the Home Secretary making the order.

**4.11**

The order will last for 12 months, unless the substance(s) subject to the order are earlier brought under the permanent control of the 1971 Act by virtue of an order made under *s 2(2)* of the 1971 Act, or the order is varied or revoked.

## Possession of a temporary class drug is not an offence

**4.12**

The drugs listed in a TCDOs will be considered a 'controlled drug' within the meaning of the *MDA 1971* and other accompanying legislation such as the *Proceeds of Crime Act 2002* (unless otherwise stated).

---

5   The role of the Advisory Council in making a recommendation for a temporary class drugs order is particularised under the provisions of *s 2B* of the 1971 Act.

**4.13**

However, those found in simple possession of a temporary class drug do not commit a criminal offence. With the exception of possession offences, all of the other drugs offences under the *MDA 1971* will apply to temporary class drugs.

**4.14**

Additionally, whilst possession of a temporary class drug is not an offence under the provisions of the Act, law enforcement officers may, nonetheless search and detain a person (or vehicle) in a number of circumstances. These are:

(a)   where there are reasonable grounds to suspect that the person is in possession of a temporary class drug;

(b)   to seize, detain and dispose of a suspected temporary class drug; or

(c)   to arrest or charge a person who commits the offence of intentionally obstructing an enforcement officer in the exercise of their powers listed above.[6]

**4.15**

Since the Secretary of State has been afforded the power to make a TCDO under the provisions of the 1971 Act, seven orders have been made.[7]

**4.16**

The first two orders listed have now lapsed and the drugs included within them have now been included within those listed under Sch 2 of the 1971 Act.[8]

**4.17**

In 2015 alone, three temporary class drug orders were made, reflecting the speed at which new drugs deemed harmful to the health of users were finding their way onto the market. For example, in April 2015 the government brought into force a TCDO making it illegal for anyone to supply or import five novel psychoactive substances (otherwise known as 'legal highs').

**4.18**

The latest order (Order 2016/1126) came into force on 27 November 2016, serving to extend by 12 months the temporary control of methiopropamine (or MPA) (as originally brought under temporary control by Order 2015/1929).

---

6   Pursuant to the provisions of *s 23A* of the *MDA 1971*.
7   They are the MDA 1971 (Temporary Class Drug) Order 2012/980; Order 2013/1294; Order 2015/102; Order 2015/1396; Order 2015/1929; Order 2016/650 and Order 2016/1126.
8   (in accordance with the provisions of the of MDA 1971 (Ketamine etc.) (Amendment) Order 2014/1106 and MDA 1971 (Amendment) Order 2013/239).

**4.19**

Such are the concerns surrounding this particular psychoactive drugs 'high risk of harm' to users, as assessed by the ACMD,[9] and acknowledging that the TCDO that serves to control it expires on 27 November 2017, an order is presently being sought to bring it under permanent control under Sch 2 of the *MDA 1971*, as a class B drug.[10]

## The burden of proof: forensic analysis

**4.20**

It is for the Crown to prove that the substance that forms the basis of a charge under *s 5(1)–(2)* of the *MDA 1971* is a controlled drug. It must be proved by the Crown that the substance in question was prohibited at the material time.

**4.21**

This is due to the provisions of Sch 2 being regularly amended or supplemented by regulations implemented by the Secretary of State under the provisions of *s 10(1)* of the 1971 Act, and further that the substance, be it controlled, was in a prohibited form.

**4.22**

This is well illustrated by *R v Hunt* [1987] A.C. 352. The appellant was charged with being in possession of a controlled drug, namely morphine. However, the provisions of reg 4(1) of the Misuse of Drugs Regulations 1973, as amended, made clear that *s 5(1) of the MDA 1971* 'shall not have effect in relation to the controlled drugs specified in Sch 1 of the 1973 Regulations.'

**4.23**

One such drug as described under para 3 of Sch 1 was:

> 'Any preparation of medicinal opium or of morphine containing … not more than 0.2 per cent. of morphine … being a preparation compounded with one or more other active or inert ingredients in such a way that the opium or … the morphine, cannot be recovered by readily applicable means or in a yield which would constitute a risk to health.'

**4.24**

The House of Lords ruled that it had been for the Crown to prove that the morphine in the appellant's possession had been in the prohibited form (being

---

9  Explanatory Memorandum to the MDA 1971 (Temporary Class Drug) (No. 3) Order 2015 No.1929', para 7.2.
10  A draft Statutory Instrument – The Misuse of Drugs Act 1971 (Amendment) (No.2) Order 2017, has been laid before Parliament for approval. It is yet to receive Royal assent.

above 0.2% in purity) rather than for the appellant to prove that the morphine on his person was not prohibited. The Crown had failed to prove the former. The evidence they relied upon identifying the drug as morphine lacked sufficient particularity as to the precise make-up of the drug. Consequently, the appeal was allowed.

**4.25**

At page 376 of the judgment Lord Griffith remarked:

> 'I do not share the anxieties of the Court of Appeal that this may place an undue burden on the prosecution. It must be extremely rare for a prosecution to be brought under the Act of 1971 without the substance in question having been analysed. If it has been analysed there will be no difficulty in producing evidence to show that it does not fall within Schedule 1 to the Regulations.'

**4.26**

Far from placing an undue burden on the Crown, Lord Griffiths went on to outline the 'very real practical difficulties' a defendant would face in proving drugs in their possession were not prohibited, given there is no statutory provision entitling the defendant to a sample of the drug for testing.

**4.27**

Most cases involving allegations of drug possession will rely on forensic/ scientific analysis to conclusively establish the identity of the drug in question. This will be particularly important in cases such as *Hunt* where the charge is only made out if it can be satisfied that the drug in question has very specific chemical attributes.

**4.28**

The failure to scientifically identify the precise makeup of a drug in cases where it is prohibited in one form but not in another must be considered a failure to prove that the drug is in a prohibited form and therefore subject to the provisions of s *5(1)–(2)* of the Act.

# Cases involving cocaine

**4.29**

The degree of precision required in an analyst's certificate to satisfy the evidential burden on the prosecution that the drug in question is prohibited will depend on the drug that is said to form the basis of the charge.

**4.30**

Where the drug in question (such as morphine), is prohibited in one form but not in another, 'absolute clarity'[11] is required in the analyst's certificate.

**4.31**

Where a defendant possesses a drug which has a number of forms, which are all prohibited, the failure to explicitly state that such a drug was a controlled drug within the meaning of *s 2(1)* of the *MDA 1971* will not render the case against the defendant unproven.

**4.32**

Cocaine, is one such drug. It can be both a natural substance, such as coca leaf, and a substance resulting from a chemical transformation, all of which are prohibited under the terms of the 1971 Act.

**4.33**

In *The Attorney General for the Cayman Islands v Roberts* [2002] UKPC 18[12] the appellant was charged with possession with intent to supply cocaine. The prosecution relied on a forensic analyst certificate. It stated that the contents of the sealed package in his possession had proved to be cocaine hydrochloride. The certificate did not, however, state that the substance known as cocaine hydrochloride was a controlled drug.

**4.34**

Consequently, on appeal against his conviction it was submitted that the certificate should have contained a statement that was a controlled drug within the meaning of s 2(1) of the Misuse of Drugs Law (the relevant statute operative in the Cayman Island at the time).

**4.35**

The Court of Appeal held that as cocaine was a controlled drug in all its forms, it was not necessary for the certificate to state that the substance was a controlled drug.

## Forensic evidence is not always required

**4.36**

Not all drugs have to be forensically analysed to establish their identity with sufficient certainty to allow a case to go before a jury.

---

11  *Hunt at* p. 378.
12  See also *R v Greensmith* [1983] 1 WLR 1124.

**4.37**

In *Gwilliam v DPP* [2010] EWHC 3312 (Admin), the court confirmed that there was nothing wrong in principle with an experienced police officer being able to give evidence as to the identity of a particular substance (in this case cannabis). However, their findings would have to be sufficiently certain to be left to a jury at the end of the prosecution's case.

**4.38**

The conviction in *Gwilliam* was set aside after the police officer conceded under cross-examination that the substance they found 'might not be cannabis'. In the absence of any other evidence dealing with what the substance was this highly equivocal evidence was deemed insufficient to support the charge alleged.

**4.39**

Similarly in *R v Hill* [1993] 96 Cr App R 456, Waterhouse J emphasised that the prosecution must establish the identity of the drug that was the subject matter of a charge with sufficient certainty to achieve the standard of proof required in a criminal case.

**4.40**

The conviction was quashed in *Hill* after the court found that the description of the substance as 'small and very dark', 'a small dark object' and 'a dark substance' was insufficient evidence to establish that the appellant was supplying cannabis resin. The Court said:[13]

> 'We do not accept that the effect of the decision in Hunt is to require scientific evidence to be adduced in every case to identify a prohibited drug because that case turned, at least in part, on the fact that the drug in question was morphine, which it was an offence to possess in one form and not an offence to possess in another form. It is clear from Hunt, however, if authority is needed for the proposition, that the prosecution must establish the identity of the drug that is the subject of a charge with sufficient certainty to achieve the standard of proof required in a criminal case.'

## Admissions

**4.41**

The prosecution may also prove the identity of a drug through admissions made by the defendant.

---

13 At p. 460.

**4.42**

In *R v Chatwood & Others* [1980] 70 Cr App R 39,[14] Forbes J ruled that where an experienced drug user identifies a substance in his possession as a controlled drug, that is sufficient prima facie evidence of both possession and the nature of the substance possessed.

**4.43**

It is clear from the cases of *Chatwood* and *Bird v Adams* that an admission made by a defendant is capable of providing proof as to the nature of the substance found in their possession. However, it will be dependent on the degree of knowledge the defendant has over the drug in question.

**4.44**

Where the admission comes from someone that had never used the substance before, one may be able to assert the opinion expressed was not sufficiently informed so as to have any evidential value.

**4.45**

Where a defendant admits to possessing one type of prohibited drug which turns out to be another type of prohibited drug, they will not be afforded a defence to a charge, based on lack of knowledge.

**4.46**

In *R v Leeson (John Anthony)* [2000] 1 Cr App R 233, the appellant appealed against a conviction of unlawful possession of cocaine with intent to supply. He had believed the drug to be amphetamine, wrongly. It was argued that the Crown could not prove that he had intended to supply cocaine, one of the elements of the offence.

**4.47**

The Court of Appeal remarked, that under a charge of possession with intent to supply, the inclusion in the particulars of offence of the words 'Class A, namely cocaine' was simply for the purposes of sentence. All the prosecution had to establish was that the accused had in his possession a controlled drug with intent to supply the substance which is in his possession to another. Significantly, it was not necessary to prove possession of a particular controlled drug notwithstanding that a specific drug had been named on the charge.

---

14 See also *Bird v Adams* [1972] Crim LR 174.

# Defences

### 4.48

When the *MDA 1971* came into force, it afforded those accused of being in possession of a controlled drug defences that had not previously existed in law. Consequently, it mitigated the harshness of the law as it had stood previously, as noted by Lord Reid in *Warner*.

### 4.49

The statutory defences available to an accused charged with possession under *s 5(1)* of the Act are found under *s 5(4)* and *s 28*.

## Section 5(4): lawful intention

### 4.50

*Section 5(4)* of the *MDA 1971* states as follows:

'In any proceedings for an offence under subsection (2) above in which it is proved that the accused had a controlled drug in his possession, it shall be a defence for him to prove—

(a)  that, knowing or suspecting it to be a controlled drug, he took possession of it for the purpose of preventing another from committing or continuing to commit an offence in connection with that drug and that as soon as possible after taking possession of it he took all such steps as were reasonably open to him to destroy the drug or to deliver it into the custody of a person lawfully entitled to take custody of it; or

(b)  that, knowing or suspecting it to be a controlled drug, he took possession of it for the purpose of delivering it into the custody of a person lawfully entitled to take custody of it and that as soon as possible after taking possession of it he took all such steps as were reasonably open to him to deliver it into the custody of such a person.'

### 4.51

*Section 5(4)* contains a defence which is available in the case of a charge of simple possession under *s 5(2)* of the Act. In simple terms, it assumes that the accused knew or suspected that the thing which was in their possession was a controlled drug but having discovered that, took reasonable steps to either destroy it or deliver it to someone lawfully entitled to possess it.

### 4.52

The provisions of *s 5(4)* of the Act have been subjected to very little noteworthy judicial analysis. In *R v Murphy* [2002] EWCA Crim 1768, the Court of Appeal stressed that in order for a defence to succeed under *s 5(4)(a)*, a defendant must show that he did more than leave it to the forces of nature to destroy the drug in question.

**4.53**

In *Murphy* the defendant had buried cannabis in a hole. The court took the view that although this may have indicated he had no intention to possess such, the cannabis was ultimately recoverable. Longmore LJ noted that 'destruction requires a great deal more finality about it than what the defendant did'. [15]

**4.54**

It should be noted that, unlike a defence under the provisions of *s 5(4)(b)*, *s 5(4) (a)* further required evidence that the act of destruction or deliverance to a lawful possessor was done for the purposes of preventing another from making unlawful use of the drugs in question.

**4.55**

No such requirement is found under the provisions of *s 5(4)(b)*. It provides a defence to those who having discovered and taken possession of a control drug, knowing or suspecting it to be such, as soon as possible thereafter take all such steps as were reasonably open to them to deliver the said controlled drug into the custody of a person lawfully entitled to take custody of it. For example, a police officer acting in the course of his duty, given they are exempt from the provisions of *s 5(1)* of the 1971 Act.[16]

## Section 28: lack of knowledge

**4.56**

Lord Roskill in *R v Ashton-Rickardt* [1977] 65 Cr App R 67 noted[17] that 'whatever the precise scope of the various subsections of section 28 may be, their manifest purpose is to afford a defence to an accused person where no defence had previously existed.'

**4.57**

*Section 28* states as follows:

> 'This section applies to offences under any of the following provisions of this Act, that is to say section 4(2) and (3), section 5(2) and (3), section 6(2) and section 9.

---

15 At p. 425.
16 See s 6(7)(a) of the Misuse of Drugs Regulations 2001/3998).
17 At p. 43.

(2)   Subject to subsection (3) below, in any proceedings for an offence to which this section applies it shall be a defence for the accused to prove that he neither knew of nor suspected nor had reason to suspect the existence of some fact alleged by the prosecution which it is necessary for the prosecution to prove if he is to be convicted of the offence charged.

(3)   Where in any proceedings for an offence to which this section applies it is necessary, if the accused is to be convicted of the offence charged, for the prosecution to prove that some substance or product involved in the alleged offence was the controlled drug which the prosecution alleges it to have been, and it is proved that the substance or product in question was that controlled drug, the accused—

(a)   shall not be acquitted of the offence charged by reason only of proving that he neither knew nor suspected nor had reason to suspect that the substance or product in question was the particular controlled drug alleged; but

(b)   shall be acquitted thereof—

(i)   if he proves that he neither believed nor suspected nor had reason to suspect that the substance or product in question was a controlled drug; or

(ii)   if he proves that he believed the substance or product in question to be a controlled drug, or a controlled drug of a description, such that, if it had in fact been that controlled drug or a controlled drug of that description, he would not at the material time have been committing any offence to which this section applies.'

## The parameters of section 28 (2)–(3)

**4.58**

The provisions of *s 28* allow for a defendant to demonstrate sufficient ignorance of an essential part of the prosecution's case so as to exculpate themselves. However, the provisions are not easy to understand and the scope of each subsection is often misunderstood.

**4.59**

Broadly speaking, subs (2) applies in circumstances where a defendant states he was unaware of the very existence of the 'substance or product' that turns out to be controlled drug. The scope of this general defence under *s 28(2)* is qualified by defences under *s 28(3)*.

**4.60**

Subsection (3), applies in circumstances where the defendant was aware of the 'substance or product' but where he states that he did not believe it to be a controlled drug [(3)(b)(i)]. Alternatively, to circumstances where the defendant believed the 'substance or product' to be a controlled drug but one that were it so, he was entitled to possess – by virtue of a legal exemption for example [(3)(b)(ii)].

**4.61**

The interplay between the subsections of *s 28* and their respective scope are helpfully explored in the case of *Salmon v HM Advocate* 1999 JC 67.

**4.62**

In this case, Lord Rodger uses the following example. The police search an accused's house, where he lives with other people. In the course of the search, the police find a bag containing ecstasy tablets. The accused is charged with possession of the ecstasy tablets.

**4.63**

In this situation, Lord Rodger identified three potential defences open to the accused. All involve a lack of knowledge, to varying degrees.

**4.64**

The first defence is an assertion from the accused that they were completely unaware that the drugs were in the house and that, if they were present, they must have belonged to one of the other occupants.

**4.65**

In this case Lord Roger's emphasises that it is for the prosecution to establish that the accused knew that the bag was in the house, that he had control of it and that the bag contained ecstasy. If they fail to establish any of these elements, then the prosecution will fail.

**4.66**

Put simply, if any of the evidence leaves the jury with a reasonable doubt as to whether the accused knew that the bag was in the house or as to whether he had it under his control, then the accused must be acquitted.

**4.67**

The second defence is that the accused knew that the bag was in the house and contained something. However, although he had control to it, he did not know that it contained tablets.

**4.68**

Here, Lord Rodger observed that the Crown have discharged their burden of proof and the accused would be convicted, unless he proves that he did not know nor suspect nor have reason to suspect that the tablets were in the bag.

**4.69**

If the accused can prove that, then, even though he was in legal possession of the tablets, he must be acquitted as set out in *s 28(2)*. As Lord Rodger observed:

> 'In a case like that the trial judge should direct the jury to consider whether they are satisfied, on a balance of probabilities, that the accused did not know nor suspect nor have reason to suspect that the tablets were in the bag. If they are so satisfied, they must acquit; if they are not so satisfied, they must convict.'[18]

**4.70**

Finally, the accused may say that he knew that the bag was in the house and in his control and he knew that it contained tablets. Nonetheless, he did not know that the tablets comprised ecstasy.

**4.71**

In that scenario, the accused will be convicted unless he can rely on *s 28(3)*. It will not be enough for him to prove that he thought that the tablets were a different controlled drug, such as heroin, as *s 28(3)(a)* makes clear. Under *s 28(3)(b)(i)*, he must prove that he neither knew nor suspected nor had reason to suspect that the tablets *were a controlled drug* of any kind. In that scenario, Lord Rodger explained that:

> '…therefore the trial judge should direct the jury to consider whether they are satisfied, on the balance of probabilities, that the accused neither knew nor suspected nor had reason to suspect that the pills were a controlled drug. If they are so satisfied, they must acquit; if they are not so satisfied, they must convict.'[19]

# Section 28 and the burden of proof

**4.72**

With the advent of *s 28* of the 1971 Act, the Crown had previously sought to argue that the effect of *s 28(2)* had been to shift the onus of proving the mens rea of possession from the Crown to the defence.

---

18  At p. 79.
19  At p. 79.

**4.73**

As was acknowledged by Lord Rodger in *Salmon*:[20]

'... it was contended that all that the Crown was required to do was to prove that, as a matter of fact, the drugs were in the custody or control of the accused and he would then be convicted, unless he proved that he had not known that the drugs were there.'

**4.74**

Such arguments however were readily rejected by the courts in both Scotland (in *McKenzie v Skeen*, 1983 S.L.T. 121) and England (in *Ashton-Rickardt*).

**4.75**

In *Ashton-Rickardt*, the appellant's car was searched by police who found a reefer in the pocket of the driver's door. Forensic analysis subsequently revealed that the reefer contained 200 milligrams of cannabis. The appellant was charged with possessing a controlled drug, contrary to *s 5(2)* of the *MDA 1971*.

**4.76**

At trial, the appellant denied all knowledge of the reefer found and claimed it must have been put there by an acquaintance during his absence. Significantly, the judge did not direct the jury that the Crown had to prove knowledge of the presence of the controlled drug as part of possession. Instead, he directed the jury that the burden of proof was on the defendant to disprove knowledge that the thing was in his car or that it was a controlled drug, pursuant to the provisions of *s 28* of the 1971 Act.

**4.77**

On appeal, the Crown maintained that the trial judge had correctly interpreted the provisions of *s 28*. They argued that the Crown no longer has to prove beyond reasonable doubt that the accused person knew that he had 'the thing', as it has been called, in his possession.

**4.78**

Lord Justice Roskill flatly rejected the argument advanced by the Crown. He stated:[21]

'We think that argument is wrong as a matter of the construction of the section. When one construes these sections in the MDA 1971 together with section 5 (1) and (2) and one realises that section 5 (2) and indeed

---

20 At p. 76.
21 At p. 43–44.

(3) are each made subject to section 28 of the Act, it is apparent that whatever the precise scope of the various subsections of section 28 may be, their manifest purpose is to afford a defence to an accused person where no defence had previously existed.'

**4.79**

Lord Justice Roskill went on to remark:[22]

'It seems to us plain that there is nothing in section 28 which in any way alters the burden which rests upon the Crown so that when they seek to prove unlawful possession of a controlled drug, proof of possession involves proof of knowledge by the accused that he had control of the "thing" in question, as the House of Lords decided in Warner's case'

## 'To prove': not a legal burden but an evidential burden

**4.80**

Where the Crown have established that an accused was in possession of a controlled drug, by satisfying both the physical and mental elements of the offence, it is then open to an accused under the provisions of *s 28* 'to prove' that 'he neither knew of nor suspected nor had reason to suspect' the article or substance in his possession was a controlled drug.

**4.81**

As noted above, the prosecution do not need to prove that the accused knew that 'the thing' in his possession was a controlled drug (just that they knew of 'the thing' not it's particular qualities). This is a matter which must be raised by the defence.

**4.82**

One possible rationale for placing this burden on the defence is that those dealing and smuggling drugs often secrete drugs in a container, enabling the carrier to say that they were unaware of the contents.

**4.83**

In *R v Lambert* [2001] UKHL 37, it was argued that the requirement for an accused to prove a lack of knowledge under the provisions of s 28 was a breach of their art 6 rights under the European Convention of Human Rights (ECHR), in that they reversed the burden of proof in respect of an essential ingredient of the offence and consequently attacked the presumption of innocence.

---

22 At p. 72.

**4.84**

In considering the arguments advanced by the appellant, their Lordships were in broad agreement that whether or not the requirements of *s 28* were incompatible with the Convention rights of an accused was dependent on whether the words *'to prove'*, as contained in *s 28*, were to be construed as imposing a legal burden of proof on the accused or alternatively only an evidential burden.

**4.85**

Significantly, in accordance with the interpretive obligations under *s 3* of the *Human Rights Act 1998*, their Lordships concluded it was possible to read the provisions of *s 28* in a way which was compatible with an accused Convention rights, by reading that *s 28(2)–(3)* created an evidential burden only, meaning the accused was required to give no more than 'sufficient evidence' of a lack of knowledge, which the prosecution were then required to disprove.

**4.86**

Consideration was then given to what constituted 'sufficient evidence', with Lord Hope remarking:[23]

> 'an evidential burden is not to be thought of as a burden which is illusory. What the accused must do is put evidence before the court which, if believed, could be taken by a reasonable jury to support his defence.'

**4.87**

Similarly, Lord Slynn stated:[24]

> 'It is not enough that the defendant in seeking to establish the evidential burden should merely mouth the words of the section. The defendant must still establish that the evidential burden has been satisfied.'

**4.88**

Establishing an evidential burden however, is not necessarily reliant on the accused giving evidence. As Lord Rodger noted in the case of *Salmon*:[25]

> 'It is perhaps worth stating explicitly that, even though subsections (2) and (3) speak of the accused proving something, this does not imply that, to establish a defence, the accused must necessarily give evidence. Doubtless, that would often be the simplest method of proof, but the

---

23 At para 90.
24 At para 17.
25 At p. 75.

necessary evidence might come, for example, from a "mixed" statement or from witnesses speaking to what the accused was told was in the container or to the accused's apparent astonishment when the contents of the container were revealed and found to be a controlled drug.'

## Self-induced intoxication and the objective limb of a section 28 defence

### 4.89

Under the provisions of *s 28* it shall be a defence for the accused to prove that:

(a)   he neither knew of;

(b)   nor suspected;

(c)   nor had reason to suspect;

(d)   the existence of some fact alleged by the prosecution (see *s 28(2)*) or that the substance or product in question was a controlled drug (see *s 28(3)(b) (i)*).

### 4.90

The first two limbs have required little by way of judicial explanation, being subjective in nature. However, the existence of the phrase 'had reason' within the third limb has elicited debate, with it suggested that it serves to inject an objective element into the defence of a lack of knowledge.

### 4.91

The existence of this objective element is evident in cases involving self-induced intoxication. Here the courts have concluded, that if a defendant does not believe or suspect that a substance or product in their possession was a controlled drug, by reason of their self-induced intoxication, then they cannot establish a defence under *s 28*, in circumstances where it can properly be said that they would have 'had reason' to believe or suspect that a substance or product was a controlled drug, had they been sober.

### 4.92

This is illustrated in the case *R v Young* [1984] 1 WLR 654. In *Young* the appellant was convicted of possessing a controlled drug (L.S.D.) with intent to supply. The evidence clearly established that the appellant did have a controlled drug on him which he swallowed when police approached. There was further strong evidence that at the time police approached him he was seriously affected by drink. Consequently, his defence to the charge was that under the provisions of *s 28(3)(b)(i)* of the Act he did not believe, suspect or have reason to suspect that what he was in possession of was a controlled drug, by reason of his self-induced intoxication.

**4.93**

In dismissing his appeal, the Court noted that whilst the question of his lack of belief or suspicion had to be considered subjectively, the accused also had to prove that he did not have reason to suspect what he had on him was a controlled drug and that a 'reason' was not 'something entirely personal and individual, calling for an entirely subjective consideration' but rather it 'involves a wider concept of an objective rationality.'[26]

**4.94**

Consequently, the Court concluded that self-induced intoxication did not afford the appellant a defence under *s 28*.

## Section 28 Does Not Apply To Those Charged With Conspiracy

**4.95**

As stipulated by the provisions of subs (1) of *s 28*, the statutory defences afforded by its provisions only apply to offences charged under *ss 4(2)–(3), 5(2)–(3), 6(2)* and *9* of the *MDA 1971*.

**4.96**

Accordingly, those charged with a conspiracy to commit one of the drugs offences identified in the 1971 Act cannot benefit directly from its provisions.[27]

# Lawful possession

## Section 7 of the MDA 1971

**4.97**

Perverse results would follow if there were a blanket prohibition on the possession of all controlled drugs, applicable to all, irrespective of the professional capacity a person was acting under whilst in possession of such drugs.

**4.98**

For example, a doctor would be liable to prosecution for possessing any controlled drug for the purposes of being able to prescribe such to patients.

---

26  At p. 658.
27  See, eg, *R v McGowan* [1990] Crim LR 399.

Equally, a police officer tasked with seizing a controlled drug from an offender would find themselves in illegal possession of such drugs once the act of seizure was completed.

**4.99**

Consequently, the *MDA 1971* contains provisions allowing the Secretary of State to make regulations exempting various professionals from the prohibitions enshrined in the Act.

**4.100**

Under the provisions of *s 7(1)(b)*, the Secretary of State may by regulations:

> 'make such other provision as he thinks fit for the purpose of making it lawful for persons to do things which under any of the following provisions of this Act, that is to say sections 4(1), 5(1) and 6(1), it would otherwise be unlawful for them to do.'

**4.101**

*Section 7(2)* goes on to stipulate that:

> 'Without prejudice to the generality of paragraph (b) of subsection (1) above, regulations under that subsection authorising the doing of any such thing as is mentioned in that paragraph may in particular provide for the doing of that thing to be lawful—
>
> (a)    if it is done under and in accordance with the terms of a licence or other authority issued by the Secretary of State and in compliance with any conditions attached thereto; or
>
> (b)    if it is done in compliance with such conditions as may be prescribed'.

**4.102**

*Section 7(3)* lists various professionals that are exempt from the legal prohibitions contained within the act, providing that at the point of possessing and/or supplying controlled drugs they are acting in their professional capacity. These professionals include, doctors, dentists, veterinary practitioners, and pharmacists.

## Self-Treatment

**4.103**

The legal parameters of *s 7(3)*, and the accompanying provisions of regs 8 and 10 of the Misuse of Drugs Regulations 1973, were considered in *R v Dunbar* [1981] 1 WLR 1536.

**4.104**

In *Dunbar* the appellant was a registered medical practitioner, who obtained a quantity of diamorphine hydrochloride and pethidine from a chemist. He was subsequently charged with unlawful possession of controlled drugs, contrary to *s 5(1)* of the 1971 Act.

**4.105**

The appellant's defence was that he had obtained such drugs whilst acting in his professional capacity as a registered doctor. He had acquired them for self-treatment in order to lift himself out of a severe depression, as legally permitted under *s 7(3)*.

**4.106**

The trial judge ruled that a doctor could not lawfully possess the drugs on his own authority to treat himself, and accordingly he invited the jury to convict the appellant based on his own evidence. However, the Court of Appeal concluded that the trial judge had erred in his direction to the jury and ordered that the appellant's conviction be quashed. It found that it was a matter for the jury to decide whether the doctor was acting 'in a professional capacity', with Lord Lane CJ commenting:[28] 'To say, as the judge did, that because the doctor had no patient, because the only patient was the doctor himself, ergo he was not acting in his capacity as a doctor, was wrong.'

## The failed defence of medical necessity

**4.107**

Those who are not registered medical practitioners, who have self-administered controlled drugs for the sole purpose of pain relief have however been treated less sympathetically than the appellant in the case of *Dunbar*.

**4.108**

In *R v Quale and Others* [2005] EWCA Crim 1415 for example, the Court of Appeal ruled unequivocally, that the defence of medical necessity in respect of cannabis use was not available to offenders who had cultivated, produced and imported cannabis for medical use, contrary to the provisions of the 1971 Act.[29]

**4.109**

The five appellants in *Quale* were either users of cannabis for the purpose of alleviating severe pain caused to them by various illnesses, or the suppliers of cannabis to other sufferers of such illnesses from a holistic centre.

---

28 At p.1541.
29 Although the court did note the exception of ongoing trials for medical research purposes.

**4.110**

It was argued on their behalf that a failure to recognise necessity as a defence in these circumstances would be a breach of art 8 of the ECHR. It was further submitted that the current law was unjustified and unsustainable, and that sufferers from pain were entitled to have a jury determine their guilt or innocence.

**4.111**

The Court of Appeal did not agree. It noted the that under the provisions of the Misuse of Drugs Regulations 2001 and the Misuse of Drugs (Designation) Order 2001, cannabis, cannabis resin and most cannabinoids are designated as drugs which may only be used for medical or scientific research and as drugs to which *s 7(4)* of the 1971 Act applies.

**4.112**

Consequently, the Court formed the view that the necessitous medical use on an individual basis of cannabis (which lay at the root of all of the defences raised) was in conflict with the purpose and effect of the legislative scheme. Expanding upon this assessment, Mance LJ stated:[30]

> 'First, no such use is permitted under the present legislation, even on doctor's prescription, except in the context of the ongoing trials for medical research purposes. Secondly, the defences involve the proposition that it is lawful for unqualified individuals to prescribe cannabis to themselves as patients or to assume the role of unqualified doctors by obtaining it and prescribing and supplying it to other individual "patients". This is contrary not only to the legislative scheme, but also to any recommendation for its change made by the Select Committee and Runciman Reports. Further, it would involve obvious risks for the integrity and the prospects of any coherent enforcement of the legislative scheme. A parallel but lawful market in the importation, cultivation, prescription, supply, possession and use of cannabis would have to come into existence, which would not only be subject to no medical safeguards or constraints, but the scope and legitimacy of which would in all likelihood be extremely difficult to ascertain or control.'

**4.113**

Despite the Court of Appeal's unambiguous ruling in *Quayle* and others, the question of whether the Convention rights of an accused were unlawfully interfered with in prosecuting those using controlled drugs on alleged medical grounds, was revived in the case of *R v Altham (Lee)* [2006] EWCA Crim 7.

---

30 At para 56.

**4.114**

In *Lee,* the appellants attempted to distinguish the case from *Quayle.* The appellants sought to persuade the Court that the prosecution of a man who used cannabis to obtain pain relief (having been left in chronic pain following a road accident) was a violation of his art 3 Convention rights. Namely, prohibiting acts of torture, inhumane or degrading treatment or punishment.

**4.115**

However, Scott Baker LJ highlighting the factual similarities between *Lee* and *Quayle,* stated:[31]

'As Mance LJ pointed out in *R v Quayle* [2005] 1 WLR 3642, para 54, the defence of necessity advocated by the defendants in these cases would, if it exists in law, enable individuals to undertake otherwise unlawful activities without medical intervention or prescription.... The defence of necessity on an individual basis as advocated by this defendant, as it was by the defendants in *Quayle,* is in conflict with the purpose and effect of the legislative scheme. The reasoning of Mance LJ in *Quayle* applies with equal force to the present case. In our view article 3 adds nothing to the extensive arguments that were dealt with by Mance LJ in *Quayle.*'

**4.116**

Further, the Court ruled that art 3 did not require the State to take any steps to alleviate the appellant's condition. Consequently, art 3 did not assist the defendant in running a defence of necessity to an offence of possession of a controlled drug under the *MDA 1971.*

**4.117**

A further example of an unsuccessful attempt to challenge the legality of prosecuting a cannabis user came in *R v Taylor* [2001] EWCA Crim 2263.

**4.118**

Here, the appellant was a practising Rastafarian. He argued that his prosecution for possession with intent to supply cannabis, interfered with his right to religious freedom under art 9 of the ECHR. Cannabis was, he argued, linked inextricably to his religious beliefs.

**4.119**

The Court of Appeal allowed his appeal against sentence. It acknowledged that the appellants' supply of cannabis for religious purposes, as opposed to for

---

31 At para 28–29.

commercial gain, was material to the length of sentence imposed. However, his appeal against conviction was refused.

**4.120**

The Court of Appeal stressed that in light of the UK's subscription to the Single Convention on Narcotic Drugs 1961 and the United Nations Convention against Illicit Traffic in Narcotic Drugs and Psychotropic Substances 1988, the trial had been justified in inferring that such subscription was convincing evidence of an international consensus on the necessity of an unqualified ban on the supply of cannabis so as to ensure the protection of public health and safety. Accordingly, any infringement of the right to religious freedom was justified, proportionate and necessary under the public health and safety limitations given by art 9(2).

## Section 10 of the Misuse of Drugs Act 1971

**4.121**

The provisions of *s* 7 of the Act are supplemented by those found under *s* 10. The latter allows the Secretary of State to put in place controls/'provisions' (through the making of regulations) designed to ensure the legal exemptions afforded to certain professionals under the Act are not misused, such as requirements that all drug transactions are documented, and the records of such are available for inspection, and that the prescribing of controlled drugs by doctors is only done under license at a specific address specified on the license[32].

## The misuse of drugs regulations

**4.122**

A comprehensive analysis of all of the regulations (as amended) made under the provisions of *ss* 7 and *10* of the Act is beyond the scope of this book.

**4.123**

A useful overview of the some of the more significant regulations made, however, can be found within the combined policy paper of the Department of Health and the Home Office, entitled '*2010 to 2015 Government Policy: Drug Misuse and Dependency*', which outlines the scope of the Misuse of Drugs Regulations 2001 (allowing for the lawful possession and supply of controlled drugs for legitimate purposes).

---

32 See *MDA 1971, s 10(2)*.

# The Psychoactive Substances Act 2016

### 4.124

Whilst the *MDA 1971* remains the principal piece legislation in the UK,[33] designed to control the use, production and supply of harmful drugs, since 26 May 2016 it has been supplemented by the provisions of the *Psychoactive Substances Act 2016* (*PSA 2016*), controlling newly emerging psychotic drugs not covered by the MDA's provisions.

### 4.125

The *PSA 2016* is a response to the proliferation of new products and substances entering the market, mimicking the effect of traditional drugs but deliberately designed to evade the controls of the *MDA 1971* (so called 'legal highs', such as synthetic drugs known as spice and mamba).

### 4.126

By capturing substances that are defined widely by the effects they have on those who consume them rather than listing the drugs affected according to their precise chemical structure (as is the case with the *MDA 1971*), the *PSA 2016* 'intends to pre-empt new substances emerging onto the drugs market.'[34]

### 4.127

The *PSA 2016* makes it an offence to produce (see *s 4*), supply or offer to supply (see *s 5*), possess with intent to supply (see *s 7*), import or export (see *s 8*) psychoactive substances for human consumption. Each offence is triable either-way and carries a maximum sentence, on indictment, of seven years' imprisonment (see *s 10(1)(d)*).

### 4.128

*Section 6* of the *PSA 2016* (largely mirroring the provisions of *s 4A* of the *MDA 1971*, explored in **Chapter 6**) creates a statutory aggravating factor when sentencing someone for an offence of supplying, or offering to supply, a psychoactive substance, where the supply, or offer to supply:

(a)   took place at or in the vicinity of a school;

(b)   involved the use of a courier under the age of 18; or

(c)   took place in a custodial institution.

---

33  Controlling a wide range of harmful drugs (including over 500 psychoactive substances).

34  See para 3 – 'Psychoactive Substances Act 2016: guidance for retailers' – Published 20 May 2016 (Home Office Guidance).

## *The Meaning of Psychoactive Substance*

**4.129**

Psychoactive substances are defined under the provisions of *s 2(1)(a)* of the *PSA 2016* as meaning 'any substance', other than those specifically exempted under the PSA),'which is capable of producing a psychoactive effect in a person who consumes it'.

**4.130**

A substance producing a psychoactive effect in a person, is further defined under *s 2(2)* as one that if, 'by stimulating or depressing the person's central nervous system, it affects the person's mental functioning or emotional state'. This would include effects associated with controlled drugs such as, hallucinations, changes in alertness, perception of time and space and drowsiness.

**4.131**

Similarly, *s 2(3)* further defines consumption as causing or allowing 'the substance, or fumes given off by the substance, to enter the person's body in any way.' Consequently, injecting, eating, drinking, snorting, inhaling and smoking would all be captured by this provision.

**4.132**

In-line with the PSA's 'Forensic Strategy', developed by the Home Office and the ACMD, proving that a substance is capable of producing a psychoactive effective in a person who consumes it, will require use of evidence, such as:

(a)   The results of 'in-vitro testing' into a substances effect (testing that takes place outside of the human body), conducted in accordance with the Home Office's Centre for Applied Science and Technology's specifications;

(b)   Evidence from suitably qualified experts commenting on published literature and/or studies into the effects of a substance;

(c)   Accounts from witnesses into the behaviour exhibited by an individual who has consumed the substance in question.

## *The Offences in Brief Overview*

*Section 4*

**4.133**

As noted above, *s 4* of the *PSA 2016* provides for an offence of producing a psychoactive substance. The actus reus of the offence is satisfied if a person produces a psychoactive substance. By virtue of *s 59(2)(a)* 'producing' a psychoactive substance includes 'producing it by manufacture, cultivation or any other method.'

**4.134**

The mens rea of *s 4* offences, compromises of three distinct mental elements. The prosecution must prove that:

(a)   The production was intentional (see *s 4(1)(a)*).

Were a psychoactive substance to be inadvertently created (the unintended by-product of research, for example) a *s 4* offence would not be made out.

(b)   The defendant must have known or suspected that the substance produced was a psychoactive substance (see *s 4(1)(b)*).

For a person to have known that a substance is a psychoactive substance, their knowledge must be based on a true belief. A person cannot be convicted under *s 4* on the basis that they 'knew' the substance was a 'pyschoactive substance' when in fact it was another substance.

The lesser standard of suspicion involves a subjective assessment of a person's state of knowledge, not an objective assessment of reasonableness. Suspicion involves a possibility that is more than fanciful, that the relevant facts exist.[35]

(c)   The defendant must intend to consume the psychoactive substance for its psychoactive effects, or know, or be reckless as to whether it is likely to be consumed by another for its psychoactive effects (see *s 4(1)(c)*).

The onus is on the prosecution to prove recklessness. A person acts recklessly when they are aware of a risk that exists or will exist and, in circumstances known to them, it was unreasonable to take the risk but nonetheless they did so.

*Section 5*

**4.135**

*Section 5* of the *PSA 2016* creates two separate offences, namely, supplying a psychoactive substance and offering to supply a psychoactive substance.

**4.136**

For supply offences under *s 5* the prosecution must prove that a person has supplied a substance to another person and that substance is a psychoactive

---

35 See: *R v Da Silva* [2006] EWCA Crim 1654 – *'a vague feeling of unease'* does not constitute suspicion but it need not be based on *'clear'* or *'firmly'* grounded facts.

substance (see *s 5(1)(a)–(b)*). Akin to the provisions of *s 37(1)* of the *MDA 1971*, *s 59(2)(b)* of the *PSA 2016* notes that 'supplying a substance includes… distributing.'

## 4.137

A detailed analysis of what constitutes an act of supply and an offer to supply is found in **Chapter 5** of this book. Whilst this chapter focuses on the provisions of the *MDA 1971*, the analysis is equally applicable to the provisions of the *PSA 2016*.

## 4.138

For an offence of supply under *s 5* to be made out, the prosecution must also prove three mental elements, namely that:

(a)   The supply was intentional (see *s 5(1)(a)*).

Were a person to unknowingly drop a psychoactive substance that was then picked up and consumed by another, for example, this would not be captured by the provisions of the *PSA 2016*.

(b)   The defendant must have known or suspected or ought to have known or suspected that the substance supplied was a psychoactive substance (see *s 5(1)(c)*).

Interestingly, the *PSA 2016* does not include provisions analogous to *s 28* of the *MDA 1971* (considered earlier in this chapter), whereby a defendant can raise a defence based on a lack of knowledge, under which they carry an evidential burden; but rather, stipulates that the prosecution must prove a person charged under *s 5* had the requisite state of knowledge noted above.

If an offence of supplying a psychoactive substance is prosecuted on the basis that a defendant 'ought to have known' that the psychoactive substance they supplied was a psychoactive substance, this will involve an objective assessment of what a 'reasonable man' in possession of the same information as a defendant would have thought.

(c)   The defendant must know, or be reckless as to whether the psychoactive substance is likely to be consumed by the person to whom it is supplied or another person, for its psychoactive effects (see *s 5(1)(d)*).

## 4.139

For offences of offering to supply a psychoactive substance, under *s 5(2)* of the *PSA 2016*, the prosecution must prove that the defendant offers to supply a psychoactive substance to another person. An advertisement can be considered an offer, including a catalogue of psychoactive substances displayed on a website with facility to purchase such online.

**4.140**

The mental element of a *s 5(2)* offence is that the defendant knows or is reckless as to whether, the substance being offered for supply, is likely to consume for its psychoactive effects. This involves an analysis of the intentions of the recipient as opposed to the person making the offer. Accordingly, there is no defence in purporting a lack of intention to fulfil the offer made, or an intention to supply something other than a psychoactive substance. Under *s 5(2)* the offence lies in the offer, not the act of supply. For further relevant analysis of such see **Chapter 5**.

*Section 7*

**4.141**

*Section 7* of the *PSA 2016* makes it an offence to possess a psychoactive substance (see *s 7(1)(a)*) with a view to supplying it to another person for consumption. **Chapter 3** of this book contains analysis of what constitutes possession under the provisions of the *MDA 1971*. Such is also of relevance to the provisions of the *PSA 2016*.

**4.142**

*Section 59(3)* of the *PSA 2016* supplements the provisions of *s 7*, noting that, a 'person's possession include any items which are: (a) subject to that person's control, but (b) in the custody of another person,' analogous to the provisions of *s 37(3)* of the *MDA 1971*.

**4.143**

As with *s 5* offences, it is for the prosecution to prove that a defendant charged under *s 7* knew or suspected that the substance in their possession was a psychoactive substance (see *s 7(1)(b)*). Unlike *s 5* offences however, it is not enough for the prosecution to prove that a defendant 'ought' to have known that such a substance was a psychoactive substance (based on an objective assessment).

**4.144**

The prosecution must further prove that a defendant intended to supply the psychoactive substance in their possession to another person for its psychoactive effective. It is inconsequential however, whether such a substance is eventually consumed by the intended recipient or some other person.

## Simple Possession is not an Offence

**4.145**

As with TCDOs the provisions of the *PSA 2016* are designed to capture those involved in the production and supply of harmful drugs. Consequently, being in simple possession of a psychoactive substance is not a criminal offence.

**4.146**

However, if a person is found to possess a psychoactive substance in a 'custodial institution' providing it is further proved that they knew or suspected it was a psychoactive substance and intended to consume it for its psychoactive effects, they are liable to be prosecuted under *s 9* of the *PSA 2016*.

**4.147**

The provisions of this section are aimed to a large extent at combatting the escalating problem of drug use within the UK's prison population and consequently, carry a maximum penalty, on indictment, of two years' imprisonment (see *s 10(2)(d)*).

**4.148**

As defined in *s 6(10)* of the Act, a custodial institution includes a prison, a young offender institution, and a removal centre.

## Exemptions

**4.149**

Pursuant to *s 3(1)* of the *PSA 2016* all substances listed in Sch 1 are exempt from its provisions. Such substances include:

(a)    Those already controlled under the provisions of the *MDA 1971;*

(b)    Medicinal products[36];

(c)    Alcohol and alcoholic products[37];

(d)    Nicotine and tobacco products;

(e)    Caffeine; and

(f)    Food, meaning any substance (including drink) that is ordinarily consumed as food (or drink), and does not contain a prohibited ingredient.[38] '

**4.150**

The provisions of *s 3* of the *PSA 2016* have been subject to recent judicial scrutiny in the case of *R v Chapman* [2017] EWCA Crim 1743. In this case four appellants sought to argue that their convictions for under the provisions of *s 7* of the *PSA 2016* should be quashed on the grounds that the nitrous oxide

---

36   Within the meaning of the Human Medicines Regulations 2012 (SI 2012/1916).

37   Defined under *s 1* of the *Tobacco Products duty Act 1979.*

38   A prohibited ingredient, in relation to a substance, is further defined under Sch 1, para 7, as meaning 'any psychoactive substance which is not naturally occurring in the substance, and the use of which in or on food is not authorised by an EU instrument.

(commonly known as laughing gas) possessed by each was a medicinal product and accordingly an exempted substance under the provisions of s 3.

**4.151**

Whilst the Court of Appeal readily acknowledged that nitous oxide was a substance 'undoubtedly used for medicinal purposes', it further noted that the definition of a 'medicinal product', as provided under the provisions of Sch 1 of the *PSA 2016*, borrowed from the Human Medicines Regulations 2012, and accordingly had to be interpreted in conformity with European Law (namely Directive 2001/83/EC).

**4.152**

Having done so, and in particular having adopted the analysis provided in the case of D & G (C–358/13, C–181/4), the Court of Appeal concluded that where a drug capable of being used for medicinal purposes is put to an alternative, entirely recreational use, then it fell outside the concept of a medicinal product and accordingly could not be considered exempt from the provisions of the PSA 2016. As the Lord Chief Justice noted:[39]

'The canisters in question were in fact manufactured for use unconnected with medical purposes, widely available and distributed for use in catering, which in itself is a strong indicator that they were not medicinal products. Furthermore, the purpose for which it was intended to supply the canisters was purely recreational with nothing whatsoever to do with health. This last feature coupled with the fact that the gas was intended to be used in circumstances which were not beneficial to health, indeed import some risk to health, was sufficient to take it outside the definition of medicinal product whatever label may have been on the boxes in which the canisters were originally packed.'

**4.153**

Similar to the provisions of the *MDA 1971*, those who carry out activities captured under *ss 4–9* of the *PSA 2016*, but do so as 'a health care professional', 'acting in the course of his or her profession' or 'in the course of, or in connection with, approved scientific research', commit no offence. Such, constitute 'Exempted Activities' under the provisions of Sch 2 of the *PSA 2016*.

## Summary of key points

**4.154**

- Any offence involving possession of a controlled drug, requires the prosecution to prove that the drug possessed was a controlled/prohibited

---

39  At para 32.

drug, at the time it was possessed (be it under the provisions of Sch 2 of the *MDA 1971*, a TCDO or the *PSA 2016*).

- The prosecution must establish the identity of the drug with 'sufficient certainty' to achieve the standard of proof required in a criminal case.

- It is not necessary to prove possession of the specific drug named on an indictment, so long as it is proved the drug was controlled/prohibited.

- Statutory defences to a charge of possession are found under *ss 5(4)* and *28* of the *MDA 1971*.

- *Section 5(4)* defences involve a defendant proving they took reasonable steps to destroy the drug they possessed or deliver it to someone lawfully entitled to possess it.

- *Section 28* defences involve a defendant proving they lacked the requisite knowledge of the drugs possessed to be considered in legal possession of them.

- The requirement that a defendant proves a lack of knowledge under any one of the statutory defences imposes no more than an evidential burden on them (ensuring the provisions are compatible with art 6 of the ECHR). This means raising no more than 'sufficient evidence' that the prosecution must then disprove.

- *Section 28* defences involve an objective consideration of what a defendant had 'reason' to suspect. Consequently, a lack of knowledge/suspicion based on self-induced intoxication will not constitute a defence.

- *Section 28*, does not remove the initial burden of proving the mental element of possession, examined in **Chapter 3**, from the prosecution.

- The *MDA 1971* allows for the lawful possession of controlled drugs by those acting in a professional capacity (such as those listed in *s 7(3)*).

- Supplementing the provisions of the *MDA 1971*, the *PSA 2016* prohibits the production and supply of newly emerging psychoactive substances, used for human consumption.

# 5 Supply and Being Concerned in Supply

Tom Stevens

## The offences

### 5.1

*Section 4(1)(b)* of the *Misuse of Drugs Act 1971* (*MDA 1971*) provides that:

'Subject to any regulations under section 7 of this Act for the time being in force, it shall not be lawful for a person— to supply or offer to supply a controlled drug to another.'

### 5.2

*Section 4(3)* of the same Act stipulates further that:

'Subject to section 28 of this Act, it is an offence for a person—

a) to supply or offer to supply a controlled drug to another in contravention of subsection (1) above; or

b) to be concerned in the supplying of such a drug to another in contravention of that subsection; or

c) to be concerned in the making to another in contravention of that subsection of an offer to supply such a drug.'

### 5.3

*Section 4(3)* of the *MDA 1971* consequently creates four offences, they are:

(1) Supplying a controlled drug to another (contrary to *s 4(3)(a)*);

(2) Offering to supply a controlled drug to another (this offence is also captured by *s 4(3)(a)* but given the offences of supplying and offering to supply are evidentially distinct, when charged, the indictment must specify which offence is being alleged);

(3) Being 'concerned' in the supply of a controlled drug to another (contrary to *s 4(3)(b)*); and

(4) Being 'concerned' in the making of an offer to supply a controlled drug to another (contrary to *s 4(3)(c)*).

**5.4**

Additionally, *s 5(3)* of the *MDA 1971* makes it an offence to be in possession of a controlled drug with 'an intention' of supplying it another. More specifically, the provision stipulates that:

> 'Subject to section 28 of this Act, it is an offence for a person to have a controlled drug in his possession, whether lawfully or not, with intent to supply it to another in contravention of section 4(1) of this Act.'

**5.5**

Whilst the five offences listed above are evidentially distinct, a consistent ingredient in each is the 'supply' of drugs, with each offence drawn in terms of supply in contravention of *s 4(1)* of the Act.

**5.6**

Accordingly, this chapter seeks to shed light on what constitutes an act of supply under the provisions of the *MDA 1971*, as well as attempting to elucidate other important concepts covered by the provisions of *ss 4* and *5(3)*, such as what constitutes 'being concerned in' the supply or an 'offer' to supply a controlled drug.

## A brief overview

**5.7**

Supplying or offering to supply controlled drugs covers a wide spectrum of transactions. There is no qualification on the quantity of drugs that need to be involved to be captured by the provisions of the *MDA 1971*.

**5.8**

Consequently, those who are involved in social supply, which may amount to no more than the passing of a cannabis joint to a fellow user[1] are prosecuted under precisely the same provisions as those involved in the supply of industrial quantities of controlled drugs for commercial gain. Although they will be differentiated at the point of sentencing.

**5.9**

When considering what an act of supply involves, the provisions of the *MDA 1971* offer little assistance. *Section 37(1)* of the Act simply notes that supplying a drug includes 'distributing' it. This is explored further later in this chapter.

---

1   See, eg, *R v Moore* [1979] Crim. L.R. 789.

**5.10**

It is now settled judicial opinion that the term 'supply' connotes more than the mere transfer of physical control of an object from one person to another. As Lord Keith articulated in the leading case of *R v Maginnis* [1987] AC 303, there is an additional concept involved in supply, 'that of enabling the recipient to apply the thing handed over to purposes for which he desires or has a duty to apply it.'

**5.11**

The consequence of this determination is that those that hand over drugs to others for safekeeping are not considered to be guilty of supplying drugs. This is because the custodian is not able to use the drugs transferred to them for their own purposes.

**5.12**

Conversely, a custodian who holds drugs for another is guilty of supplying them when they return the drugs to the person who deposited them with them, thereby enabling the drug to be used by the depositor for their own purposes.

**5.13**

The decision made in *Maginnis* is still binding. However, it has not been immune from criticism. For example, in the case of *R v Carey* [1990] 20 NSWLR 292, the Court of Criminal Appeal in Australia refused to apply the 'extended' meaning of supply adopted in *Maginnis*.

# The meaning of supply

## *A physical transfer of control is required*

**5.14**

An early case involving judicial consideration of the meaning of supply was *R v Mills* [1963] 2 WLR 137.

**5.15**

In *Mills*, it was noted that 'supply must denote the parting of possession from one person to another'[2] with no further qualifications added.

**5.16**

This simplistic analysis of supply appeared to be adopted by the Court of Appeal in *R v Delgado* [1984] 1 WLR 89. The appellant was charged with possession

---

2   At p. 527.

with intent to supply a controlled drug, namely 6.31 kilogrammes of cannabis, contrary to *s 5(3)* of the *MDA 1971.*

**5.17**

The defence advanced by the appellant was that he was simply holding the drugs found for a friend whom he intended to return them to at a future date. It was submitted that the word 'supply' within *s 5(3)* of the *MDA 1971* should be confined to acts of providing drugs to third parties, meaning those who did not already have ownership or control over them.

**5.18**

The Court of Appeal rejected the argument. It found that that 'supply' covered a wide range of transactions, the common feature of which was the transfer of physical control of a drug from one person to another. In the Court's judgment, 'questions of the transfer of ownership or legal possession of those drugs are irrelevant to the issue whether or not there was intent to supply'.[3]

## Issuing a Prescription is not an act of Supply

**5.19**

The supply of drugs involves a transfer of physical control. Consequently, the issuing of a prescription for controlled drugs, even if done in bad faith, is not regarded as an act of supply. This was acknowledged in *R v Taylor* [1986] Crim LR 680.

**5.20**

The defendant in *Taylor* was a doctor, who had issued hundreds of prescriptions of Methadone, allegedly unlawfully and in bad faith (ie to known drug users not eligible for the drugs prescribed). He was consequently charged with supplying a controlled drug contrary to *s 4* of the *MDA 1971.*

**5.21**

The defendant was acquitted at trial. The court noted that supplying within the meaning of the *MDA 1971* involved the physical passage of a controlled drug from the supplier to the supplied. Consequently, the issuing a prescription, which could not be equated with the actual handing over of a controlled drug, could not be considered supplying within the meaning of the act.

**5.22**

However, if drugs prescribed by a doctor, unlawfully and in bad faith, are eventually dispensed to a 'patient' by a pharmacist (even when the pharmacist

---

3   At p. 92.

acts in good faith, in accordance with the prescription provided), the dispensing of the drug constitutes an act of supply, that in this scenario, the doctor could theoretically be considered criminally liable for.

### 5.23

Here, the doctor, with the relevant mens rea (knowing the prescriptions were unlawful), could be considered the aider and abettor of an act of supply, unknowingly committed by the pharmacist. The cases of *R v Bourne* (1952) 36 Cr App R 125, C.C.A. and R *v Cogan* [1976] QB 217, CA, be they wholly unrelated to drug supply, provide authority for imposing liability on this basis.

## The supply must be to the benefit of/for the purposes of the recipient

### 5.24

Whilst the supply of drugs involves their physical transfer from one person to another, proof of this alone is not enough to satisfy the meaning of supply within the provisions of the *MDA 1971*.

### 5.25

Additionally, it must be shown that the act of supply in question was designed to benefit the transferee as opposed to simply the transferor. Consequently, those who hand over drugs to another for their safekeeping are not considered to be supplying that other with the drugs in question.

### 5.26

This scenario was considered carefully in *R v Demsey* (1986) 82 Cr App R 291. Here, the appellant was a heroin addict who had legitimately obtained from his doctor 25 ampoules of Physeptone (a substitute for heroin but nonetheless still classified as a controlled drug).

### 5.27

Shortly after receiving these drugs, he was observed by police officers handing them over to his wife before entering a lavatory within Paddington train station. He was subsequently charged with supplying a controlled drug to another contrary to *s 4(3)(a)* of the *MDA 1971*.

### 5.28

It was argued on appeal that his conviction for such should be quashed on the basis that handing over a drug to someone to temporarily look after it for you could not properly be considered an act of supply.

**5.29**

The Court of Appeal agreed with the proposition advanced on behalf of the appellant, with the then Lord Chief Justice noting:

'The word "supply" is defined in the Shorter Oxford Dictionary as follows: …To fulfil, satisfy (a need or want) by furnishing what is wanted. To furnish, provide, afford (something needed, desired or used)…."Those are the two definitions which seemed to be relevant to the particular circumstances. It is an act, so it seems, which is designed to benefit the recipient. It does not seem to us that it is apt to describe the deposit of an article with another person for safe keeping, as was the case here'.[4]

**5.30**

The Court of Appeal then made the following parallel:

'It could scarcely be said that the person handing the coat supplies it to the cloakroom attendant. Nor do we think it makes any difference that the cloakroom attendant wishes in one sense to get the coat, thinking that he may get a tip at the end of the evening.That is not the sort of wish or need which is envisaged by the definition of the offence.That sort of transfer is a transfer for the benefit of the transferor rather than the transferee.'[5]

**5.31**

The definition of supply adopted in *Dempsey* was endorsed by the House of Lords in the leading case of *Maginnis*. In this case the appellant was stopped driving a vehicle which when searched by the police was found to contain 227 grams of cannabis resin, with a street value of £500. The appellant's case was that the package containing the cannabis had been left in his car by a friend who he expected would return at a future date to collect it.

**5.32**

Lord Keith noted as follows:

'The word "supply," in its ordinary natural meaning, conveys the idea of furnishing or providing to another something which is wanted or required in order to meet the wants or requirements of that other. It connotes more than the mere transfer of physical control of some chattel or object from one person to another. No one would ordinarily say that to hand over something to a mere custodian was to supply him with it'.[6]

---

4   At p. 293.
5   At p. 293.
6   At p. 309.

**5.33**

Similarly, Lord Goff remarked that he 'would not describe the delivery by the depositor to the depositee as a supply of goods, because the goods are not being made available to him but are rather being entrusted to him'.[7]

## The transfer of drugs to a custodian or courier is not an act of supply

**5.34**

As is evident from the judicial analysis provided in *Dempsey* and *Maginnis* above, those who transfer drugs to others for temporary safekeeping [so called custodians] are not deemed to be guilty of supplying the drugs concerned.

**5.35**

The rationale for such a conclusion is that the custodian does not benefit from the arrangement to the extent that they are able to use the drugs for their own purposes. Whilst a custodian may be in possession of drugs they cannot be said to have acquired ownership of them.

**5.36**

By logical extension, the act of passing a drug onto a courier is not deemed to be an act of supply contrary to the provisions of the *MDA 1971*. Like a custodian, a courier is not able to use the drugs received for their own purposes, having no legal ownership over them, a point that was illustrated in *R v Hussain (Shabbir)* [2010] EWCA Crim 970.

**5.37**

The appellant in this case ran a business purchasing and selling medicines. During a search of his business premises, the police found large quantities of class C drugs that the appellant was not licensed to possess. He was convicted of various counts of possessing a controlled drug with intent to supply them to another.

**5.38**

The appellant appealed on the basis that he had only ever intended to supply the drugs seized to customers outside of the UK, making use of a professional courier service to do so.

**5.39**

It was argued that such would involve two transfers. First, from himself to the courier and then a second transfer from the courier to the customer outside

---

7  At p. 314.

of the UK. It was contended on behalf of the appellant that neither of these transfers fell foul of the provisions of the *MDA 1971*.

**5.40**

In respect of the second transfer from the courier to customers based outside of the UK, the Court of Appeal agreed with the argument advanced on behalf of the appellant. It accepted that such a transfer did not amount to an act of supply contrary to the provisions of the Act because the provision was of territorial effect within the UK only.

**5.41**

In respect of the first intended transfer, it was argued on behalf of the appellant that such did not amount to supply within the meaning of *ss 4* and *5(3)* of the *MDA 1971* because the transfer from the owner to the courier was akin to a deposit with a custodian; it was not a transaction where ownership passed to the courier.

**5.42**

Acknowledging the argument advanced, Laws LJ observed that:[8]

> '... might it be said there is a distinction between transfer to a custodian or temporary keeper who is to transfer the drugs back to the person he got them from and transfer to a courier, whose obligation is to pass them on to a third party? That is a factual distinction from *R v Maginnis*. It seems to us the fact that the custodian may act for profit does not turn the transfer to him into a supply for the purpose of 1971 Act. The essence of a supply on Lord Keith's reasoning is "the transfer must be for the purposes of the transferee". We conclude that it is in effect beyond argument that the prospective transfer to the courier is not a statutory supply.'

## A custodian who returns drugs is guilty of supplying them

**5.43**

What is the position of a custodian who returns the drugs to the original depositor? In short, those who return (or intend to return) drugs to the person who originally deposited them with them are liable to conviction under the provisions of *ss 4* or *5(3)* of the *MDA 1971*.

---

8   At para 12.

**5.44**

Originally, as is evident from the case of *R v Greenfield* (1984) 78 Cr App R 179, it had been assumed that in returning drugs to a person who originally deposited them, a custodian was not supplying such drugs contrary to the provisions of the *MDA 1971*.

**5.45**

In this case the appellant was stopped by the police and the vehicle he was driving was searched. The search revealed the presence of a plastic bag containing cannabis on the floor of the car. The appellant's case was the cannabis seized did not belong to him but a friend of his whom he knew was a drug dealer. He was charged with possession with intent to supply cannabis, contrary to *s 5(3)* of the *MDA 1971*.

**5.46**

The focus of the appeal was whether A, knowing it was B's intention to supply the drugs that A was holding for them, was guilty of an offence contrary to *s 5(3)* of the Act. The Court of Appeal concluded that A would not be, 'with intent to supply' referring to the intent of the person in possession of the drugs and not the intent of some other who was not in possession of them.

**5.47**

However significantly, the Court of Appeal's decision was predicated on an assumption that the handing back of the drugs to their owner by the appellant was not an act of supply.

**5.48**

This assumption was not applied in *Delgado* considered above. The Court of Appeal concluding that an intention on the part of a custodian to return drugs to their owner was an intention to supply them, with questions over who owned the drugs irrelevant to the question of supply.

**5.49**

The opinions expressed by the Court of Appeal in *Delgado* have since been the subject of criticism, with it now accepted that supply within the context of *s 4(1)* of the *MDA 1971* involves more than the mere transfer of property, for the reasons already outlined.

**5.50**

That said, as in *Delgado*, in addressing the central question of 'whether a person in unlawful possession of a controlled drug which has been deposited with him for safe keeping has the intent to supply that drug to another if his intention is to return the drug to the person who deposited it with him', the House of Lords in *Maginnis* has answered this question affirmatively.

## The decision in *Maginnis*

### 5.51

In *Maginnis*, having avowed that supply under the provisions of the *MDA 1971* connoted 'more than the mere transfer of physical control of some chattel or object from one person to another', Lord Keith outlined an 'additional concept' to the act of supply, namely:[9]

> 'that of enabling the recipient to apply the thing handed over to purposes for which he desires or has a duty to apply it.'

### 5.52

Applying this analysis to the case of a custodian who returned (or intended to return – as was the case in this instance) drugs to the person who originally deposited them with them, Lord Keith concluded unequivocally, that:[10]

> 'If on a later occasion the defendant had handed the drugs back to his friend, he would have done so in order to enable the friend to apply the drugs for the friend's own purposes. He would accordingly, in my opinion, have supplied the drugs to his friend in contravention of section 4(1).'

### 5.53

In reaching this view Lord Keith drew an important distinction between a cloakroom assistant who returns an item of clothing to its owner (referred to previously by Mr Justice Mann when the case was earlier considered in the Court of Appeal), and a custodian who returns drugs to the person who originally deposited them with them.

### 5.54

In the case of the latter, it was stressed that the custodian was under a legal obligation not to return the drugs to the person who deposited them, thereby potentially facilitating the drugs wider distribution. 'The custodian in choosing to return the drugs to the depositor does something which he is not only not obliged to do, but which he has a duty not to do.'[11]

---

9   At p. 309.
10  At p. 309.
11  At pp. 312–313.

**5.55**

Accordingly, there appear to be strong public policy considerations for concluding a custodian who returns drugs to the original depositor is guilty of supplying drugs under the provisions of the Act.

**5.56**

When considering the case of *Maginnis*, three key principles (which remain binding) can be extracted from the opinions (favoured by the majority) expressed by Lord Keith, they are:

(1)   Supply involves more than the mere physical transfer of drugs from one person to another;

(2)   To constitute supply the physical transfer must enable the recipient to apply the drugs handed over to them for purposes which he desires; and

(3)   The drugs supplied need not come out of the supplier's own resources.[12]

**5.57**

The views expressed by Lord Keith were not however entirely immune from criticism. Described as 'too legalistic' in the dissenting opinion of Lord Goff, he remarked:[13]

> '...I would not describe the redelivery by the depositee to the depositor as a supply of goods, because the goods are simply being returned to him, rather than being made available to him from resources other than his own....I find myself, with all respect, unable to agree with my noble and learned friend that it is a sufficient qualification to characterise a transfer of possession as a supply that it should be made in order to meet the wants or requirements of the recipient, such expression being understood to include circumstances where the want or requirement of the recipient is simply to get his own goods back again.'

**5.58**

Significantly, the criticisms expressed by Lord Goff, have since found favour with the Court of Criminal Appeal of New South Wales. Here in *Carey*, the court concluded that supply does not include temporary possession of a prohibited drug with the intention of returning it to the owner of the drug. Justice Hunt, at page 295G of his judgment remarked:

> 'For my own part, I frankly find that decision [Maginnis] to be a surprising one. If my neighbour lends me his lawnmower and,

---

12   See p. 309.
13   At pp. 314–315.

after using it myself, I return it to him to enable him to use it for whatever purposes he may desire, the use of the word "supply" in its ordinary meaning to describe my act of returning the mower to its owner seems to me, with all due respect, to be entirely inappropriate.'

## Involuntary possession and intent to supply

**5.59**

Attempts have been made since the ruling in *Maginnis* to limit its scope. For example, in *R v Panton* [2001] EWCA Crim 611 those who appeared on the part of the appellant attempted to persuade the Court of Appeal that the decision in *Maginnis,* that an act of returning drugs to their owner on the part of a custodian constituted supply, was limited to cases where the custodian had obtained the drugs voluntarily.

**5.60**

In *Panton* the police found a quantity of controlled drugs in the appellant's house during the course of a search. The appellant, relying on a defence of duress, stated that the drugs did not belong to him and that he intended to return them to the depositor. He stated that he had come into possession of the drugs involuntarily as they had been deposited by drug dealers to whom he was indebted.

**5.61**

The Court of Appeal disagreed with the argument advanced, stating that:[14]

'The present case cannot be distinguished from *Maginnis.* The ratio of that decision is that the word "supply" in section 5(3) of the 1971 Act means "furnishing or providing a person with something that that person wants or requires for that person's purposes". Thus, as the facts of *Maginnis* demonstrate, when a custodian of drugs returns the drugs to the person who deposited them with him for safekeeping he "supplies" them to the depositor whether a custodian is in possession voluntarily or involuntarily is irrelevant to the question whether he intends to supply the drugs to the depositor. Either way, if he intends to return them to the depositor, *Maginnis* makes it clear that he intends to supply them.'

---

14 At paras 15–16.

**5.62**

It is worth noting however, that the Court did acknowledge that whether or not a custodian is a voluntary custodian may be relevant to the issue of possession, with Dyson LJ noting:[15]

'... if he is unaware that the drugs have been deposited with him, he may be said in a sense to be an involuntary custodian. Without such knowledge, he will not be guilty of an offence under section 5(3), but that will be because he is not in possession of the drugs and will not have the knowledge which is requisite to having an intention to supply them to another person. Moreover, if he is an involuntary custodian, he may have a defence of duress.'

## Territorial restrictions on the provisions of the Misuse of Drugs Act

**5.63**

Clearly, those involved in the transportation of drugs (couriers), may be tasked with delivering them to 'customers' living outside of the UK. In this scenario, given the act of supply, or intended act is to take place outside of the UK, does the courier, notwithstanding the controlled drugs were first received by them within this jurisdiction, fall foul of the provisions of *s 5(3)* of the Act? Given the presumption against extra-territorial effect, the answer is no.

**5.64**

Importantly, there are no explicit provisions within the *MDA 1971*, in which Parliament has provided for it to have extra-territorial effect. Consequently, the Act is not designed to make conduct taking, or intended, to take place outside of the UK an offence.

**5.65**

The case of *Hussain*, considered previously makes specific reference to the jurisdictional parameters of the *MDA 1971*.

**5.66**

As previously noted, the appellant in this case argued that his intention was to supply drugs to those outside of the UK by use of a professional courier service. With the Court of Appeal concluding that the first intended transfer from the appellant to the couriers was not to be regarded as supply (for reasons already

---

15 At para 17.

explored), the Court then went on to consider whether the second intended transfer from the courier to the eventual customer (who was significantly based outside of the UK) was an act of supply captured by the provisions of the *MDA 1971*.

**5.67**

The Court of Appeal, placing reliance on the Privy Council's ruling in the case of *Seymour v The Queen* [2007] UKPC 59, ruled that it was not, with Laws LJ stating:[16]

> 'There can, in our judgment, be no basis for not applying the reasoning in *Seymour v The Queen* to this present case. Accordingly, if the intention may have been to supply customers outside the jurisdiction, no offence such as those charged… could be committed.'

**5.68**

The case of *Seymour,* concerned Bermudan legislation whose terms were identical to the relevant provision of the *Misuse of Drugs Act 1971*. In this case the appellant had swallowed various wrapped pellets of heroin before booking a flight from Bermuda to Miami. The appellant was subsequently hospitalised in Bermuda, as a result of one of these pellets becoming unwrapped. Upon discovery of the controlled drugs within his system the appellant was charged with possession with intent to supply a controlled drug contrary to the *Bermudan Misuse of Drugs Act 1972*.

**5.69**

In agreeing with the argument advanced on the appellant's behalf, that given his intention was to supply controlled drugs to those outside of Bermuda he had not acted contrary to the provisions of the relevant act, the Privy Council held that a supply, if it were to fall within the Bermudan statute, had to take place within the jurisdiction because of the presumption of territorial effect, being a general rule of interpretation of all criminal statutes.

**5.70**

It is worth noting however, that within the scenarios considered, whilst the courier does not fall foul of the provisions of *s 5(3)* of the Act, it would theoretically be open to the Crown to charge them with an offence of attempted exportation.[17]

---

16 At para 14.
17 Exportation of controlled drugs being prohibited under *s 3(1)(b)* of the *MDA 1971*.

# Supplying includes distributing

### 5.71

Whilst the term 'supply' is not strictly defined under the provisions of the *MDA 1971, s 37(1)* of the Act does offer some assistance by noting that supplying includes 'distributing'.

### 5.72

As can be seen from the cases explored below, the courts have concluded that someone who is in joint possession of drugs (where they have been purchased on behalf of themselves and others) may nonetheless be found guilty of supplying those drugs when they are distributed by them amongst the others.

## *Being in Joint Possession is no Defence*

### 5.73

In *Holmes v Chief Constable of Merseyside* [1976] Crim LR 125, the Court of Appeal considered the proposition that if there is joint possession between the actual custodian of the drugs and others who have some title to those drugs, a separation or division of them cannot be a supply under the provisions of the *MDA 1971*.

### 5.74

In rejecting this proposition, the then Lord Chief Justice, stressed the word 'supply' should be given its ordinary everyday meaning. He stated[18]:

'... the question of joint possession can become highly relevant on a charge of possessing, but I do not believe that the question of possession... is a satisfactory route to an answer in the type of case we are dealing with at the present time where the charge is of supplying or possession with intent to supply. The word "supply" in this context is determined by the Act itself as including "distributing". Section 37 of the Misuse of Drugs Act 1971 in terms says "supplying" includes distributing, and in my judgment when a Court has to consider an allegation of supply under this Act it must give the word "supply" its perfectly ordinary natural everyday meaning. I have no doubt at all that a man who goes to market shopping for drugs on behalf of himself and others will often properly be regarded as supplying those drugs when he brings them home and distributes them because distribution is by statute a form of supply and that in itself is enough to cover such a case.'

---

18   Referred to by Lane LJ at p.374 of *R v Buckley & Lane* (1979) 69 Cr App R 371.

**5.75**

The opinions expressed in *Holmes* were later applied in *R v Buckley & Lane* (1979) 69 Cr App R 371. The appellant and another male named Gilchrist agreed to jointly purchase a quantity cannabis resin, with each thereafter taking their agreed share.

**5.76**

Accordingly, the appellant and Gilchrist pooled their money which was then used by the appellant to purchase cannabis resin from a supplier. After the appellant had purchased the cannabis he divided it up, giving three-quarters of it to Gilchrist and retaining the remaining quarter for himself.

**5.77**

The appellant sought to appeal his subsequent conviction for supplying Gilchrist with cannabis, contrary to *s 4(3)(a)* of the *MDA 1971*. He argued there could not have been a supply to Gilchrist because at the point of transferring cannabis to him, he was already in possession of it as a joint purchaser. Consequently, one cannot be said to have supplied a person with something which they already possess.

**5.78**

In support of the argument, the Court was asked to consider the provisions of *s 37(3)* of the *MDA 1971*, stating that 'For the purposes of this Act the things which a person has in his possession shall be taken to include any thing subject to his control which is in the custody of another.'

**5.79**

Lord Justice Lane, dismissed the argument, relying on the case of *Holmes*. In doing so he observed that *s 37(1)* defined 'supplying' as 'including distributing', concluding the appellant was clearly distributing the cannabis, irrespective of who could be said to have owned or been in possession of it.

**5.80**

Facts akin to those in *Buckley & Lane,* have since been considered by the Court of Appeal in *R v Denslow* [1998] Crim LR 566. In this case the appellant and another bought heroin, pooling their money evenly in order to do so.

**5.81**

Both were physically present at the point of acquisition but it was the appellant who conducted the negotiations and it was he who handed the whole of the money over to the dealer. In return the appellant received two bags of heroin, one of which he handed immediately to his friend. The appellant was subsequently convicted for supplying his friend with heroin, contrary to *s 4(3) (a)* of the *MDA 1971*.

**5.82**

The appellant sought to distinguish his case from *Buckley* with it argued that he and his friend were both physically present at the point of the initial transaction, with the transfer of drugs by the appellant to the other following almost immediately afterwards.

**5.83**

Mr Justice Mantell, noting that the facts in this case were clearly analogous with those in *Buckley*, dismissed the appeal.

**5.84**

However, it is worth noting the remarks of Mr Justice Mantell in relation to the appropriateness of charging the appellant with supply in circumstances where at the point of sentence they would clearly be dealt with on the basis they were in no more than possession of drugs for their own use. He stated:[19]

'...we wonder why it was thought necessary to charge supply in the circumstances of this case. How could it possibly serve the interests of the public that there should be either a trial or if not a trial as conventionally understood a hearing to determine this matter of law? It was inevitable that the appellant would be dealt with at worst as though he were in possession of the drugs and, as turned out in this case, as though he were without any criminal responsibility for that particular part of the transaction. We are told that a plea had been offered to a charge of possession. It ought to have been accepted. We hope that those words will be borne in mind by prosecuting authorities in the future.'

## The case of *Harris*: administering is not supplying

**5.85**

In the case of *R v Harris (Janet Marjorie)* [1968] 1 WLR 769, the Court of Appeal was asked to consider the following question: If A injects B with B's own heroin (having previously been purchased by B), is A supplying heroin to B?

**5.86**

Be it, this case was considered before the enactment of the *MDA 1971*, the answer provided by the Court is still applicable to consideration of such scenarios today. The answer provided was straightforward, with Lord Parker CJ stating:[20]

---

19 At para 12.
20 At p. 771.

'This court is quite unable to accept that proposition as a matter of law. If B has obtained in some way the possession of the heroin, and all that A is doing is to assist in injecting that heroin into B, then A is not supplying heroin… it seems… quite impossible as a matter of ordinary common sense and law to say that a person administering heroin in those circumstances is supplying the heroin.'

**5.87**

Lord Parker went on to remark however, that had there been evidence in the case which would have entitled the jury to come to the conclusion that the heroin injected by A into B had in fact belonged to A, the conclusion reached by the court would have be quite different, with A in that scenario 'clearly' 'guilty of supplying'.

## Making an offer to supply

**5.88**

The mischief that an offence of offering to supply a controlled drug is designed to punish, is the offer itself. As Lord Justice Staughton said in *R v Mitchell* [1992] Crim LR 723, 'an offer may be by words or conduct. If it by words, one has to judge from the words whether it is an offer to supply a controlled drug. If a person knowingly makes an offer to supply in words which have that effect, that is the offence.'[21]

**5.89**

As the offence is the making of an offer, the prosecution need not prove that a defendant had in his possession a controlled drug at the time of making an offer. Nor need it be proved that the offer to supply drugs was a genuine offer.

**5.90**

Consequently, those who offer to supply a particular controlled drug, knowing what they are in fact intending to supply is not in a controlled drug, are not afforded a defence in law. Nor are those that claim they had no intention of carrying out the offer made.

**5.91**

In analysing the legal parameters of the offence of 'offering to supply' a controlled drug, the following three scenarios are worthy of consideration.

---

21  At para 12.

## Scenario 1

*The Accused Offers to Supply One Controlled Drug but in Fact Supplies Another*

### 5.92

No defence exists under the provisions of *s 28(3)* where an offer is made to supply a specific drug (such as heroin), which when supplied turns out to be a controlled drug of a wholly different description.

### 5.93

As previously noted, the offence that is captured under the provisions of *s 4(3) (a)* of the *MDA 1971* is the making of an offer to supply a controlled drug. Consequently, it is immaterial whether the controlled drug offered is in fact actually supplied.

## Scenario 2

*The Accused Offers to Supply a Controlled Drug, Believing it to be Controlled, but in Fact Supplies a Substance Which is Not Controlled*

### 5.94

What is the position when an accused offers to supply a controlled drug, believing it to be such, which in fact turns out to be a substance that is not controlled at all? This was discussed in the case of *Haggard v Mason* [1976] 1 WLR 187.

### 5.95

In this case, the appellant possessed a substance which he believed to be LSD. He offered to sell it to another and at the time of supplying it both he and the purchaser believed it to be LSD. The substance supplied was in fact another drug, but not one that was controlled under the provisions of the *MDA 1971*, and accordingly a substance that it was legal to possess.

### 5.96

Following his conviction for offering to supply a controlled drug, contrary to *s 4(3)(a)* of the *MDA 1971*, the Court of Appeal considered whether the fact the substance supplied was not in fact a controlled drug afforded the appellant a defence.

**5.97**

The Court concluded that it was irrelevant that the drug supplied was not controlled. Lawson J said:[22]

> 'In my judgment the offence was completed at the time when, to follow the findings of the justices, the defendant met H and offered to sell him a quantity of Lysergide. To my mind that was a clear situation in which the justices were right to find that there was an offer to supply a controlled drug, an offer made by the defendant to H. It matters not in relation to the offence of offering to supply that what is in fact supplied pursuant to that offer, the offer having been accepted, is not in fact a controlled drug.'

## Scenario 3

*The Accused Makes a Bogus Offer to Supply a Controlled Drug in That he Either Knows That a Substance That is Not Controlled Will be Supplied or he Has no Intention Of Supplying Anything at All*

**5.98**

In *R v Goodard* [1992] Crim LR 588, the appellant was arrested in relation to an alleged robbery. During the course of his police interview, he admitted to obtaining money from a man by offering to supply him with cannabis. He was subsequently charged with an offence of offering to supply a controlled drug contrary to the provisions of *s 4* of the *MDA 1971*.

**5.99**

At trial, a submission of no case to answer was made on his behalf. It was suggested that the offence charged was not made out because the appellant had never intended to supply cannabis and had accordingly obtained money by deception. The recorder who presided over the trial rejected the submissions advanced, which then became the subject matter of his appeal against conviction.

**5.100**

The appellant's appeal was roundly dismissed. After analysing the provisions of *s 4(1)(b)*, Mr Justice Swinton-Thomas, concluded that:[23]

> '... there is nothing in the section which provides that the person who makes the offer must intend to supply the controlled drug. The section does not say that a person is guilty of an offence if he offers to

---

22 At p.190.
23 At p. 4A.

supply a controlled drug to another with the intent of supplying that drug. If Parliament had so intended, no doubt the section would have incorporated those words. In our judgment it is quite plain that the offence is complete when the offer to supply a controlled drug is made, quite regardless of whether the offerer intends to carry the offer into effect by actually supplying the drug. Any other construction would not only offend common sense but would also offend the ordinary canons of construction.'

### 5.101

Similarly, in *Mitchell* the appellant sought to overturn his conviction for offering to supply a controlled drug on the basis that he never intended to supply such a drug. The only substance he had on him was a grassy substance, which he knew was not a controlled drug.

### 5.102

The Court of Appeal found that had a verbal offer to supply cannabis been made by the appellant in the terms alleged, then this constituted an offence of offering to supply a controlled drug 'whether or not the defendant either had any controlled drug in his possession or had easy access to any controlled drug round the corner.'

### 5.103

Highlighting important public policy considerations were the Court to have ruled differently, Lord Justice Staughton went on to remark:[24]

'Police officers and others who have to detect offences can scarcely be required, whenever they hear someone offering to supply a controlled drug, to pause and consider whether that person has got any of that drug on him or has got access to it round the corner from a friend or in some place of storage. The offence is making the offer'.

### 5.104

The Court of Appeal in *Mitchell* deemed it immaterial whether or not the accused was actually in possession of controlled drugs, or had easy access to them at the time of making a verbal offer to supply them. However, Lord Justice Staughton acknowledged that had the offer been made by way of conduct, 'such as holding a packet in one's hand and in the other hand a placard saying "£20", it might be another question; there it might be relevant whether what was in the packet was a controlled drug or not.'[25]

---

24  At para 13.
25  At para 12.

**5.105**

Finally, the case of *Mitchell* made it clear that a defence under the provisions of *s 28(3)* of the *MDA 1971* did not apply to an offer to supply drugs. The offence was embedded in the making of the offer and not the quality of the substance offered (if the substance existed at all).

**5.106**

Latterly, *Goodard* was applied, and *Mitchell* was approved, in the case of *R v Gill* [1993] 97 Cr App R 215, in which the appellant was charged with a conspiracy to offer to supply controlled drugs.

**5.107**

The defence advanced was that no meaningful offer existed as the appellant had intended to cheat customers by offering ecstasy tablets but in fact supply vitamin pills instead. Here at page 217 of his judgment, Lord Justice McCowan stated:

> 'We see no reason to think that the cases of *Goodard* and *Mitchell* were wrongly decided but in any event in our judgment they are clearly binding upon us. The fact that what is charged here is a conspiracy rather than a substantive offence cannot make any difference. In those circumstances this appeal must be dismissed.'

**5.108**

The fact that an offence of offering to supply a controlled drug is committed whether or not the offer is genuine has been reaffirmed in the more recent case of *R v Prior* [2004] EWCA Crim 1147.

**5.109**

Here, the Court observed that to rule otherwise would make it almost impossible for the prosecution to meet a defence that an accused did not intent to carry out the offer, with Lord Justice Auld noting:[26]

> '... the important thing is the effect of the words ... having regard also to the way in which they were said and any other relevant circumstances apparent to the offeree at the time. In short, whether the words uttered and the manner in which they were uttered had the appearance of an offer for this purpose is essentially a matter of fact for the jury. The genuineness or otherwise of the offer, or indeed whether, notwithstanding appearances, it was meant as a joke, would be irrelevant.'

---

26 At para 24.

**5.110**

The case of *Prior* also considered the effect of the withdrawal of an offer, in the context of the provisions of *s 4* of the *MDA 1971*. Here the court found:[27]

> '... that when the offer is made, the offence is complete, whatever lies behind it, and that its subsequent withdrawal or revocation cannot affect that. This has nothing to do with the meaning of "offer" in the law of contract, which in any event would be of little help in this context. Although in contract an offeror may withdraw his offer at any time up to acceptance, if he does so it does not mean that he never made such an offer, simply that he is not bound by acceptance, if there is one, after withdrawal'.

## An offer to supply remains until it is either resiled from or has been completed

**5.111**

The applicability of the law on contract to an offence of offering to supply a controlled drug was considered in *R v Dhillon* [2000] Crim LR 760.

**5.112**

In *Dhillon,* the appellant had been convicted of an offence of offering to supply a class A drug contrary to *s 4(3)(a)* of the *MDA 1971*. He was charged on a joint enterprise basis with his brother, who had made an offer to supply an undercover police officer with heroin which would be delivered a few days after the offer was made. On this agreed latter date the appellant's brother directed the officer to the appellant who handed over a substance that forensic analysis subsequently revealed to be nothing more than flour.

**5.113**

As has already been considered, the fact the bag delivered by the appellant did not contain controlled drugs did not afford him a defence to the charge faced. Instead he sought to argue that he could not be found guilty of an offence of offering to supply drugs on the date he passed a substance to the undercover officer, as the offer to supply a controlled drug had been made by his brother a few days previously. It was asserted, applying the law of contract, that as this offer was accepted by the undercover police officer at the time it was first made, the 'offer' ceased to exist at the point of it being accepted.

---

27  At para 28.

**5.114**

The Court of Appeal rejected the technical argument advanced on behalf of the appellant and instead accepted a broader construction of the expression 'offering to supply', concluding that the initial offer made by the appellant's brother was a continuing offer and one that remained in place until it had either been resiled from or had been completed.

**5.115**

Mr Justice Hooper in providing the judgment of the court noted:[28]

> 'We take the view that it would be quite wrong to introduce into the trial of a person charged with this offence the principles of the law of contract. It is clear to us that this appellant was either offering heroin or taking part in such an offer, as the jury so found. We reject therefore that ground of appeal.'

**5.116**

Interestingly, be it the decision taken by the Court of Appeal in *Dhillon* is of superior authority to the decisions taken in the Divisional Court, Mr Justice Hooper's rejection of the principles of the law of contract appear to be inconsistent with the cases of *Fisher v Bell* [1961] 1 QB 394, *Mellor v Monahan* [1961] Crim LR 175 and *Partridge v Crittenden* [1968] 1 WLR 1204, in which the Divisional Court held that it was bound to construe the word 'offer' in a criminal statute in the sense which it bears in the law of contract. Significantly however, none of these authorities were brought to the Court of Appeal's attention in *Dhillon* and accordingly were not considered.

## An offer of consumption is an offer to supply

**5.117**

The case of *R v Moore* [1979] Crim LR 789 provides authority for the proposition that an offer to consume a drug is an offer to supply it. In this case, the defendant persuaded two girls to 'go for a smoke' with him and consequently he began rolling a cannabis cigarette with the intension that the girls would share it with him. He was charged with possession of cannabis resin with intent to supply and with offering to supply the drug to another contrary to *ss 4(3)(a)* and *5(3)* of the *MDA 1971* respectively.

**5.118**

His submission of no case to answer in respect of both counts was rejected, with the Crown Court at Surbiton concluding that an offer of consumption comfortably equated to an offer of supply.

---

28  At para 7.

**5.119**

Significantly, the court declined to follow the earlier decision in *R v King* [1978] Crim LR 228, in which the Crown Court at Maidstone had ruled that the passing of a cannabis joint within a circle of fellow smokers should not be considered a 'supply' of it under the provisions of the *MDA 1971*.

## Being concerned in the supply/offer to supply drugs

**5.120**

Being concerned in either the supply of a controlled drug, or the making of an offer to supply a controlled drug, requires that an accused is involved in some identifiable act of participation.

**5.121**

The courts have been dissuaded from attempting to define exhaustively what an act of participation is. However, the prevailing view is that the provisions of *s 4(3)(b)–(c)* should be construed broadly, with the provisions designed to cover a great variety of activities both at the centre and also on the fringes of dealing controlled drugs.

**5.122**

Further, it is now settled judicial opinion that being concerned in supplying a controlled drug involves the whole process of supplying to others, which can include things done before any actual supply has taken place, such as their preparation. Accordingly, the prosecution need not prove there has been a supply of drugs in order for an accused to be found guilty of being concerned in the supply of such.[29]

**5.123**

Following the ruling in the leading case of *R v Hughes* (1985) 81 Cr App R 344, it will be for the trial judge to assist the jury as to the meaning of 'being concerned in', although there is not currently any illustrative example of a suitable direction to be found within the 'Crown Court Compendium Part 1: Jury and Trial Management and Summing Up'.[30]

---

29 See also: *R v Nguyen (Khin Quoc)* [2010] EWCA Crim 2658, and the comments of Lord Justice Hooper at para 8 of his judgement: 'that act of "concerning" can either take place before or after the substantive offence'

30 Last updated in February 2017. See: www.judiciary.gov.uk/publications/crown-court-bench-book-directing-the-jury-2.

# A broad construction

### 5.124

The term 'being concerned in' is not defined under the provisions of the *MDA 1971*. Its meaning has accordingly been the subject of much judicial analysis. In *R v Blake* (1979) 68 Cr App R 1, the Court of Appeal, formed the view that the term should be construed in such a way that those charged with being concerned in an offer to supply drugs contrary to the provisions of *s 4(3)(c)* of the *MDA 1971*, could still be found guilty of the offence without it being necessary to prove a specific and close involvement in the making of a particular offer.

### 5.125

In *Blake,* police officers observed male A approach a group of people in Piccadilly Circus. They then overheard male A ask this group whether they liked cannabis. When the group asked male A where they could get some, he replied that he had a friend who lived in a flat nearby who could 'fix them.' Consequently, the group attended a flat belonging to the appellant, who claimed not to know male A and left his flat.

### 5.126

Both he and male A were later convicted of being concerned in the making of an offer to supply a controlled drug. On appeal, it was said that given he did not know of the initial offer made by Male A at Piccadilly Circus, he could not be guilty of the offence charged.

### 5.127

The Court of Appeal disagreed. It stated that it was clear that *s 4(3)(c)* had been widely drawn to involve people who may be at some distance from the actual making of the offer. Unfortunately, it went no further in offering any precise meaning of *s 4(3)(c)*.

## *The Hughes Definition*

### 5.128

A more precise definition of the term 'being concerned in' was provided subsequently by Lord Justice Goff, in the case of *R v Hughes* (1985) 81 Cr App R 344.

### 5.129

In this case an appeal was advanced on the basis that the Recorder had failed to provide any direction to the jury on the meaning of 'being concerned in', despite having been asked to do so.

**5.130**

Importantly, *Hughes* now stands as authority[31] for the proposition that a trial judge must direct the jury on the meaning of 'being concerned in', where an accused is charged under the provisions of *s 4(3)(b)* and/or *(c)*.

**5.131**

Helpfully, Lord Justice Goff identified three elements which need to be proved for an offence under section 4(3) to be made out. They are:[32]

'(1)  the supply of a drug to another, or as the case may be the making of an offer to supply a drug to another, in contravention of section 4(1) of the Act;

(2)  participation by the defendant in an enterprise involving such supply or, as the case may be, such offer to supply; and

(3)  knowledge by the defendant of the nature of the enterprise, i.e. that it involved supply of a drug or, as the case may be, offering to supply a drug.'

**5.132**

Whilst *Hughes* remains a leading authority on the definition of 'being concerned in' recent judicial opinion has warned against slavishly following the judicial interpretations of *s 4(3)(b)* contained within it.

**5.133**

For example, in *R v Baker,* [2009] EWCA Crim 535, the then Lord Chief Justice, in considering the three elements involved in 'being concerned in', as highlighted in Hughes, noted:[33] 'However closely section 4(3)(b) of the 1971 Act is looked at, neither the word "enterprise" nor the word "participate" appears.'

**5.134**

Having regard to the factual particulars of the case under consideration, it was suggested that the provisions of *s 4(3)(b)* required no additional elucidation, in that[34]:

'The language of the subsection is straightforward. In our judgment, if a person introduces someone who wants to obtain heroin to someone who he knows is willing and able to supply it, and together they obtain heroin for which the person introduced to the vendor pays, on the basis that in due course the introducer will pay for his share, it is open

---

31  See *R v Martin (Dwain Ashley)* [2014] EWCA Crim 1940.
32  At p. 348.
33  At para 14.
34  At para 14.

to a jury to conclude that the introducer is concerned in the supplying of the heroin to the other person.'

### 5.135

Importantly, the Lord Chief Justice went on to caution against the danger of treating language used in the course of a judgment (in this case *Hughes*) which involves the interpretation of a criminal statute, *'as if it were the statute, or as if it replaced or amended the statute, at any rate certainly where the statute is plain enough in its language and uses ordinary English to describe the offence'*.[35]

## Is proof of an actual supply of controlled drugs required to be found guilty of being concerned in it?

### 5.136

Before defining the term 'being concerned in', Lord Justice Goff in *Hughes* sought to differentiate between the offences of being concerned in the supply of drugs, contrary to *s 4(3)(b)* of the *MDA 1971* and being concerned in 'an offer' to supply, contrary to *s 4(3)(c)*. In doing so he noted:[36]

'... the difference between (b) and (c) is that in (b) there has to be an actual supply in which the accused was concerned, whereas under (c) it is enough that there was an offer to supply in which the accused was concerned.'

### 5.137

This particular passage has been cited up until recently as authority for the proposition that the actus reus of an offence of being concerned in the supply of a controlled drug requires the prosecution to prove that 'an actual supply' has taken place.

### 5.138

The courts in Scotland however, have long rejected such a narrow construction of the provisions of *s 4(3)(b)*. In the leading case of *Kerr v HM Advocate* 1986 J.C. 41, for example, Lord Hunter, adopting a purposive approach to statutory interpretation, remarked:[37]

'... the offence created by sec. 4(3)(b) is that of being concerned in the "supplying" of a controlled drug to another. This covers in my opinion the whole process of supplying to others, a process which may not be

---

35 At para 18.
36 At p. 347.
37 At para 47.

completed and which, fortunately, is sometimes interrupted by police and other action. It would be strange indeed if Parliament, having used the very wide language which was enacted in sec. 4(3)(b), should be held to have imposed a limitation which would often deprive the provision of practical effect. In my opinion the actual language used in the provision points strongly against any such narrow construction. I am satisfied that the provision is designed to catch any person who is concerned at any stage in the process of supplying to others from the beginning of that process to the end.'

### 5.139

Significantly, the views expressed by Lord Hunter above have more recently been echoed by the Court of Appeal in *R v Akinsete* [2012] EWCA Crim 2377 and *R v Martin & Brimecome* [2014] EWCA Crim 1940.

### 5.140

In *Akinsete* the two appellants had been stopped by the police. Cannabis, a substantial amount of cash and two mobile telephones were found in the car. The appellants were then charged with being concerned in the supply of both Class A and Class B drugs as part of a joint enterprise.

### 5.141

The prosecution relied on an expert's interpretation of text messages found on the mobile phone that had been seized. The Crown contended that the messages related to drug supply, the cash found and the fact that the cash was contaminated with a higher than normal derivative of cannabis, cocaine and heroin. Both appellants were convicted.

### 5.142

One of the subsequent grounds on appeal was that the trial judge was wrong to have directed the jury that an actual supply of drugs could have been inferred from circumstantial evidence in the case.

### 5.143

Significantly, this argument was advanced on the assumption that evidence of actual supply involving the accused was required in order for an offence under *s 4(3)(b)* to be made out. The Court of Appeal disagreed stating that:[38]

'The words "concerned in" relate to the participation of the particular defendant in the enterprise. It is not necessary in respect of an offence that is charged under section 4(3)(b) for the prosecution to prove that the defendant himself physically supplied the controlled drug to

---

38  At para 24.

another. His participation in the enterprise could take other forms. He could set up a meeting, be a middleman, provide the finance, or arrange the contacts and so forth. If the defendant is involved in the actual supply itself he can be charged under section 4(3)(a).'

## 5.144

Later the Court noted that:[39]

'... there is no rule of law that there has to be direct evidence of a supply of drugs in a case brought under section 4(3)(b). The leading case of *R v Hughes* to which we have referred is certainly not authority for such a proposition and we have been shown none that is. The prosecution can rely on circumstantial evidence.'

## 5.145

*Akinsete*, demonstrated that the prosecution need not prove an accused was involved in an actual supply of controlled drugs to be found guilty of being concerned in their supply. Nor did the prosecution need to produce direct evidence of actual supply having taken place. However, the Court fell short of stating explicitly that the Crown need not prove actual supply at all, whether with circumstantial evidence or not.

## 5.146

*Martin & Brimecome*, however, went further than *Akinsete* in aligning itself more closely with the interpretation of *s 4(3)(b)* provided in *Kerr.* In *Martin*, the Court of Appeal emphasised that the word 'supply' within the meaning of *s 4(3)(b)* was a broad term and was not confined to the expressions 'actual delivery' or 'past supply', but referred to the entire process of supply.

## 5.147

Lord Thomas noted the words within the statute made reference only to 'supply to another', noting that the statute 'does not say "actual supply to another"; nor does it say "delivered to another"... This case illustrates the importance of courts looking at and applying the simple language of the statute.'[40]

# Supply to 'another'

## 5.148

The another to whom a drug is supplied may be a co-accused providing it is sufficiently clear that this is what is being alleged by the Crown in the particulars of the offence that are drafted. This is dealt with in greater detail in **Chapter 6**.

---

39  At para 47.
40  At paras 14–16.

# Summary of key points

**5.149**

- Supply offences are captured by the provisions of *ss 4(3)* and *5(3)* of the *MDA 1971*.

- Supply involves the physical transfer of drugs from one person to another.

- It also involves an additional concept of enabling the recipient to apply/ use the drugs transferred to them for their own purposes.

- The drugs supplied need not come out of the supplier's own resources to be found guilty under the provisions of the *MDA 1971*.

- Consequently, those who hand over drugs to custodians for temporary safekeeping (with an expectation they will be returned in full) are not considered to have supplied the drugs, but a custodian who then hands the drugs back to the original depositor is.

- To be captured by the provisions of *s 4(3)* the act of supply must take place within the UK given the presumption against extra-territorial effect.

- Supply includes distributing drugs amongst those who can be said to be in joint possession of them.

- The offence of offering to supply a controlled drug under *s 4(3)* lies in the offer itself.

- Consequently, it need not be proved that an offeror is in possession of a controlled drug at the time an offer is made, nor that their offer was genuine in that they intended to supply a controlled drug, nor where a substance was transferred to another, the substance was in fact a controlled drug.

- Being concerned in the supply/offer to supply of a controlled drug, involves some identifiable act of participation, not limited to the physical transfer of drugs to another.

- To be concerned in the supply/offer to supply a controlled drug, the prosecution need not prove that a physical transfer of drugs has taken place.

# 6 Possession With Intent To Supply

Tom Stevens

## The offence

**6.1**

Section 5(3) of the Misuse of Drugs Act 1971 (MDA 1971) provides that:

> 'Subject to section 28 of this Act, it is an offence for a person to have a controlled drug in his possession, whether lawfully or not, with intent to supply it to another in contravention of section 4(1) of this Act.'

**6.2**

Paragraph 1(b) of Sch 2 to the Proceeds of Crime Act 2002 (POCA), further provides that s 5(3) of the MDA 1971 is a 'lifestyle offence' meaning POCA proceedings are triggered following on from conviction.[1]

## Overview

**6.3**

An offence under s 5(3) consists of three elements. Firstly, the prosecution must prove that the individual charged is in possession of a drug. Secondly, that the drug in question is controlled; and lastly that the person who possesses it intends to supply it to another.

**6.4**

A detailed analysis of what constitutes possession is found in **Chapters 3** and **4**. However, the phrase, 'whether lawfully or not' in s 5(3) means that those who are in legal 'possession' of drugs would still be found guilty of an offence under s 5(3) if they intended to supply those drugs on to another, without having lawful authority to do so.

**6.5**

Section 5(3) is designed to punish an individual's intention to supply drugs in the future. Consequently, where there is only evidence of past supply an individual

---

1   See Ch 12.

would be more appropriately charged with supplying a controlled drug under the provisions of *s 4(3)(a)* of the Act.

**6.6**

An intention to supply involves supply at any time in the future. Consequently, it need not be proved that the individual charged had a present or immediate intention to supply to another, as evident in the Scottish case of *Lockhart v Hardie* 1994 SCCR. 722.

**6.7**

Additionally, the case of *R v Ibrahima* [2005] EWCA Crim 1436 highlights that the prosecution need not prove the identity of the intended recipient. Neither is it required to prove whether the supply intended was to be carried out on a commercial basis.

**6.8**

An individual who intends to supply a small amount of drugs to a friend without any financial gain is no less guilty of an offence under the provisions of *s 5(3)* than those who intend to supply drugs on an industrial scale for considerable profit. However, the scale of the supply intended and the likely remuneration are clearly factors that will influence the sentence length imposed following conviction.[2]

## An intention to supply does not require an intention to make financial gain

**6.9**

In *Ibrahima*, the appellant was charged with possession with intent to supply ecstasy tablets. There had been no issue at his trial that he was in possession of the drugs in question. The issue concerned his intent, with the appellant asserting that the 32 tablets in his possession were for his personal use only.

**6.10**

Significantly, this assertion was at odds with comments made by the appellant in his interview in which he indicated he had intended to give a few of the tablets to his friend who had jointly purchased them.

**6.11**

The Crown contended that the appellant had intended to sell the 32 tablets on a commercial basis. However, it also suggested an alternative basis for a finding

---

2   See Ch 11.

of guilt, raised by the appellant himself in interview. Namely, that even if the appellant had intended to consume some of the drugs in his possession and pass a small portion of the tablets onto a friend, he would still be guilty of an offence contrary to *s 5(3)* of the *MDA 1971*.

### 6.12

It was argued on appeal that these two bases were inconsistent. Having 'nailed its colours to the mast of commercial supply'[3], it was submitted that the Crown should not have been allowed to seek to advance the alternative case.

### 6.13

Furthermore, it was contended that having been left with two factual bases to consider, the jury should have been directed that they had to be unanimous as to which set of facts formed the basis of any verdict of guilty, which the trial judge had failed to do.

### 6.14

Lord Justice Keene rejected the arguments advanced on behalf of the appellant. He noted that:[4]

'The particulars of offence here alleged, and only had to allege, that the appellant possessed the tablets "with intent to supply to another". That was the ingredient which had to be proved. The jury did not have to be satisfied as to the identity of the intended recipient, nor as to whether it was to be carried out on a commercial basis or not. The necessary ingredient of the offence, apart from possession, was the intent to supply to another. That would be sufficient. The jury had to be sure that that mental element on the part of the appellant existed at the relevant time, but in our judgment they did not have to be satisfied beyond that.'

## An intention to supply a different drug to the one charged affords no defence

### 6.15

In the case of *R v Leeson* [2000] 1 Cr App R 233 the appellant appealed against a conviction of possessing cocaine with intent to supply contrary to *s 5(3)* of the *MDA 1971*. He argued that he had believed, mistakenly that the drugs in his possession were amphetamine and not cocaine. Consequently, the Crown could not prove that he intended to supply cocaine and accordingly, as cocaine was the drug named on the charge, the Crown had failed to establish one of the elements of the offence.

---

3  At para 8.
4  At para 18.

**6.16**

In dismissing the appeal, and following the principles enunciated in the earlier cases of *R v McNamara* (1988) 87 Cr App R 246 and *Warner v Commissioner of Police of the Metropolis* [1969] 2 A.C. 256,[5] the Court of Appeal noted that all that was required by *s 5(3)* was for the Crown to establish that the accused has in his possession a controlled drug with intent to supply the substance which was in his possession to another. More particularly, Lord Justice Roch stated:[6]

> 'It is to be noticed that section 5(3) of the Act does not distinguish between classes of controlled drugs, nor does the section require the person to know that what he has in his possession and what he intends to supply to another is a controlled drug. The only relevance of the different classes of drug and the only purpose of specifying the class of drug concerned in the particulars of offence is that that factor affects the sentence that can be passed on conviction.'

**6.17**

Further, the Court of Appeal found that no defence was available to the appellant under the provisions of *s 28* of the Act. This was because given proof of the specific identity of the drug in question was not a matter which had to be proved. The appellant could not allege that he had no knowledge of a fact which fell to be proved by the Crown.

**6.18**

In considering the social mischief that the provisions of the *MDA 1971* were designed to address Lord Justice Roch concluded:[7]

> 'Parliament clearly intended that a person in possession of a controlled drug with intent to supply should not be able to say "I did not know it was cocaine. I thought it was another controlled drug." That Parliament should have such an intention is hardly surprising in view of the social problems and evils that the use of controlled drugs brings in its wake.'

## An intention to supply need not be an intention to supply immediately

**6.19**

In the case of *Lockhart*, the defendant was charged with possession with intent to supply cannabis resin. The particulars of the offence specified an intention

---

5   See Ch 5.
6   At p. 238.
7   At p. 240.

to supply the drug at two separate locations including the Grampian Police Station where cannabis resin wrapped into recognisable deals was found on his person.

**6.20**

The Court noted that that it 'could not sensibly deduce any sane person could have intent to supply anyone when locked up in a police cell.' Having considered that a conviction under *s 5(3)* of the *MDA 1971* could only be sustained in circumstances where there was a present or immediate intent to supply another, the Court consequently acquitted the defendant.

**6.21**

The Sheriff's decision to acquit the defendant and the rationale behind it was subsequently scrutinised by the High Court of the Justiciary, following an unopposed appeal made by the Crown.

**6.22**

Significantly, the High Court held that the Sheriff had erred in acquitting the defendant. It noted that an intention to supply simply denoted supply taking place at some time in the future. The Crown, it noted, were not required to prove that at the particular time when the accused was found in possession, he has some intent to make an immediate supply to some other person.

## Section 5(3) and possessing drugs not ready for harvest

**6.23**

Although the Crown need not prove an immediate intention to supply, they must prove an intention to supply 'the thing' that the accused possessed at the time they were charge.

**6.24**

This was illustrated in *R v Wright* [2011] 2 Cr App R 15. A charge of possession with intent to supply drugs was found to be inappropriate in circumstances where the drugs found on a person were in an immature state and the supply allegedly intended is a supply at a future date when the drugs have been harvested and are in a usable state.

**6.25**

In *Wright,* 35 cannabis plants were found and then seized during a police search of the appellant's home address, along with equipment used in cannabis cultivation. The appellant consequently pleaded guilty to one count of producing cannabis, contrary to *s 4(2)(b)* of the *MDA 1971.*

**6.26**

However, having rejected the appellant's contention that he intended to use the cannabis, once mature, only for his own personal use, the prosecution added a further charge of possession with intent to supply the cannabis seized, contrary to *s 5(3)* of the *MDA 1971*.

**6.27**

At trial, agreed expert evidence stated that the seized plants were two to three months away from being harvested. Consequently, they were not in a usable state at the time of their seizure. Despite that evidence, the appellant was found guilty of possession with intent to supply.

**6.28**

It was asserted on appeal that *s 5(3)* of the *MDA 1971* required the prosecution to prove that the defendant possessed a controlled drug with a then present intention of supplying what he 'then' possessed. Possession and intention needing to be 'co-terminus'.

**6.29**

Further, it was asserted that as the appellant was in possession of immature cannabis plants any intention to sell the yield or harvest from those plants once they matured, did not amount to an intention to sell the plants which he then possessed. Rather it demonstrated an intention to supply that which might come into being and be possessed in the future.

**6.30**

In response, the Crown contended that if the jury concluded that the appellant's intention was to supply all or part of the crop for others to use, once the cannabis plants were ready for harvesting then, they were entitled to convict him of the offence charged. Furthermore, to rule that a defendant cannot be convicted of possession with intent to supply unless and until the crop has reached maturity and is suitable for harvesting was a 'perverse interpretation of the statute'[8].

**6.31**

The Court of Appeal held that on the facts, the appellant was not in possession of cannabis with intent to supply within the meaning of *s 5(3)*, with Lord Justice Richards noting:[9]

'There was no suggestion in this case that the appellant intended to supply the immature plants of which he was in possession at the

---

8   At para 18.
9   At paragraphs 19–20.

material time. As the full court said in granting leave, the useable part of each plant would have been the flowering heads, but since these plants were in their infancy there were as yet no flowering heads. The case against the appellant was that he intended to grow the plants to maturity and then to harvest a crop from them and then to supply the harvested crop, or some of it, to others. Thus the intended supply was a supply of the harvested product of the process of cultivation, not a supply of the plants as they existed and were in his possession at the time to which the charge related.'

## Motive is irrelevant

**6.32**

In the case of *R v Finch* (1993) 14 Cr App R 226, the appellant was convicted of possessing nearly 250 grams of amphetamine, a class B drug, with intent to supply it.

**6.33**

When interviewed, the appellant claimed that he was a registered police informant. He claimed he had acquired the drugs with the knowledge of another officer and with a view to supplying them to another and then to inform upon that other.

**6.34**

The Court of Appeal noted that notwithstanding that the appellant intended to give the information to assist the police arresting someone involved in drug supply, on the appellants own version of events he was guilty of possession with intent to supply.

**6.35**

*Finch* was then considered in *R v X* [1994] Crim L 827. In this case the appellant, X, was a registered police informer who was convicted by a jury of possession with intent to supply amphetamine. The jury added a rider to their verdict, indicating that they accepted that X had intended that the person to whom he had intended to sell the drugs would then sell them to an undercover officer, so that they would eventually get into police hands.

**6.36**

The appellant argued that his motivation had only been to prevent drug circulation. He had acted in accordance with a police arrangement. His appeal was dismissed with the Court of Appeal concluding that as he had intended to 'supply' the drugs in his possession to another his conviction was safe and that he motive for the supply was irrelevant to whether or not a charge under *s 5(3)* had been established.

## Proving intention

### 6.37

Where an individual, seeks to challenge that they had an intention to supply drugs, the Crown will invariably rely on inferential evidence in rebuttal. Such evidence may include:[10]

- Possession of a quantity of drugs that is said to be inconsistent with personal use;

- Possession of drugs that have not yet been adulterated/drugs with a high purity value, thereby indicating a proximity to their manufacturer or importer;

- Evidence that the drug has been prepared for sale, for example where the drugs seized have been cut and wrapped into small portions;

- Evidence of drugs paraphernalia, typically used in drugs supply, such as electronic weighing scales, cutting agents, bags or wraps of foil and so-called dealers lists documenting amongst other things the names and telephone numbers of customers; and

- Evidence of large amounts of money/evidence of an 'extravagant lifestyle' said to be the proceeds of drug dealing. The admissibly of such evidence is considered later in this chapter.

## The quantity of drugs possessed

### 6.38

In contested cases brought under *s 5(3)* of the *MDA 1971*, the jury will frequently be invited to consider whether the drugs possessed are consistent with personal use. Alternatively, whether the quantities involved are too large thereby inferring an intention to supply the drugs on to another.

### 6.39

Interestingly, pursuant to the provisions of *s 2* of the *Drugs Act 2005*, Parliament had previously contemplated inserting three new subsections [4A–4C], into the provisions of *s 5* of the *MDA 1971*.

---

10 As referred to in the Crown Prosecution Services' guidance on 'Drugs Offences': www.cps.gov.uk/legal/d_to_g/drug_offences/.

**6.40**

This would have provided that in circumstances in which an accused was found to be in possession of a quantity of drugs above a 'prescribed amount', it was then to be assumed that they possessed such with an intention to supply them. The defence would then have the opportunity to rebut the assumption.

**6.41**

*Section 4A* stipulated that: 'In any proceedings for an offence under subsection (3) above, if it is proved that the accused had an amount of a controlled drug in his possession which is not less than the prescribed amount, the court or jury must assume that he had the drug in his possession with the intent to supply it as mentioned in subsection (3).'

**6.42**

Significantly however, that statutory presumption has never come into force. Furthermore, the provisions of *s 2* of the *Drugs Act 2005* have now been repealed.[11]

**6.43**

The issue of whether the amount of drugs is consistent with personal use accordingly remains a matter for the jury to decide. In order to help the jury grapple with such a question reliance is frequently placed on expert evidence addressing matters such as typical consumption patterns of drug users.

**6.44**

The suitability (and therefore the admissibility) of an individual to give such evidence is a matter for a trial judge to resolve. The absence of academic qualifications need not be a barrier to providing such evidence. Experience derived from working with and encountering drug users can provide grounds for offering expert opinion on matters relevant to drug use and supply.[12]

## Expert evidence on consumption patterns

**6.45**

In *R v Bryan,* unreported, 8 November 1984, the appellant was charged with possession with intent to supply cannabis. At trial the Crown had placed reliance on evidence from a police officer who had two years' experience in a drug squad.

---

11  Sch 8, Pt 13, para 1 of the *Policing and Crime Act 2009* as of the 12 January 2010.
12  See the judgment of Lord Justice Keene at para 29 of *Ibrahima*.

**6.46**

In light of this experience, the Crown put him forward as an expert who was sufficiently qualified to offer his opinion on whether or not the amount of cannabis possessed by the accused was consistent with personal use alone and further, to give evidence on the cost of an average street deal.

**6.47**

The defence argued that he was not a suitable expert. The Court of Appeal in rejecting the argument advance by the defence concluded that the evidence of the police officer had been properly admitted as expert evidence, stating:[13]

'The view of this Court is that police officers with their experience of dealing with these problems, being on the streets and with their knowledge and meeting with those having a drug problem and those pushing the drugs, have a very wide experience and can give evidence of fact of what takes place on many occasions on the streets.'

**6.48**

In the subsequent case of *R v Edwards* [2001] 9 Archbold News, the Court of Appeal adopted a much stricter approach to the question of the admissibility of expert evidence relating to drug consumption habits.

**6.49**

The experience of a police officer, and a drugs charity worker of eight years' experience, called on behalf of the defence, were both deemed to be insufficient. Neither were considered qualified to provide expert evidence on the consumption habits of ecstasy users and the effects upon them in terms of developing tolerance or suffering serious harm.

**6.50**

Neither the police officer nor the drugs worker had a medical or toxicological qualification. Consequently, the Court of Appeal found that their opinions were based entirely on experience gained through speaking with many drug users as part of their work. The Court agreed with the trial judge's decision to exclude the evidence of both. The court further noted that the opinions of the officer and the drugs worker were based on hearsay evidence that was potentially unreliable.

**6.51**

The divergent opinions expressed by the Court of Appeal in the cases of *Bryan* and *Edwards* have since been considered in *R v Hodges* [2003] 2 C App R 15.

---

13 At para 3E.

Lord Justice Rose, approving and following the approach taken in *Bryan*, allowed the inclusion of expert evidence provided by a serving police officer based on the experience he had gained whilst serving in matters relevant to drugs supply. His evidence was permitted, despite his lack of academic qualifications in the field.

### 6.52

In *Hodges*, the two appellants were convicted of conspiracy to supply. One of them was found in possession of 14 grams of heroin and £350 in cash. Part of the defence was that the heroin was for the personal use of both accused. The Crown asserted that such drugs were intended for commercial distribution and sought to rely on the evidence of a police officer.

### 6.53

His opinion was based on the experience he had gained through his work with the police as a drugs liaison officer, carrying out observations of drugs supply and from speaking to both prisoners and informants. One of the grounds of appeal was the admissibility of the officer's evidence.

### 6.54

The Court of Appeal held that the evidence was admissible. In contrast to *Edwards*, it noted that the fact that the Detective Constable's opinion was based on hearsay evidence was not a barrier to it being fairly admitted:[14]

> 'He had, in his statement served on the defence given the categories of his sources of information and, of course, any witness who is tendered as an expert must do that. But that does not mean, as was submitted, that it is necessary to call the various people to whom the witness has spoken, before the witness can give expert evidence based upon what they have said.'

### 6.55

Lord Justice Rose went on to conclude that the evidence provided by the Detective Constable also satisfied the 'dual test' of admissibility of opinion evidence of an expert as identified by the South Australian Supreme Court in *R v Bonython* (1984) 38 SASR 45.

### 6.56

In that case Chief Justice King said that, in deciding whether a witness is competent to give evidence there are two questions for judges to decide:[15]

> 'The first is whether the subject matter of the opinion falls within the class of subjects upon which expert testimony is permissible. This may

---

14  At para 31.
15  At para 5.

be divided into two parts (a) whether the subject matter of the opinion is such that a person without instruction or experience in the area of knowledge or human experience would be able to form a sound judgment on the matter without the assistance of witnesses possessing special knowledge or experience in the area, and (b) whether the subject matter of the opinion forms part of a body of knowledge or experience which is sufficiently organised or recognised to be accepted as a reliable body of knowledge or experience, a special acquaintance with which by the witness would render his opinion of assistance to the court. The second question is whether the witness has acquired by study or experience sufficient knowledge of the subject to render his opinion of value in resolving the issues before the court.'

### 6.57

In *Ibrahima*, the Court of Appeal followed the approach taken to expert evidence in *Hodges*, with the expert evidence provided by a deputy director of a drugs charity as to the consumption habits of ecstasy users held to be admissible. The Court were critical of the decision of the trial judge not to allow the defence to adduce such evidence at the accused trial noting that the expert in question had very substantial experience. Although he did not have formal medical qualifications, the Court took the view that 'experience itself may form the basis for an expert opinion. The same, after all, would often be true of an experienced police officer called by the Crown on such matters'.[16]

## The admissibility of evidence of an extravagant lifestyle/possession of money

### 6.58

Just as the prosecution may seek to highlight the quantity of drugs involved in a particular case as being consistent with an intention to supply (ie being more than is associated with personal use alone), evidence of drugs paraphernalia used to prepare and divide drugs for onward supply, or telephone evidence said to contain messages related to drug supply, so too might they attempt to highlight evidence of lavish material possessions/quantities of cash, belonging or linked to an accused, with the accompanying assertion that such are the spoils of drug supply (particularly in circumstances where no legitimate source of income for the accused has been identified).

### 6.59

The admissibility of evidence alleged to be the proceeds of drug dealing, namely a quantity of money prima facie under the accused control, in a case where

---

16  At para 29–32.

they were charged with possession with intent to supply controlled drugs, was considered in the case of *R v Batt* [1994] Crim LR 592.

## 6.60

In *Batt* police officers arrived at the appellant's home with a search warrant. During the course of their search they found just over 500 grams of cannabis, a set of scales with traces of cannabis resin on them, and £150 in notes, secreted in an ornamental kettle.

## 6.61

On appeal against conviction, it was submitted that the Recorder had been wrong to allow evidence of the money to go before the jury. It was argued that such evidence was highly prejudicial and of no probative value, not assisting the jury will the central issue in the case, namely, whether the appellant had an intention to supply the cannabis seized.

## 6.62

The Court of Appeal endorsed the defence submissions and concluded that the evidence of the money found was inadmissible, noting its inclusion was unfair and prejudicial to the appellant because it raised the suggestion that she was in the business of drug dealing generally.

## 6.63

The case of *Batt* should not however be considered authority for the proposition that evidence of money seized is never admissible when the charge is one of possession of a drug with intent to supply. In the same year that *Batt* was decided, the Court of Appeal in *R v Wright* [1994] Crim LR 55 adopted a very different approach to the question of the admissibility of evidence of money.

## 6.64

In *Wright*, packets of cocaine were found concealed in the defendant's car. He denied that the car was anything to do with him. A search of his flat revealed £16,000 in cash and a gold necklace valued at £9,000.

## 6.65

As in *Batt*, evidence relating to the £16,000 and the gold necklace found at the accused flat was allowed to go before the jury. The decision to adduce such evidence was the subject of a subsequent appeal against conviction. It was argued that the money found was irrelevant to the question of whether the accused had an intention to supply the cocaine seized at some future date.

**6.66**

The Court of Appeal rejected the Appellant's argument. It found that those who deal drugs are found frequently to have large quantities of cash either from the sale of drugs or to purchase more to supply. It stated further that:[17]

'The question for decision is... does the fact of the possession of the large amount of cash tend to prove or render more probable the other facts the prosecution have to prove, that is that the drugs were in his possession for the purpose of supplying them to another? It may be that in some cases the finding of a large quantity of cash, or the fact that there is a large quantity of cash available, is of comparatively little relevance; in others it may be a much more significant feature ... no doubt that the finding of a large quantity of cash is capable of being relevant to an issue the jury had to consider in this case, and we reject the submission that this evidence was inadmissible because it was irrelevant.'

**6.67**

The decisions in *Batt* and *Wright* were later scrutinised in *R v Morris* [1995] 2 Cr App R 69, where the appellant had also been found guilty of possession with intent to supply and where evidence of large quantities of money said to belong to her was been adduced at her trial.

**6.68**

As in the case of *Wright*, Justice Morland rejected the conclusions in *Batt*. Criticising the approach, and citing *DPP v P* (1991) 93 Cr App R 267, he remarked that 'merely because evidence of possession of money might tend to show the commission of offences other than that charged would not, of itself, render the evidence inadmissible in law'.[18]

**6.69**

Ultimately, he said, it was a matter of judicial discretion whether or not to allow such evidence to go before a jury:[19]

' ... evidence of large amounts of money in the possession of a defendant or an extravagant life style on his part, *prima facie* explicable only if derived from drug dealing, is admissible in cases of possession of drugs with intent to supply if it is of probative significance to an issue in the case.

---

17  At p.75.
18  At p. 45.
19  At p. 76.

The fact that a defendant gives an explanation for possession of large sums of money does not of itself render such evidence inadmissible; the Crown may be able to rebut such an explanation. If the Crown can establish that explanations, such as winnings from the Irish Sweep, cash profits from market trading, the proceeds of bank robbery or the proceeds of dealing in jewelry and stolen clothes are false, the false explanation may be of significance—if a defendant is in control of a house, car or bag in which drugs are found—to prove that the defendant was knowingly in possession of the drugs and had the drugs in his possession for supply.'

### 6.70

Justice Morland went on to emphasise the need for the judge to clearly direct the jury on how they may use such evidence in considering the case against the accused.[20]

## Directing the Jury

### 6.71

The need to properly direct a jury on how they are to use evidence of an extravagant lifestyle or money has since been emphasised in *R v Grant* [1996] 1 Cr App R 73, and more recently in *R v Malik* [2000] 2 Cr App R 8. In the latter, the then Lord Chief Justice said:[21]

'… it is necessary, in the circumstances, for the judge to indicate that any explanation for the money which has been put forward by way of an innocent explanation by the accused would have to be rejected by the jury before they could regard the finding of the money as relevant to the offence. Again the jury should be directed that if there was any possibility of the money being in the accused's possession for reasons other than drug dealing, then the evidence would not be probative. If, on the other hand, the jury were to come to the conclusion that the presence of the money indicated not merely past dealing, but an ongoing dealing in drugs, then finding the money, together with the drugs in question, would be a matter which the jury could take into account in considering whether the necessary intent had been proved.'

### 6.72

In *R v Lovelock* [1997] Crim LR 821, a similar question arose regarding an alleged 'dealers list'. The Court of Appeal stressed that, as this note had been

---

20  ibid.
21  At p. 78.

adduced as part of the prosecution's case, it was then incumbent on the judge to give a scrupulously fair direction. That direction should note that before the jury used it as evidence of the appellant's intention to supply, they must be satisfied that it was not only demonstrative of past dealing, but also capable of going to intention to supply in the future.

**6.73**

The court further emphasised that the cases requiring such a direction applied also to cases where documents said to be linked to drug dealing had been adduced as well as those adducing evidence of drugs paraphernalia more generally.

## Where a guilty plea to possession is offered

**6.74**

In cases where possession with intent to supply is charged, it is not uncommon for the accused to admit being in possession of the drugs but deny any intention to supply them to another.

**6.75**

In such cases, and in the absence of an alternative charge of possession being added to the indictment, a judge is precluded from sentencing an accused for possession of a controlled drug where they have been acquitted of possession with intent to supply after trial.

**6.76**

In *R v Yeardley* [2000] 2 Cr App R 141, the appellant was charged with a single count of possessing heroin with intent to supply and entered a plea of not guilty. The accused had offered to plead guilty to the offence of possessing the drug, but this was rejected by the Crown. Following a trial in which the jury were only invited to reach a verdict in respect of a single count of possession with intent to supply, contrary to *s 5(3)* of the *MDA 1971*, a not guilty verdict was returned.

**6.77**

Despite the appellant's acquittal, the trial judge then proceeded to sentence the appellant to three years' imprisonment for the offence of possession on the basis that he had offered to plead guilty to that offence before trial.

**6.78**

At the subsequent appeal, it was contended that the judge had no power to sentence for an offence with which the appellant had not been charged.

Further, that the charge was one which the Crown had refused to accept a guilty plea for.

**6.79**

The Court of Appeal concluded that the jury had returned only one verdict of not guilty of possession with intent to supply. Consequently, there was no conviction and no basis on which the defendant could have been lawfully sentenced.

**6.80**

Lord Justice Roch made two further observations:[22]

'First, it may well be sensible in cases of persons charged with dealing in drugs or being in possession of drugs with intent to supply, to include a separate count for simple possession where the quantity of the drugs involved is not such that simple possession is wholly out of the question. It would probably be sensible to draft the indictment with that alternative on a separate sheet so that in cases where an accused pleads guilty to simple possession, and that plea is unacceptable either to the court or to the prosecution, the trial can proceed on the more serious charge and the jury supplied with a copy of the more serious charge on its own. Such a course would avoid the situation which has arisen in this case and the prosecution will not have to weaken the presentation of their case on the more serious charge by inviting the jury to consider the alternative of simple possession where the prosecution are convinced that the accused is a dealer in drugs'.

# Aggravated supply

**6.81**

As a result of the provisions of Pt 1, *s 1(1)* of the *Drugs Act 2005*, *s 4A* has been added to the *MDA 1971* to supplement the provisions of *s 4(3)*.

**6.82**

It stipulates that where certain conditions are met, then the court 'must' treat them as an aggravating feature, increasing the seriousness of the offence, and accordingly the likely sentence to be imposed (see **Chapter 11**). *Section 4A* provides that:

'(1)   This section applies if –

(a)   a court is considering the seriousness of an offence under section 4(3) of this Act, and

---

22 At p. 147.

(b)   at the time the offence was committed the offender had attained the age of 18.

(2)   If either of the following conditions is met the court–

(a)   must treat the fact that the condition is met as an aggravating factor (that is to say, a factor that increases the seriousness of the offence), and

(b)   must state in open court that the offence is so aggravated.

(3)   The first condition is that the offence was committed on or in the vicinity of school premises at a relevant time.

(4)   The second condition is that in connection with the commission of the offence the offender used a courier who, at the time the offence was committed, was under the age of 18.'

## 6.83

Subsection (5) stipulates further that the 'relevant time' referred to in subs (3) is:

(a)   any time when the school premises are in use by persons under the age of 18;

(b)   one hour before the start and one hour after the end of any such time.

## 6.84

Furthermore, subs (6) provides that for the purposes of subs (4), a person uses a courier in connection with an offence under *s 4(3)* of this Act if he causes or permits another person (the courier):

(a)   to deliver a controlled drug to a third person; or

(b)   to deliver a drug related consideration to himself or a third person.

## 6.85

'A drug related consideration' referred to in subs (6), is defined in subs (7) as a consideration of any description which:

(a)   is obtained in connection with the supply of a controlled drug; or

(b)   is intended to be used in connection with obtaining a controlled drug.

## 6.86

Finally, subs (8) defines 'school premises' as land used for the purposes of a school excluding any land occupied solely as a dwelling by a person employed at the school; and that the word 'school' has the same meaning in England and Wales, as in *s 4* of the *Education Act 1996*; meaning, 'an educational institution which is outside the further education sector and the higher education sector' and is an institution for providing primary education, secondary education, or both.

**6.87**

Importantly, rather than create a distinct offence of aggravated supply, the provisions of *s 4A* simply note factors that must be taken into account, increasing the seriousness of any offence committed under the provisions of *s 4(3)*.

**6.88**

The necessity of this statutory addition to the *MDA 1971* has been the subject of debate, given factors increasing the seriousness of any offence can be effectively addressed in guidance provided by the Sentencing Council.

The content of the Sentencing Council's 'Drug Offences Definitive Guideline', applicable to all drugs offences committed after 27 February 2012 is considered in detail in **Chapter 11**.

## Lawful supply

**6.89**

As raised in **Chapter 4**[23], *s 7* of the *MDA 1971* enables the Secretary of State to make regulations exempting certain groups (including doctors acting in their professional capacity) from the provisions of the Act, including the prohibition on supplying controlled drugs under *s 4(1)*.

**6.90**

A detailed analysis of the various regulations that have been enacted to supplement the provisions of the Act since its inception is beyond the scope of this book. However, it is nonetheless worth noting the existence of certain regulations that presently govern the lawful supply of controlled drugs. These regulations include:

(a) The Misuse of Drugs Regulations 2001 (as amended)[24], allowing for the lawful possession and supply of controlled drugs for legitimate purposes. The regulations cover matters such as prescribing, administering, dispensing, record keeping, destruction and the disposal of controlled drugs to prevent misuse;

(b) The Misuse of Drugs (Safe Custody) Regulations 1973 (as amended)[25] set the minimum storage requirements for some controlled drugs, applicable

---

23  See Ch 4, Lawful Possession, para 4.97–4.102.
24  For the most recent amendment see: Misuse of Drugs (Amendment) (England, Wales and Scotland) Regs 2017/631.
25  For the most recent amendment see: Misuse of Drugs and Misuse of Drugs (Safe Custody) (Amendment) (England, Wales and Scotland) Regs 2014/1275.

to care homes and retail pharmacies, and setting minimum standards in other healthcare settings; and

(c)   The Misuse of Drugs (Supply to Addicts) Regulations 1997 (as amended)[26] restricting the prescribing of cocaine, diamorphine and dipipanone for the treatment of addiction, to doctors licensed by the Home Office (and in Scotland, by the Scottish government).

## Summary of key points

**6.91**

- *Section 5(3)* of the *MDA 1971* makes it an offence to be in possession of a controlled drug with an intent to supply it.

- An intention to supply need not be a present or immediate intention but an intention to supply at any time in the future.

- The prosecution need not prove the identity of the intended recipient of the controlled drugs.

- The prosecution need not prove that an accused intended to profit from the intended supply.

- An intention to supply a different controlled drug to the actual drug found in an accused possession is no defence.

- The motive for supplying controlled drugs is irrelevant when determining whether the elements of a *s 5(3)* offence have been made out.

- An intention to supply drugs may be inferred where a jury conclude that the amount of drugs possessed is inconsistent with personal use.

- Evidence of past drug supply/the proceeds of past drugs supply may be admissible in cases alleging a future intention to supply.

- Expert evidence on consumption habits of drug users (designed to rebut assertions that drugs possessed were for personal use only) may be based on a witness's experience of contact with drug users rather than academic/medical qualifications.

- Certain persons are exempt from the provisions of *s 5(3)* pursuant to the provisions of *s* 7 of the *MDA 1971*.

- *Section 4A* of the *MDA 1971* aggravates supply offences, for the purpose of sentencing, where offences are committed on or in vicinity to a school, or the offence made use of a courier under the age of 18.

---

26  For the most recent amendment see: Misuse of Drugs (Supply to Addicts) (Amendment) Regs 2012/2394.

# 7    Occupiers of Premises

Abigail Bright

## Overview

### 7.1

Occupiers of premises are liable for a host of criminal conduct. Conduct that is criminal because it is, in some material way, connected to the premises in question. 'Occupiers' of premises should be understood as a matter of plain English. An occupier can be an individual person or (which may, in some cases, express and have the same result) a body corporate.

### 7.2

'Occupier' is not limited to a person with legal possession of premises. 'Occupier' includes any person who has a licence which entitles him to exclusive possession, ie anyone who has the requisite degree of control over the premises to exclude from them those who might otherwise use them for the purposes forbidden by s 8 of the *Misuse of Drugs Act 1971* (*MDA 1971*).

### 7.3

*Degree of control* is key. What is required to create liability in law is a sufficient degree of control over the premises such that a person/occupier is capable of excluding anyone likely to commit an offence on the premises.

## Being the occupier or concerned in the management of the premises

### 7.4

An early case, which remains good law, demonstrates this: *Tao (Ben Nien) v The Queen* [1977] QB 141. The appellant, an undergraduate at King's College, University of Cambridge, lived in a room in a hostel. The college owned the hostel. The appellant had paid a sum of money in rent to the college, for the use of the room in which he lived. Police were called to the hostel.

### 7.5

A small fire had started in the room. The appellant was not in the room when police arrived: he was in the college itself. Police found traces of cannabis resin in the room. Police saw a young man, standing outside, but near to, the room. That young man was later convicted of unlawful possession of cannabis. The appellant was tried. He was convicted of an offence contrary to *s 8(d)* of *MDA 1971*.

**7.6**

The case for the prosecution at his trial was that he had occupied, and had been the occupier of, the room. He had permitted the premises to be used for the smoking of cannabis. The appellant's appeal against conviction was dismissed. He had had an exclusive contractual licence to use the room.

**7.7**

He was the '*occupier*' of that room within the meaning of *s 8* of *MDA 1971*. It did not matter that he did not have legal possession of the premises (property of the college). He was in occupation of the premises. He had a degree of control over the premises such that he could exclude (and had not excluded) anyone likely to commit an offence under the Act.

**7.8**

The Court of Appeal distinguished on its facts, if not, in reality, disapproved as wrong, the earlier decision in 1970 of *Mogford v The Queen* (Assizes at Glamorgan, unreported). *Mogford* was decided pursuant to the *Dangerous Drugs Act 1965, s 5*, and not the *MDA 1971*.

**7.9**

*Mogford* had decided that, for a person to be an occupier of premises, within the meaning of the *Dangerous Drugs Act 1965, s 5*, he must have legal possession of, and control over, the premises. In *Mogford*, two sisters, aged twenty and fifteen, were charged with permitting premises to be used for the purpose of smoking cannabis at their parents' home whilst their parents were away on holiday.

**7.10**

The Court held that such control over premises did not amount to the nature and measure of control envisaged by the *Dangerous Drugs Act 1965, s 5*. The reality underpinning *Mogford* is that the Court in that case did not have regard to what feature had decided the outcome in *Tao (Ben Nien)*: degree of control itself could be sufficient minus any requirement for legal possession.

## Permitting premises to be used for drug offending

**7.11**

Co-tenancy of premises is sufficient basis to found criminal liability as an occupier. A co-tenant who, knowingly, permitted another co-tenant to smoke cannabis was safely convicted of permitting the premises to be used for smoking cannabis. All four appellants, co-tenants of a flat, had, thereby, been safely convicted. A co-tenant enjoyed what the Court observed was *'no special immunity'*; if that co-tenant knowingly permitted his co-tenant to smoke cannabis on the premises: *Ashdown (Robert James); Howard (Leonard Edward); Howard (Judith Mary); Stuart (Michael Adrian)* (1974) 59 Cr App R 193, CA, cor. Roskill LJ; James LJ; Milmo J.

### 7.12

If there is no *legal right* to be on the premises, what degree of management of the premises is sufficient to show that an accused person, in some way, ran or organised (from) the premises? Mere squatting or trespassing does not prevent a person from coming within the terms of criminal liability for which *s 8* of *MDA 1971* provides. *Josephs (Ivan Dick) and Christie (Ransford) v The Queen (1977)* 65 Cr App R 253, CA, cor. Lord Widgery LCJ; Caulfield J; Gibson J. On the facts, the appellants could be so *'knowingly concerned in the management of premises'* – despite neither having had a legal right to be present. The appellants were squatters or trespassers in a building. Cannabis was found on a man present at the premises whilst the appellants were present. The appellants were convicted of *'being concerned in the management of premises'* in that the appellants knowingly permitted cannabis to be smoked on the premises.

### 7.13

Power of a person to exclude others is a hallmark or indication of sufficient control. An occupier may be a person concerned in the management of premises, however cursory the function and role is, who has the power to exclude someone who is apparently involved in one of the prohibited activities listed in *s 8* of *MDA 1971*.

## Liability pursuant to section 8 of the 1971 Act

### 7.14

*Section 8* of *MDA 1971* covers and controls a range of conduct relevant to persons or groups who are deemed occupiers of premises. Specifically, *MDA 1971* covers consumption, production, and supply of controlled drugs on premises.

### 7.15

The *Psychoactive Substances Act 2016 (PSA 2016)* materially and significantly revises liability of occupiers of premises. *PSA 2016* received Royal Assent and was enacted on 28 January 2016. It was conceived as 'an Act to make provision about psychoactive substances; and for connected purposes'.[1]

---

1   Preamble to the Act.

## 7.16

Additionally, to stop and search powers applicable to persons, *PSA 2016* conceives of powers to enter and search *vehicles* (*s 37*) and to board and search *vessels or aircraft* (*s 38*).

## 7.17

*Section 8* of *MDA 1971* creates criminal liability for occupiers or managers who permit their premises to be used for controlled drug-related activities. *PSA 2016* closely tracks and maps equivalent powers and proscriptions in the context of legislating for parliamentary control of psychoactive substances.

## 7.18

*Section 8* of *MDA 1971* (in force from 27 May 1971) is the enabling statutory provision that creates and confers the potential for criminal liability of occupiers of premises:

> 'Occupiers etc. of premises to be punishable for permitting certain activities to take place there
>
> A person commits an offence if, being the occupier or concerned in the management of any premises, he knowingly permits or suffers any of the following activities to take place on those premises, that is to say –
>
> (a)  producing or attempting to produce a controlled drug in contravention of section 4(1) of this Act;
>
> (b)  supplying or attempting to supply a controlled drug to another in contravention of section 4(1) of this Act, or offering to supply a controlled drug to another in contravention of section 4(1);
>
> (c)  preparing opium for smoking;
>
> (d)  smoking cannabis, cannabis resin or prepared opium.'

## 7.19

A parent of a person who is using cannabis within the private and family home is readily caught within the ambit of *s 8* of *MDA 1971*. The overriding issue is one of control.

## 7.20

Evidence of control of premises may be established (for example) by showing the *role* that a person has in connection with the premises; the *proximity* of a person to the premises, which may include a person's *presence* at the premises or the presence at the premises of a person or persons *nominated* by them (whether or not for payment).

# What constitutes premises, in section 8?

### 7.21

What constitutes premises, for the purpose and purposes of *s 8* of *MDA 1971*, has not been defined in law. Seemingly, *'premises'* would be an apt description of *any* property – providing that there exists an element of control exerted by a person in respect of any such property.

### 7.22

Broadly stated, a raft of case law demonstrates the point that *s 8* has been recognised as applying to hostels and other services accessed by drug users as well as nightclubs.

## *Knowledge*

### 7.23

In order for an offence to be committed pursuant to *s 8*, the occupier and/or manager of premises 'must knowingly permit or suffer' one of the prohibited activities. The definition of 'permit' is actual knowledge of the act(s).

### 7.24

The definition of 'suffer' is less straightforward. To 'suffer' means to 'allow': to fail to take action, which may, in essence, amount to turning a blind eye, deliberately, to the activity or activities taking place on the premises. This constructive, purposive approach clearly places an obligation on occupiers and/or managers of premises to take action to stop the act(s), or risk criminal prosecution.

# Investigatory powers; entry, search and seizure

### 7.25

The starting-point is the *Police and Criminal Evidence Act 1984 (PCA 1984)*, *s 17*.

### 7.26

*Section 17* of *PCA 1984* specifies:

'Entry for purpose of arrest, etc.

(1)　Subject to the following provisions of this section, and without prejudice to any other enactment, a constable may enter and search any premises for the purpose—

> (a)   of executing—
>
> > (i)   a warrant of arrest issued in connection with or arising out of criminal proceedings; or
> >
> > (ii)   a warrant of commitment issued under section 76 of the Magistrates' Courts Act 1980;
>
> (b)   of arresting a person for an indictable offence;
>
> (c)   of arresting a person for an offence under [provisions of statutes there specified]'

**7.27**

The powers relevant to criminal liability of occupiers as specified in *s 17* of *PCA 1984* are to be read together with the equivalent powers in the Act pertaining to search upon arrest (*s 32*).

**7.28**

Additionally, to intrusive investigatory powers of entry search and seizure, there exists provision for the Secretary of State to specify circumstances in which a special caution may be given at certain premises.

**7.29**

*Section 11* of *MDA 1971* reserves this power to the Secretary of State ('Powers of Secretary of State for Preventing Misuse of Controlled Drugs; Directions relating to special precautions at certain premises'):

> '(1)   Without prejudice to any requirement imposed by regulations made in pursuance of section 10(2)(a) of this Act or by provision made in a temporary class drug order by virtue of section 7A that is of a corresponding description to such regulations, the Secretary of State may by notice in writing served on the occupier of any premises on which controlled drugs are or are proposed to be kept give directions as to the taking of precautions or further precautions for the safe custody of any controlled drugs of a description specified in the notice which are kept on those premises.
>
> (2)   It is an offence to contravene any directions given under subsection (1) above.'

**7.30**

Codes of Practice and Attorney-General's Guidelines were introduced to advance and consolidate the statutory powers per *PCA 1984*. The Codes apply to applications for warrants made after midnight on 27 October 2013. The Codes apply to searches and seizures taking place after midnight on 27 October 2013.

**7.31**

One such Code is the *'Code of Practice for Searches of Premises by Police Officers and the Seizure of Property Found by Police Officers on Persons or Premises'*. It specifies:

'Introduction

B:1.1 This code of practice deals with police powers to:

- search premises

- seize and retain property found on premises and persons.

B:1.1A These powers may be used to find:

- property and material relating to a crime

- wanted persons

- children who abscond from local authority accommodation where they have been remanded or committed by a court.

[…]'

## Enlarged investigatory powers: the Psychoactive Substances Act 2016

**7.32**

Legal liability of occupiers of premises extended remarkably with enactment of the *PSA 2016*. Specifically: *ss 36–48*, inclusive, of the Act confer an armoury of additional powers on police and other kinds of investigators.

**7.33**

*Section 36* of *PSA 2016* concerns the power to stop and search persons. The balance of the remaining sections, *ss 37–48*, relate to powers of entry to and search of kinds of premises. This is the now current and immediate context of the criminal prosecution (and other sanction-based regulation) of occupiers of premises in terms of their (alleged) involvement in drug offences.

**7.34**

Parliament has enacted, and has brought into force, or has committed to saying it shortly will do so, several key legislative provisions that are specifically directed at occupiers of premises. An immediate and convenient example is the newly conferred power on a 'relevant enforcement officer', conferred by *s 42(2)* of *PSA 2016*, to require production of documents.

**7.35**

*Section 42(2)* provides [emphasis by underlining here added]: 'The [relevant enforcement] officer may require <u>any</u> person in or on the premises to produce <u>any</u> document or record that is in the person's possession or control'.

**7.36**

Practically, such a statutory duty of production upon lawful request may well operate, in some cases, as a requirement to give up information and/or make a comment or other statement against because adverse to interest.

**7.37**

Those provisions are, variously, intended to increase the range of powers of entry, search, seizure, arrest and prosecution in connection with persons who are deemed in law to be the occupiers of premises.[2]

**7.38**

This expansion of scope for the criminal liability of occupiers of premises overlays what legislative enactments already exist – including a panoply of anti-social behaviour (interim) orders and other preventive-based measures. In principle, there is a (seamless) cross-over and enmeshing of criminal and civil provisions to control – and thereby regulate and criminalise, the conduct of occupiers and premises.

**7.39**

*PSA 2016* creates a blanket ban on the production, distribution, sale, and supply of psychoactive substances in the UK. *Section 2* defines a *'psychoactive substance'* for the purposes of the Act. Schedule 1 lists substances, such as food, alcohol, tobacco, caffeine, medicinal products and controlled drugs, which are excluded from the definition.

**7.40**

The Act is not a replacement for the *MDA 1971*. Some psychoactive substances will continue to be classified pursuant to *MDA 1971*, as statutorily specified. In territorial extent and application, the provisions of the *PSA 2016* extend to the whole of the UK.

**7.41**

The increased panoply of powers contemplated and newly created by the Act conferred on law enforcement and investigating officers is particularly significant in the context of occupiers' liability.

---

2   See further, Ch 9.

**7.42**

The *PSA 2016* is intended to introduce newly conceived powers for a police officer or customs officer who has 'reasonable grounds to suspect' that a person has committed, or is likely to commit, an offence under the Act.

**7.43**

Powers for dealing with what *PSA 2016* specifies are *'prohibited activities'* are found in *ss 12–35* of the Act, inclusive – in particular: powers to give prohibition notices and powers to make prohibition orders. Powers of entry, search and seizure are found in *ss 36–48* of *PSA 2016*, inclusive.

**7.44**

Occupiers of premises beware: *s 56* of *PSA 2016* gives rise to offences committed by directors and corporate partners. *Section 56* specifies:

'(1)   Where an offence under this Act has been committed by a body corporate and it is proved that the offence—

(a)   has been committed with the consent or connivance of a person falling within subsection (2), or

(b)   is attributable to any neglect on the part of such a person,

that person (as well as the body corporate) is guilty of that offence and liable to be proceeded against and punished accordingly.

(2)   The persons are—

(a)   a director, manager, secretary or similar officer of the body corporate;

(b)   any person who was purporting to act in such a capacity.

(3)   Where the affairs of a body corporate are managed by its members, subsection (1) applies in relation to the acts and defaults of a member, in connection with that management, as if the member were a director of the body corporate.

(4)   Where an offence under this Act has been committed by a Scottish firm and it is proved that the offence—

(a)   has been committed with the consent or connivance of a partner in the firm or a person purporting to act as such a partner, or

(b)   is attributable to any neglect on the part of such a person,

that person (as well as the firm) is guilty of that offence and liable to be proceeded against and punished accordingly.'

**7.45**

Occupiers of premises are key targets for national and international law enforcement. Brought into force on 3 March 2015, the *Serious Crime Act 2015 (SCA 2015)* was intended, among other purposes, 'to make provision about involvement in organised crime groups and about serious crime prevention orders; to make provision for the seizure and forfeiture of drug-cutting agents'.

**7.46**

The *SCA 2015* amended various existing legal provisions governing the liability of occupiers of premises – including, for example, the *Proceeds of Crime Act 2002*, the *Computer Misuse Act 1990*, Pt 4 of the *Policing and Crime Act 2009*, s 1 of the *Children and Young Persons Act 1933*, the *Sexual Offences Act 2003*, the *Street Offences Act 1959*, and the *Terrorism Act 2006*.

# Prohibition orders: the 2016 Act

**7.47**

The *PSA 2016* introduced the concept of *'prohibition orders'*: orders by which certain types of conduct were specified. The sections of the 2016 Act pertinent to prohibition orders had legal effect from 26 May 2016 [see SI 2016/553]. No transitional provisions were introduced.

**7.48**

Creation of prohibition orders is subject to the list of exceptions to offences (see *PSA 2016, s 11*). 'Prohibition order' means, per *s 17(1)* of the *PSA 2016*, an order prohibiting the person against whom it is made from carrying on any prohibited activity or a prohibited activity of a description specified in the order.

**7.49**

There, Parliament specified that 'prohibited activity' means any of the following activities:

(a)   producing a psychoactive substance that is likely to be consumed by individuals for its psychoactive effects;

(b)   supplying such a substance;

(c)   offering to supply such a substance;

(d)   importing such a substance;

(e)   exporting such a substance;

(f)    assisting or encouraging the carrying on of a prohibited activity listed in any of para (a)–(e), *PSA 2016, s 12(1)*.

## Anti-social behaviour (interim) orders

### 7.50

The *Anti-Social Behaviour Act 2003*, which received Royal Assent on 20 November 2003, gives police the power to close premises where there are reasonable grounds to suspect there has been disorder or serious nuisance and involvement on or from the premises of use or supply of controlled drugs.

### 7.51

The raft of available anti-social measures police may invoke include the issue of a notice of closure where authorised by a police officer of at least the rank of Superintendent and in consultation with the local authority.

### 7.52

Police may then apply to the courts for a closure order for the premises. Use of such orders will be susceptible to challenge where (for example): there has been no, or inadequate, consultation; the required level and type of authorisation does not underpin the order; application for, and issue of, such an order was not a measure of last resort; reliance on such orders was not, in all the circumstances, proportionate.

### 7.53

Interim orders will be subject to self-limiting conditions: interim orders will be applicable until expiry of a stated time and date or *'until further [Court] order'*.

## Summary of key points

### 7.54

- Degree of control is key. It is what creates liability of occupiers in law.

  - The language of *s 8* of *MDA 1971* prompts questions about its scope. Who is (in law deemed to be) an occupier of premises? What constitutes (requisite and sufficient) knowledge? At which category of persons is *s 8* aimed?

- *Section 8* is targeted at any person who is the 'occupier or concerned in the management of any premises'. This has been interpreted by the appellate courts to include any person who has (what the courts deem to be) a sufficient degree of control – of any kind – of the premises in question.

- Examples of categories of occupiers of premises whose convictions were upheld as safe and correct include co-tenants who knowing permitted other co-tenants to offend on the premises; and squatters and trespassers of premises who did not deter or prevent others from offending whilst on the premises.

- Powers of entry, search and seizure are of especial significance for occupiers.

- Powers for dealing with what *PSA 2016* specifies are 'prohibited activities' are found in *ss 12–35* of the Act, inclusive. In particular, powers to give prohibition notices and powers to make prohibition orders.

- Legal liability of occupiers of premises extended remarkably with enactment of the *PSA 2016*. Specifically, *ss 36–48*, inclusive, of the Act confer an armoury of additional powers on police and other kinds of investigators.

- *Sections 41–48*, inclusive, contain limitations on the exercise by a 'relevant enforcement officer' of powers connected to the issue and execution of search warrants and the making and recording of searches.

- Anti-social behaviour orders, pursuant to the *Anti-Social Behaviour Act 2003*, also serve to control the conduct of occupiers of premises.

# 8 Conspiracy and Cross-Jurisdictional Offences

Paul Mason

## Introduction

### 8.1

There are three principal types of conspiracy. These is conspiracy to commit an offence under the *Criminal Law Act 1977* (*CLA 1977*); conspiracy to commit a crime abroad; and conspiracies at common law.

### 8.2

The *CLA 1977* replaced almost all forms of common law conspiracy. Those that remain concern conspiracy to defraud, to corrupt public morals and to outrage public decency. This chapter is concerned with statutory conspiracy to commit drugs offences, and issues arising from international jurisdictions.

### 8.3

The key issues around conspiracy are neatly summarised by Sir Anthony May in *R v D* [2009] EWCA Crim 584:[1]

> 'The essence of an unlawful conspiracy, as it may be a conspiracy to defraud, is an agreement between two or more people to act unlawfully. The offence is committed upon the making of the agreement, the conspirators do not have to be proved to have proceeded to commit the unlawful act or acts which they agreed to commit. Any analysis will therefore need to concentrate on the agreement, its nature and to determine such matters as: who made the agreement? When did they make it? What was the unlawful ambit of that which they agreed to do?'

---

1   At para 1.

# The indictment

### 8.4

*Section 1* of the *CLA 1977* defines the offence of conspiracy as follows:

'(1)   Subject to the following provisions of this Part of this Act, if a person agrees with any other person or persons that a course of conduct shall be pursued which, if the agreement is carried out in accordance with their intentions, either—

(a)   will necessarily amount to or involve the commission of any offence or offences by one or more of the parties to the agreement, or

(b)   would do so but for the existence of facts which render the commission of the offence or any of the offences impossible, he is guilty of conspiracy to commit the offence or offences in question.

(2)   Where liability for any offence may be incurred without knowledge on the part of the person committing it of any particular fact or circumstance necessary for the commission of the offence, a person shall nevertheless not be guilty of conspiracy to commit that offence by virtue of subsection (1) above unless he and at least one other party to the agreement intend or know that that fact or circumstance shall or will exist at the time when the conduct constituting the offence is to take place.

(3)   [repealed]

(4)   In this Part of this Act *"offence"* means an offence triable in England and Wales.'

### 8.5

Conspiracy is an indictable only offence. This remains the case where the conspiracy is to commit a summary offence. In these cases the consent of the Director of Public Prosecutions (DPP) is required (*CLA 1977, s 4(1–3)*).

### 8.6

Under the Criminal Procedure Rules,[2] an indictment for conspiracy must identify the individual offences concerned.

### 8.7

A single count of conspiracy may relate to an agreement to commit several offences without being duplicitous. As the Court of Appeal noted in *R v Roberts*

---

2   At 10.2.

[1998] 1 Cr App R 441, such a count does not amount to several conspiracies where there is a single agreement to engage in a course of conduct.

**8.8**

Further, an indictment may cite the commission of alternative offences as forming the subject of the conspiracy. These are sometimes referred to as 'either/or conspiracies'.

**8.9**

In *R v Hussain* [2002] EWCA Crim 06, the Court of Appeal was invited to consider whether it was permissible for an indictment to contain a conspiracy to either one offence or another. There were three indictments against multiple defendants. Each had the following as count 1 'Conspiracy to contravene s 49(2) of the Drug Trafficking Act 1994 alternatively s 93C(2) of the Criminal Justice Act 1988, contrary to s 1(1) of the Criminal Law Act 1977'.

**8.10**

The Court of Appeal noted that it was necessary to distinguish between the statutory offence, which the Court termed 'the Conspiracy Offence', and the offence or offences, which the agreement contemplates – 'the Agreed Offence or Offences'. The Court went on to find that:[3]

'… there can be an agreement constituting a Conspiracy Offence where the agreed course of conduct, if it is carried out in accordance with the conspirators' intentions, will necessarily amount to or involve the commission by one or more of the conspirators of more than one Agreed Offence.'

**8.11**

Further, *Hussain* noted that an agreement to commit crime A or crime B is entirely possible. Such an agreement was capable of falling within *s 1(1)* of the *CLA 1977*.

**8.12**

It remains open to the prosecution to break down an indictment into a number of separate counts. As Lord Bridge noted in *R v Cooke* [1986] AC 909:[4]

'A single agreement to pursue a course of conduct which involves the commission of two different specific offences could perfectly properly be charged in two counts alleging two different conspiracies, *e.g.* a

---

3   At para 26.
4   At 919 G–H.

conspiracy to steal a car and a conspiracy to obtain money by deception by selling the car with false registration plates and documents.'

## 8.13

Can the defendant be 'another' and therefore guilty of conspiracy to supply a controlled drug to another, where the case for the Crown is that he himself was the person to be supplied? That was the question for the Court of Appeal in the cases of *R v Jackson* [2000] 1 Cr App R 97, and *R v Drew* [2000].

## 8.14

In both cases, the defendant was charged as one of the co-conspirators to supply drugs to himself. In *Jackson*, the defendant was in prison at the time; and in *Drew*, he was in police custody. In both cases, the Court found that it was an offence known to law to conspire to supply a co-conspirator.

## 8.15

However, *Drew* made clear that if the prosecution were going to allege a conspiracy to supply to one of the co-conspirators, that had to be made clear in the particulars. If the allegation is a conspiracy between A, B and C to supply to 'another', then the prosecution are alleging supply to someone other than A, B or C. Consequently, if the prosecution can establish only a supply by A and B to C then the Crown will not have to established the offence with which A, B and C have been charged.

## 8.16

Conversely, and as in the particulars of *Drew*, the conspiracy charged is a conspiracy to supply to one of the conspirators, then there is no difficulty.

# What is an agreement?

## 8.17

As *s 1* of the *CLA 1977* makes clear, the central element of conspiracy is agreement. However, the *CLA 1977* is of no further help in defining what such an agreement must consist of.

## 8.18

In *R v Mehta* [2012] EWCA Crim 2824, the Court of Appeal distilled the definition of agreement from previous authorities to the following principles:[5]

---

5   At para 36.

(1)   A conspiracy requires that the parties to it have a common unlawful purpose or design.

(2)   A common design means a shared design. It is not the same as similar but separate designs.

(3)   In criminal law (as in civil law) there may be an umbrella agreement pursuant to which the parties enter into further agreements which may include parties who are not parties to the umbrella agreement. So, A and B may enter into an umbrella agreement pursuant to which they enter into a further agreement between A, B and C, and a further agreement between A, B and D, and so on. In that example, C and D will not be conspirators with each other.

### 8.19

Similarly, in *R v Shillam* [2013] EWCA Crim 160, it was held that:

'... for two or more persons to be convicted of a single conspiracy each of them must be proved to have a shared common purpose or design ... there must be a shared criminal purpose or design in which all have joined, rather than merely similar or parallel ones.'[6]

### 8.20

It follows that there is no conspiracy where individuals conspire separately. An example of this principle was given in *R v Griffiths* (1966) 1 QB 589. In that case several farmers had each conspired separately with Mr Griffiths without any knowledge of each other, or having ever met.

### 8.21

In finding that there was no agreement between the parties, Paull J gave the following example:[7]

'I employ an accountant to make out my tax return. He and his clerk are both present when I am about to sign the return. I notice an item in my expenses of £100 and say: "I don't remember incurring this expense." The clerk says: "Well, actually I put it in. You didn't incur it, but I didn't think you would object to a few pounds being saved." The accountant indicates his agreement to this attitude. After some hesitation I agree to let it stand. On those bare facts I cannot be charged with 50 others in a conspiracy to defraud the Exchequer of £100,000 on the basis that this accountant and his clerk have persuaded 500

---

6   At para 19.
7   At pp. 598G–599C.

other clients to make false returns, some being false in one way, some in another, or even all in the same way. I have not knowingly attached myself to a general agreement to defraud.'

### 8.22

That is not to say there cannot be an agreement simply because the parties have not met. It is the course of conduct – the common purpose – that is crucial. The prosecution must demonstrate that the parties are aware of that criminal design.

### 8.23

As noted in *R v Reid* [2013] EWCA Crim 1844, this can take the form of a 'wheel' conspiracy with A at the centre and B, C, D part of a common design to (in the case of *Reid*) supply cocaine.

### 8.24

Alternatively, the conspiracy could be a chain, in which A agrees with B, B with C, C with D and so on. The fact that B, C and D have never met is irrelevant, if they share the common design with A (*R v Meyrick and Ribuffi* (1930) 21 Cr App R 94; *R v D* [2009] EWCA Crim 584).

### 8.25

In *Reid*, the difficulty arose when the trial judge directed that the conspiracy could be between any of A, B and C and persons unknown. The Court of Appeal described that approach as 'misleading', because it suggested that all three defendants could be convicted of separate conspiracies with different people.

## Qualified agreements

### 8.26

Does an agreement amount to a conspiracy where that agreement *may not necessarily* require the commission of an offence? Would this form of contingency planning amount to a conspiracy?

### 8.27

In *R v Reed* [1982] Crim LR 819, Donaldson LJ gave two contrasting examples. In the first A and B agree to drive from London to Edinburgh in a time which may or may not require them to exceed the speed limit depending on traffic. Their agreement will not necessarily involve the commission of any offence and does not amount to a conspiracy.

**8.28**

In Lord Donaldson's second example A and B agree to rob a bank, if it seems safe to do so when they get there. Their agreement will necessarily involve the commission of the offence of robbery if it is carried out in accordance with their intentions. Accordingly, they are guilty of conspiracy.

**8.29**

Lord Nicholls in *R v Saik* [2006] UKHL 18 summarised the approach as follows:[8]

> 'An intention to do a prohibited act is within the scope of s 1(1) even if the intention is expressed to be conditional on the happening, or non-happening, of some particular event. The question always is whether the agreed course of conduct, if carried out in accordance with the parties' intentions, would necessarily involve an offence ... In the nature of things, every agreement to do something in the future is hedged about with conditions, implicit if not explicit. In theory if not in practice, the condition could be so far-fetched that it would cast doubt on the genuineness of a conspirator's expressed intention to do an unlawful act. If I agree to commit an offence should I succeed in climbing Mount Everest without the use of oxygen, plainly I have no intention to commit the offence at all. Fanciful cases apart, the conditional nature of the agreement is insufficient to take the conspiracy outside s 1(1).'

## Parties to the agreement

**8.30**

By definition, an agreement requires at least two people. However, a single defendant may be charged with conspiracy even if their conspirators remain unknown.

**8.31**

*Section 2(2)* of the *CLA 1977* provides that a person will not be guilty of conspiracy if the only other person or persons with whom they agree are either their spouse or civil partner; a person under the age of criminal responsibility; or an intended victim of the offence.

**8.32**

*Section 2(2)* does not apply to long-term partners. The terms 'spouse' and 'civil partner' are ordinary and well-understood (*R v Suski* [2016] EWCA Crim 24; *R v Pearce* [2001] EWCA Crim 2834).[9]

---

8   At para 5.
9   See also *R v Bala* [2016] EWCA Crim 560.

**8.33**

While spouses or civil partners cannot be guilty of conspiracy if they are the only parties to the agreement, that is not the case where there are other co-conspirators.

**8.34**

In *R v Chrastny (No. 1)* (1992) 94 Cr App R 283, the Court of Appeal clarified that where a wife, knowing that her husband is involved with others in a particular conspiracy, agreed with her husband to join the conspiracy and play her part, she is thereby agreeing with all those whom she knows are the other parties to the conspiracy.[10]

**8.35**

A company may be a party to a conspiracy (*R v ICR Haulage Ltd* [1944] KB 551). However, where the only parties to the conspiracy are the company and one of the directors of that company, there is no conspiracy. This is because although a director and company are separate legal personalities, there are not two separate minds (*Cassel v The Queen* [2016] UKPC 19).

**8.36**

As Nield J stated fifty years earlier in *R v McDonnell* [1966] 1 QB 233, 'the true position is that a company and a director cannot be convicted of conspiracy when the only human being who is said to have broken the law or intended to do so is the one director'.[11]

**8.37**

The acquittal of the only other alleged conspirator does not mean, necessarily that the defendant cannot be convicted.[12] If the evidence admissible against A proves that A and B conspired together, A may be convicted of conspiracy with B. This may be the case even though B, his alleged co-conspirator is acquitted because there is no sufficient evidence admissible against him.

**8.38**

Conversely, where there is evidence of equal weight, the jury should be directed to return the same verdict on both defendants, to avoid the risk of inconsistency (*R v Longman & Cribben* [1981] 72 Cr App 121; *R v Testouri* [2003] EWCA Crim 3735). It is a matter for the judge to decide, as a matter of law, whether or not it is possible for one of the accused to be convicted and the other acquitted (*R v Roberts* [1987] 78 Cr App R 41).

---

10 At p. 1384 E–F.
11 At p.246 A–B.
12 *Section 8(2)* of the *CLA 1977*. See further below at 8.80–8.84.

**8.39**

Where only one party to the conspiracy is capable of committing the offence, a co-defendant may still be liable for that conspiracy. In *R v Sherry* [1993] Crim LR 536, E and S were convicted of conspiracy to abduct S's son. E appealed on the ground that as he was not a parent, he could not be charged with conspiracy to abduct under *s 1* of the *Child Abduction Act 1984*. E's appeal was dismissed. He had agreed to a course of conduct that amounted to an offence, namely that S would abduct the child.

# Criminal conduct

**8.40**

A conspiracy requires an agreement that one of the parties will commit a substantive offence. A conspiracy to aid, abet or procure an offence is not a conspiracy of the purposes of *s 1* of the 1977 Act. Hodgson J, in *R v Hollinshead* (1985) 80 Cr App R 285 cited *Smith and Hogan's Criminal Law* to explain the position:[13]

> 'If E uses the ladder and commits burglary, D1 and D2 will be guilty of aiding and abetting him to do so. Are they guilty of conspiracy to commit burglary? If the course of conduct is placing the ladder, it seems clear that they are not. Placing the ladder is not an offence, not even an attempt to aid and abet burglary, since the Criminal Attempts Act 1981 makes it clear that this is not an offence known to the law ... E is not a party to the agreement, so the question becomes, do the words "commission of any offence" include participation in the offence as a secondary party? Since all the parties to a conspiracy to commit an offence will be guilty of that offence if it is committed, but s 1(1) contemplates that it may be committed by only one of them, it is clear that "commission' means commission by a principal in the first degree."'[14]

**8.41**

The question was further ventilated in two drugs offences cases. In *R v Kenning* [2008] EWCA Crim 1534, the appellants were owners of a business selling hydroponic equipment. They had been convicted of conspiracy to aid and abet the conspiracy of cannabis, after their equipment had been used by several cannabis producers, who were subsequently prosecuted.

---

13  At p.293.
14  Ormerod and Laird (2015) *Smith and Hogan's Criminal Law* (14<sup>th</sup> edn), at pp. 500–501.

**8.42**

It was argued on appeal (and in a submission of no case to answer during the trial) that no conspiracy had been made out because none of the conspirators had agreed to cultivate cannabis.

**8.43**

The Court of Appeal agreed. The course of conduct to which the appellants agreed were no more than as accessories to the offence intended to be committed by the primary offender:

> 'They do not amount to an offence unless the primary offender commits the primary offence. There can be no certainty that he will do so. Thus, even if the aiders and abettors do all that they agree to do, their course of conduct will not necessarily amount to the commission of an offence.'[15]

**8.44**

A similar set of facts arose in *R v Dang* [2014] EWCA Crim 348. The case concerned 24 defendants, who were said to be engaged in a conspiracy to supply hydroponic and other products and equipment for the purpose of assisting others to grow cannabis plants. The indictment contained two counts: conspiracy to be concerned in the production of cannabis; and conspiracy to produce cannabis.

**8.45**

Among the various grounds of appeal, it was submitted that the importing and selling of hydroponic and other equipment did not necessarily amount to, or involve the commission of any offence within the meaning of *s 1(1)* of the 1977 Act. Count 1 was therefore bad in law. The appellants relied upon the reasoning in *Kenning* and *Hollinshead*.

**8.46**

In dismissing the appeal, the Court of Appeal drew a distinction between the agreement and the substantive offence of being concerned in production. To establish the substantive offence the prosecution had to prove that cannabis was produced and that the defendants were concerned in its production.

**8.47**

However, to establish a conspiracy to commit the substantive offence the prosecution had to prove an agreement that cannabis will be produced by

---

15 At para 18.

another with the conspirators' assistance. The offence charged was the making of the agreement to be concerned in the production of cannabis by others.

**8.48**

Further, the Court distinguished the offence of being concerned in the production of a drug under *s 4(2)(b)* of the *Misuse of Drugs Act 1971* (*MDA 1971*) from that of aiding and abetting the production of a drug as was the case in *Kenning*. It said that 'a person who is concerned in the production of cannabis contrary to s 4(2)(b) MDA 1971 is a principal offender, just as the producer himself is a principal offender contrary to s 4(2)(a)'.[16]

**8.49**

In *Kenning,* none of the conspirators intended to act as a principal offender in the production of a controlled drug. In *Dang*, the prosecution case was that the appellants had agreed to be personally concerned in the production of cannabis by supplying equipment for that purpose.

**8.50**

The appellants had argued that an agreement simply to supply equipment which may be used in the production of cannabis did not satisfy *s 1(1)(a)* of the 1977 Act. This was because *s 1(1)(a)* requires an agreement which would 'necessarily amount to or involve the commission of any offence or offences'. The appellants cannot have known whether the principal offender (who was not a co-conspirator) intended to produce cannabis or not.

**8.51**

However, as Fortson notes[17] the word 'unnecessary' in *s 1(1)(a)* is misleading. It gives the impression that only infallible agreements will amount to conspiracy. Fortson suggests[18] that a conspiracy under *s 1* extends to plans that have intended consequences and foreseen circumstances. Conspirators may be unconcerned about the method of a murder (for example poison, bullet, or bomb) but they are agreed as to the consequence (death).

**8.52**

This is why the Court in *Dang* found that no question arose as to whether the defendant aided and abetted the production of cannabis. This was because an offence under *MDA 1971, s 4(2)(b)* does not require proof of involvement in any particular process of production.

---

16 At para 19.
17 Fortson QC, R. (2014) '*R v Dang (Manh Toan):* Conspiracy – Conspiracy to be Concerned in the Production of a Controlled Drug to Another', *Criminal Law Review* vol. 9, pp. 675–678.
18 See also *Smith and Hogan's Criminal Law* (2011), pp.433–434, and Glanville Williams *Textbook of Criminal Law*, 2nd edn (1983), pp. 428–429.

## Mens rea of conspiracy

### 8.53

The mens rea of conspiracy is the intention to be party to the agreement. However, the law has been far from clear on the point. In *R v Anderson* [1986] AC 27, the appellant had agreed with another prisoner that he would help him escape from prison when he, the appellant, was released. He was charged under *CLA 1977, s 1* with conspiracy to effect the escape of a prisoner.

### 8.54

The appellant said that he never intended that the escape should take place, nor did he think the plan could succeed. The question for the House of Lords was whether *s 1* of the 1977 Act required an intention on the part of each conspirator that the offence or offences in question should in fact be committed.

### 8.55

Lord Bridge said:

> 'I am clearly driven by consideration of the diversity of roles which parties may agree to play in criminal conspiracies to reject any construction of the statutory language which would require the prosecution to prove an intention on the part of each conspirator that the criminal offence or offences ... is fully carried out should in fact be committed'[19]

### 8.56

He added:[20]

> 'But, beyond the mere fact of agreement, the necessary *mens rea* of the crime is, in my opinion, established if, and only if, it is shown that the accused, when he entered into the agreement, intended to play some part in the agreed course of conduct in furtherance of the criminal purpose which the agreed course of conduct was intended to achieve. Nothing less will suffice; nothing more is required.'

### 8.57

However, *Anderson* has been largely ignored in later cases, or at least it has been qualified. This is because of a number of seemingly contradictory passages in Lord Bridge's judgment. Instead, it has been held that there must be an intention that the offence be carried out (*R v Edwards* [1991] Crim LR 45).[21]

---

19 At p. 38D.
20 At p. 39E.
21 For further discussion of undercover officers in drugs offences, see Ch 10.

**8.58**

*Yip ChieuChung v The Queen* [1995] 1 AC 111 was a Privy Council case, concerning conspiracy to traffic a dangerous drug, in this case heroin. Although conspiracy was a common law offence under Hong Kong law, the Privy Council did not distinguish between that and statutory conspiracy in its discussion of intention.

**8.59**

The appellant had agreed with an undercover drug enforcement officer, N that N would carry five kilos of heroin from Hong Kong to Australia. N had agreed to smuggle the heroin out of Hong Kong, and had informed both the Hong Kong and Australian authorities.

**8.60**

The plan had been for the arrest to take place when the heroin arrived in Australia. N missed his flight and decided not to proceed with the plan. The appellant was arrested at Hong Kong airport.

**8.61**

The question for the Court was whether the undercover agent could be a co-conspirator. It was suggested by the appellant that because N had no intention of carrying out the agreement but only to frustrate the objectives of the conspiracy, there was no conspiracy.

**8.62**

The Privy Council dismissed the appeal. They found that N did have the intention to traffic the drugs from Hong Kong and therefore the necessary mens rea for the offence. The fact that the authorities in Hong Kong and Australia were aware of N's plan did not negate that intention. If N's plan had been simply to prevent any trafficking of the drugs from Hong Kong, then there would not have been any conspiracy.

**8.63**

On the question of intention and conspiracy more broadly, Lord Griffiths said:[22]

'The crime of conspiracy requires an agreement between two or more persons to commit an unlawful act with the intention of carrying it out. It is the intention to carry out the crime that constitutes the necessary mens rea for the offence. As Lord Bridge pointed out, an undercover agent who has no intention of committing the crime lacks the necessary mens rea to be a conspirator.'

22 At p. 118A.

**8.64**

Further, it is not necessary that <u>each</u> conspirator play an active part in the conspiracy. In *R v Siracusa* (1989) 90 Cr App R 340, four appellants had been convicted of importation of cannabis from Kashmir and heroin from Thailand.

**8.65**

It was accepted by both sides that the mens rea was the same for both offences. The prosecution did not have to prove that a defendant knew what the goods imported were. It was no defence to a charge of importing Class A drugs for a defendant to say he believed he was bringing in a Class C drug.[23]

**8.66**

However, the appellant's argued the position was different when the offence was a conspiracy. It was asserted that for each defendant, the prosecution had to prove that they knew that the Kashmir operation involved cannabis and that the Thailand operation involved heroin.

**8.67**

The Court of Appeal discussed *Anderson* at some length. It noted the following on the nature of conspiracy:[24]

'The present case is a classic example of such a conspiracy. It is the hallmark of such crimes that the organisers try to remain in the background and more often than not are not apprehended ... Participation in a conspiracy is infinitely variable: it can be active or passive ... Consent, that is the agreement or adherence to the agreement, can be inferred if it is proved that he knew what was going on and the intention to participate in the furtherance of the criminal purpose is also established by his failure to stop the unlawful activity.'

**8.68**

In *R v Patel*, unreported 7 August 1991, Lord Woolf summarised the position set out in *Siracusa* as follows:[25]

'(i)  a defendant will not be guilty of that offence unless the jury are satisfied that he knew that the drugs to which the conspiracy related were prohibited drugs. If the jury are so satisfied then he will only be entitled to be acquitted, so far as his intent is concerned, if the jury consider that, although he agreed to join the conspiracy, he may have mistakenly believed that the

---

23 See Ch 2.
24 At p. 349.
25 At para 17, as cited in *R v Taylor* [2002] Crim LR 205, paras 33–34.

conspiracy related to a different drug from that named in the Particulars of Offence and that different drug is of a Class, the maximum punishment in relation to which (for the substantive offence) is less than that for drugs of the Class specified in the Particulars of Offence. Thus if a person enters into a conspiracy believing it concerns cannabis (Class B) he will not be guilty of an offence charging him with being a party to a conspiracy concerning heroin (Class A) ...

(ii) a defendant will be guilty of the offence if he joined the conspiracy alleged in the mistaken belief it involved a drug which, while different from, belongs to the same Class as the drug named in the Particulars of Offence.

(iii) ... a defendant will be guilty if he joins the conspiracy knowing that prohibited drugs are involved but without knowing what drugs are involved. In such a situation he would in fact have agreed to be a party to a conspiracy irrespective of what drugs are involved'.[26]

### 8.69

Ignorance of the law is irrelevant. A defendant cannot say that they did not know what they agreed to do was unlawful because they did not know it was a criminal offence.[27]

### 8.70

If the agreement is nothing more than a fantasy, then it is not a conspiracy. In *R v Goddard* [2012] EWCA Crim 1756, the appellants were convicted of conspiracy to rape a child under 13. The Crown relied upon a text exchange between the two men.

### 8.71

In allowing the appeal, the Court of Appeal found that the evidence had been equivocal, and consistent with fantasy. The men never met at any stage, not were there any other practical details discussed. There had been no 'executory intent'.[28]

## Impossibility

### 8.72

As noted above, *s 1(1)(b)* of the *CLA 1977* has removed the defence of impossibility. It states that a person is guilty of conspiracy if the agreement to

---

26  See also *R v Ayala* [2003] EWCA 2047 and *R v Hanif* [2012] EWCA Crim 1968.
27  See, eg, *Churchill v Walton* [1967] 2 AC 224; and *R v Broad* [1997] Crim LR 666.
28  At para 40.

carry out a course of conduct amounts to an offence 'but for the existence of facts which render the commission of the offence or any of the offences impossible'.

**8.73**

*Section 1(1)(b)* was added by the *Criminal Attempts Act 1981*. Prior to the amendment, where the course of conduct was impossible, there could be no conspiracy.

**8.74**

The leading case had been *DPP v Nock* [1978] AC 979, two defendants had been convicted of conspiracy to produce cocaine. They had separated what they thought was cocaine from other substances in a powder. The powder did not contain any cocaine, and hence cocaine could not have been produced from it.

**8.75**

The House of Lords upheld the Court of Appeal's decision. It confirmed that when two or more persons agreed on a course of conduct with the object of committing a criminal offence but unknown to them, it was not possible to do so, then they did not commit the crime of conspiracy.

**8.76**

Now, under *s 1(1)(b)*, parties can be found guilty of conspiracy where, for example, they handle stolen goods, which are not in fact, stolen.

## Proving agreement

**8.77**

Proving a conspiracy is usually a matter of inference.[29] As Willes J noted in *Mulcahy v R* (1868) LR 3 HL 306, such an inference is 'deduced from certain criminal acts of the parties accused, done in pursuance of an apparent criminal purpose in common between them'.[30]

**8.78**

As with other offences, the actions and/or statements of one conspirator may be adduced as evidence against both that conspirator and any co-conspirators. That is provided those words and/or actions were said done in relation to the common purpose.

---

29 For judicial directions to a jury on proving conspiracy, see *The Crown Court Compendium*, Feb 2017 at pp.14-30 to 14-31, available at www.judiciary.gov.uk/publications/crown-court-bench-book-directing-the-jury-2/.
30 At para 11, citing *R v Brissac* 4 East, 164 at 171.

## *Acquittal of the Co-Conspirator*

### 8.79

*Section 5(8)* and *(9)* of the *CLA 1977* states as follows:

'(8)    The fact that the person or persons who, so far as appears from the indictment on which any person has been convicted of conspiracy, were the only other parties to the agreement on which his conviction was based have been acquitted of conspiracy by reference to that agreement (whether after being tried with the person convicted or separately) shall not be a ground for quashing his conviction unless under all the circumstances of the case his conviction is inconsistent with the acquittal of the other person or persons in question.

(9)    Any rule of law or practice inconsistent with the provisions of subsection (8) above is hereby abolished.'

### 8.80

This means that where there is evidence admissible against A but not B (such as a confession) which demonstrates A conspired with B, a jury could be sure that A conspired with B, but not sure that B conspired with A.[31]

### 8.81

However, as the Court of Appeal noted in *R v Longman & Cribben* [1981] 72 Cr App 121, where the evidence against both A and B is of equal weight, then a judge should direct the jury to acquit both or find both guilty. He must be careful to add, however, that if they are unsure about the guilt of one, then both must be found not guilty.[32]

### 8.82

The question of the similarity or difference in the evidence against co-conspirators is a matter of law for the judge (*R v Roberts* (1987) 78 Cr App R 41). But how is a judge to assess that degree of difference or similarity?

### 8.83

In *Longman*, the level of difference required to allow for separate verdicts was described as 'marked'. In *Roberts*, the Court of Appeal summarised the approach in this way:[33]

---

31  *R v Longman* (1980) 72 Cr App R 121 at p. 125.
32  ibid. See also *R v Testouri* [2003] EWCA Crim 3735.
33  At p. 47.

'When a judge has to sum up in a conspiracy case, involving only two accused, he has to make up his mind, on the evidence, whether or not it is possible, as a matter of law, for one of the accused to be convicted and the other acquitted. That must necessarily be a matter for the judge to decide. Once he has decided it, he must direct the jury accordingly. When he comes to decide it, a factor he should keep in mind is whether the two cases are different to a substantial degree; but that is a matter for his assessment and not for the jury's'.

## 8.84

Where only one party to the conspiracy is capable of committing the offence, a co-defendant may still be liable for that conspiracy. In *R v Sherry* [1993] Crim LR 536, E and S were convicted of conspiracy to abduct S's son. E appealed on the ground that as he was not a parent, he could not be charged with conspiracy to abduct under *s 1* of the *Child Abduction Act 1984*. E's appeal was dismissed. He had agreed to a course of conduct that amounted to an offence, namely that S would abduct the child.

# Jurisdiction

## 8.85

Conspiracies that span other jurisdictions can give rise to difficulty. For example, where a co-conspirator is based in another country; or where the conspiracy is to commit a crime abroad; or where, conversely, the conspiracy is formed abroad to commit a crime in England and Wales.

## *Co-Conspirator Based Abroad*

## 8.86

A conspiracy to commit an offence domestically, where a co-conspirator is based outside the domestic jurisdiction, is indictable under English law. In *R v Parnell* (1881) 14 Cox 508, Mr Justice Fitzgerald explained, in reference to conspiracies between defendants in Ireland and the United States that:[34]

'It may be that the alleged conspirators have never seen each other, and have never corresponded. One may have never heard the name of the other, and yet by the law they may be parties to the same common criminal agreement.'

---

34  At p. 515. See also *R v Meyrick and Ribuffi* (1930) 21 Cr App R 94.

## Domestic Conspiracies to Commit an Offence Abroad

### 8.87

An agreement made in England and Wales to commit an offence abroad is deal with by *s 1A* of the *CLA 1977*.[35] It provides that where each of four conditions are met, the conspiracy falls within domestic conspiracies under *s 1(1)*, as already set out.

### 8.88

Those four conditions are that:

(1) the agreed conduct would involve an act or event intending to take place outside England and Wales;

(2) the act or event constitutes an offence under the law of that country;

(3) it would be an offence triable in England and Wales but for the fact that it was committed abroad; and

(4) a part to the agreement did anything in England and Wales in relation to the agreement before its formation; or became a party in England in Wales; or did anything in England and Wales in pursuance of the agreement.

### 8.89

The assessment of these conditions is a question of law to be decided by the Judge. The provisions of *s 1A* are an extension to *s 1(1)* rather than an offence in itself.

### 8.90

As Smith and Hogan note,[36] this is a significant extension of the offence of conspiracy because it broadens the scope of the criminal law beyond the physical limits of the jurisdiction of English law.

## Conspiracy Formed Abroad to Commit an Offence in England and Wales

### 8.91

There are no provisions in the *CLA 1977* for conspiracies formed abroad to commit offences in the UK. However, at common law such conspiracies can be indicted under *s 1* of the *CLA 1977*.

---

35 The provision was inserted by the *Criminal Justice (Terrorism and Conspiracy) Act 1998* and amended by *s 72* of the *Coroners and Justice Act 2009*.

36 At p. 511.

**8.92**

In *Somchai Liangsiriprasert v Government of the United States of America* [1991] 1 AC 225, the Privy Council held that a conspiracy formed in Thailand to traffick heroin in Hong Kong was indictable in Hong Kong. This was the case even when there had been no overt act pursuant to the conspiracy in Hong Kong itself.

**8.93**

In *R v Smith* [2004] EWCA Crim 631, the Court of Appeal recognised conspiracy, which does not require proof of any harmful consequence, 'a broader approach has undoubtedly been adopted as to jurisdiction'.[37]

**8.94**

*Smith* approved the comments of Lord Griffiths in *Somchai*, in which he said that:[38]

> 'Unfortunately in this century crime has ceased to be largely local in origin and effect. Crime is now established on an international scale and the common law must face this new reality. Their Lordships can find nothing in precedent, comity or good sense that should inhibit the common law from regarding as justiciable in England inchoate crimes committed abroad which are intended to result in the commission of criminal offences in England.'[39]

**8.95**

Earlier, Pt 1 of the *Criminal Justice Act 1993* introduced particular rules to address difficulties of cross-frontier offences such as fraud, forgery and blackmail.

**8.96**

There are two groups of offences are listed in *s 1* as Group A and Group B. Group A offences include theft, fraud, forgery and blackmail. Group B offences include conspiracies to commit Group A offences.

**8.97**

Where a 'relevant event' occurs within England and Wales, a person may be found guilty of the offence in this jurisdiction (*s 3(1)*. A relevant event is as any event that is an essential element of the offence in question.

---

37 At para 61.
38 At p. 251.
39 See also *R v Sansom* (1991) 2 QB 130☒ *R v Manning* [1999] QB 980; and *R (AlFawwaz) v Governor of Brixton Prison* [2002] 1 AC 556.

## Conspiracy Formed Abroad to Commit an Offence Abroad

### 8.98

*Smith and Hogan* suggest that where for example, D1 and D2, British citizens in France, agree to kill V in France, the offence contemplated is triable in England even if committed in France.

### 8.99

However, they note that 'the presumption against the extraterritorial application of the criminal law will exclude agreements not made within the jurisdiction and not intended to have any effect therein, but this seems less likely after *Liangsiriprasert*'.[40]

## Summary of key points

### 8.100

- Statutory conspiracy is dealt with by the *CLA 1977*.

- The central element of conspiracy is agreement. It is not defined in the 1977 Act.

- Case law has defined agreement for the purposes of conspiracy as (1) the parties to it have a common unlawful purpose or design; (2) a common design means a shared design; (3) there is no conspiracy where individuals conspire separately.

- Conspiracies can be 'wheels' with A at the centre and B, C, D part of a common design. They can also be 'chains' where A agrees with B, B with C, C with D and so on.

- A person will not be guilty of conspiracy if the only other person or persons with whom they agree are either their spouse or civil partner; a person under the age of criminal responsibility; or an intended victim of the offence.

- A conspiracy requires an agreement that one of the parties will commit a substantive offence. A conspiracy to aid, abet or procure an offence is not a conspiracy.

- The mens rea of conspiracy is the intention to be party to the agreement to commit an unlawful act with the intention of carrying it out.

- A person can still be guilty of conspiracy even if the course of conduct is impossible.

---

40 At p. 512.

- A conspiracy to commit an offence domestically, where a co-conspirator is based outside the domestic jurisdiction, is indictable under English law.

- An agreement made in England and Wales to commit an offence abroad also falls under English law, provided the four conditions in *s 1A* of the *CLA 1977* are met.

- Conspiracies formed abroad to commit offences in the UK can be indicted under English common law.

# 9    Search and Seizure

Harriet Johnson

## Powers of search and seizure

### 9.1

General powers of search and seizure are contained within the *Police and Criminal Evidence Act 1984 (PACE)*[1]. Part I addresses police powers to stop and search persons and vehicles, and Part II sets out powers of entry, search and seizure, including search warrants, entry and search without warrant, and retention of seized items. Further powers of search and seizure are contained within the *Criminal Justice and Police Act 2001 (CJPA)*[2]. The majority of statutes relating to public health and safety also include provision for search and seizure.

### 9.2

*Section 1* of Pt I of *PACE* provides the power for a constable to stop and search any person or vehicle, or anything which is in or on a vehicle, for stolen or prohibited articles, and to detain a person or vehicle for the purpose of the search[3]. Such powers may only be exercised if he has reasonable grounds for suspecting that he will find stolen or prohibited articles. *Section 1* also sets out the parameters for where such searches may be carried out, and the circumstances in which an officer may seize articles discovered during the course of the search.

### 9.3

*Howarth v Commissioner of Police of the Metropolis* [2012] A. C. D. 41, DC confirmed that the lawfulness of a search conducted under *s. 1* of *PACE* is dependent on three factors:

(1)    that the officer did suspect that he would find stolen or prohibited articles;

(2)    that there was reasonable cause for that suspicion; and

(3)    that the officer exercised his discretion reasonably[4].

---

1    Pt II, ss 8-23.
2    Pt 2.
3    Per *Lewis v Cattle* [1938] 2 K. B. 454, any police officer in England and Wales of any rank holds the office of constable.
4    *Howarth v Commissioner of Police of the Metropolis* [2012] A. C. D. 41, DC, para 26.

**9.4**

*PACE* Code A sets out a subjective and objective test for 'reasonable suspicion' in two parts. The first part is that the officer must have a genuine suspicion that they will find the object for which the search power being exercised allows them to search. The second is that the suspicion that the object will be found must be reasonable; meaning that it must be based on facts, information and/or intelligence relevant to the likelihood of finding the object in question, which would entitle a reasonable person to reach the same conclusion based on the same information[5]. Further examples of what may or may not constitute reasonable grounds for suspicion are found elsewhere within Code A:2.

**9.5**

Part II of *PACE* effectively consolidates a range of previously existing powers of search and seizure. *Section 8* provides the conditions required for the issuing of warrants by a justice of the peace on application by a constable, including:

- That there are reasonable grounds for believing that an indictable offence has been committed; and

- That there is material on the premises in question that is likely to be of substantial value to the investigation,

along with other criteria. *Section 8* also provides the circumstances in which an officer may seize and retain anything found during the course of the search. *Sections 19–22* set out more general powers of seizure and retention. Powers of entry and search without a warrant are found at *ss 17* and *18*.

**9.6**

Part 2 of *CJPA* significantly extended the powers of seizure found under *PACE*, in part in an effort to address some of the limitations of *PACE* when it came to seizure of evidence stored digitally. In particular, *s 50(1)* of *CJPA* allows a person exercising search powers to seize anything that might contain something that he is entitled to seize, for the purpose of determining that question later. *Section 50(2)* allows a person exercising search powers to seize material that does not in itself fall to be seized, but which is inextricably connected to material that does.

**9.7**

Specific powers of search and seizure relating to drugs offences are set out in *s 23* of the *Misuse of Drugs Act 1971 (MDA 1971)*[6]. *Section 23* gives constables powers to enter the premises of a person in business as a producer or supplier

---

5   PACE Code A: 2.2.
6   As amended by the *Criminal Justice (International Co-operation) Act 1990, s 23(1), (4)*; the *DTA 1994, s 65 (1)*, and Sch 1, para 4; the *PCA 2002, s 457*, and Sch 12; the *Policing and Crime Act 2009, ss 111* and *112(2)*, and Sch 8, Pt 12; and the *Police Reform and Social Responsibility Act 2011, s 151*, and Sch 17, paras 1 and 15.

of any controlled drugs and inspect related documents and stock. It also allows a constable with reasonable grounds to suspect a person of being in possession of a controlled drug to search that person, and to search any vehicle or vessel in which the constable suspects the drug may be found. It also provides powers for the officer to seize and detain anything found during the course of the search which appears to be evidence of an offence under the Act. *Section 23(3)* provides for magistrates to issue warrants in respect of vehicles and premises for officers investigating drugs searches.

### 9.8

*Section 23A* of the *MDA 1971* provides powers of search, seizure and detention in respect of temporary class drugs.

### 9.9

The powers of entry and inspection set out at **9.1** also apply for the purposes of the execution of art 3 of Council Regulation (EC) 273/2004, which sets out requirements for operators who possess or sell 'drug precursors': specified substances used for the manufacture of controlled drugs, listed in Category 1 of the Annex to Council Regulation (EC) No. 111/2005[7].

### 9.10

Where a suspect had a valid reason to be at the home of a known drug dealer (such as the drug dealer being his brother) the suspect's presence alone did not provide reasonable grounds for suggesting that the suspect was in possession of drugs. Nor was the suspect's aggressive behaviour upon being detained by police capable of retrospectively providing reasonable grounds (*Black v DPP* [1995] COD 381).

### 9.11

In *R v Littleford* [1978] Crim LR 48 a police officer searched L's car, believing that it had been used in drug trafficking. Cannabis resin was found in the car. However, the search was deemed unlawful as the terms of the MDA give officers a power to search any person or vehicle only when they had reasonable grounds to suspect that the *person* was in possession of a controlled drug.

### 9.12

Here, it was the vehicle that was suspected, not the person. However, although illegally obtained, the evidence of the presence of cannabis resin in the car was deemed admissible as the Court considered the officer's actions understandable.

---

7    Regulation 8 of the Controlled Drugs (Drug Precursors) (Intra-Community Trade) Regulations 2008 (SI 2008/295).

**9.13**

The officer conducting the search must himself have reasonable grounds to suspect that a person is in possession of a controlled drug. It is insufficient for the officer to rely solely on information received from persons with no personal knowledge of the circumstances of the alleged possession (*French v DPP* [1997] COD 174, DC).

**9.14**

Once entry to premises has been effected using any lawful power to do so, an officer is lawfully on those premises for all purposes (*Foster v Attard* (1986) 83 Cr App R 214). In *R v Longman* [1988] 1 WLR 619, the Court of Appeal considered a case in which police officers attended in plain clothes at the address in respect of which they had obtained a warrant. An officer knocked at the door holding a bunch of flowers, which she told the occupant she had tried to deliver to the adjacent property. The Court held that where a search warrant was issued under the *MDA 1971*, and the constable executing the warrant had reasonable grounds for believing that any delay in entry would frustrate the search, he was entitled to use subterfuge or force to gain entry before complying with the requirements of *PACE 1984, s 16(5)*.

**9.15**

While the right conferred by *MDA 1971, s 23(2)(a)* to detain a suspect for a search necessarily involves the right to detain, question and search, the fact of the detention itself does not confer an obligation to search (*R v Geen* [1982] Crim LR 604).

**9.16**

As to the effect of unlawful searches, under *s 78* of the *Police and Criminal Evidence Act 1984* (*PACE 1984*) evidence that was obtained improperly or unlawfully may be excluded if its admission would have such an adverse effect on the fairness of the proceedings that the court ought not to admit it. However, it is well established that even where a search is unlawful, the evidence obtained through such a search will not necessarily be inadmissible (*R v Delaney* (1989) 88 Cr App R 388; *R v Absolam* (19890 88 Cr App R 332)). Though there is a discretion to exclude evidence obtained as a result of unlawful searches, this will only be exercised in exceptional cases (*Jeffrey v Black* [1978] QB 490).

**9.17**

As to the manner of search to be conducted, when searching an individual under *MDA 1971, s 23*, the requirements of *PACE 1984, s 2* apply (*R v Bristol* [2007] EWCA Crim 3214).

**9.18**

Where a police officer failed to comply with *PACE 1984, s 2* prior to commencing a drug search, that search was unlawful despite the fact that the officer and suspect were well known to each other (*Michaels v Highbury Corner Magistrates' Court* [2009] EWHC 2928 (Admin)).

**9.19**

Similarly, a search was unlawful where an officer failed to comply with the requirements of *s 2* even where his status as a police officer must have been obvious to the suspect, and where the officer had sincere concerns for the safety of another officer (*Bonner v DPP* [2004] EWHC 2415).

**9.20**

An officer executing a warrant under subs (3) has the power to detain persons in the premises for the purpose of searching the premises, and to use reasonable force in doing so.

**9.21**

While it was for the police to show that the use of force was necessary and reasonable, it was not unreasonable for officers to restrict the movement of those occupying premises while the premises were being searched, as long as no more force was used than was necessary (*DPP v Meaden* [2003] EWHC 3005).

## Obstruction of searches

**9.22**

*Section 23(4)* of the *MDA 1971* provides as follows:

'(4)   A person commits an offence if he—

intentionally obstructs a person in the exercise of his powers under this section; or

conceals from a person acting in the exercise of his powers under subsection (1) above any such books, documents, stocks or drugs as are mentioned in that subsection; or

without reasonable excuse (proof of which shall lie on him) fails to produce any such books or documents as are so mentioned where their production is demanded by a person in the exercise of his powers under that subsection.'

**9.23**

The elements of the offence were set out in *R v Forde* (1985) 81 Cr App R 19 and clarified in *R v Garjo* [1985] EWCA Crim 1169. In *Forde,* the Appellant was a self-confessed drug addict who had been searched by the police on a number of occasions. Police observed that the Appellant was handed something by another person he was with. On being stopped by police the Appellant placed something in his mouth and swallowed it. He later claimed that it was a prescribed drug.

**9.24**

In *Garjo*, the Appellant was alleged to have offered to supply cannabis to an undercover police officer, and recovered three bags of the drug from a nearby hiding place. When the officer told the Appellant that he was being detained for under MDA, the Appellant was alleged to have run away, ripping open one of the bags of cannabis. The Appellant was also alleged to have resisted arrest. The Judge directed in summing up that running away, ripping/attempting to dispose of the bag of cannabis and physically resisting arrest amounted to an obstruction. Allowing the appeal, the Court held that the minimum requirements for a conviction of obstruction are:

(i)     that the accused has knowledge that he is being detained for the purpose of a search under *s 23(2)(a)*;

(ii)    that viewed objectively, the accused did in fact obstruct the detention and search; and

(iii)   the accused intended by his actions to obstruct the detention or search.

**9.25**

Under *s 23(4)(a)* the search must be lawful for the offence to be made out (see above). The burden of proof concerning the lawfulness of the search rests with the Crown.

**9.26**

Where an officer searched a suspect under *s 23* at the request of other officers, the question of whether a search is lawful will be dependent to some degree on the reasonableness of the suspicion of the officers at the beginning of the chain.

**9.27**

Where the Crown had not called those officers to give evidence about their grounds for suspicion in order to allow the court to assess their reasonableness, it could not be established that the subsequent search was lawful, nor that an obstruction to it was unlawful (*French v DPP* [1997] C. O. D. 174).

# Return of seized property

**9.28**

*Section 22* of *PACE* provides as follows:

'(1)   Subject to subsection (4) below, anything which has been seized by a constable or taken away by a constable following a requirement made by virtue of section 19 or 20 above may be retained so long as is necessary in all the circumstances

(2)   Without prejudice to the generality of subsection (1) above—

    (a)   anything seized for the purposes of a criminal investigation may be retained, except as provided by subsection (4) below—

        (i)   for use as evidence at a trial for an offence; or

        (ii)   for forensic examination or for investigation in connection with an offence; and

    (b)   anything may be retained in order to establish its lawful owner, where there are reasonable grounds for believing that it has been obtained in consequence of the commission of an offence.

(3)   Nothing seized on the ground that it may be used—

    (a)   to cause physical injury to any person;

    (b)   to damage property;

    (c)   to interfere with evidence; or

    (d)   to assist in escape from police detention or lawful custody,

may be retained when the person from whom it was seized is no longer in police detention or the custody of a court or is in the custody of a court but has been released on bail.

(4)   Nothing may be retained for either of the purposes mentioned in subsection 2 (a) above if a photograph or copy would be sufficient for that purpose.'

## 9.29

*Section 1* of the *Police (Property) Act 1897* provides:

'Where any property has come into the possession of the police in connexion [with their investigation of a suspected offence] a court of summary jurisdiction may, on application, either by an officer of police or by a claimant of the property, make an order for the delivery of the property to the person appearing to the magistrate or court to be the owner thereof, or, if the owner cannot be ascertained, make such order with respect to the property as to the magistrate or court may seem meet.'

An order under this section shall not affect the right of any person to take within six months from the date of the order legal proceedings against any person in possession of property delivered by virtue of the order for the recovery of the property, but on the expiration of those six months the right shall cease.

## 9.30

As a matter of fundamental constitutional principle, circumstances where articles seized by the police may be retained are strictly limited (*Ghani v Jones* [1970] 1 QB 693).

## 9.31

Where police had seized a video tape as part of a criminal investigation, they had no power to retain the tape under s 22 following the completion of the investigation, even where it was believed that the return of the tape might lead to the owner of the tape committing a serious criminal offence (*Chief Constable of Mersyside v Owens* [2012] EWHC 1515 (Admin); see also *McCarthy v Chief Constable of Northern Ireland* [2016] NICA 36).

## 9.32

Where the person entitled to possession of money seized under *MDA 1971, s 23* has not been convicted of a drug trafficking offence, the money must be returned to him; even where it has been established in civil proceedings that the money represented the proceeds of drug trafficking (*Webb v Chief Constable of Merseyside Police* [2000] QB 427, CA.

## 9.33

Police may retain property after the CPS decide not to prosecute in the event that a private prosecution is being contemplated or is underway (*Scopelight Ltd v Chief Constable of Northumbria* [2010] 1 Cr App R 19, CAN).

## 9.34

Property may be retained for a short period after detention is no longer necessary under *s 22* while the police consider their position (*Gough v Chief Constable of the West Midlands Police, The Times*, 4 March 2004, CAN).

## 9.35

*Section 22(2)* is to be read in conjunction with the rest of *s 22* and therefore only relates to material that has been lawfully seized or that has been removed following a requirement made under *ss 19(4)* or *20(1)*. The police do not have a general right to retain unlawfully seized material for use as evidence (*R v Chief Constable of Lancashire, ex p. Parker* 97 Cr App R 90, DC). In the event that property is not returned, redress is to the Magistrates' Court under *s 1* of the *Police (Property) Act 1897* (see **9.29**).

# Forfeiture and destruction of seized property

**9.36**

Provisions for forfeiture and destruction of property seized in respect of offences under the *MDA 1971* are found at *s 27*:

'(1)  Subject to subsection (2) below, the court by or before which a person is convicted of an offence under this Act [...] may order anything shown to the satisfaction of the court to relate to the offence, to be forfeited and either destroyed or dealt with in such other manner as the court may order.

(2)  The court shall not order anything to be forfeited under this section, where a person claiming to be the owner of or otherwise interested in it applies to be heard by the court, unless an opportunity has been given to him to show cause why the order should not be made.

(3)  An offence falls within this subsection if it is an offence which is specified in—

(a)  paragraph 1 of Schedule 2 to the Proceeds of Crime Act 2002 (drug trafficking offences), or

(b)  so far as it relates to that paragraph, paragraph 10 of that Schedule.'

**9.37**

*Section 27(1)* may include money. In such cases, the court had a discretion, to be exercised judicially, as to the manner in which it was dealt with. In *R v Beard,* [1975] Crim LR 92 the arresting officer had clung onto a car travelling at speed in the course of apprehending suspects who later pleaded guilty to charges relating to the importation of drugs. The Judge directed that part of forfeited money was to be paid as a reward to the officer in question.

**9.38**

Notably, provisions for forfeiture of money under *s 27* are more narrowly drawn than those for confiscation under the *Proceeds of Crime Act 2002*. For example, in *R v Morgan* [1977] Crim LR. 488, the defendant had arranged to meet two others with the intention of selling them cocaine and cannabis. On arrest he was found in possession of the drugs in question as £393. An order for the forfeiture of the money, which was certainly part of his working capital, was quashed as ultra vires as there was no evidence that it related to the offence.

**9.39**

In *R v Cuthbertson* [1981] AC 470, HL the Appellants were convicted of a common law conspiracy to contravene the provisions of *MDA 1971, s 4*. The trial judge made orders of forfeiture against them in respect of British and foreign currency, the contents of various safe deposit boxes situated abroad, and money in foreign bank accounts. The House of Lords overturned the orders, ruling that the power of forfeiture conferred by s 27 does not apply to intangible things or choses in action. Further, an English court has no jurisdiction either in a criminal or a civil matter to make orders purporting *ipso jure* to transfer property situated abroad into the jurisdiction.

**9.40**

In *R v Pearce* [1996] Crim LR 442, CA, the Appellant had pleaded guilty to cultivation of cannabis. The Court imposed an order for forfeiture of the Appellant's house, held to have been purchased solely for use in producing the drug. The Court held that the power under s 27 to order the forfeiture of 'anything' connected with the offence did not include real property. By way of alternative, the Court proposed imposing a fine in a sum equal to or less than the value of the property, which could thereafter be enforced by the property's sale.

# Summary of key points

**9.41**

- *Section 1* of Pt I of *PACE* provides 'stop and search' powers relating to persons and vehicles.

- For a search to be lawful, it is necessary that the officer suspected he would find stolen or prohibited articles; that there was reasonable cause for that suspicion; and that the officer exercised his discretion reasonably.

- The test for 'reasonable suspicion' as set out by *PACE* Code A is a subjective and objective test: the officer must have a genuine suspicion that they will find the object in question; and the suspicion must be based on facts, information and/or intelligence that would entitle a reasonable person to reach the same conclusion.

- Specific powers of search and seizure concerning drugs offences are contained in s 23 of the *MDA 1971*.

- When searching a person using powers found under *MDA 1971, s 23*, the requirements of *PACE, s 2* apply.

- It is an offence under *MDA 1971, s 23(4)* to obstruct an officer exercising his powers under s 23.

- For the offence to be made out the search obstructed must be lawful. The burden of proof concerning lawfulness rests with the Crown.

- *PACE, s 22* makes provision for the retention of seized property.

- Where seized property has not been returned in accordance with the requirements of *PACE, s 22* the appropriate remedy is an application to the Magistrates' Court under *s 1* of the *Police (Property) Act 1897.* Circumstances where the police may retain seized articles are strictly limited.

# 10 Forensic and Covert Evidence

Harriet Johnson

## Expert forensic evidence

### 10.1

There is no need for scientific testing and analysis to be undertaken to identify a prohibited drug. As is the case for other expert evidence, an experienced police officer or other person may give evidence as an expert in a criminal trial to identify a substance suspected to be a prohibited drug (*Gwilliam v DPP* [2010] EWHC 3312).

### 10.2

In many cases, an admission is adequate to identify a substance as being a prohibited drug.[1] While evidence from a person who had a great deal of familiarity with a substance is admissible as evidence to prove the substance in question is a prohibited drug, that does not remove the requirement that the evidence has to be capable of satisfying the criminal standard of proof.[2]

### 10.3

The factors for the court to consider when determining the reliability of expert opinion, and in particular of expert scientific opinion, are set out in the *Criminal Practice Directions 2015* [2015] EWCA Crim 1567 at paras 19A.5 and 19A.6. They include factors relating to: the available data set (both in the area in question and in terms of the case as a whole); methodology; and the expert's own expertise.

### 10.4

In *R v Dlugosz & Ors* [2013] EWCA Crim 2, the Court of Appeal observed that:

'It is essential to recall the principle which is applicable, namely in determining the issue of admissibility, the court must be satisfied that

---

1   *R (on the application of Wright) v Crown Prosecution Service* [2015] EWHC 628 (Admin).
2   ibid.

there is a sufficiently reliable scientific basis for the evidence to be admitted'.[3]

## Forensic analysis of drugs and drug traces

### 10.5

CPS guidance states that any substance suspected to be a controlled drug must be sent to a forensic science laboratory, with the exception of certain cannabis seizures.[4]

### 10.6

Forensic evidence is rarely controversial where the substance being tested is itself suspected to be a controlled drug. Controversy arises, however, when 'trace' evidence is relied upon to establish whether a tested item, such as a banknote or an item seized from the premises of a suspect, has come into contact with controlled drugs.

### 10.7

If the test for drug traces is positive, the evidence is then used to invite an inference; for example, that the suspect was involved in the supply of drugs.

### 10.8

The chief limitation of expert evidence concerning drug traces is that 'it is not possible to establish when or how the item being tested became contaminated. Nor is it possible to determine whether the person in possession of the [in this case] banknotes was in possession at the time when the contamination occurred or knew of that contamination (or had reason to consider such contamination may have occurred)'.[5]

### 10.9

In his 2009 report to the Forensic Science Regulator, Dr. Jeff Adams recommended that:

> 'This form of evidence should be used by the prosecution in criminal cases very carefully and in circumstances where the information it can provide is of direct relevance and value. Using this form of evidence, without more, to found a prosecution appears a high risk strategy'.[6]

---

3   *R v Dlugosz & Ors* [2013] EWCA Crim 2 at para11.

4   CPS guidance on drug offences, www.cps.gov.uk/legal/d_to_g/drug_offences/, accessed 17 June 2017.

5   Adams, J (2009) *'Analysis of Currency for Target Controlled Drugs, Report to the Forensic Science Regulator'*, para 5.1.16.

6   ibid, para 5.1.17.

**10.10**

Reliance on trace evidence concerning drugs has been the subject of academic criticism. Such criticism has been directed in part at what is seen as a lack of sufficient empirical research into transfer of drug traces themselves, and at an assumption within the scientific community that drug traces will deplete over time.

**10.11**

As Amber Marks of Queen Mary, University of London put it:

'The scientific basis for the assumption that traces will deplete over time is unclear and yet it forms the foundation for the hypothesis that a higher level of contamination suggests proximity (in terms of the handling steps or number of transactions) between the defendant's acquisition of the notes and their contamination'.[7]

**10.12**

Judicial treatment of drug trace evidence has varied. In *R v Compton* [2002] EWCA Crim 2835, the Court of Appeal held that the difference between the levels of heroin contamination found on the bank notes in question and those in ordinary circulation was so significant that, even if the database from which the control samples had been collected had been deficient (which the Court did not necessarily accept) an explanation was still required as to the high levels of heroin contamination.

**10.13**

In *R v Fleur* [2004] EWCA Crim 2372 the jury heard evidence that forensic analysis of two cars associated with the defendant had revealed traces of heroin. No statistics were available from which any conclusion could be drawn as to how common it might be to find traces of heroin in a car.

Though the appeal was ultimately refused on the basis that the evidence as a whole was overwhelming, the Court accepted that the evidence concerning the traces of heroin found in the cars was inadmissible. Without statistical context the evidence that traces of heroin had been found in the car only invited impermissible speculation.

**10.14**

In *Smith v HM Advocate* [2008] HCJAC 7 bank notes seized from the appellant's address were found to be contaminated with heroin in quantities much greater than those typically found on banknotes in general circulation. No other drugs or associated paraphernalia were found. While the Court accepted that the

---

7   ibid, Crim LR 814.

evidence of the contamination of the banknotes was sufficient to establish that the bank notes had been in close proximity to heroin in the course of illegal drug dealing, it was deemed insufficient to find an inference that the appellant knew he was a participant in a drug dealing enterprise.

## 10.15

Failure to account for drug traces found on the property of a defendant can result in a direction to the jury that they may draw an adverse inference under *s 36* of the *Criminal Justice and Public Order Act 1994*, which provides:

'36.— Effect of accused's failure or refusal to account for objects, substances or marks.

(1) Where—

    (a) a person is arrested by a constable, and there is—

        (i) on his person; or

        (ii) in or on this clothing or footwear; or

        (iii) otherwise in his possession; or

        (iv) in any place in which he is at the time of his arrest, any object, substance or mark, or there is any mark on any such object; and

    (b) that or another constable investigating the case reasonably believes that the presence of the object, substance or mark may be attributable to the participation of the person arrest in the commission of an offence specified by the constable; and

    (c) the constable informs the person arrested that he so believes, and requests him to account for the presence of the object, substance or mark; and

    (d) the person fails or refuses to do so, then if, in any proceedings against the person for which the offence so specified, evidence of those matters is given, subsection (2) below applies.

(2) Where this subsection applies—

    (a) a magistrates' court inquiring into the offence as examining justices;

    (b) a judge, in deciding whether to grant an application made by the accused under—

        (i) section 6 of the Criminal Justice Act 1987 (application for dismissal of charge of serious fraud in respect of which notice of transfer has been given under section 4 of that Act); or

(ii) paragraph 5 of Schedule 6 to the Criminal Justice Act 1991 (application for dismissal of charge or violent or sexual offence involving child in respect of which notice of transfer has been given under section 53 of that Act);

(c) the court, in determining whether there is a case to answer; and

(d) the court, in determining whether the accused is guilty of the offence charged, may draw such inferences from the failure or refusal as appear proper.'

## 10.16

The granting of an application for a direction under *s 36* arising from failure to account for trace evidence of drugs was challenged in *R v Compton* (above). The defendant gave an account in interview in which he stated that the contaminated money found in his property was his personal money, and that it had been contaminated through his own drug habit. The Court upheld the granting of a *s 36* direction, ruling:

'In the circumstances of Robert's money, stowed away in a safe, the presence of heroin on it is far from accounted for by a bare statement that Robert was a heroin user'[8].

## 10.17

It is submitted that *s 36* applications in respect of trace evidence of drugs ought to be considered within the context of the ruling of the European Court of Human Rights in *Murray v United Kingdom* (1996) 22 E. H. R. R. 29, and in particular, paragraph 51 of the judgment:

'The question in each particular case is whether the evidence adduced by the prosecution is sufficiently strong to require an answer. The national court cannot conclude that the accused is guilty merely because he chooses to remain silent. It is only if the evidence against the accused "calls" for an explanation which the accused ought to be in a position to give that a failure to give an explanation "may as a matter of common sense allow the drawing of an inference that there is no explanation and that the accused is guilty'[9].

---

8   *R v Compton* [2002] EWCA Crim 2835, para 32.
9   *Murray v UK* (1996) 22 E. H. R. R. 29, para 51.

Given the limitations of expert evidence on how or when a bank note might have become contaminated (see paragraph **10.2** above), it is questionable whether a defendant 'ought to be in a position to give' an explanation on the same point. As the Council for the Registration of Forensic Practitioners put it:

'By its very nature, trace evidence at very low concentrations has to be treated very carefully. If MSA scientists cannot offer such an explanation, how can anyone else (the defendant, for example)?'[10]

## Covert evidence

**10.18**

Covert entry to, and interference with, property or wireless telegraphy by the police and other bodies is governed by Pt III of the *Police Act 1997*. All other forms of covert surveillance are regulated by Pt II of the *Regulation of Investigatory Powers Act 2000 (RIPA)*.

**10.19**

'Directed surveillance' is defined by *RIPA, s 26(2)* as covert surveillance undertaken for the purposes of a specific investigation or operation that is likely to result in private information being obtained about a person (including those not identified for the purposes of the operation). 'Intrusive surveillance' is defined by *s 26* (3–5) as covert surveillance conducted in relation to anything occurring on residential premises. The crucial practical difference between 'directed' and 'intrusive' surveillance is that the authorisation requirements for 'intrusive' surveillance are significantly more stringent than those required for 'directed' surveillance.

**10.20**

The Regulation of Investigatory Powers (extension of Authorisation Provisions: Legal Consultation) Order 2010 (SI 2010/461) directed that from February 2010 surveillance carried out concerning anything taking place on a specified premises that is, at any point during the surveillance, used for the purpose of legal consultations, is to be treated as 'intrusive surveillance' for the purposes of Pt II, *RIPA*.

**10.21**

In *R v Turner* [2013] EWCA Crim 642, the Court upheld the admission of surveillance evidence, even when such evidence had amounted to a breach of

---

10  Council for the Registration of Forensic Practitioners' reference to the Forensic Science Regulator, as cited in Adams, J (2009) '*Analysis of Currency for Target Controlled Drugs, Report to the Forensic Science Regulator*', para 4.5.1.

legal professional privilege. However, the Court emphasised the need for those arranging covert evidence to pay meticulous attention to the need to preserve legal professional privilege and, where any precautions have failed, to ensure that there is no prejudice to the defendant during the investigation or in any subsequent trial.

## 10.22

In *R.E. v United Kingdom* 63 EHRR 2, the European Court of Human Rights held that the fact that SI 2010/461 allowed for the covert surveillance of legal consultations did not render it incompatible with art 8 of the European Convention on Human Rights. It further held that consultations that took place between a detainee and an appropriate adult were not subject to legal professional privilege and therefore did not carry the same expectation of privacy. Accordingly, covert surveillance of such conversations could be classified as 'directed' rather than 'intrusive' surveillance.

## 10.23

In *R v Plunkett (Daniel) & Plunkett (James)* [2013] 2 Cr App R 2, CA, the Court held that a police van was not a private vehicle as defined by *s 48* of *RIPA*. The covert recording of conversations between prisoners held in the van therefore amounted to 'directed' rather than 'intrusive' surveillance.

## 10.24

No comprehensive definition of 'surveillance' is given in *RIPA*, but in *Re. a Complaint of Surveillance* [2014] 2 All ER 576 the Investigatory Powers Tribunal held that the correct approach was to give the word its ordinary meaning.

## 10.25

*RIPA* also provides for the use of 'covert human intelligence sources'. In relation to *s 26 (8)*, this is a person who establishes or maintains a relationship with a person for the covert purpose of using the relationship to obtain information or provide access to any information to another person, or to covertly disclose information obtained by the use of the relationship or as a consequence of the existence of the relationship. In *R v Hardy* [2003] 1 Cr App R 30, CA, the Court held that 'covert human intelligence sources' included an undercover police officer.

## 10.26

*Sections 28* and *29* of *RIPA* state that covert activity as set out above must be both necessary and proportionate. In both sections, an authorisation is deemed necessary within the terms of the Act if it is necessary:

(a)　　in the interests of national security;

(b)    for the purpose of preventing or detecting crime or of preventing disorder;

(c)    in the interests of the economic well-being of the United Kingdom;

(d)    in the interests of public safety;

(e)    for the purpose of protecting public health;

(f)    for the purpose of assessing or collecting any tax, duty, levy or other imposition, contribution or charge payable to a government department; or

(g)    for any purpose (not falling within paras (a) to (f)) which is specified for the purposes of this subsection by an order made by the Secretary of State.

**10.27**

The existence of lawful authority for covert surveillance will normally be sufficiently demonstrated by the production of the surveillance commissioner's signed approval forms, or through evidence of the senior officer who had authorised and obtained approval of the surveillance to that effect. Only in exceptional cases would the defence be entitled to see the authorisations or any underlying material (*R v GS* [2005] EWCA Crim 887).

**10.28**

Failure to obtain authorisation is not criminalised by *RIPA*, but the Act's explanatory notes recognise that a failure to obtain authorisation may mean the law enforcement agency had acted unlawfully under *s* 6 of the *Human Rights Act 1998*[11]. Revised codes of practice for use of covert human intelligence sources and covert surveillance and property interference came into force in December 2014[12].

## Impact of non-compliance

**10.29**

As to the impact on a prosecution of non-compliance with the above requirements, in *R v Harmes & Crane* [2006] EWCA Crim 928 the Court held that the conduct of officers involved in a covert operation had involved serious breaches of *RIPA* and of the Code of Practice. However, although the conduct of the officers in question had been criminal and was not properly authorised, it should not be seen as so seriously improper as to require the court to intervene to prevent the prosecution for conspiracy. The Court held that the conduct of

---

11  *RIPA* explanatory notes, para 180.
12  Regulation of Investigatory Powers (Covert Human Intelligence Sources: Code of Practice) Order 2014 (SI 2014/3119); Regulation of Investigatory Powers (Covert Surveillance and Property Interference: Code of Practice) Order 2014 (SI 2014/3103).

the officers, when considered as a whole, did not stray beyond that which was permissible to investigate.

**10.30**

In *R v Khan* [2013] EWCA Crim 2230, the Court held that the trial judge had been correct not to exclude a covertly-obtained recording of a conversation between two defendants, despite the fact that the circumstances in which the recording was made exceeded the authority granted under *RIPA*.

**10.31**

As neither the *Police Act 1997* nor *RIPA* addresses the matter of the admissibility of evidence obtained, the question of admissibility is governed by the *Police and Criminal Evidence Act 1984, ss 76* and *78*. The crucial factor to consider is the effect of the conduct of the police on the fairness of the proceedings, rather than the legality of their conduct (*R v Khan (Sultan)* [1997] A. C. 558). That said, the definition of fairness should not be confined to procedural fairness, and evidence may be excluded because it has been obtained by unfair means (see *R v Looseley* [2001] UKHL 53, below).

**10.32**

Similarly, lack of authorisation will rarely lead the court to accede to an argument for abuse of process owing to entrapment. However, in *R v Moon* [2004] EWCA Crim 2872, an undercover officer acting without authorisation under the relevant Code of Practice approached the appellant and asked to buy drugs. The Court held that on the particular facts of the case, including but not limited to the lack of the safeguards provided by proper authorisation, the operation had the effect of causing crime rather than simply providing the opportunity for it, and the trial ought to have been stayed as an abuse of process.

**10.33**

Surveillance evidence obtained by a party other than those named in *RIPA*, but nonetheless relied upon in a criminal prosecution, does not fall within the scope of the Act. In *R v Rosenberg* [2006] EWCA Crim 6, the appellant had been convicted after trial of possession of class A drugs with intent to supply and possession of a class A drug. The prosecution had relied at trial on CCTV footage taken by the neighbour of the appellant through a camera aimed at the appellant's house. The police had been aware that the appellant's neighbour had been filming her, and had warned the neighbour against it. On appeal, the Court held that while the police were complicit in the surveillance in so far as they knew of its existence and were prepared to use it in a criminal prosecution, for the purposes of the Act it could not be regarded as police surveillance. The police had not initiated the surveillance, nor had they encouraged it, and the warning given to the neighbour by the police did not have the effect of converting it into a police operation.

## Admissibility of covert evidence

### 10.34

Prior to *RIPA*, a series of cases demonstrated that covert evidence would be admitted in all but the most exceptional cases; including when police deception or trickery was used to obtain it. In *R v Buchan* [1964] 1 WLR 365, the defendant, while in a police cell, gave an account to a police officer on the express understanding that nothing was being written down. The Court upheld the admissibility of the evidence of a second officer, who had been in an adjoining cell, taking notes.

### 10.35

In *R v Bailey & Smith* [1993] 3 All ER 513, the police had represented to the two appellants that they were being forced to house them in the same cell, against the wishes of the officers in question. The appellants' conversation was then covertly recorded and admitted in evidence. The appeal, founded on the breach of Code C 8.1, failed. The Court held that the appellants did not have to be protected from the opportunity to speak incriminatingly amongst themselves if they chose, though it was observed that such methods ought only to be used in 'grave cases', and that nothing ought to be done to render unreliable any admissions made.

### 10.36

In *R v Roberts* [1997] 1 Cr App R 217, CA, the appellant was suspected of a number of armed robberies. He and another man, C, were both charged with a particular robbery. C requested to be put in the same cell as the appellant, believing he could get the appellant to confess, so exculpating himself. Authority was obtained to bug the cell and the appellant, during conversation, admitted a number of offences. The Court upheld the decision of the trial judge to admit the evidence obtained from the cell recordings. C was not a police agent, and was still a suspect at the time that the recordings were made. The *PACE* Codes of Practice did not exist to protect one suspect against another, and, there being no causal link between the breaches of the codes and the admissions of the appellant, the trial judge was right to consider such breaches as insignificant to the appellant. The test in such cases was whether the conduct of the police had, wittingly or unwittingly, let to unfairness or injustice.

### 10.37

In *Chalkley & Jeffries* [1998] 2 Cr App R 79, CA, the police wished to install a listening device in the defendant's home. In order that they might obtain the necessary authorisation, they arrested him for unrelated offenses about which they had earlier been given information but upon which they had decided not to act. There was no realistic prospect of proceedings in any of the matters for which he had been arrested. The Court held that a collateral motive for an arrest on otherwise good grounds did not render the arrest unlawful. The evidence obtained through the listening device did not result from incitement, entrapment or inducement, and the police's conduct did not affect the quality of the evidence.

## Covert policing and agents provocateurs

### 10.38

Historically, the Courts have been reluctant to interfere with prosecutions arising through the actions of agents provocateurs. In *R v Mealey* (1974) 60 Cr App R 59 the Court held that it was legitimate for police to infiltrate suspect societies, and, if an undercover officer were to discover that the society was contemplating a crime, it would be necessary for the officer to show a degree of enthusiasm to avoid exposure. The court stressed the need for officers to avoid themselves procuring the commission of crimes that would not otherwise take place, but emphasised that, even if a crime were procured by such an agent provocateur, that of itself does not provide a defence to the accused.

### 10.39

The key case on entrapment and agents provocateurs remains *R v Looseley* [2001] UKHL 53. The House of Lords ruled that it was acceptable for officers to provide a person with an unexceptional opportunity to commit a crime, and that if that person then freely took advantage of the opportunity provided there was no unfairness caused. However, it was unfair, and an abuse of process, to allow officers to instigate an offence by offering inducements, and luring a person into a course of action he would not normally have followed. In making the assessment as to the propriety of police action in such undercover operations, it was especially important to consider the nature of the offence, the requirement of good faith on the part of the officers, and the nature and extent of police involvement in the commission of the offence.

### 10.40

In undercover drug operations the use of test purchase officers is relatively common and has been repeatedly upheld, even when the methods of the officers have strayed far beyond the conduct authorised at the outset of the investigation. In *R v Harmes* [2006] EWCA Crim 928 an officer had supplied the appellant with soft drinks in exchange for a small amount of drugs worth half the value of the drinks. The appellant later revealed to another officer a system where drugs could be imported into Heathrow Airport with the assistance of his friend who worked there, and that the appellant could import 44 kilos of cocaine every other day. A test run for the importation of 200 kilos of cocaine was successful. The Court held that the suggestion by the officers that they should be supplied with drugs in exchange for the soft drinks did not trap the appellants into the agreement to import substantial quantities of drugs. It was not the supply of drinks that persuaded the appellant to become involved in the importation, but the prospect of significant remuneration for himself. The officers' conduct, viewed as a whole, did not stray beyond that which was permissible. The officers' activities were insignificant in comparison to the offers made by the appellant to import large amounts of drugs of a high value.

**10.41**

In *R v Chandler* [2002] EWCA Crim 3167 the Court upheld the decision of the trial judge not to stay proceedings where the appellant had supplied drugs as part of an undercover operation, despite some evidence of pressure, bordering on threats, being issued by the officers in question. The Court concluded that 'we do not even consider that this was a borderline case'.

**10.42**

In *R v Byrne* [2003] EWCA Crim 1073, the appellant was a heroin addict who supplied undercover officers, themselves posing as heroin addicts suffering from withdrawal, with heroin. She maintained that she had done so only out of sympathy for the suffering of fellow addicts. The appellant relied on a passage from the speech of Lord Hoffman in *Looseley* in which he noted:

> 'Nor is the fact that a person is a drug addict and therefore likely to know a supplier a sufficient ground in itself for tempting him to move altogether outside his usual way of life and act as intermediary in the supply of a substantial quantity of drugs. Such persons may be particularly vulnerable to unfair pressures of this kind.'[13]

The Court distinguished by finding that the appellant had demonstrated a propensity:

> 'The likelihood is she would have done what she did for anyone whom she felt was suffering from heroin withdrawal.'[14]

**10.43**

The exception is found in the case of *R v Moon* [2004] EWCA Crim 2872, which turned on similar facts to *R v Byrne*. The appellant was a heroin addict who was approached by an undercover police officer. The officer pleaded with the appellant to supply her with heroin. After being asked a number of times the appellant relented, out of sympathy for a fellow addict. She went to her own dealer and obtained a wrap of heroin for £10, which she then gave to the officer for £10. She told the officer never to contact her again. The Court allowed the

---

13  *R v Looseley* [2001] UKHL 53, at para 68.
14  *R v Byrne* [2003] EWCA Crim 1073, at para 12.

appeal, noting that the appellant had no predisposition to dealing drugs and no previous history of doing so. The officer had made the first approach to the appellant, and had been persistent in her requests. The Court held that the officer had caused the crime, rather than merely providing the opportunity for it. On that basis the case ought to have been stayed as an abuse of process.

**10.44**

Conversely, in *R v Jones* [2010] EWCA Crim 915, the appellant had been convicted on four counts of incitement to produce cannabis. The appellant ran a shop which sold hydroponics equipment and smoking paraphernalia. An undercover officer attended the shop and purchased equipment posing as a novice cannabis grower. The officer sought cultivation advice from the appellant, who provided it willingly but with reference to tomatoes, rather than cannabis. The jury accepted the prosecution case that, taken as a whole, the appellant had been giving advice on the cultivation of cannabis. The Court of Appeal held that the persistence of the officer's questioning did not go too far, noting:

> 'a dealer in drugs will not voluntarily offer drugs to a stranger unless first approached and that this approach may need to be and can be persistent without crossing the line.'[15]

While it was submitted on behalf of the appellant that an ordinary customer would have abandoned the conversation once the appellant had made it clear he could not discuss the cultivation of cannabis, the Court held that, given the obvious specialisation of the shop, the proper test was to view the conduct of the officer as against that of a member of the public who would be prepared to break the law.

## Summary of key points

**10.45**

- It is not necessary to subject a drug to scientific analysis for it to be identified as a prohibited drug for the purposes of court proceedings.

- An experienced police officer or other person may give expert evidence to identify a prohibited drug.

- Where trace evidence is relied upon to invite an inference it should be relied upon carefully and only where the information it can provide is of direct relevance and value.

- Whether or not trace evidence is admissible to found an inference will depend on the facts of the case.

---

15  *R v Jones* [2010] EWCA Crim 915.

- Failure to account for drug traces on a defendant's property can in certain circumstances found a direction for an adverse inference under *s 36* of the *Criminal Justice and Public Order Act 1994.*

- Covert surveillance is regulated by Pt III of the *Police Act 1997* and by Pt II of the *Regulation of Investigatory Powers Act 2000* (*RIPA*).

- *RIPA* distinguishes between 'directed surveillance' and 'intrusive surveillance'. 'Intrusive surveillance' has significantly more stringent authorisation requirements than 'directed surveillance'.

- Surveillance carried out on specified premises that are at any point during surveillance used for the purpose of legal consultations is to be treated as 'intrusive surveillance'.

- Even where surveillance has amounted to a breach of legal professional privilege, it has still been held to be admissible in criminal proceedings.

- *RIPA* does not specifically define 'surveillance' and the Investigatory Powers Tribunal has held that the word ought to be given its ordinary meaning.

- 'Covert human intelligence sources' are defined at *RIPA, s 26(8)*. Covert activity must be both necessary and proportionate (*RIPA, ss 28* and *29*).

- Failure to obtain authorisation for covert surveillance is not criminalised by *RIPA* but may mean the law enforcement agency in question has acted unlawfully under *s 6* of the *Human Rights Act 1998.*

- Even where the conduct of officers involved in surveillance involves serious breaches of *RIPA* and the Code Of Practice it will not necessarily render the evidence obtained inadmissible.

- The question of admissibility of evidence obtained covertly falls under *PACE, ss 76* and *78.*

- It is acceptable for officers to act as *agents provocateurs* in so far as they provide a person with an unexceptional opportunity to commit a crime; but it is unfair and an abuse of process for officers to instigate an offence.

# 11 Sentencing For Drugs Offences

Tim Moloney QC and Paul Mason

## The sentence guidelines

### 11.1

Prior to 2012, the sentencing of offences related to drugs was governed by a wealth of case law. But since 27 February 2012, the sentencing of any offender aged 18 and over has been governed by the Sentencing Council's Definitive Guideline[1] (the Guideline). The Guideline applies, irrespective of when the offence took place.

### 11.2

The Guideline substitutes for, and supersedes previous sentencing authorities. This has been made clear by the Court of Appeal on many occasions. For example, in *R v Dyer* [2014] 2 Cr App R 11, a case which concerned sentencing for offences of supplying class A drugs, Leveson LJ, as he then was, said:[2]

'Against the background of this Guideline, the earlier authorities have only very limited (if any) relevance; there is no point in referring (as a number of skeleton arguments do in this case) to cases such as *R v Djahit* [1999] 2 Cr App R 142: the pre-Guideline authorities have been overtaken by the Guideline itself.'

### 11.3

The Guideline covers offences of:[3]

(a)    the fraudulent evasion of a prohibition by bringing in or taking out of the UK, a controlled drug;

(b)    supplying or offering to supply, a controlled drug;

(c)    production of a controlled drug;

(d)    permitting premises to be used for consumption of a controlled drug; and,

(e)    possession of a controlled drug.

---

1    Sentencing Council, *Drugs Offences: Definitive Guideline*, February 2012.
2    At para 8.
3    See App 4.

# Applying the guidelines

### 11.4

In *R v Healey* [2013] 1 Cr App R 33, Hughes LJ, as he then was, gave important guidance as to how the Guideline should operate in practice. He said:[4]

> 'The format which is adopted by the Sentencing Council in producing its guidelines is to present the broad categories of offence frequently encountered pictorially in boxes. That is perhaps convenient, especially since it is necessary to condense the presentation as much as possible and to avoid discursive narrative on so wide a range of offending. It may be that the pictorial boxes which are part of the presentation may lead a superficial reader to think that adjacent boxes are mutually exclusive, one of the other. They are not. There is an inevitable overlap between the scenarios which are described in adjacent boxes. In real life offending is found on a sliding scale of gravity with few hard lines. The guidelines set out to describe such sliding scales and graduations. We wholeheartedly endorse the approach of Mr Wyatt, counsel for one of these defendants (Brearley), who asked us to find that a particular case was to be located on examination somewhere between two of the pictorial boxes.'

In these guidelines, as in almost all such, there is a recognition that the two principal factors which affect sentencing for crime can broadly be collected together as, first, the harm the offence does, and secondly, the culpability of the offender. Those two root factors are often linked but not always. In some other contexts from that which we are now considering, such as for example offences of impromptu violence or offences which are committed carelessly, the two factors may not march together. In the context of offences which involve a considerable degree of deliberation and planning, such as will normally be the case for the production of drugs, they generally do march broadly together and certainly the one is likely to colour the other. Quantity, which is a broad appreciation of harm, may well colour participation, which is a broad appreciation of culpability, and vice versa. What we have just said about sliding scales applies equally to both elements, both to culpability and to harm. In neither case do the boxes have hard edges.

### 11.5

Step One of the Guideline requires the sentencer to determine the offence category by reference to three factors:

(1)    the class of controlled drug;

(2)    the culpability of the offender; and

(3)    the harm caused by the offending.

---

4   At para 8.

## *Culpability*

### 11.6

In all three drug classes A, B and C, culpability is determined by the role of the offender.

### 11.7

As the Guidelines note, where factors fall between or across more than one role, 'the court should balance these characteristics to reach a fair assessment of the offender's culpability'.[5]

## *Harm*

### 11.8

Harm is determined by quantity of the drug. The amounts listed are indicative and form a starting point. The quantities stated in the Guidelines 'are not thresholds; they are indications of the general region of weight which goes into the relevant category. It is not exclusively an arithmetical process'.[6]

### 11.9

Purity of the drug is not taken into account at Stage 1. As noted in *Boakye*, pre-Guideline cases were sentenced on the basis of 100% purity. The change in approach by the Sentencing Council appears to have been based, at least partially, on the unavailability of scientific analysis of purity, particularly at the lower end of offences.[7]

### 11.10

After determining the relevant category of the offence, Step Two is for the sentencer to find the initial appropriate sentence in the range available by reference to the corresponding starting point.

### 11.11

Having identified that initial appropriate sentence, the sentencer should lastly adjust that sentence accordingly by reference to relevant aggravating and mitigating factors. Some of these are set out in a list which is not intended to be exhaustive, in order to determine the ultimate sentence to be imposed.

---

5   Guidelines, p.4.
6   *R v Boyake* [2012] EWCA Crim 838, at para 39. See also *Healey, Att-Gen's Ref Nos 15-17 of 2012* 2012 EWCA Crim 1414; and *R v Faruqe and Anwar* 2015 EWCA Crim 179.
7   See *Banks on Sentence* (2017) at para 340.17.

**11.12**

This general sentencing framework applies to all classes of controlled drugs.

## Conspiracy Offences

**11.13**

The Guidelines do not make explicit provision for conspiracy offences related to drugs. However, the Court of Appeal have held that the Guidelines do apply to conspiracies.

**11.14**

The issue was raised in *R v Khan and others* [2013] EWCA Crim 800. The Court of Appeal were considering an appeal against sentence by four defendants for conspiracy to supply Cocaine and Heroin.

**11.15**

The offences came to light following undercover police officers making test purchases from street dealers. Those deals amount to the supply of more than 5 kilos in over 100 deals of £20 each. The issue for the Court of Appeal was whether a large-scale conspiracy should be limited to harm category 3, as street dealing.

**11.16**

The Court of Appeal were clear that the Guidelines should apply to conspiracy cases.[8] It gave several reasons for reaching that decision.

**11.17**

Firstly, that there is no explicit exclusion of the Guidelines in application to conspiracy cases. This was in contrast to the Sentencing Guidelines on fraud which expressly excluded conspiracies to defraud.[9]

**11.18**

Secondly, many supply offences could be charged either substantively or as a conspiracy. It cannot be the case, the Court found, that the application of the Guidelines should be decided by how the prosecution chose to frame the offence.

---

8   Paras 21–35.
9   The sentencing Guidelines the Court of Appeal referred to have since been superceded by the *Fraud, Bribery and Money Laundering Offences: Definitive Guideline*, in force from 1 October 2014.

**11.19**

Thirdly, the language of the Guidelines was consistent with multi-offender conspiracies. References to roles, management functions, knowledge of the operation and links to the original source were clearly applicable to conspiracies.

**11.20**

The reasoning in *Khan* was applied also in *R v Pitts and Others* [2014] EWCA Crim 1615, where the Court of Appeal said:[10]

'We bear in mind the parameters of the definitive sentencing guidelines on drug offences which do not explicitly encompass the offences of conspiracy to import, supply or produce drugs. We see no error in the judge seeking to derive some assistance from relevant entry points into sentencing categories by virtue of the relevant weights of drugs recovered subject to the recognition that the criminality of the conspiracy is not necessarily thereby confined. That which must also be considered is the degree of participation in the illegal agreement and its scope. We accept that the broad brush of defining leading, significant and lesser roles may be an helpful indicator as to participation but these categories will themselves likely be subject to further refining on the facts. In summary, in sentencing for the conspiracies indicted, caution should be exercised against a slavish following of the guidelines on the basis of weights of drugs discovered at the conclusion of a surveillance operation.'

# Importation

**11.21**

For any offender playing a leading role in such an offence, the starting point for Class A drugs is one of 14 years' imprisonment for a Category 1 case. For a Category 2 case the starting point is one of 11 years and for a Category 3 case, eight years six months imprisonment.

**11.22**

The starting points are ten years, eight years and six years imprisonment respectively for an offender playing a significant role.

**11.23**

For an offender playing a lesser role, the starting points are eight years, six years and four years six months respectively.

---

10  At para 6.

## 11.24

But in *Attorney-General's References (Nos. 15, 16 and 17 of 2012)* [2013] 1 Cr App R 52, the Court of Appeal made clear that those starting points must not always be slavishly adhered to. Giving the judgment of the Court, Hallett LJ observed:[11]

'... first, the Definitive Guideline is not a statute requiring strict statutory construction; second, the Council's clear intention was certainly to maintain if not increase the level of sentences for drugs offences (save in the case of the so-called "drugs mules"— a very special category of offender); and third, as we have already indicated, the Guideline does not provide a series of boxes into which every offender and every offence must be squeezed with no exceptions permitted. A judge must obviously explain any departure from the ranges provided but departures are possible, as the Council makes plain in the words "where the operation is on the most serious and commercial scale involving a quantity of drugs significantly higher than Category 1 sentences of twenty years and above may be appropriate depending on the role of the offender."

18. The focus for sentencing in drugs offences remains the same: it is on culpability and harm and massive importations of drugs have the potential to cause immense harm. If therefore an offender plays a lesser role in an operation on a serious and commercial scale involving a quantity of drugs significantly higher than Category 1, a sentence significantly higher than the range indicated (six to nine years) must be appropriate.'

## 11.25

As the Guideline itself notes, 'where the operation is on the most serious and commercial scale, involving a quantity of drugs significantly higher than Category 1, sentences of 20 years and above may be appropriate, depending on the role of the offender'.[12]

## 11.26

Subsequently, in *R v Sanghera and Others* 2016 EWCA Crim 94, 2 Cr App R 15, the Court of Appeal noted that previous authorities suggested there was a ceiling of thirty years as a starting point.[13]

---

11 At paras 17–18.
12 *Drugs Offences Guideline*, p. 4.
13 At para 25. See also *R v Black* [2009] EWCA Crim 754; *R v Clough* [2009] EWCA Crim 1669, [2010] 1 Cr App R 53; and *R v Kahn* [2011] EWCA Crim 2049.

**11.27**

As highlighted in *AG's Refs. (Nos. 15, 16 and 17 of 2012)* above, 'drug mules' have received specific attention in the Guideline. The press release accompanying the issuing of the new Guideline explained that:

> 'Sentences for drug mules – who are usually vulnerable and exploited by organised criminals – will have a starting point of six years imprisonment ... A drug mule should not be confused with other types of offender sentenced for importation offences – if the court decides that he or she has a more significant role in importing drugs, then a longer prison sentence would be passed.'[14]

**11.28**

That was reiterated in *R v Boakye* [2013] 1 Cr App R 2, where the Court of Appeal made clear that there is a real distinction to be made between an ordinary courier and a drug mule. The Court observed:[15]

> '... the Guideline does not treat all couriers the same. On the contrary, it invites the Court to assess each case individually according, first, to the harm done by the offence (which is very broadly measured by the quantity and type of drug concerned), and, secondly, according to the culpability of the offender (which is very broadly measured by the role or function of the offender in the offence).
>
> [...]
>
> 35 The objective of distinguishing between different couriers has been accomplished by Step One of the new Guideline. A third-world offender exploited by others will be likely to be assessed by the judge as having a lesser role: see the expressions "performs a limited function under direction", "engaged by pressure, coercion, intimidation" and "involvement through naivety, exploitation".
>
> 36       By contrast, the courier who is worldly-wise, who knows what he (or she) is doing, and does it as a matter of free choice for the money, is likely to be assessed as having a significant role: see the expressions "motivated by financial or other advantage, whether or not operating alone" and sometimes "some awareness and understanding of the scale of operation".

---

14 Sentencing Council – *Courts Issued With New Guideline For Sentencing Drug Offenders*, 24 January 2012, available at www.sentencingcouncil.org.uk/news/item/courts-issued-with-new-guideline-for-sentencing-drug-offenders/.
15 At para 34.

37      These two classes of offender may both attract the generic label "courier", but that is not the test. There will be different ranges of sentencing for the two groups. Indeed, sometimes there are such offenders whose role is properly to be assessed as a leading one, for example, those who are an integral part of the importation business and have a substantial financial stake in the consignment.'

## 11.29

A similar approach was taken in *R v Jaramillo* [2013] 1 Cr App R 110. The Appellants, who were persons of good character prior to their arrest, were suffering severe financial problems and may not have known that the drugs they were carrying were in such large quantities. However, the Court of Appeal felt unable to go beyond classifying them as couriers to recognise them as mules particularly because:[16]

'these appellants were Spanish nationals who voluntarily journeyed to the Dominican Republic, knowing that when they did so they would become Class A drug couriers, for substantial sums of money. They therefore exposed themselves to the risk of intimidation on arrival.'

## 11.30

In *Boakye*, the Court of Appeal also made clear that the Guideline could not apply retrospectively in order to give rise to grounds for appeal against a sentence passed on a drug mule prior to 27 February 2012.[17]

## 11.31

Opium is not specifically covered in the Guideline. In *R v Talebi* [2013] 2 Cr App R 49, the Court of Appeal followed the approach taken in *R v Mashaollahi* [2001] 1 Cr App R 6 and proceeded on the basis that 40 kg of opium equates to about 5 kg of heroin.

## 11.32

It should be noted that a minimum custodial sentence of seven years applies for a third Class A drug trafficking offence.[18]

## 11.33

For those playing a leading role in the importation of Class B drugs, the starting point for an offence within Category 1 is eight years. For an offence within Category 2 the starting point is six years and an offence within Category 3 attracts a starting point of four years.

---

16 At para 27.
17 See paras 13–23.
18 s *110* of the *Powers of Criminal Courts (Sentencing) Act 2000 (PCCSA 2000)*. See further Ch 2 at 2.25.

**11.34**

For offenders playing a significant role, the starting points are five years six months (Category 1), four years (Category 2) and two years (Category 3).

**11.35**

For offenders playing a lesser role, the starting points are four years (Category 1), two years (Category 2) and one year (Category 3).

**11.36**

In *AG's Refs (Nos. 15, 16 and 17 of 2012),* the Court of Appeal increased the sentence imposed on a man who had pleaded guilty to the importation of 240 kg of methylethcathinone, 4 kg of cannabis resin and 971g of amphetamine sulphate from 42 months to six years. Giving the judgment of the Court, Hallett LJ said:[19]

> 'In our judgment, the quantity, unadulterated nature and value of the methylethylcathinone alone tell their own story. This was a highly professional, commercial operation in which very substantial quantities of Class B drugs were to be brought into the United Kingdom and eventually distributed on the streets. The offender was a trusted part of that chain of supply and played a very significant role. There is little mitigation other than his previous good character and his plea.'

**11.37**

For an offender playing a leading role in the importation of Class C drugs, the starting points are five years (Category 1), three years six months (Category 2) and 18 months (Category 3).

**11.38**

In respect of an offender playing a significant role, the corresponding starting points are three years, 18 months and 26 weeks respectively. For an offender playing a lesser role, the starting points are 18 months, 26 weeks and a high level community order respectively.

## Supplying or offering to supply a drug

### *Class A Drugs*

**11.39**

For those playing a leading role in the offence, the starting point for an offence within Category 1 is 14 years. For an offence within Category 2 the starting

---

19  At para 64.

point is 11 years and an offence within Category 3 attracts a starting point of eight years six months. For an offence within Category 4, the starting point is five years six months.

**11.40**

For offenders playing a significant role, the starting points are 10 years (Category 1), eight years (Category 2), four years six months (Category 3) and three years six months (Category 4).

**11.41**

For offenders playing a lesser role, the starting points are seven years (Category 1), five years (Category 2), three years (Category 3) or 18 months (Category 4).

**11.42**

In *Dyer*, Leveson LJ explained that, in contrast to other drugs offences, the harm caused by the offence was not to be assessed by reference to the quantity of drugs involved in the offence. Moreover, the fact that an offender was supplying in order to feed his own habit meant that they were motivated by a financial advantage. He explained:[20]

> 'In relation to selling directly to users ("street dealing"), harm is not categorized by quantity: the fact of street dealing is sufficient to put the offending into Category 3 irrespective of the quantity of the drugs involved. It will inevitably be the case that street dealing will be in quantities far smaller than those listed in the Guideline. Furthermore, the fact that supply is to a test purchase or undercover police officer is equally not a reason to reduce the category: the position is put beyond doubt in the lowest category (Category 4) which identifies indicative quantities of drugs of different class and goes on to provide an alternative in identical language: "where the offence is selling directly to users* ("street dealing") the starting point is not based on quantity—go to Category 3." The footnote to which the asterisk refers includes within the Guideline selling to test purchase officers.
>
> It is appropriate to say a few words about the asterisk and the explanation. The Council consulted widely on the issue of supply to undercover (or test purchase) officers: in reality, there is no question of a street dealer deliberately approaching an undercover officer (intending less harm) and the identity of the person with whom the defendant engages when supplying or offering to supply drugs is entirely a matter of chance. The respondents to the consultation agreed and in the Council's published response, the conclusion was reached:

---

20  At para 4.

The Council agrees that 'supply to an undercover officer' should not be a factor for consideration at either step 1 or step 2 and it will not be included in the definitive Guideline.

As to the culpability of the offender as demonstrated by his or her role, it is important to emphasise that the descriptions cover a wide range of activities and circumstances in which the offence of supplying a controlled drug might be committed. For that reason one or more of the characteristics may demonstrate the role and the lists are not exhaustive. Among the descriptors for a significant role is included "motivated by financial or other advantage, whether or not operating alone". Lesser role, on the other hand, includes "involvement through naivety/exploitation", "if own operation, absence of any financial gain, for example joint purchase for no profit, or sharing minimal quantities between peers on a non-commercial basis." Street dealers funding their own habit, or, perhaps, an extremely meagre living for food and the like are motivated by financial or other advantage and are not the same as those who, for example, are funded by friends to purchase for the group without any question of financial or other reward.

## 11.43

The supply of drugs to prisoners is a serious aggravating factor. In respect of the supply of Class A drugs, that was made clear in a number of pre-Guideline authorities including *R v Happe* [2011] 1 Cr App R 14 and *AG's Ref (No. 34 of 2011)* [2012] 1 Cr App R (S) 288.

## 11.44

In *R v Sanchez-Canadas* [2013] 1 Cr App R 114, a sentence of 45 months was upheld in respect of a man who had attempted to supply heroin and cannabis to a serving prisoner by sending the drugs concealed in training shoes. A starting point of five years after trial could not be criticised.

## 11.45

Hughes LJ, observed:[21]

'… supply of drugs into prison is in itself inherently more serious than the supply of drugs generally is. That is because drugs in prison are a currency, an instrument of power, extortion and oppression and they fundamentally undermine the discipline and good order which is essential to running a prison properly

[…]

---

21  At paras 10–11.

It is correct that among the examples of a significant role there appears this short case, "supply other than by a person in a position of responsibility to a prisoner for gain without coercion". That was clearly intended to identify the well-known fact of the special evil of supply of drugs into prison.'

## 11.46

Subsequent authority has emphasised that the supply of drugs within or into prison by a non-prison employee is to be regarded as a highly aggravating feature, placing the level of sentence at the top end of the appropriate range in the guidelines.[22]

## *Class B or Class C drugs*

### 11.47

For a leading role in the supply of Class B drugs, the starting points are eight years (Category 1), six years (Category 2), four years (Category 3) and 18 months (Category 4).

### 11.48

For a significant role in the supply of Class B drugs, the starting points are five years six months imprisonment (Category 1), four years (Category 2), one year (Category 3) and a high level community order (Category 4).

### 11.49

For a lesser role, the starting points are three years, one year, a high level community order and a low level community order respectively. For an offender playing a leading role, the starting points are five years (Category 1), three years six months (Category 2), 18 months (Category 3) and 26 weeks (Category 4).

### 11.50

In respect of an offender playing a significant role, the corresponding starting points are three years, 18 months and 26 weeks and a high level community order respectively. For an offender playing a lesser role, the starting points are 18 months, 26 weeks a high level community order and a low level community order respectively.

---

22 See, eg, *R v Adcock* [2016] EWCA Crim 1272; *R v Melim* [2014] EWCA Crim 1915; and *R v Bayliss* [2013] EWCA Crim 1067.

## Prevalence of Supply

### 11.51

Judges may not take into account the social harm of supply by increasing a sentence simply because there is a 'perceived' increased prevalence in the area served by the Court.

### 11.52

In *R v Bondzie* [2016] EWCA Crim 552, the Court of Appeal considered the role that prevalence of drugs supply should have in any sentencing exercise. The appellant has been sentenced to nearly five years for supply and possession of Class A drugs offences. It had been common ground he was a Level 3 street dealer and had pleaded guilty at a relatively early stage.

### 11.53

The sentencing judge's remarks noted that the supply of drugs was 'such a desperately serious problem in the East Kent and Thanet area in particular'.

### 11.54

The Court of Appeal adopted a clear approach in dealing with the issue of prevalence. First, it made clear that social harm had already been taken into account in the sentencing levels set by the Guidelines. Consequently, the social harm caused by supplying drugs should not be considered an aggravating factor.

### 11.55

Secondly, it was 'not open to the judge to increase sentence for prevalence in ordinary circumstances or in response to his own personal view that there is "too much of this sort of thing going on in this area"'.[23]

### 11.56

Instead, the following approach should be adopted when considering prevalence:[24]

'Firstly, there must be evidence provided to the court by a responsible body or by a senior police officer. Secondly, that evidence must be before the court in the specific case being considered with the relevant statements or reports having been made available to the Crown and defence in good time so that meaningful representations about that material can be made. Even if such material is provided, a judge will only be entitled to treat prevalence as an aggravating factor if (a) he

---

23 At para 10.
24 At para 11.

is satisfied that the level of harm caused in a particular locality is significantly higher than that caused elsewhere (and thus already inherent in the guideline levels); (b) that the circumstances can properly be described as exceptional and (c) that it is just and proportionate to increase sentence for such a factor in the particular case before him. It is clear therefore, that a court should be hesitant before aggravating a sentence by reason of prevalence. Judges will be only too well aware of the types of harm which are caused by drug dealing and will not be assisted by statements of the obvious. Only if the evidence placed before the court demonstrates a level of harm which clearly exceeds the well understood consequences of drug dealing by a significant margin should courts be prepared to reflect this in sentence. If judges do so, they must clearly state when sentencing that they are doing so.'[25]

## *Cuckoo-ing*

### 11.57

"Cuckooing" is a recent term for drug dealers from large cities who move into smaller provincial areas to sell drugs. This is achieved by setting up in local premises and taking control of local drug networks and users.

### 11.58

In 2016, the National Crime Agency described the practice as follows:[26]

'Urban Street Gangs (USGs) continue to play an important role in the distribution of Class A drugs (heroin and crack cocaine) into county and coastal towns outside the major big cities where they normally operate. In these scenarios, groups from large cities are taking control of local markets outside the city, supplying high-frequency deliveries of mid-market quantities. This form of criminality almost always involves the exploitation of children and vulnerable adults coerced to assist with accommodation and supply.'

### 11.59

The question of how to address sentencing for cuckooing-type supply offences was discussed by the Court of Appeal in *R v Ajayi and Others* [2017] EWCA Crim

---

25 This approach to prevalence in supply case sentencing has been adopted by the Court of Appeal in a number of cases. See, eg, *R v Khalid* [2017] EWCA Crim 592; *R v Johncock* [2016] EWCA Crim 2218; and *R v Duncanson* [2016] EWCA Crim 1537.

26 National Crime Agency – *National Strategic Assessment of Serious and Organised Crime 2016*, 9 September 2016, available at www.nationalcrimeagency.gov.uk/publications/731-national-strategic-assessment-of-serious-and-organised-crime-2016/file, at para 128.

1011. The Court observed that the phenomenon had developed after the Guidelines had been published and, as such was not dealt with explicitly.

## 11.60

The Court of Appeal suggested the following approach to applying the Guidelines to cuckooing cases:

'The practice of cuckooing is commonly achieved by exploiting local drug users, either by paying them in drugs, or by building up drug debt, or by the use of threats and/or violence to coerce. The exploitation and use of young people as couriers of drugs or money, or as minders of drugs and money, as well as salespeople, is not uncommon … [a person organising such an operation] would appear clearly to fall within a leading role in the drug supply guideline … Judges will need to consider carefully the evidence placed before them, considering such factors consistent with a leading role as expectation of substantial financial gain, substantial links to, and influence on, others in the chain, and directing or organising buying and selling on a commercial scale.

Those who do not fall within a leading role, but who are involved in the process of cuckooing will ordinarily fall into a significant role. Where there is evidence of involvement of others in the operation by pressure, influence, intimidation or reward, that should be given particular weight in the assessment of culpability and in determining whether a move upward from the starting point is appropriate. This particular type of offending carries with it the hallmarks of professional crime above and beyond that in ordinary street dealing, so that judges should pay particularly close attention to the assessment of role and the offender's place within a category range. Equally, those who work within such an operation and who seek to have a lesser role ascribed to them, should expect to have those claims (based, for example, on coercion or lack of awareness of the scale of the operation) examined with care.'

## 11.61

The Court noted that such an approach was not to downgrade local street dealing, which it observed, 'remained a pernicious crime, seriously damaging individuals and society, and should continue to be recognised as such'.

## 11.62

However, the Court noted that the additional sophistication of cuckooing 'reflected a further degree of criminality, which judges should be astute to recognise, and to reflect in a particularly careful examination of the three roles by which culpability in drug supply offending is assessed'.

**11.63**

Finally, the Court reiterated the importance of the Guidelines. If the offence established a cuckooing operation, then that should be reflected either in role or as an aggravating feature at Step 2 of the Guideline. Care should be taken to avoid double counting and ensure the sentence remained just and proportionate.

# Production and/or cultivation

**11.64**

For the purposes of the Guidelines, the tariffs for production of drugs and cultivation of cannabis are set out together.

**11.65**

For a leading role in the production of Class A drugs, the starting points are 14 years imprisonment (Category 1), 11 years (Category 2), eight years six months (Category 3) and five years six months (Category 4).

**11.66**

For a significant role in the production of Class A drugs, the starting points are 10 years (Category 1), eight years (Category 2), four years six months (Category 3) and three years six months (Category 4). For a lesser role, the starting points are seven years, five years, three years and 18 months respectively.

**11.67**

As with importation, the most serious and commercial production of drugs that is significantly higher than the amounts set out in Category 1, sentences of 20 years and above may be appropriate, depending on the role of the offender.[27]

**11.68**

For a leading role in the production of Class B drugs, the starting points are eight years (Category 1), six years (Category 2), four years (Category 3) and one year (Category 4).

**11.69**

For a significant role in the production of Class B drugs, the starting points are five years six months imprisonment (Category 1), four years (Category 2), one year (Category 3) and a high level community order (Category 4). For a lesser role, the starting points are three years, one year, a high level community order and a low level community order respectively.

---

27 Guidelines, p. 18.

**11.70**

For Class C drugs, For an offender playing a leading role, the starting points are five years (Category 1), three years six months (Category 2), 18 months (Category 3) and 26 weeks (Category 4).

**11.71**

In respect of an offender playing a significant role, the corresponding starting points are three years, 18 months and 26 weeks and a high level community order respectively.

**11.72**

For an offender playing a lesser role, the starting points are 18 months, 26 weeks a high level community order and a Band C fine respectively.

**11.73**

In *R v Bamford* [2013] 1 Cr App R 4, the appellant had been sentenced to six months' custody for production of herbal cannabis. The sentencing judge identified as aggravating features the fact that the electricity had been bypassed and that the operation was a continuing one.

**11.74**

The continuing nature of the operation was demonstrated by the presence of specialist equipment and whilst the judge accepted that this was the first crop, he concluded that there was a plan to produce more. A further aggravating feature was that the appellant had a six-year-old son who visited him at his home. In terms of mitigating factors, the judge identified the absence of previous convictions as a mitigating factor and accepted that the appellant had shown genuine remorse and had a positive good character.

**11.75**

The pre-sentence report identified a low risk of re-offending and suggested a community sentence. The judge's overall conclusion was that this was a Category 3 'significant role' case, with a category range of 26 weeks to three years' custody and a starting point of one year. Full discount for a guilty plea was reflected in the six months sentence.

**11.76**

Allowing the appeal against sentence, Burnett J said:[28]

---

28 At para 22.

'We respectfully disagree with the judge that the aggravating features of this case, serious though they are, moved it into the next level of culpability. However, we consider that the custody threshold was passed. A professional set up, albeit to provide cannabis for personal use, with the capacity for crop after crop, is likely to result in the custody threshold being passed in cases such as this. Nonetheless, the very significant adverse consequences of an immediate custodial sentence would, in our judgment, have justified a suspended sentence in this case.'

## 11.77

The Court of Appeal upheld a sentence of 40 months imprisonment in a case following a plea of guilty where the sentencing judge had concluded that the appellant had conducted a commercial operation in cultivating 60 cannabis plants in an outbuilding.

## 11.78

In *R v Descombre* [2013] 2 Cr App R 51, the appellant had played a leading role in that commercial operation. The sentencing judge concluded that the starting point from the Guideline was six years' imprisonment with a sentencing range of four-and-a-half years to eight years.

## 11.79

The aggravating features of the offence were that the electricity supply had been bypassed and it was an ongoing operation producing high profits. The mitigating features included that the appellant was of previous positive good character, he had been under financial pressure because the family engineering business had collapsed and there was genuine remorse for his own behaviour and for involving his partner.

## 11.80

In addition, there was a previous and continuing background of mental health problems and the appellant had been open and frank with the police at the outset. His early guilty plea justified full credit.

## 11.81

The Court of Appeal dismissed the appeal. It concluded that:[29]

'... the cultivation was commercial in the ordinary sense. It fell into the uppermost category of culpability. By identifying the role as leading role the judge was identifying [the Appellant's] role as falling into the

---

29 At para 21.

uppermost category of culpability. The judge balanced the aggravating and mitigating features. By reducing the starting point of six years to five prior to reduction for the guilty plea, it is clear that he did have significant regard to the mitigation in the case.'

## 11.82

Giving the judgment of the Court of Appeal in *Healey*, Hughes LJ (as he then was) explained the underlying rationale of the Guideline in saying:[30]

'The defendant who has half a dozen plants or so in a grow-bag alongside his tomatoes outside the back window is no doubt contemplated as engaged in what the Guidelines would call a domestic operation (see category 4 of the harm). Assuming he is growing only for his own use, he would clearly have what they envisage as the lowest level of culpability within the range of offences of this kind. However, those who create a purpose-built room in the loft or the cellar or the garage, or who dedicate a bedroom to the exclusive purpose of cultivating cannabis, having invested substantially in professional equipment for watering, for lighting and/or for electronically controlled timing of those operations and others, cannot sensibly be described as having a lesser role.

Nor can they sensibly be bracketed with people who perform a limited function under direction, who were engaged through coercion or intimidation or who were involved through naivety or exploitation. People with the kind of determined approach to cultivation which we have described and who are prepared to make the investment, do so because they are contemplating repeated cropping under professional or semi-professional conditions with dedicated apparatus which has been bought for the purpose, usually at a cost of some hundreds of pounds. Those people can perfectly properly be described, and in our view should be described, as having the kind of level of culpability which is the next level up from those who are at the lowest level, i.e. that labelled "significant role."

Also in significant role will be those who like the defendants we have just described have the apparatus and the dedicated space for cultivation but in whose case there is a real likelihood of additional wider circulation, in other words supply, whether for money or not. That latter group is clearly higher up in the sliding scale and higher up in the significant category than those who do not. There is an essential and important distinction between cases where there is likely to be circulation or supply and cases where there is not.'

---

30 At para 17.

# Permitting premises to be used for consumption of a drug

### 11.83

For Category 1 offences (where there is higher culpability and greater harm) the starting point is two years six imprisonment. For Category 2 offences (where there is either higher culpability and lesser harm or lesser culpability and greater harm) the starting point is 36 weeks. For Category 3 offences (where there is lesser culpability and lesser harm) the starting point is a medium level community order.

### 11.84

The Guideline provides that the starting point is 12 months custody for a Category 1 offence within a range of sentences from 26 weeks to 18 months. For a Category 2 offence, the starting point is a high level community order and the range is from a low level community order to 26 weeks. For a Category 3 offence, the starting point is a Band C fine in a range from a Band A fine to a low level community order.

### 11.85

The Guideline provides that the starting point is one to 12 weeks custody for a Category 1 offence within a range of sentences from a high level community order to 26 weeks. (It should be noted that the maximum sentence when the offence is tried summarily is 12 weeks imprisonment).

### 11.86

For a Category 2 offence, the starting point is a low level community order and the range is from a Band C fine to a high level community order. For a Category 2 offence, the starting point is a Band A fine in a range from a discharge to a Band C fine.

# Possession of a controlled drug

### 11.87

The starting point for possession of a Class A drug is a Band C fine and the range of sentence is from a Band A fine to 51 weeks custody. It is an aggravating factor for the offender to be a serving prisoner.

### 11.88

For Class B, The Guideline provides that the starting point is a Band B fine in a range from a discharge to 26 weeks custody.

**11.89**

In respect of an offence of possession of a Class C drug, the Guideline provides that the starting point is a Band A fine within a range of sentences from a discharge to a medium level community order.

## Sentences for servicemen and women

**11.90**

Like other offences, sentencing in the Court Martial for drugs offences is distinct from that in civilian courts. Guidance on sentencing is issued by the Judge Advocate General.[31]

**11.91**

The Guidance states its underlying approach to drugs offences is set out in Joint Service Publication 835[32] as follows:[33]

'... the misuse of drugs is incompatible with the demands of Service life and poses a significant threat to operational effectiveness. The implications of drug misuse are particularly damaging and the illegal possession and use of controlled drugs is an offence under both Service and civil law ... It is Service Personnel Board policy that there is no place in the Armed Forces for those who misuse drugs. Only in exceptional circumstances will any member of the Armed Forces be retained following drug misuse ... They must expect to be punished more severely for breaching those high standards.'

**11.92**

The Guidance notes that dismissal on conviction or administrative discharge is inevitable where the offence concerns Class A drugs.

**11.93**

For simple possession, the sentence entry point before mitigating and aggravating factors are considered is dismissal and 90 to 180 days detention.

**11.94**

For all other drug related offences, including supplying drugs, the sentence is dismissal and imprisonment. There is a Service Community Order as

---

31  See *Guidance On Sentencing in the Court Martial,* Version 4, October 2013, available at www.judiciary.gov. uk/wp-content/uploads/2015/05/guidance-sentencing-court-martial.pdf.

32  Ministry of Defence – *JSP 835: Alcohol and Substance Misuse and Testing Version 2.0,* 1 November 2013, available at www.gov.uk/government/uploads/system/uploads/attachment_data/file/425401/20131101-JSP_835-V2_0-U.pdf.

33  para 5.7.1.

an alternative to imprisonment, 'where the offender needs treatment for addiction'.[34]

## Psychoactive Substances Act 2016

### 11.95

The *Psychoactive Substances Act 2016 (PSA 2016)* came into force on 26 May 2016.[35] It creates a number of offences, set out as 'prohibited activities' in *s 12* and detailed further in *ss 4–8*. These are as follows:

(a) producing a psychoactive substance that is likely to be consumed by individuals for its psychoactive effects;

(b) supplying such a substance;

(c) offering to supply such a substance;

(d) importing such a substance;

(e) exporting such a substance; and

(f) assisting or encouraging the carrying on of a prohibited activity listed in any of paragraphs (a) to (e).

### 11.96

These offences are all triable either way. They carry a maximum sentence of seven years on indictment; and six months and/or an unlimited fine summarily. They are lifestyle offences for the purposes of the Proceeds of Crime Act 2002.[36]

### 11.97

The offence of supply or offering to supply a psychoactive substance under *s 5* of the *PSA 2016* is aggravated for sentencing purposes by any of three conditions set out in *s 6*. These are:

Condition A – offence committed on, or in the vicinity of a school; or

Condition B – the offender used a courier who was under 18; or

Condition C – the offence was committed in a custodial institution

### 11.98

*Section 9* of the *PSA 2016* creates a separate offence of possessing a psychoactive substance in a 'custodial institution' for consumption for its psychoactive effect.

---

34 para 5.7.5.
35 For further details see Chs 2 to 5.
36 Para 2 (2) of Sch 5 to the *PSA 2016*.

The offence carries a maximum of two years imprisonment on indictment, or six months or a fine on summary conviction or both.

## Ancillary orders

### *Confiscation*

**11.99**

This is dealt with in **Chapter 12**.

### *Forfeiture*

**11.100**

Under *s 143(1)* of the *PCCSA 2000*, courts have the power of the courts to order the forfeiture of property connected to the commission on an offence.

**11.101**

However, there are specific provisions relating to drugs offences set out in the *MDA 1971*. *Section 27* states that

'(1)  Subject to subsection (2) below, the court by or before which a person is convicted of an offence under this Act or an offence falling within subsection (3) below or an offence to which section 1 of the Proceeds of Crime (Scotland) Act 1995 relates or a drug trafficking offence, as defined in Article 2(2) of the Criminal Justice (Confiscation) (Northern Ireland) Order 1990 may order anything shown to the satisfaction of the court to relate to the offence, to be forfeited and either destroyed or dealt with in such other manner as the court may order.

(2)  The court shall not order anything to be forfeited under this section, where a person claiming to be the owner of or otherwise interested in it applies to be heard by the court, unless an opportunity has been given to him to show cause why the order should not be made.'

**11.102**

The offences listed in subs (3) are drug trafficking offences, or inchoate offences of attempt, conspiracy or incitement to commit drugs offences.

**11.103**

*Section 27* refers to the forfeiture of 'anything' related to the offence. This may include money (*R v Beard* [1974] 1 WLR 1549). However, as Lord Diplock noted in *R v Cuthbertson* [1981] AC 470, there are two limits to the ambit of forfeiture of property in drugs cases.

## 11.104

The first is that property must be tangible. The purpose of *s 27*, he said was:[37]

> '... to enable things to be forfeited so that they may be destroyed or dealt with in some other manner as the court thinks fit. The words are apt and, as it seems to me, are only apt to deal with things that are tangible, things of which physical possession can be taken by a person authorised to do so by the court and which are capable of being physically destroyed by that person or disposed of by him in some other way.'

## 11.105

Secondly, it is well established that 'an English court has no jurisdiction either in a criminal or a civil matter to make orders purporting ipso jure to transfer moveable property situate abroad'.[38]

## 11.106

The property must be shown to be connected with the offence of which the offender is convicted. *Section 27* cannot be used to seek forfeiture of intended to be used to facilitate the commission of other offences.

## 11.107

In *R v Llewellyn* (1985) 7 Cr App R 225, the appellant pleaded guilty to possession with intent to supply cannabis and two other counts of possession. £400 discovered in the handbag of the appellant's wife was ordered to forfeited under *s 27*.

## 11.108

The Court of Appeal quashed the order. It found that it was impossible to see how the £400 related to the cannabis which he had in his possession with intent to supply.[39]

## 11.109

Further, forfeiture does not apply to real property. In *R v Kahn* (1983) 76 Cr App R 29, the Court of Appeal set aside an order for forfeiture of the appellant's house following his conviction for supplying heroin.

---

37 At p. 483 B-E.
38 At p. 485 D.
39 See also *Haggard v Mason* [1976] 1 WLR 187; *R v Morgan* [1977] Crim LR 488⊠ *R v Ribeyre* (1982) 4 Cr App R 165; *R v Boothe* (1987) 9 Cr App R 8; and *R v Simms* (1987) 9 Cr App R (S) 8; and *R v Askew* [1987] Crim LR 584.

**11.110**

Similarly, in *R v Pearce* [1996] Crim LR 442, a forfeiture order on the appellant's house was quashed by the Court of Appeal. The appellant had been convicted of cultivating cannabis, having converted the upstairs of his house and installing an irrigation system. Following *Cuthbertson* and *Khan*, the Court reiterated that 'anything' under *s 27* did not include a house.

**11.111**

However, it suggested one potential solution to forfeiture of real property in such cases. The Court could impose a fine, which would be equal to or less than the value of the property in question.

## Summary of key points

**11.112**

- Drugs sentences are now governed by the *Drugs Offences: Definitive Guideline*, published in February 2012. The Guideline substitutes for and supersedes previous sentencing authorities.

- The Guidelines apply to conspiracies to commit drug offences, despite there being no explicit reference in the Guidelines.

- As with other definitive guidelines, Judges are permitted to move outside them provided there is good reason for doing so.

- For importation offences, the Court of Appeal have interpreted the Guidelines as differentiating between drug couriers and drug 'mules' in length of sentence. An individual who is exploited is more likely to be assessed as undertaking a lesser role, than a worldly wise courier, who would be considered as having a significant role.

- Social harm is not an additional factor to consider in drugs offence sentencing. It has been accounted for in the Guidelines. Where prevalence of drug supply in an area is being considered as an aggravating factor, the guidance set out in *Bondzie* should be adopted.

- The recent development of 'cuckoo-ing' requires particular attention by sentencing judges. Defendants may well fall into a leading role in the Guidelines where there is evidence of exploitation of local drug users and/or young people as couriers. Those found to be involved in the practice of cuckoo-ing who are not considered to have a leading role will ordinarily fall into a significant role.

- Sentencing in the Court Martial for drugs offences is set out in Guidance issued by the Judge Advocate General. Where the offence concerns Class A drugs, dismissal on conviction or administrative discharge is inevitable

- For simple possession, the sentence entry point before mitigating and aggravating factors are considered is dismissal and 90 to 180 days detention.

- The Psychoactive Substances Act 2016 post-dates the Guidelines. All offences carry a maximum sentence of seven years on indictment; and six months and/or an unlimited fine summarily.

- The offence of supply or offering to supply a psychoactive substance is aggravated if the offence is committed on or near a school, uses a courier under the age of 18 or was committed in prison.

- The Act creates a separate offence of possessing a psychoactive substance in a 'custodial institution' for consumption for its psychoactive effect. The offence carries a maximum of two years imprisonment on indictment, or six months or a fine on summary conviction or both.

- Forfeiture relating to drugs offences is dealt with by *s 27* of the *MDA 1971*. Forfeiture applies only to tangible property. It does not apply to real property. Nor can a forfeiture order be made relating to property outside the jurisdiction of England and Wales. *Section 27* cannot be used to seek forfeiture of property intended to be used to facilitate the commission of other offences.

# 12 Restraint and Confiscation

Steven Bird

## Introduction

### 12.1

Confiscation proceedings in drugs cases were introduced by the *Drug Trafficking Offences Act 1986 (DTOA 1986)*. This was amended subsequently by the *Drug Trafficking Act 1994 (DTA 1994)*. The confiscation provisions of the *DTA 1994* were replaced for offences taking place on or after 24 March 2003 by the *Proceeds of Crime Act 2002 (POCA 2002)*.

### 12.2

It is unlikely that any practitioner will have to deal with any confiscation proceedings now which relate as far back as the *DTOA 1986*. However, if any count on the indictment is to be included in confiscation proceedings and the date on that count pre-dates 24 March 2003, the confiscation proceedings should be held under the *DTA 1994* and not *POCA 2002* in relation to that count.

### 12.3

If the offence charged is a conspiracy, the important date is the start date of the conspiracy as stated on the indictment. If that date is before 24 March 2003, confiscation proceedings have to be held under the *DTA 1994* and not *POCA 2002*.

### 12.4

This principle was most recently articulated by the Court of Appeal in *R v Boughton-Fox* [2014] EWCA Crim 227 (a fraud case). In that case, the pre-POCA confiscation regime applied although no criminal conduct was relied upon in evidence before 24 March 2003 because the indictment start date had been extended back to 1 March 2003.

### 12.5

Given that the vast majority of cases after the publication of this book will not date back as far as March 2003, this chapter will only consider the procedure under *POCA 2002*.

# Restraint orders

## 12.6

The provisions of *POCA 2002* can take effect even before a suspect is charged with an offence and will affect the ability of the individual to live their normal life during the pre-charge period and during the trial. The prosecuting authorities may apply to the Crown Court for a Restraint Order to prohibit an individual from dealing with any realisable property that they hold.[1]

## 12.7

A Restraint Order may only be granted if any of the prescribed conditions apply.[2] Most commonly, a Restraint Order is applied for either before charge or after charge but before conviction.

## 12.8

A Restraint Order may be granted before charge where a criminal investigation has been started in England and Wales with regard to an offence and there are reasonable grounds to suspect that the alleged offender has benefited from his criminal conduct.[3]

## 12.9

Post charge, an Order can be made where proceedings for an offence have been started in England and Wales and not concluded and there is reasonable cause to believe that the defendant has benefited from his criminal conduct.[4]

## 12.10

There is a caveat to the post charge condition. It will not be satisfied if the court believes there has been undue delay in continuing the proceedings or that the prosecutor does not intend to proceed.[5]

## 12.11

A Restraint Order can also be imposed post conviction in a number of circumstances. Firstly, where an application has been made by the prosecutor but not concluded for reconsideration of the case or the benefit figure where no confiscation order was originally made or in certain situations where the defendant has absconded.[6]

---

1   *POCA 2002, s 41.*
2   ibid, *s 40.*
3   ibid, *s 40(2).*
4   ibid, *s 40(3).*
5   ibid, *s 40(7).*
6   ibid, *s 40(4).*

## 12.12

An Order can be made where the court believes that such an application is to be made. In both instances there has to be reasonable cause to believe that the defendant has benefited from his criminal conduct. In the case of an absconding defendant, a Restraint Order can be imposed if the prosecution is seeking a confiscation order even where there has been no conviction.

## 12.13

Secondly, where an application has been made by the prosecutor and not concluded or the court believes that an application is to be made to reconsider the benefit of the defendant after a confiscation order has been imposed. There must be reasonable cause to believe that the court will decide that the amount found under the new calculation of the defendant's benefit exceeds the previous benefit figure[7].

## 12.14

Finally, where an application has been made by the prosecutor and not concluded or the court believes that an application is to be made to reconsider the available amount after a confiscation order has been imposed. There has to be reasonable cause to believe that the court will decide that the amount found under the new calculation of the available amount exceeds the previous figure[8].

## 12.15

These post-conviction applications are subject to the court believing that there has been no undue delay in continuing the application or that the prosecutor intends to proceed.[9]

## 12.16

When a Restraint Order is received, it should be considered carefully. The format of Restraint Orders is generally very similar but each will be tailored to the individual case. In some instances the Restraint Order will apply solely to the specific property referred to in it.

## 12.17

However, in the majority of cases the Order will apply to all realisable property held by the individual whether or not it is specifically described in the Order as well as to realisable property transferred to the individual after the Order has been made.[10]

---

7  ibid, *s 40(5)*.
8  ibid, *s 40(6)*.
9  ibid, *s 40(8)*.
10  ibid, *s 41(2)*.

**12.18**

The terms of the Restraint Order will usually allow the individual to withdraw reasonable living expenses and to enable them to carry on their trade or profession.[11].

**12.19**

For instance, if the individual is on bail, the Restraint Order ought to allow for reasonable living expenses (usually in the region of £250 per week) and for payment from restrained accounts for such items as household bills, mortgage repayments, insurance premiums and school fees. Any allowance specified in the Order can be varied either by agreement with the prosecution or by application to the Crown Court.

**12.20**

The Act does not allow for funds to be released for legal expenses incurred by the defendant or a recipient of a tainted gift which relate to the offences in respect of which the Restraint Order is made.[12]

**12.21**

However, funds can be released from restraint in order to satisfy any legal aid contribution imposed by the Legal Aid Agency in relation to the offence.[13]

**12.22**

Before an individual is charged with an offence, public funds for legal advice are severely restricted. The person restrained but not yet charged may find that they do not qualify for publicly funded legal advice about the matter under investigation except when questioned at the police station (where the non-means tested Police Station Advice and Assistance scheme is available from any firm of solicitors holding a Standard Crime Contract with the Legal Aid Agency).

**12.23**

However, public funding for advice prior to a police station attendance or during any period on police bail or having been released under investigation is only available under the Legal Advice and Assistance Scheme which is very strictly means tested.

**12.24**

Any person receiving £250 per week under the Restraint Order is most unlikely to qualify under the means test for advice under the scheme. They

---

11  ibid, *s 41(3)*.
12  ibid, *s 41(5)*.
13  ibid, *s 41(2A) & (2B)*.

will also be unable to pay for the advice from their own funds, given the prohibition on the release of funds for legal advice about the subject matter of the offence.

### 12.25

If an application is to be made to vary a Restraint Order, civil legal help or civil legal aid may be available if the individual is financially eligible. Such work is associated civil work for any firm of solicitors holding a Standard Crime Contract and therefore can be undertaken notwithstanding that the firm may not hold a contract for civil work.

### 12.26

The restriction on using restrained funds to fund legal expenses extends to advice about the Restraint Order as legal expenses for proceedings in connection with a Restraint Order are 'related to' the underlying offence.[14]

### 12.27

The fact that this restriction may produce harsh results in some cases does not mean that it is incompatible with the defendant's right to peaceful enjoyment of his possessions under Art 1 of the First Protocol to the ECHR.[15]

### 12.28

In making a pre-charge Restraint Order, the Crown Court judge must be satisfied that there is a real risk that but for the order the assets are liable to be dissipated. If the individual has had ample opportunity to dissipate assets prior to the application for the Restraint Order such a risk may not be demonstrated.

### 12.29

The imposition of a Restraint Order can have serious personal and professional consequences for the individual concerned and it is therefore very important for the court to be satisfied that there are good reasons and a proper basis for making such an order especially pre-charge.[16]

### 12.30

Often the only way to access legal advice once a Restraint Order has been imposed and before charges have been brought is to have an untainted and genuine third party pay the legal fees.

---

14  *Re S. (Restraint Order)* [2005] 1 W.L.R. 1338, CA.
15  *R. v A.P.; R. v U. Ltd* [2008] 1 Cr. App.R. 39, CA.
16  *R v B [2008]* EWCA Crim 1374.

**12.31**

Once charged, criminal legal aid becomes available to defend the proceedings. The grant of legal aid for the criminal proceedings may be subject to a contribution from income which can be paid from restrained funds.

**12.32**

However, in reality this is unlikely. Most Restraint Orders will not allow the release of sufficient funds for the defendant to pass the threshold at which a contribution from income applies.

**12.33**

If convicted, a defendant may be subject to a contribution from capital up to the full value of the legal aid costs if they have capital above £30,000. Such contribution will not take precedence over confiscation of assets and an assessment will be postponed until the conclusion of the confiscation proceedings.

# Confiscation proceedings

## *Instigation of confiscation proceedings*

**12.34**

After conviction the Crown Court must embark on confiscation proceedings if the defendant–

(a)    has been convicted of an offence or offences in proceedings before the Crown Court; or

(b)    is committed by the magistrates' court to the Crown Court for sentence in the normal way; or

(c)    is committed by the magistrates' court to the Crown Court with a view to a confiscation order being made in a case where committal for sentence would not be appropriate but for the need to consider confiscation; and

(d)    the prosecutor asks the court to proceed under *s 6 of POCA 2002* or the court believes that it is appropriate to do so.[17]

**12.35**

Unless there has been any abuse of the court's process in the making of an application for confiscation, the court has no discretion but to proceed if the above criteria are met.

---

17  *POCA 2002, s 6(2) & (3).*

## 12.36

There may be situations where it may be inappropriate (or arguably an abuse of process) for the prosecution to request the initiation of confiscation proceedings.

## 12.37

For instance, where the prosecution has previously agreed with the defendant not to proceed to confiscation and then seeks to renege on that agreement. Other instances where the court has found the instigation of confiscation proceedings to be inappropriate are unlikely to feature in drugs cases but can briefly be summed up as cases where there has been full restitution to the victim of the offence[18] or where legitimately obtained property has to be treated as benefit.[19]

## 12.38

Although it is possible to make a Confiscation Order before sentence, it is usual for the confiscation proceedings to take place after sentence has been passed.

## 12.39

The making of the Confiscation Order can be postponed but should take place within two years of the date of the conviction[20] unless there are exceptional circumstances[21] or any appeal against conviction takes the case beyond the two-year period. The Confiscation Order must be made within three months of the conclusion of the appeal proceedings.[22]

## 12.40

Any application to extend the time period for the determination of confiscation proceedings must be made before that period expires, although the application can be heard afterwards.[23]

## 12.41

Once confiscation proceedings are commenced, the court must make the following determinations:

(a)    It must first decide whether the defendant has a criminal lifestyle;

(b)    If so, the court must decide whether he has benefited from his general criminal conduct;

---

18  *R v Morgan* [2009] 1 Cr App R (S) 60.
19  *R v Shabir* [2008] EWCA 1809.
20  *POCA 2002*, s 14(5).
21  ibid, *s 14(4)*.
22  ibid, *s 14(6)*.
23  ibid, *s 14(8)*.

(c)    If he has no criminal lifestyle, the court has to decide whether he has benefited from his particular criminal conduct;[24]

(d)    If the court decides that there is benefit to the defendant from such conduct, it must decide the '*recoverable amount*';

(e)    The court must make a confiscation order in the recoverable amount unless it would be disproportionate to require the defendant to pay that amount;[25] and

(f)    If the defendant shows that the '*available amount*' is less than the benefit figure, the Confiscation Order is made in the sum of the available amount or a nominal figure if the available amount is zero.[26]

## Procedure

### 12.42

The court will set a timetable for the confiscation proceedings after conviction starting with an order that the defendant provide information as to their assets.[27] If there has been a pre-charge Restraint Order which required a disclosure of assets by the suspect, the provision of such information may not be required, although often the court makes the order in any event.

### 12.43

Following receipt of this document, the prosecution will produce a statement of information[28] to which the defendant will be required to provide a response.[29]

## Provision of information by defendant: section 18

### 12.44

Where the court is proceeding or considering whether to proceed with confiscation proceedings, it may at any time order the defendant to provide specific information about their financial situation within a specified time frame set by the court.[30]

---

24  ibid, s 6(4).
25  *POCA 2002, s 6(5)(b)* as amended by the *Serious Crime Act 2015. c. 9, Sch. 4, para. 19* to give effect to the ruling of the Supreme Court in *R v Waya* [2012] UKSC 51.
26  *POCA 2002, s 7(2)*.
27  ibid, *s 18*.
28  ibid, *s 16*.
29  ibid, *s 17*.
30  ibid, *s 18(1)–(3)*.

**12.45**

If the defendant fails without reasonable excuse to comply with such an order, the court may draw such inference as it believes is appropriate in future proceedings.[31]

**12.46**

If the prosecutor accepts what the defendant says in his s 18 document or in any other statement given to the court concerning either the available amount, whether to make a determination as to interest in property or what determination to make, the court may treat the acceptance as conclusive of the matters to which it relates.[32]

**12.47**

If the court makes an order under s 18 it may at any time vary it by making another order. It is important to note that no information given by the defendant in compliance with the requirements of s 18 which amounts to an admission by the defendant that he has benefited from criminal conduct is admissible in evidence in proceedings for an offence.[33]

**12.48**

The defendant should bear in mind when providing information under s 18 that it will be used as the starting point for the prosecution's statement of information. In addition, should the prosecution discover that the information provided was incomplete or misleading, it will severely undermine the credibility of the defendant in the following confiscation proceedings.

## *Prosecutor's Statement of Information: section 16*

**12.49**

The statement of information must be provided in every case and it should be provided within the time limit set by the court.

**12.50**

The statement should include all relevant matters to the confiscation enquiry including whether the prosecutor believes that the defendant has a criminal lifestyle, whether he has benefited from his general criminal conduct and his benefit from the conduct[34].

---

31 ibid, s *18(4)*.
32 ibid, s *18(6)*.
33 ibid, s *18(9)*.
34 ibid, s *16(3)*.

**12.51**

The prosecutor should set out what is believed to be relevant in relation to the making by the court of any required assumption under *s 10* of *POCA 2002* including information to enable the court to decide if the circumstances are such that it must not make such an assumption.[35]

**12.52**

If the prosecutor does not believe that the defendant has a criminal lifestyle, the statement of information should set out the matters which the prosecutor believes are relevant in connection with deciding whether the defendant has benefited from his particular criminal conduct and his benefit from the conduct.[36]

**12.53**

The prosecutor must set out any information known to him which he believes is or would be relevant for the purpose of enabling the court to decide whether to make a determination as to the extent of the defendant's interest in property. If the court decides to make such a determination, the prosecutor should provide such information as is relevant to the making of that determination.[37]

**12.54**

It is possible that as the proceedings develop, the prosecutor may prepare and serve more than one s 16 statement of information or may be required to do so by the court.

## *Defendant's response to statement of information: section 17*

**12.55**

The court may order the defendant to reply to the s 16 statement of information in writing within a certain time frame. In the statement the defendant should indicate the extent to which he accepts each allegation in the prosecutor's statement, and in so far as he does not accept any allegation, he should give particulars of any matters he proposes to rely on.[38]

**12.56**

It is important that the defendant's reply is carefully drafted and that each and every allegation made in the prosecutor's statement is dealt with in the reply. If

---

35  ibid, *s 16(4)*.
36  ibid, *s 16(5)*.
37  ibid, *s 16(6A)*.
38  ibid, *s 17(1)*.

the defendant accepts to any extent an allegation in a statement of information, the court may treat his acceptance as conclusive of the matters to which it relates for the purpose of deciding the issues as to whether and by how much he has benefited from general and particular criminal conduct.[39]

**12.57**

If the defendant fails in any respect to comply with the court order to provide a response in the above terms, he may be treated as accepting every allegation in the statement of information. The exception being any allegation in respect of which he has complied with the requirement to respond or any allegation that he has benefited from his general or particular criminal conduct[40].

**12.58**

It should be noted that no acceptance made in such a response that the defendant has benefited from conduct is admissible in evidence in proceedings for an offence.[41]

**12.59**

On service of the defendant's response the issues often narrow in the case and a period of discussion with the prosecution may ensue in an effort to come to an agreement over the extent of any order to be made.

## The determinations to be made by the court

**12.60**

As stated above, the court has to make a number of determinations in the course of confiscation proceedings. The first such determinations is whether the defendant has a criminal lifestyle.

### *Criminal Lifestyle*

**12.61**

A defendant will be deemed to have a criminal lifestyle in any of three specified ways.[42] Firstly, if the offence or any of the offences concerned is specified in *Sch 2 of POCA 2002*.

---

39  ibid, *s 17(2)*.
40  ibid, *s 17(3)*.
41  ibid, *s 17(6)*.
42  ibid, *s 75(1)*.

**12.62**

Schedule 2 includes the following drugs offences at para 1:

- unlawful production or supply of controlled drugs;[43]

- possession of controlled drug with intent to supply;[44]

- permitting certain activities relating to controlled drugs;[45]

- assisting in or inducing the commission outside the UK of an offence punishable under a corresponding law;[46]

- importation of drugs;

- manufacture or supply of a substance useful for manufacturing controlled drugs and specified in *Sch 2* of the *Criminal Justice (International Co-operation) Act 1990*;[47] and

- using a ship for illicit traffic in controlled drugs.[48]

Schedule 2 also includes the following offences under the *Psychoactive Substances Act 2016* under para 1A:

- producing a psychoactive substance;[49]

- supplying, or offering to supply, a psychoactive substance;[50]

- possession of psychoactive substance with intent to supply;[51]

- importing or exporting a psychoactive substance.[52]

**12.63**

The most common drugs offences of production, supply, possession with intent to supply and importation are included within *Sch 2* of *POCA 2002* and therefore automatically bring the defendant within the definition of having a criminal lifestyle. Equally the main offences under the *Psychoactive Substances Act 2016* are also automatically criminal lifestyle offences.

**12.64**

Possession of drugs is not included within the schedule and is not a criminal lifestyle offence. It will rarely be necessary to look further than Sch 2 in drugs cases.

---

43 *Misuse of Drugs Act 1971, s 4(2) or (3).*
44 ibid, *s 5(3).*
45 ibid, *s 8.*
46 ibid, *s 20,*
47 *Criminal Justice (International Co-operation) Act 1990, s 12.*
48 ibid, *s 19.*
49 *Psychoactive Substances Act 2016, s 4.*
50 ibid, *s 5.*
51 ibid, *s 7.*
52 ibid, *s 9.*

**12.65**

However, the other routes to a *'criminal lifestyle'* are where the offence or any of the offences constitute conduct forming part of a course of criminal activity[53] or the offence or any of the offences are committed over a period of at least six months and the defendant has benefited from the conduct which constitutes the offence.[54]

**12.66**

If the defendant has benefited from conduct, it forms part of a course of criminal activity in two ways.

**12.67**

Firstly, if in the proceedings in which he has been convicted, he was convicted of three or more other offences from which he has benefited.

**12.68**

Secondly, if in the period of six years before charge (or, if there is more than one such day, the earliest day), he was convicted on at least two separate occasions of an offence constituting conduct from which he has benefited[55].

**12.69**

Whether by virtue of a course of conduct or because the offence spans at least six months, the benefit has to exceed £5,000 to bring the offence(s) within the criminal lifestyle provisions[56].

## Criminal conduct

**12.70**

The effect of the defendant being deemed to have a criminal lifestyle is that benefit is calculated from his general criminal conduct as opposed to his particular criminal conduct which is limited to benefit from the index offence(s) and any offences for which he was convicted at the same time or had taken into consideration.

**12.71**

Criminal conduct is conduct which constitutes an offence in England and Wales or would constitute an offence if it occurred in England and Wales[57].

---

53  *POCA 2002, s 75(2)(b)*.
54  ibid, *s 75(2)(c)*.
55  ibid, *s 75(3)*.
56  ibid, *s 75(4)*.
57  ibid, *s 76(1)*.

**12.72**

General criminal conduct is all of the defendant's criminal conduct including conduct in the current proceedings and any other proven criminal conduct whether or not related to the current proceedings. This includes conduct which is alleged against a defendant but upon which he is not tried.

**12.73**

In *R v Briggs-Price* [2009] UKHL 19, the Crown's case was that the appellant had been brought into a conspiracy to import heroin because he had an existing network for the transportation and distribution of cannabis which could be used for the distribution of heroin.

**12.74**

He was not charged in relation to the distribution of cannabis. The judge ruled that on the evidence given at trial it had been proved to the criminal standard that the defendant had been trafficking in cannabis and that he had benefited as a result. The figure for the cannabis importations was included in the benefit figure and this was upheld by the Court of Appeal and the House of Lords.

**12.75**

Subsequent decisions have held that where other conduct is alleged and to be included in calculating the benefit, the Crown does not have to comply with anything more than the civil standard of proof.[58].

**12.76**

In *Bagnall*, the Court of Appeal held that the Crown was entitled to adduce evidence of a defendant's involvement in a missing trader fraud, even though he had not been convicted of such an offence. The information was relevant to the making of assumptions under *s 10* of *POCA 2002* and the Crown was not obliged to prove the offences beyond reasonable doubt.

**12.77**

The fact that the Crown accused the defendant of specific offences and adduced evidence to support that accusation did not amount to the bringing of a new charge and he was not at risk of any further conviction. There was no finding of guilt and the findings reached by the judge on the assumptions under *s 10* of *POCA 2002* merely went to the amount of the order the court was obliged to make. The Crown was obliged to include in its statement of information matters relevant to the making of assumptions and was, accordingly, obliged to set out the information it had relevant to the fraudulent activity.

---

58  *R v Gale* [2011] 1 WLR 2760 and *R v Bagnall* [2012] EWCA Crim 677.

## Benefit

### 12.78

A person benefits from conduct if he obtains property as a result of or in connection with the conduct.[59] If a person benefits from conduct his benefit is the value of the property obtained.[60]

### 12.79

Calculating the benefit obtained by a defendant is not always as straightforward as it may appear from the definition of benefit contained in *s 76* of *POCA 2002*. Issues often arise as to whether or how to divide up potential benefit between co-defendants and whether the defendant actually obtained anything at all.

### 12.80

The House of Lords set out the broad principles to be followed in determining benefit under *POCA 2002* in the case of *R v May* [2008] UKHL 28. The section is often quoted and is important to any assessment of benefit.

### 12.81

The Court set out the principles as follows:

'(1) The legislation is intended to deprive defendants of the benefit they have gained from relevant criminal conduct, whether or not they have retained such benefit, within the limits of their available means. It does not provide for confiscation in the sense understood by schoolchildren and others, but nor does it operate by way of fine. The benefit gained is the total value of the property or advantage obtained, not the defendant's net profit after deduction of expenses or any amounts payable to co-conspirators.

(2) The court should proceed by asking:

(i)   Has the defendant benefited from relevant criminal conduct?

(ii)   If so, what is the value of the benefit that the defendant has so obtained?

(iii)   What sum is recoverable from the defendant?

Where issues of criminal lifestyle arise the questions must be modified. These are separate questions calling for separate answers, and the questions and answers must not be elided.

---

59  *POCA 2002, s 76(4)*.
60  ibid, *s 76(7)*.

(3) In addressing these questions the court must first establish the facts as best it can on the material available, relying as appropriate on the statutory assumptions. In very many cases the factual findings made will be decisive.

(4) In addressing the questions the court should focus very closely on the language of the statutory provision in question in the context of the statute and in the light of any statutory definition. The language used is not arcane or obscure and any judicial gloss or exegesis should be viewed with caution. Guidance should ordinarily be sought in the statutory language rather than in the proliferating case law.

(5) In determining, under the 2002 Act, whether the defendant has obtained property or a pecuniary advantage and, if so, the value of any property or advantage so obtained, the court should (subject to any relevant statutory definition) apply ordinary common law principles to the facts as found. The exercise of this jurisdiction involves no departure from familiar rules governing entitlement and ownership. While the answering of the third question calls for inquiry into the financial resources of the defendant at the date of the determination, the answering of the first two questions plainly calls for a historical inquiry into past transactions.

(6) The defendant ordinarily obtains property if in law he owns it, whether alone or jointly, which will ordinarily connote a power of disposition or control, as where a person directs a payment or conveyance of property to someone else. He ordinarily obtains a pecuniary advantage if (among other things) he evades a liability to which he is personally subject. Mere couriers or custodians or other very minor contributors to an offence, rewarded by a specific fee and having no interest in the property or the proceeds of sale, are unlikely to be found to have obtained that property. It may be otherwise with money launderers.'

**12.82**

From *May* we can extract the following principles in relation to benefit calculations:

- Where a benefit is jointly obtained by a group, each is liable for the whole;

- Benefit gained is the total value of property obtained and not the net profit after deduction of expenses or amounts payable to co-conspirators;

- The defendant obtains property if he owns it alone or jointly which connotes a power of disposition or control; and

- Mere couriers rewarded by a specific fee have not obtained the property.

## Couriers and custodians

### 12.83

In drugs cases there are often defendants who have played relatively minor roles such as acting as a courier or custodian for drugs within the wider operation. Such defendants are usually paid a fee for their services and it was recognised in *May* that such defendants do not obtain the value of the drugs which are temporarily within their possession when it comes to calculating benefit.

### 12.84

The principle in *May* was also followed in the cases of *R v Sivaramen* [2009] 1 Cr App R (S) 80 and *R v Allpress* [2009] EWCA Crim 8. In the latter case the Court of Appeal held the defendant who was paid a fee to take cash abroad in relation to drug transactions did not benefit by the value of the money transported but by the value of the fees they were paid to do so.

### 12.85

It is submitted that for any drug courier bringing drugs into the UK or transporting drugs around the UK and for any defendant who is holding drugs as a temporary custodian for a third party who has the ultimate control over the drugs, their benefit should not be calculated on the basis of the value of the drugs but the value of the fee they were paid to provide the service.

### 12.86

It will be important when representing defendants of this nature to ensure that it is clear to the court considering confiscation what was paid to the individual for their part in the criminal enterprise and it may also be advisable to put such information into a written basis of plea which if accepted by the Crown should be binding on them in confiscation proceedings.[61]

### 12.87

The concept of a mere courier or custodian being a 'bailee who receives physical possession of property for another'[62] may possibly be extendable to the defendant who provides storage facilities for larger amounts of drugs if it can be demonstrated that they were not a major player in the operation and obtained payment for the service rather than a cut of the proceeds of the operation.[63]

---

61 *R v Lunnon* [2004] EWCA Crim 1125, *R v Lazarus* [2004] EWCA Crim 2297, *R v Fowles* [2005] EWCA Crim 97.
62 *Allpress* para 30.
63 See also Ch 3.

**12.88**

In *R v Clark* [2011] EWCA Crim 15 the Court of Appeal held that the appellant who had assisted in the shipping of numerous stolen vehicles to east Africa had not been a principal conspirator but a bailee of the cars for the purpose of containerising and transporting them in preparation for shipment. He was an integral facilitator but there was nothing to link him either with the original thefts, or with the onward sales in Africa or the proceeds of such sales. His role was an important part of the overall handling conspiracy, but there was nothing apart from the importance of that role to suggest that the cars were jointly owned by him with other principal conspirators.

## The Corporate veil

**12.89**

Although more common in fraud cases, it may be relevant to some drugs cases that an individual acts through a company to commit an offence. In such circumstances, in confiscation proceedings the corporate veil can be lifted so that the benefit figure relates to the turnover of the company rather than the income of the individual.

**12.90**

The corporate veil is more likely to be lifted in drugs cases given that the court is likely to find that the convicted defendant has either sheltered behind the company to attempt to hide the crime, committed the acts in the name of the company or used the company to carry out transactions which are ultimately a sham to deceive others.[64]

**12.91**

However, in any case where a legitimate company has been used in a drugs case and it can be argued that the illegal activity was not the main purpose for the company, it may be possible to keep the corporate veil in place.

**12.92**

In *R. v Boyle Transport (Northern Ireland) Ltd [2016]* 2 Cr App R (S) 11, CA. it was said that where an issue of lifting the corporate veil arises, the principles to be applied are the same as in the civil courts[65]. The court urged that any conclusion on lifting the corporate veil will require a careful examination of all the relevant facts and that it was more likely where the entire undertaking is unlawful than where a legitimate operation is tainted by associated illegality.

---

64  *R v Sale* [2013] EWCA Crim 1306; *R v Seager and Blatch* [2009] EWCA Crim 1303.
65  As laid down originally in *Salomon v A. Salomon & Co. Ltd* [1897] A.C. 22, HL, and restated in *Prest v Petrodel Resources Ltd* [2013] 2 A.C. 415, SC.

## *Joint benefit*

### 12.93

In any case the amount of the benefit has to be proportionate. In multi-handed cases the benefit figure for co-defendants might be the total amount obtained which on the face of it could lead to multiple recovery by the Crown.

### 12.94

In *May* the House of Lords held that there might be circumstances where confiscation orders for the full amount against several defendants might be disproportionate and contrary to Article 1, Protocol 1 and an apportionment might be preferable.

### 12.95

In *R v Ahmad* [2014] UKSC 36 the Supreme Court has shifted effectively the problem from the Crown Court (in making the orders) to the magistrates' court in enforcing the orders.

### 12.96

The Supreme Court held that defendants who had jointly obtained a benefit through criminal conduct were each separately liable for the whole amount of that benefit and confiscation orders had to be made against each of them for the whole of it. However, each order could only be enforced to the extent that the sum had not been recovered in satisfaction of another confiscation order made in respect of the same joint benefit. This provides the possibility of defendants paying orders and releasing other defendants from the requirement to pay parts of their orders and may be a recipe for confusion and argument at the enforcement stage of proceedings.

## *Value*

### 12.97

Commonly in drugs cases an assessment has to be made as to the market value of the drugs in order to calculate the benefit figure, Drugs have a value on the black market, there being no legitimate value, and it is this value which will be used for the calculation of benefit.

### 12.98

However, the same value cannot be taken into account when the available amount is being calculated as the drugs have no legitimate market value and have often been seized in any event and are not therefore available to the defendant.[66]

---

66  *R v Islam* [2009] UKHL 30.

## Assumptions as to benefit

**12.99**

When the defendant is deemed to have a criminal lifestyle, the assumptions set out in *s 10* of *POCA 2002* must be applied when the court is considering whether the defendant has benefited from his general criminal conduct. If so, those assumptions must be applied also to the value of that benefit, unless the assumption is shown to be incorrect or there would be a serious risk of injustice if the assumption were made.

**12.100**

The assumptions are:

(a)    any property transferred to the defendant at any time after the 'relevant day' was obtained by him as a result of his general criminal conduct;

(b)    any property held by the defendant at any time after the date of conviction was obtained by him as a result of his general criminal conduct;

(c)    any expenditure incurred by the defendant at any time after the relevant day was met from property obtained by him as a result of his general criminal conduct;

(d)    for the purpose of valuing any property obtained (or assumed to have been obtained) by the defendant, he obtained it free of any other interests in it.

**12.101**

The 'relevant day' is calculated by going back six years from the date that proceedings for the offence concerned were started against the defendant or, if there are two or more offences and proceedings for them were started on different days, the earliest of those dates.

**12.102**

The calculation of the relevant day may be complicated if there has been a previous confiscation order made within that six-year period.

**12.103**

If this is the case, the relevant day is the day when the defendant's benefit was calculated for the purposes of the last confiscation order. In practice this would normally mean that the relevant day is the day that the last confiscation order was made as the benefit would have been calculated on the day that the confiscation order was made.

**12.104**

It is for the defendant in the confiscation proceedings to demonstrate that any such assumption applied by the prosecution is incorrect or, if made, would lead to a serious risk of injustice to the defendant.

**12.105**

It is not a simple task for the defendant to demonstrate that either of these exceptions applies. It often requires a forensic examination of the finances of the defendant over a period extending back more than six years.

**12.106**

Defendants in such cases rarely keep good financial records and the lack of documentary evidence to support assertions made by the defendant causes a problem in demonstrating that the assumptions should not apply.

**12.107**

On the face of it, this burden on the defendant may appear unfair. However, in *Bagnall* the Court of Appeal held that whilst Art 6(1) of ECHR applied to confiscation proceedings, the proceedings were not unfair to the appellant.

**12.108**

The statutory assumption applied to assess the amount of the confiscation order. The defendant was entitled to rebut the assumption that the source of the assets was criminal on the balance of probabilities. There was nothing unfair in requiring him to demonstrate that two of the companies through which he was trading were carrying out lawful business. There was no basis for contending that to impose the burden upon the defendant of showing that the source of his property was legitimate was unfair or contrary to Art 6 of ECHR.

## Recoverable Amount

**12.109**

The recoverable amount is the benefit figure unless the defendant shows that the available amount is less than that benefit in which case the recoverable amount will be the available amount or a nominal amount (usually £1) if the available amount is shown to be zero.[67].

**12.110**

The House of Lords made a number of comments in *May* about the importance of confiscation orders being made within the available means of defendants and

---

67  *POCA 2002, s 7.*

the unfairness of imprisoning a defendant for failing to pay a sum which they cannot pay.

**12.111**

However, courts frequently make confiscation orders beyond the means of defendants where the defendant has failed to persuade the court that their available assets are lower than the benefit figure. In these circumstances, the recoverable amount remains higher than the amount available to the defendant.

**12.112**

The prosecution will often claim that a defendant has hidden assets – assets which may not have been disclosed in proceedings or identified by the Crown. Such an assertion by the Crown is difficult to meet as it involves proving a negative. The burden is on the defendant to prove the value of his available assets.

**12.113**

The Court of Appeal has shown little sympathy for appellants caught by the notion of hidden assets. In *R v Whittington* [2009] EWCA Crim 1641 the Court of Appeal held that, once a criminal lifestyle had been established, it was for the prosecution to prove on a balance of probabilities that the defendant had obtained the property (in this case £8.8 million of cocaine based on entries in a notebook).

**12.114**

The burden shifted to the defendant to explain what had happened to those assets or how much profit they represented to him. In the absence of an explanation the court was compelled to conclude that the available amount was no less than the amount of the benefit. If a defendant gives no explanation or no acceptable explanation, he will fail to discharge the burden of establishing that a lesser amount is available.

**12.115**

In *R v McIntosh* [2011] EWCA Crim 1501 it was held that the court imposing the order must answer the statutory question in *POCA 2002, s* 7 in a just and proportionate way. The court is not bound to reject a defendant's case that his current realisable assets are less than the full amount of the benefit, merely because it concludes that the defendant has not revealed their true extent or value, or has not participated in any revelation at all. The court may conclude that a defendant's realisable assets are less than the full value of the benefit on the basis of the facts as a whole.

**12.116**

A defendant who is found not to have told the truth or who has declined to give truthful disclosure will inevitably find it difficult to discharge the burden imposed upon him. However, it may not be impossible for him to do so. Other sources of evidence, apart from the defendant himself, and a view of the case as a whole, may persuade a court that the assets available to the defendant are less than the full value of the benefit.

**12.117**

This is often one of the most pernicious and difficult parts of dealing with a confiscation matter. The defendant is a convicted criminal and is expected to explain where assets have gone which may not have existed in the first place with the burden of proof on him. His credibility as a convicted person is not high and it will frequently be impossible to demonstrate anything with documents in cases where records of transactions are not kept. Inferences from handwritten notes (such as in *Whittington*) can and frequently are wrong either entirely or in terms of the figures they create.

## Available Amount

**12.118**

The available amount is the total of the values of all free property then held by the defendant less the total amount payable in relation to any obligations which have priority plus the value of all tainted gifts.[68] The value is assessed at the time that the Confiscation Order is made.

**12.119**

An obligation has priority if it is an obligation of the defendant to pay an amount due in respect of a fine or other court order imposed on conviction for an offence at any time before the confiscation order is made or an obligation to pay a sum which would be included in the preferential debts if the defendant were made bankrupt at that time. Preferential debts are as stated in *s 386* and *Sch 6* of the *Insolvency Act 1986*.[69]

**12.120**

Consequently, the defendant has to show what assets he has and what the value of those assets is after certain interests such as mortgages have been deducted. Tainted gifts are defined as any transfer for a consideration whose value is significantly less than the value of the property[70].

**12.121**

In criminal lifestyle cases a gift is tainted if it was given up to six years before the proceedings commenced or at any time in the case if it was the proceeds of

---

68  ibid, *s 9(1)*.
69  ibid, *s 9(2)*.
70  ibid, *ss 77* and *78*.

crime. In non-lifestyle cases the gift is tainted if it were given after the offence was committed.

### 12.122

The value of the tainted gift is the greater of the value at the time that it was obtained (adjusted for the change in the value of money) and the value at the time of the confiscation hearing[71]. Clearly some items will increase in value and some decrease over time.

### 12.123

If it is claimed that the defendant has made a tainted gift, the value of the gift remains part of their assets and is included in the available amount even though they no longer have access to the asset itself. The purpose is clearly to prevent defendants passing on their assets to third parties in order to avoid losing them in confiscation.

## Determination of extent of defendant's interest in property

### 12.124

If the court considers that the defendant may hold property that might be realised or otherwise used to satisfy the order and another person holds (or may hold) an interest in the property, the court may determine the extent of the defendant's interest in the property at the time the confiscation order is made[72]. The 'extent' of the defendant's interest in property means the proportion of the value of the defendant's interest in relation to the value of the property itself.

### 12.125

The court must not exercise this power unless it gives a reasonable opportunity to make representations to anyone who is or may be a person holding an interest in the property.

### 12.126

If the court makes such a determination, it is conclusive in relation to the extent of the defendant's interest in the property that arises in connection with the realisation of the property. Further, it is conclusive in relation to the transfer of an interest in the property, with a view to satisfying the confiscation order, or any action or proceedings taken for the purposes of any such realisation or transfer. It is obviously not binding on a court of appeal.

---

71  ibid, *s 81*.
72  ibid, s 10A.

**12.127**

Often in cases involving confiscation orders, one of the main assets is the 'matrimonial home'. Issues arise concerning the interest of the defendant's partner.

**12.128**

In cases where the property is held in joint names, the court should start with the presumption that it is held in equal share between the parties. However, it may be that the partner's share comes from tainted gifts from the defendant and the court should consider whether a greater than 50% share should be included within the available amount.[73]

**12.129**

Equally, if the defendant can demonstrate that his partner has contributed more than 50% towards the cost of the property or that others have contributed towards its purchase, the defendant's share should be reduced accordingly.

**12.130**

In cases where the property is held in the name of the defendant but the partner claims an equitable interest (usually 50%), the principles to be followed were set out by the Administrative Court in *CPS v Piper* [2011] EWHC 3570 Admin.

**12.131**

The starting point is that equity follows the law and that the defendant who is the sole registered owner of the property holds the beneficial interest. The burden of proof is upon the partner to displace that presumption or starting point on the balance of probability.

**12.132**

The court should first ask whether there was a common intention by the defendant and the partner that the partner should have any beneficial interest in the property at all. Their common intention is to be deduced objectively from their conduct.

**12.133**

In answering the question, if the partner has made some financial contribution referable to the transfer of the property to the defendant, it can readily be inferred that it was intended that the partner should have a beneficial interest in that property.

---

73 *R v Buckman* [1997] 1 Cr App R (S) 325. This was a case decided under the *DTA 1994*.

**12.134**

If it is decided that the partner does have a beneficial interest in the property, and the court can also deduce a common intention as to the size of that interest by direct evidence or by inference, then that is the partner's interest.

**12.135**

If it is not possible to ascertain by direct evidence or by inference what the common intention as to the size of that interest is, then the size of that interest is that which the court considers fair having regard to the whole course of dealing between the couple in relation to the property. The whole course of dealing in relation to that property is to be given a broad meaning.

**12.136**

In some cases, the defendant is divorcing, and the spouse may claim a greater interest in the matrimonial home in the matrimonial proceedings. It was held in *Webber v CPS* [2006] EWHC 2893 (Fam) that there has to remain a separation between the family and the criminal proceedings.

**12.137**

It would be appropriate for the ancillary relief application in the matrimonial proceedings to be disposed of before the confiscation proceedings in the criminal court. By that means, the Crown Court judge hearing the confiscation proceedings would be in a position to judge whether the amount available was 50% of the proceeds of sale of the matrimonial home or whether the amount required adjustment in the light of the findings of the High Court judge hearing the ancillary relief application.

## Legal aid contributions from capital

**12.138**

A legal aid contribution from capital does not have priority over a Confiscation Order. However, in cases where the partner of the defendant retains a share in the property, the Legal Aid Agency can seek to enforce a capital contribution against that share assuming that it exceeds £30,000. This has the effect of fixing the partner with the debt of the defendant.

**12.139**

It is submitted that in such situations, the potential legal aid capital contribution should be deducted from the equity share of the defendant for the purposes of the confiscation proceedings despite not being a preferential debt. Even if the debt were treated as a mortgage and deducted before the division of the property between the parties, the partner would be left with half of the defendant's debt.

**12.140**

This situation arose in *R v Flynn* [2016] EWCA Crim 201 where the principal asset of the appellant was his 50% share in the equity of the matrimonial home. The prosecution and defence agreed that in calculating the available amount, certain charges against the property had to be deducted before the shares of the appellant and his wife could be calculated. There was disagreement over the treatment of two charges incurred solely by Mr Flynn including an interim charging order in favour of the Legal Aid Agency related to the costs of his representation in the criminal proceedings.

**12.141**

The judge at first instance treated all charges the same and deducted them before calculating the value of each party's interest in the equity. On appeal it was argued that this led to a disproportionate result whereby the appellant's wife had to pay half of the appellant's debt to the Legal Aid Agency. The Legal Aid Agency could enforce against the whole property and would enforce if the value of the equity held by either party was sufficient.

**12.142**

In *Flynn*, the Crown did not oppose the appeal given that a charge in favour of the Legal Aid Agency on the appellant's share of the equity would lead to the full amount of his share going to the public purse in any event. The Court reduced the available amount so that in effect the debt to the Legal Aid Agency was taken into account only against the appellant's share of the equity.

## Making the order

**12.143**

Either by agreement between the parties or following a contested confiscation hearing, the judge will make the confiscation order setting out the benefit figure and the recoverable amount. The Confiscation Order will be the lower of the benefit figure and the recoverable amount if the defendant has shown that the available amount is less than the benefit figure.

**12.144**

It should be noted that if the available amount is below the benefit figure, the prosecution can make an application to recalculate the available amount in the future up to the amount of the benefit if it comes to their attention that the assets of the defendant have increased beyond the previously assessed available amount.[74]

---

74 *POCA 2002, s 22.*

**12.145**

There is no time limit on such an application but it is subject to reasonableness in terms of any undue delay on the part of the prosecutor.[75] The benefit figure is not therefore an academic figure in cases where the order is to be made at a lower figure, although such applications are relatively rare they are anecdotally on the increase.

## Time to pay

**12.146**

The Confiscation Order is due for payment on the day that it is made[76] unless the court is satisfied that the defendant is unable to pay the full amount on that day. It would in practice be unusual for the court not to allow some time to pay an order.

**12.147**

The court may make an order requiring whatever cannot be paid on that day to be paid in a specified period, or in specified periods each of which relates to a specified amount. However, the specified period must start with the day on which the confiscation order is made, and must not exceed three months.[77]

**12.148**

It is possible to apply to extend the time for payment. This must be done before the time period expires although the application can be heard after expiry, unless that would take the time beyond six months from the date of the order.[78]

**12.149**

If the court is satisfied that, despite having made all reasonable efforts, the defendant is unable to pay the amount to which the specified period relates within that period, the court may make an order extending the period. The extended period cannot take the time for payment beyond six months from the day on which the confiscation order was made.[79]

**12.150**

The court must not make an order allowing or extending time to pay unless it gives the prosecutor an opportunity to make representations.[80]

---

75  *R v Griffin* [2009] Cr App R (S) 587.
76  *POCA 2002, s 11(1).*
77  ibid, *s 11(2)-(3).*
78  ibid, *s 11(6).*
79  ibid, *s 11(5).*
80  ibid, *s 11(8).*

**12.151**

If the order requires the sale of assets or property, it would be reasonable to expect the maximum time to settle the order.

## Interest on unpaid sums

**12.152**

Interest on unpaid sums starts to run once the time to pay period has ended.[81] If that period is extended, interest does not start to run until the extended period has passed. The rate of interest is the same rate as that for the time being specified in *s 17* of the *Judgments Act 1838* (interest on civil judgment debts) and the amount of the interest must be treated as part of the amount to be paid under the confiscation order.

## Period in default

**12.153**

The period of time to be served in default of payment is set by the judge at the confiscation hearing using the figures set out in *POCA 2002, s 35(2A)*. The periods are maximum periods and the court has discretion to set the period below the maximum.[82]

**12.154**

The maximum periods in default are:

| Amount | Maximum term |
|---|---|
| £10,000 or less | 6 months |
| More than £10,000 but no more than £500,000 | 5 years |
| More than £500,000 but no more than £1 million | 7 years |
| More than £1 million | 14 years |

**12.155**

The purpose of the default term is to secure payment of the confiscation order. It is not a simple arithmetical calculation as to where the amount of the order comes within the band but all the circumstances of the case have to be considered.

---

81  ibid, *s 12*.
82  *R v Szrajber* 15 Cr App R (S) 821, CA.

**12.156**

The court should not be influenced by the overall totality of the sentence should the default term be served. In some cases, the term in default may be higher than the term for the offence itself.

**12.157**

If the default term is served, the defendant will be released having served one half of the term unless the Confiscation Order was made in the sum of £10 million or more.[83]

**12.158**

The debt of the confiscation order is not extinguished by serving the term but having served it and still not having paid, the defendant cannot be returned to prison again. If the order is paid in part, the default term ordered to be served is reduced mathematically in relation to the amount of the order that has been paid.

## Variation of an order

### *Application by the defendant*

**12.159**

Should the defendant have realised all of his available assets and the amount realised not reach the amount of the Confiscation Order, it is possible to make an application to the Crown Court to reduce the available amount and therefore reduce the amount of the Confiscation Order.[84]

**12.160**

In such a case, the court must calculate the available amount at the date of the application and, if it finds that the available amount is inadequate for the payment of any amount remaining to be paid under the confiscation order, it may vary the order by substituting for the amount required to be paid such smaller amount as the court believes is just.

**12.161**

The court may disregard any inadequacy which it believes is attributable (wholly or partly) to anything done by the defendant for the purpose of preserving property held by the recipient of a tainted gift.

---

83  *CJA 2003, s 258(2B).*
84  *POCA 2002, s 23.*

## *Applications by the prosecution*

### 12.162

Equally, the prosecution is able to make an application to reconsider the benefit figure[85] or the available amount figure.[86].

### 12.163

An application to reconsider the benefit figure can be made where there is evidence which was not available to the prosecutor at the relevant time, which suggests that the benefit figure should have been calculated differently. This application has to be made within six years of the date of conviction.

### 12.164

An application to reconsider the available amount can be made without the limit of time. Such applications are likely to be made where it is known that the defendant has subsequently obtained assets after the date of the confiscation order or where he has satisfied the order without using all of his assets (perhaps by borrowing money to pay the order). The court must make the new calculation with figures calculated as at the time of the application and if the amount found under the new calculation exceeds the relevant amount the court may vary the order by substituting for the amount required to be paid such amount as it believes is just, but does not exceed the amount found as the defendant's benefit from the conduct concerned.

## Enforcement

### 12.165

Confiscation orders are treated as though the amount to be paid is a fine imposed on the defendant by the Crown Court.[87] However, whereas the amount of a fine can be remitted (under *s 85* of the *Magistrates Court Act 1980*), there is specifically no such corresponding power with a confiscation order.[88]

### 12.166

The collection and enforcement of the confiscation order is undertaken by the magistrates' court from which the defendant was sent for trial. If the defendant is in default of payment of all or part of the order, the magistrates court will institute enforcement proceedings which could lead to the committal to prison

---

85  ibid, *s 21*.
86  ibid, *s 22*.
87  ibid, *s 35*.
88  ibid, *s 35(3)(b)*.

of the defendant to serve the default period (or part thereof if the order is part paid).

**12.167**

Separate legal aid is available in these circumstances to represent the defendant at enforcement proceedings before the magistrates' court. These proceedings will involve, among other things, an investigation into the defendant's means and consideration of the defendant's means to pay; whether the non-payment to date is due to wilful or culpable neglect; and whether other methods of enforcement have proved unsuccessful or are inappropriate.

**12.168**

Enforcement proceedings should be instigated within a reasonable time otherwise they may amount to a breach of a defendant's right to a fair trial within a reasonable time under Art 6(1) of ECHR.[89]

## Public funding for confiscation proceedings

**12.169**

The original trial legal aid representation order covers the work done in confiscation proceedings. Advocates are paid on a fee which is based on the amount of pages in the confiscation proceedings but solicitors are paid for the work done on confiscation in addition to the trial litigators' graduated fee.

**12.170**

The payment is on the pre-litigator fee structure whereby the claim is made on a time-spent basis and assessed by the National Taxing Team at the conclusion of the case. Uplift of 100% can be claimed on the work done if the case meets the criteria for such uplift and there are different hourly rates for different levels of fee earner from A to C, albeit that these rates are lower than they were in 1996 not even taking into account the effect of inflation in the intervening period.

**12.171**

Bills should be submitted within six months of the conclusion of the confiscation proceedings. The trial bill should not await the conclusion of the confiscation proceedings but be submitted within three months of the end of the trial (ie after the sentencing hearing).

---

89 *Lloyd v Bow Street Magistrates' Court* [2003] EWHC 2294 Admin.

### 12.172

Public funding is available by extension of the original legal aid order for any application to vary an order or seek further time to pay and no new legal aid application is required.

### 12.173

For enforcement proceedings a new application for legal aid has to be made to the Legal Aid Agency using the CRM14 and CRM 15 application forms.

## Summary of key points

### 12.174

- Restraint Orders can be obtained against an individual pre-charge, before or after conviction.

- Money can be released from restraint for the payment of living expenses but not for legal fees relating to the offence.

- Legal aid may be available to apply to vary the conditions of a Restraint Order.

- In confiscation proceedings, the court must first decide whether the defendant has a criminal lifestyle.

- In most drugs cases, including offences under the *Psychoactive Substances Act 2016*, the defendant will be deemed to have a criminal lifestyle.

- If the court considers that the defendant has a criminal lifestyle, it must decide whether he has benefited from his general criminal conduct.

- Assumptions can be made that all income and expenditure in the period of six years before the date of charge has been obtained by criminal activity unless the defendant can show this to be incorrect or that it might lead to a serious risk of injustice.

- If the defendant has no criminal lifestyle, the court has to decide whether he has benefited from his particular criminal conduct.

- A person benefits from conduct if he obtains property as a result of or in connection with the conduct and the value of the benefit is the value of the property obtained.

- Where a benefit is jointly obtained by a group, each is liable for the whole but repayment by one defendant would reduce the liability of the others to pay the full amount.

- Benefit gained is the total value of property obtained and not the net profit after deduction of expenses or amounts payable to co-conspirators.

- The defendant obtains property if he owns it alone or jointly which connotes a power of disposition or control.

- Mere couriers rewarded by a specific fee have not obtained the property.

- If the court decides that there is benefit to the defendant from such conduct, it must decide the 'recoverable amount'.

- The court must make a confiscation order in the sum of the recoverable amount unless it would be disproportionate to require the defendant to pay that amount.

- If the defendant shows that the 'available amount, is less than the benefit figure, the Confiscation Order is made in the sum of the available amount or a nominal figure if the available amount is zero.

- Confiscation Orders should be made within two years of conviction unless exceptional circumstances apply.

- Time to pay the confiscation order cannot extend beyond six months from the date of the order after which date interest accrues on the unpaid amount.

- The prosecution can apply to increase a confiscation order if a defendant has acquired assets or not used assets to satisfy a confiscation order or to increase the benefit figure if new information suggests that the original figure was incorrect.

- A defendant can apply to vary a confiscation order if he has realised all of his assets but the amount falls short of the confiscation figure.

- A prison term in default of payment will be set with enforcement and imposition of such terms applied by the magistrates' court.

# Appendix A

# Misuse of Drugs Act 1971, sections 1 to 9 and Schedules 1 and 2

*The Advisory Council on the Misuse of Drugs*

**1    The Advisory Council on the Misuse of Drugs.**

(1)    There shall be constituted in accordance with Schedule 1 to this Act as Advisory Council on the Misuse of Drugs (in this Act referred to as 'the Advisory Council'); and the supplementary provisions contained in that Schedule shall have effect in relation to the Council.

(2)    It shall be the duty of the Advisory Council to keep under review the situation in the United Kingdom with respect to drugs which are being or appear to them likely to be misused and of which the misuse is having or appears to them capable of having harmful effects sufficient to constitute a social problem, and to give to any one or more of the Ministers, where either the Council consider it expedient to do so or they are consulted by the Minister or Ministers in question, advice on measures (whether or not involving alteration of the law) which in the opinion of the Council ought to be taken for preventing the misuse of such drugs or dealing with social problems connected with their misuse, and in particular on measures which in the opinion of the Council ought to be taken—

(a)    for restricting the availability of such drugs or supervising the arrangements for their supply;

(b)    for enabling persons affected by the misuse of such drugs to obtain proper advice, and for securing the provision of proper facilities and services for the treatment, rehabilitation and after-care of such persons;

(c)    for promoting co-operation between the various professional and community services which in the opinion of the Council have a part to play in dealing with social problems connected with the misuse of such drugs;

(d)    for educating the public (and in particular the young) in the dangers of misusing such drugs, and for giving publicity to those dangers; and

(e)    for promoting research into, or otherwise obtaining information about, any matter which in the opinion of the Council is of relevance for the purpose of preventing the misuse of such drugs or dealing with any social problem connected with their misuse.

(3)    It shall also be the duty of the Advisory Council to consider any matter relating to drug dependence or the misuse of drugs which may be referred to them by any one or more of the Ministers and to advise the Minister or Ministers in question thereon, and in particular to consider and advise the Secretary of State with respect to any communication referred by him to the Council, being a communication relating to the control of any dangerous or otherwise harmful drug made to Her Majesty's Government in the United Kingdom by any organisation or authority established by or under any treaty, convention or other agreement or arrangement to which that Government is for the time being a party.

(4)    In this section 'the Ministers' means the Secretary of State for the Home Department, the Secretaries of State respectively concerned with health in England, Wales and Scotland, the Secretaries of State respectively concerned with education in England, Wales and Scotland, the Minister of Home Affairs for Northern Ireland, the Minister of Health and Social Services for Northern Ireland and the Minister of Education for Northern Ireland.

*Controlled drugs and their classification*

## 2    Controlled drugs and their classification for purposes of this Act.

(1)    In this Act—

(a)    the expression 'controlled drug' means any substance or product for the time being specified[—

(i)    in Part I, II or III of Schedule 2, or

(ii)    in a temporary class drug order as a drug subject to temporary control (but this is subject to section 2A(6));][1] and

(b)    the expressions 'Class A drug', 'Class B drug' and 'Class C drug' mean any of the substances and products for the time being specified respectively in Part I, Part II and Part III of that Schedule[, and

(c)    the expression 'temporary class drug' means any substance or product which is for the time being a controlled drug by virtue of a temporary class drug order;][2]

and the provisions of Part IV of that Schedule shall have effect with respect to the meanings of expressions used in that Schedule.

(2)    Her Majesty may by Order in Council make such amendments in Schedule 2 to this Act as may be requisite for the purpose of adding any

substance or product to, or removing any substance or product from, any of Parts I to III of that Schedule, including amendments for securing that no substance or product is for the time being specified in a particular one of those Parts or for inserting any substance or product into any of those Parts in which no substance or product is for the time being specified.

(3)    An Order in Council under this section may amend Part IV of Schedule 2 to this Act, and may do so whether or not it amends any other Part of that Schedule.

(4)    An Order in Council under this section may be varied or revoked by a subsequent Order in Council thereunder.

(5)    No recommendation shall be made to Her Majesty in Council to make an Order under this section unless a draft of the Order has been laid before Parliament and approved by a resolution of each House of Parliament; and the Secretary of State shall not lay a draft of such an Order before Parliament except after consultation with or on the recommendation of the Advisory Council.

**Amendments**

1   Substituted for words by the Police Reform and Social Responsibility Act 2011, s 151, Sch 17, paras 1, 2(a).

2   Inserted by the Police Reform and Social Responsibility Act 2011, s 151, Sch 17, paras 1, 2(b).

## [2A  Temporary class drug orders

(1)    The Secretary of State may make an order (referred to in this Act as a 'temporary class drug order') specifying any substance or product as a drug subject to temporary control if the following two conditions are met.

(2)    The first condition is that the substance or product is not a Class A drug, a Class B drug or a Class C drug.

(3)    The second condition is that—

    (a)    the Secretary of State has consulted in accordance with section 2B and has determined that the order should be made, or

    (b)    the Secretary of State has received a recommendation under that section that the order should be made.

(4)    The Secretary of State may make the determination mentioned in subsection (3)(a) only if it appears to the Secretary of State that—

    (a)    the substance or product is a drug that is being, or is likely to be, misused, and

    (b)    that misuse is having, or is capable of having, harmful effects.

(5)    A substance or product may be specified in a temporary class drug order by reference to—

    (a)    the name of the substance or product, or

(b)    a description of the substance or product (which may take such form as the Secretary of State thinks appropriate for the purposes of the specification).

(6)    A substance or product specified in a temporary class drug order as a drug subject to temporary control ceases to be a controlled drug by virtue of the order—

    (a)    at the end of one year beginning with the day on which the order comes into force, or

    (b)    if earlier, upon the coming into force of an Order in Council under section 2(2) by virtue of which the substance or product is specified in Part 1, 2 or 3 of Schedule 2.

(7)    Subsection (6)—

    (a)    is subject to subsection (10), and

    (b)    is without prejudice to the power of the Secretary of State to vary or revoke a temporary class drug order by a further order.

(8)    The power of the Secretary of State to make an order under this section is subject to section 2B.

(9)    An order under this section is to be made by statutory instrument.

(10)  An order under this section—

    (a)    must be laid before Parliament after being made, and

    (b)    ceases to have effect at the end of the period of 40 days beginning with the day on which the order is made unless before the end of that period the order is approved by a resolution of each House of Parliament.

(11)  In calculating that period of 40 days no account is to be taken of any time during which Parliament is dissolved or prorogued or during which both Houses are adjourned for more than 4 days.

(12)  Subsection (10)(b)—

    (a)    is without prejudice to anything previously done or to the power of the Secretary of State to make a new order under this section;

    (b)    does not apply to an order that only revokes a previous order under this section.][1]

**Amendments**

1   Inserted by the Police Reform and Social Responsibility Act 2011, s 151, Sch 17, paras 1, 3.

## [2B  Orders under section 2A: role of Advisory Council etc

(1)    Before making an order under section 2A the Secretary of State—

    (a)    must consult as mentioned in subsection (2), or

(b)     must have received a recommendation from the Advisory Council to make the order.

(2)     The Secretary of State must consult—

(a)     the Advisory Council, or

(b)     if the order is to be made under section 2A(1) and the urgency condition applies, the person mentioned in subsection (3).

(3)     The person referred to in subsection (2)(b) is—

(a)     the person who is for the time being the chairman of the Advisory Council appointed under paragraph 1(3) of Schedule 1, or

(b)     if that person has delegated the function of responding to consultation under subsection (1)(a) to another member of the Advisory Council, that other member.

(4)     The 'urgency condition' applies if it appears to the Secretary of State that the misuse of the substance or product to be specified in the order as a drug subject to temporary control, or the likelihood of its misuse, poses an urgent and significant threat to public safety or health.

(5)     The duty of the Advisory Council or any other person consulted under subsection (1)(a) is limited to giving to the Secretary of State that person's opinion as to whether the order in question should be made.

(6)     A recommendation under subsection (1)(b) that a temporary class drug order should be made may be given by the Advisory Council only if it appears to the Council that—

(a)     the substance or product is a drug that is being, or is likely to be, misused, and

(b)     that misuse is having, or is capable of having, harmful effects.][1]

**Amendments**
1   Inserted by the Police Reform and Social Responsibility Act 2011, s 151, Sch 17, paras 1, 3.

*Restrictions relating to controlled drugs etc.*

**3     Restriction of importation and exportation of controlled drugs.**

(1)     Subject to subsection (2) below—

(a)     the importation of a controlled drug; and

(b)     the exportation of a controlled drug,

are hereby prohibited.

(2)     Subsection (1) above does not apply—

(a)     to the importation or exportation of a controlled drug which is for the time being excepted from paragraph (a) or, as the case may be, paragraph (b) of subsection (1) above by regulations under section 7 of this Act [or by provision made in a temporary class drug order by virtue of section 7A][1]; or

(b)  to the importation or exportation of a controlled drug under and in accordance with the terms of a licence issued by the Secretary of State and in compliance with any conditions attached thereto.

**Amendments**
1  Inserted by the Police Reform and Social Responsibility Act 2011, s 151, Sch 17, paras 1, 4.

## 4  Restriction of production and supply of controlled drugs.

(1)  Subject to any regulations under section 7 of this Act[, or any provision made in a temporary class drug order by virtue of section 7A,][1] for the time being in force, it shall not be lawful for a person—

(a)  to produce a controlled drug; or

(b)  to supply or offer to supply a controlled drug to another.

(2)  Subject to section 28 of this Act, it is an offence for a person—

(a)  to produce a controlled drug in contravention of subsection (1) above; or

(b)  to be concerned in the production of such a drug in contravention of that subsection by another.

(3)  Subject to section 28 of this Act, it is an offence for a person—

(a)  to supply or offer to supply a controlled drug to another in contravention of subsection (1) above; or

(b)  to be concerned in the supplying of such a drug to another in contravention of that subsection; or

(c)  to be concerned in the making to another in contravention of that subsection of an offer to supply such a drug.

**Amendments**
1  Inserted by the Police Reform and Social Responsibility Act 2011, s 151, Sch 17, paras 1, 5.

## [4A  Aggravation of offence of supply of controlled drug

(1)  This section applies if—

(a)  a court is considering the seriousness of an offence under section 4(3) of this Act, and

(b)  at the time the offence was committed the offender had attained the age of 18.

(2)  If either of the following conditions is met the court—

(a)  must treat the fact that the condition is met as an aggravating factor (that is to say, a factor that increases the seriousness of the offence), and

(b)    must state in open court that the offence is so aggravated.

(3)    The first condition is that the offence was committed on or in the vicinity of school premises at a relevant time.

(4)    The second condition is that in connection with the commission of the offence the offender used a courier who, at the time the offence was committed, was under the age of 18.

(5)    In subsection (3), a relevant time is–

   (a)    any time when the school premises are in use by persons under the age of 18;

   (b)    one hour before the start and one hour after the end of any such time.

(6)    For the purposes of subsection (4), a person uses a courier in connection with an offence under section 4(3) of this Act if he causes or permits another person (the courier)–

   (a)    to deliver a controlled drug to a third person, or

   (b)    to deliver a drug related consideration to himself or a third person.

(7)    For the purposes of subsection (6), a drug related consideration is a consideration of any description which–

   (a)    is obtained in connection with the supply of a controlled drug, or

   (b)    is intended to be used in connection with obtaining a controlled drug.

(8)    In this section–

   'school premises' means land used for the purposes of a school excluding any land occupied solely as a dwelling by a person employed at the school; and

   'school' has the same meaning–

      (a)    in England and Wales, as in section 4 of the Education Act 1996;

      (b)    in Scotland, as in section 135(1) of the Education (Scotland) Act 1980;

      (c)    in Northern Ireland, as in Article 2(2) of the Education and Libraries (Northern Ireland) Order 1986.][1]

**Amendments**
1    Inserted by the Drugs Act 2005, s 1(1).

## 5    Restriction of possession of controlled drugs.

(1)    Subject to any regulations under section 7 of this Act for the time being in force, it shall not be lawful for a person to have a controlled drug in his possession.

(2)     Subject to section 28 of this Act and to subsection (4) below, it is an offence for a person to have a controlled drug in his possession in contravention of subsection (1) above.

[(2A) Subsections (1) and (2) do not apply in relation to a temporary class drug.][1]

(3)     Subject to section 28 of this Act, it is an offence for a person to have a controlled drug in his possession, whether lawfully or not, with intent to supply it to another in contravention of section 4(1) of this Act.

(4)     In any proceedings for an offence under subsection (2) above in which it is proved that the accused had a controlled drug in his possession, it shall be a defence for him to prove—

    (a)     that, knowing or suspecting it to be a controlled drug, he took possession of it for the purpose of preventing another from committing or continuing to commit an offence in connection with that drug and that as soon as possible after taking possession of it he took all such steps as were reasonably open to him to destroy the drug or to deliver it into the custody of a person lawfully entitled to take custody of it; or

    (b)     that, knowing or suspecting it to be a controlled drug, he took possession of it for the purpose of delivering it into the custody of a person lawfully entitled to take custody of it and that as soon as possible after taking possession of it he took all such steps as were reasonably open to him to deliver it into the custody of such a person.

(5)     ...[2]

(6)     Nothing in subsection (4) ...[2] above shall prejudice any defence which it is open to a person charged with an offence under this section to raise apart from that subsection.

**Amendments**
1   Inserted by the Police Reform and Social Responsibility Act 2011, s 151, Sch 17, paras 1, 6.
2   Repealed by the Criminal Attempts Act 1981, s 10, Schedule, Pt I

**6     Restriction of cultivation of cannabis plant.**

(1)     Subject to any regulations under section 7 of this Act for the time being in force, it shall not be lawful for a person to cultivate any plant of the genus Cannabis.

(2)     Subject to section 28 of this Act, it is an offence to cultivate any such plant in contravention of subsection (1) above.

**7     Authorisation of activities otherwise unlawful under foregoing provisions.**

(1)     The Secretary of State may by regulations—

(a)  except from section 3(1)(a) or (b), 4(1)(a) or (b) or 5(1) of this Act such controlled drugs as may be specified in the regulations; and

(b)  make such other provision as he thinks fit for the purpose of making it lawful for persons to do things which under any of the following provisions of this Act, that is to say sections 4(1), 5(1) and 6(1), it would otherwise be unlawful for them to do.

(2)  Without prejudice to the generality of paragraph (b) of subsection (1) above, regulations under that subsection authorising the doing of any such thing as is mentioned in that paragraph may in particular provide for the doing of that thing to be lawful—

(a)  if it is done under and in accordance with the terms of a licence or other authority issued by the Secretary of State and in compliance with any conditions attached thereto; or

(b)  if it is done in compliance with such conditions as may be prescribed.

(3)  Subject to subsection (4) below, the Secretary of State shall so exercise his power to make regulations under subsection (1) above as to secure—

(a)  that it is not unlawful under section 4(1) of this Act for a doctor, dentist, veterinary practitioner or veterinary surgeon, acting in his capacity as such, to prescribe, administer, manufacture, compound or supply a controlled drug, or for a pharmacist or a person lawfully conducting a retail pharmacy business, acting in either case in his capacity as such, to manufacture, compound or supply a controlled drug; and

(b)  that it is not unlawful under section 5(1) of this Act for a doctor, dentist, veterinary practitioner, veterinary surgeon, pharmacist or person lawfully conducting a retail pharmacy business to have a controlled drug in his possession for the purpose of acting in his capacity as such.

(4)  If in the case of any controlled drug the Secretary of State is of the opinion that it is in the public interest—

(a)  for production, supply and possession of that drug to be either wholly unlawful or unlawful except for purposes of research or other special purposes; or

(b)  for it to be unlawful for practitioners, pharmacists and persons lawfully conducting retail pharmacy businesses to do in relation to that drug any of the things mentioned in subsection (3) above except under a licence or other authority issued by the Secretary of State,

he may by order designate that drug as a drug to which this subsection applies; and while there is in force an order under this subsection

265

designating a controlled drug as one to which this subsection applies, subsection (3) above shall not apply as regards that drug.

(5)  Any order under subsection (4) above may be varied or revoked by a subsequent order thereunder.

(6)  The power to make orders under subsection (4) above shall be exercisable by statutory instrument, which shall be subject to annulment in pursuance of a resolution of either House of Parliament.

(7)  The Secretary of State shall not make any order under subsection (4) above except after consultation with or on the recommendation of the Advisory Council.

(8)  References in this section to a person's 'doing' things include references to his having things in his possession.

(9)  In its application to Northern Ireland this section shall have effect as if for references to the Secretary of State there were substituted references to the Ministry of Home Affairs for Northern Ireland and as if for subsection (6) there were substituted—

'(6) Any order made under subsection (4) above by the Ministry of Home Affairs for Northern Ireland shall be subject to negative resolution within the meaning of section 41(6) of the Interpretation Act (Northern Ireland) 1954 as if it were a statutory instrument within the meaning of that Act.'

[(10)  In this section a reference to 'controlled drugs' does not include a reference to temporary class drugs (see instead section 7A).][1]

**Amendments**
1  Inserted by the Police Reform and Social Responsibility Act 2011, s 151, Sch 17, paras 1, 7.

## [7A Temporary class drug orders: power to make further provision

(1)  This section applies if a temporary class drug order specifies a substance or product as a drug subject to temporary control.

(2)  The order may—

(a)  include provision for the exception of the drug from the application of section 3(1)(a) or (b) or 4(1)(a) or (b),

(b)  make such other provision as the Secretary of State thinks fit for the purpose of making it lawful for persons to do things in respect of the drug which under section 4(1) it would otherwise be unlawful for them to do,

(c)  provide for circumstances in which a person's possession of the drug is to be treated as excepted possession for the purposes of this Act, and

(d)   include any provision in relation to the drug of a kind that could be made in regulations under section 10 or 22 if the drug were a Class A drug, a Class B drug or a Class C drug (but ignoring section 31(3)).

(3)   Provision under subsection (2) may take the form of applying (with or without modifications) any provision made in regulations under section 7(1), 10 or 22.

(4)   Provision under subsection (2)(b) may (in particular) provide for the doing of something to be lawful if it is done—

(a)   in circumstances mentioned in section 7(2)(a), or

(b)   in compliance with such conditions as may be prescribed by virtue of section 7(2)(b).

(5)   Section 7(8) applies for the purposes of this section.

(6)   Section 31(1) (general provision as to regulations) applies in relation to a temporary class drug order that contains provision made by virtue of this section as it applies to regulations under this Act.]¹

**Amendments**
1   Inserted by the Police Reform and Social Responsibility Act 2011, s 151, Sch 17, paras 1, 8.

*Miscellaneous offences involving controlled drugs etc.*

**8      Occupiers etc. of premises to be punishable for permitting certain activities to take place there.**

A person commits an offence if, being the occupier or concerned in the management of any premises, he knowingly permits or suffers any of the following activities to take place on those premises, that is to say—

(a)   producing or attempting to produce a controlled drug in contravention of section 4(1) of this Act;

(b)   supplying or attempting to supply a controlled drug to another in contravention of section 4(1) of this Act, or offering to supply a controlled drug to another in contravention of section 4(1);

(c)   preparing opium for smoking;

(d)   smoking cannabis, cannabis resin or prepared opium.

**9      Prohibition of certain activities etc. relating to opium.**

Subject to section 28 of this Act, it is an offence for a person—

(a)   to smoke or otherwise use prepared opium; or

(b)   to frequent a place used for the purpose of opium smoking; or

(c)    to have in his possession—

>    (i)    any pipes or other utensils made or adapted for use in connection with the smoking of opium, being pipes or utensils which have been used by him or with his knowledge and permission in that connection or which he intends to use or permit others to use in that connection; or

>    (ii)    any utensils which have been used by him or with his knowledge and permission in connection with the preparation of opium for smoking.

## [9A Prohibition of supply etc. of articles for administering or preparing controlled drugs.

(1)    A person who supplies or offers to supply any article which may be used or adapted to be used (whether by itself or in combination with another article or other articles) in the administration by any person of a controlled drug to himself or another, believing that the article (or the article as adapted) is to be so used in circumstances where the administration is unlawful, is guilty of an offence.

(2)    It is not an offence under subsection (1) above to supply or offer to supply a hypodermic syringe, or any part of one.

(3)    A person who supplies or offers to supply any article which may be used to prepare a controlled drug for administration by any person to himself or another believing that the article is to be so used in circumstances where the administration is unlawful is guilty of an offence.

(4)    For the purposes of this section, any administration of a controlled drug is unlawful except—

>    (a)    the administration by any person of a controlled drug to another in circumstances where the administration of the drug is not unlawful under section 4(1) of this Act, ...[1]

>    (b)    the administration by any person of a controlled drug[, other than a temporary class drug,][2] to himself in circumstances where having the controlled drug in his possession is not unlawful under section 5(1) of this Act[, or

>    (c)    the administration by any person of a temporary class drug to himself in circumstances where having the drug in his possession is to be treated as excepted possession for the purposes of this Act (see section 7A(2)(c)).][2]

(5)    In this section, references to administration by any person of a controlled drug to himself include a reference to his administering it to himself with the assistance of another.][3]

**Amendments**
1   Repealed by the Police Reform and Social Responsibility Act 2011, s 151, Sch 17, paras 1, 9(a).
2   Inserted by the Police Reform and Social Responsibility Act 2011, s 151, Sch 17, paras 1, 9(b), (c).
3   Inserted by the Drug Trafficking Offences Act 1986, s 34(1).

# Schedule 1 Constitution etc. of Advisory Council on the Misuse of Drugs

**1**

(1)   The members of the Advisory Council, of whom there shall be not less than twenty, shall be appointed by the Secretary of State after consultation with such organisations as he considers appropriate ...[1].

(2)   ...[1]

(3)   The Secretary of State shall appoint one of the members of the Advisory Council to be chairman of the Council.

**Amendments**
1   Repealed by the Police Reform and Social Responsibility Act 2011, s 152.

**2**

The Advisory Council may appoint committees, which may consist in part of persons who are not members of the Council, to consider and report to the Council on any matter referred to them by the Council.

**3**

At meetings of the Advisory Council the quorum shall be seven, and subject to that the Council may determine their own procedure.

**4**

The Secretary of State may pay to the members of the Advisory Council such remuneration (if any) and such travelling and other allowances as may be determined by him with the consent of the Minister for the Civil Service.

**5**

Any expenses incurred by the Advisory Council with the approval of the Secretary of State shall be defrayed by the Secretary of State.

# Schedule 2 Controlled drugs

## *Part I Class A drugs*

**1**

The following substances and products, namely:

[(a)][1]
    Acetorphine.
    [Alfentanil.][2]
    Allylprodine.
    Alphacetylmethadol.
    Alphameprodine.
    Alphamethadol.
    Alphaprodine.
    Anileridine.
    Benzethidine.
    Benzylmorphine (3-benzylmorphine).
    Betacetylmethadol.
    Betameprodine.
    Betamethadol.
    Betaprodine.
    Bezitramide.
    Bufotenine.
    ...[3]
    ...[3]
    [Carfentanil.][4]
    Clonitazene.
    Coca leaf.
    Cocaine.
    Desomorphine.
    Dextromoramide.
    Diamorphine.
    Diampromide.
    Diethylthiambutene.
    [Difenoxin (1-(3-cyano-3,3-diphenylpropyl)-4-phenylpiperidine-
        4-carboxylic acid).][5]
    Dihydrocodeinone O carboxymethyloxime.
    [Dihydroetorphine.][6]
    Dihydromorphine.
    Dimenoxadole.
    Dimepheptanol.
    Dimethylthiambutene.
    Dioxaphetyl butyrate.
    Diphenoxylate.
    Dipipanone.
    [Drotebanol (3,4-dimethoxy-17-methylmorphinan- 6β 14-diol).][7]
    Ecgonine, and any derivative of ecgonine which is convertible to
        ecgonine or to cocaine.
    Ethylmethylthiambutene.
    [Eticyclidine.][2]
    Etonitazene.
    Etorphine.

Etoxeridine.
[Etryptamine.][8]
Fentanyl.
[Fungus (of any kind) which contains psilocin or an ester of psilocin.][9]
Furethidine.
Hydrocodone.
Hydromorphinol.
Hydromorphone.
Hydroxypethidine.
Isomethadone.
Ketobemidone.
Levomethorphan.
Levomoramide.
Levophenacylmorphan.
Levorphanol.
[Lofentanil.][4]
Lysergamide.
Lysergide and other N -alkyl derivatives of lysergamide.
Mescaline.
Metazocine.
Methadone.
Methadyl acetate.
[Methylamphetamine.][10]
Methyldesorphine.
Methyldihydromorphine (6-methyldihydromorphine).
Metopon.
Morpheridine.
Morphine.
Morphine methobromide, morphine N -oxide and other pentavalent nitrogen morphine derivatives.
Myrophine.
…[11]
Nicomorphine (3,6-dinicotinoylmorphine).
Noracymethadol.
Norlevorphanol.
Normethadone.
Normorphine.
Norpipanone.
Opium, whether raw, prepared or medicinal.
Oxycodone.
Oxymorphone.
Pethidine.
Phenadoxone.
Phenampromide.
Phenazocine.

[Phencyclidine.][12]
Phenomorphan.
Phenoperidine.
Piminodine.
Piritramide.
Poppy-straw and concentrate of poppy-straw.
Proheptazine.
Properidine (1-methyl-4-phenylpiperidine-4-carboxylic acid isopropyl ester).
Psilocin.
Racemethorphan.
Racemoramide.
Racemorphan.
[Remifentanil.][6]
[Rolicyclidine.][2]
[Sufentanil.][13]
[Tapentadol.][14]
[Tenocylidine.][2]
Thebacon.
Thebaine.
[Tilidate.][13]
Trimeperidine.
[(6aR,9R)-4-acetyl-N,N-diethyl-7-methyl-4,6,6a,7,8,9-hexahydroindolo[4,3-fg]quinoline-9-carboxamide (ALD-52).][15]
[4-Bromo-2,5-dimethoxy-α-methylphenethylamine.][5]
4-Cyano-2-dimethylamino-4,4-diphenylbutane.
4-Cyano-1-methyl-4-phenylpiperidine.
[1-Cyclohexyl-4-(1,2-diphenylethyl)piperazine (MT-45).][16]
[3,4-dichloro-N-[[1-(dimethylamino)cyclohexyl]methyl] benzamide (AH-7921).
[3,4-dichloro-N-[2-(dimethylamino)cyclohexyl]-N-methylbenzamide (U-47,700).][17]
(6aR,9R)-N,N-diethyl-7-allyl-4,6,6a,7,8,9-hexahydroindolo[4,3-fg]quinoline-9-carboxamide (AL-LAD).
(6aR,9R)-N,N-diethyl-7-ethyl-4,6,6a,7,8,9-hexahydroindolo[4,3-fg]quinoline-9-carboxamide (ETH-LAD).
(6aR,9R)-N,N-diethyl-7-propyl-4,6,6a,7,8,9-hexahydroindolo[4,3-fg]quinoline-9-carboxamide (PRO-LAD).][15]
N,N-Diethyltryptamine.
[2,4-dimethylazetidinyl{(6aR,9R)-7-methyl-4,6,6a,7,8,9-hexahydroindolo[4,3-fg]quinolin-9-yl}methanone (LSZ).][15]
N,N-Dimethyltryptamine.
2,5-Dimethoxy-α 4-dimethylphenethylamine.
[N-Hydroxy-tenamphetamine][18]

1-Methyl-4-phenylpiperidine-4-carboxylic acid.

2-Methyl-3-morpholino-1,1-diphenylpropane-carboxylic acid.

[4-Methyl-aminorex][18]

[4-Methyl-5-(4-methylphenyl)-4,5-dihydrooxazol-2-amine (4,4'-
DMAR).][16]

4-Phenylpiperidine-4-carboxylic acid ethyl ester.

[[(b) any compound (not being a compound for the time being specified in sub-paragraph (a) above) structurally derived from tryptamine or from a ring-hydroxy tryptamine by modification in any of the following ways, that is to say—

(i) by substitution at the nitrogen atom of the sidechain to any extent with alkyl or alkenyl substituents, or by inclusion of the nitrogen atom of the side chain (and no other atoms of the side chain) in a cyclic structure;

(ii) by substitution at the carbon atom adjacent to the nitrogen atom of the side chain with alkyl or alkenyl substituents;

(iii) by substitution in the 6-membered ring to any extent with alkyl, alkoxy, haloalkyl, thioalkyl, alkylenedioxy, or halide substituents;

(iv) by substitution at the 2-position of the tryptamine ring system with an alkyl substituent;][19]

[(ba) the following phenethylamine derivatives, namely:—

Allyl($\alpha$-methyl-3,4-methylenedioxyphenethyl)amine

2-Amino-1-(2,5-dimethoxy-4-methylphenyl)ethanol

2-Amino-1-(3,4-dimethoxyphenyl)ethanol

Benzyl($\alpha$-methyl-3,4-methylenedioxyphenethyl)amine

4-Bromo-$\beta$,2,5-trimethoxyphenethylamine

N -(4- sec -Butylthio-2,5-dimethoxyphenethyl)hydroxylamine

Cyclopropylmethyl($\alpha$-methyl-3,4-methylenedioxyphenethyl)
amine

2-(4,7-Dimethoxy-2,3-dihydro-1 H -indan-5-yl)ethylamine

2-(4,7-Dimethoxy-2,3-dihydro-1 H -indan-5-yl)-1-
methylethylamine

2-(2,5-Dimethoxy-4-methylphenyl)cyclopropylamine

2-(1,4-Dimethoxy-2-naphthyl)ethylamine

2-(1,4-Dimethoxy-2-naphthyl)-1-methylethylamine

N-(2,5-Dimethoxy-4-propylthiophenethyl)hydroxylamine

2-(1,4-Dimethoxy-5,6,7,8-tetrahydro-2-naphthyl)ethylamine

2-(1,4-Dimethoxy-5,6,7,8-tetrahydro-2-naphthyl)-1-
methylethylamine

$\alpha$,$\alpha$-Dimethyl-3,4-methylenedioxyphenethylamine

$\alpha$,$\alpha$-Dimethyl-3,4-methylenedioxyphenethyl(methyl)amine

Dimethyl($\alpha$-methyl-3,4-methylenedioxyphenethyl)amine

N-(4-Ethylthio-2,5-dimethoxyphenethyl)hydroxylamine

4-Iodo-2,5-dimethoxy-α-methylphenethyl(dimethyl)amine

2-(1,4-Methano-5,8-dimethoxy-1,2,3,4-tetrahydro-6-naphthyl)
ethylamine

2-(1,4-Methano-5,8-dimethoxy-1,2,3,4-tetrahydro-6-naphthyl)-
1-methylethylamine

2-(5-Methoxy-2,2-dimethyl-2,3-dihydrobenzo[b]furan-6-yl)-1-
methylethylamine

2-Methoxyethyl(α-methyl-3,4-methylenedioxyphenethyl)amine

2-(5-Methoxy-2-methyl-2,3-dihydrobenzo[b]furan-6-yl)-1-
methylethylamine

β-Methoxy-3,4-methylenedioxyphenethylamine

1-(3,4-Methylenedioxybenzyl)butyl(ethyl)amine

1-(3,4-Methylenedioxybenzyl)butyl(methyl)amine

2-(α-Methyl-3,4-methylenedioxyphenethylamino)ethanol

α-Methyl-3,4-methylenedioxyphenethyl(prop-2-ynyl)amine

N-Methyl-N-(α-methyl-3,4-methylenedioxyphenethyl)
hydroxylamine

O-Methyl-N-(α-methyl-3,4-methylenedioxyphenethyl)
hydroxylamine

α-Methyl-4-(methylthio)phenethylamine

β,3,4,5-Tetramethoxyphenethylamine

β,2,5-Trimethoxy-4-methylphenethylamine;][20]

(c)   any compound (not being methoxyphenamine or a compound for
the time being specified in sub-paragraph (a) above) structurally
derived from phenethylamine, an N-alkylphenethylamine,
α-methylphenethylamine, an N-alkyl-α-methyl-phenethylamine,
α-ethylphenethylamine, or an N-alkyl-α-ethylphenethylamine by
substitution in the ring to any extent with alkyl, alkoxy, alkylenedioxy
or halide substituents, whether or not further substituted in the ring
by one or more other univalent substituents.][1]

[(d)  any compound (not being a compound for the time being specified
in sub-paragraph (a) above structurally derived from fentanyl by
modification in any of the following ways, that is to say,

(i)   by replacement of the phenyl portion of the phenethyl group
by any heteromonocycle whether or not further substituted in
the heterocycle;

(ii)  by substitution in the phenethyl group with alkyl, alkenyl,
alkoxy, hydroxy, halogeno, haloalkyl, amino or nitro groups;

(iii) by substitution in the piperidine ring with alkyl or alkenyl
groups;

(iv)  by substitution in the aniline ring with alkyl, alkoxy,
alkylenedioxy, halogeno or haloalkyl groups;

(v)   by substitution at the 4-position of the piperidine ring with any alkoxycarbonyl or alkoxyalkyl or acyloxy group;

(vi)  by replacement of the N -propionyl group by another acyl group;

(e)   any compound (not being a compound for the time being specified in sub-paragraph (a) above) structurally derived from pethidine by modification in any of the following ways, that is to say,

(i)   by replacement of the 1-methyl group by an acyl, alkyl whether or not unsaturated, benzyl or phenethyl group, whether or not further substituted;

(ii)  by substitution in the piperidine ring with alkyl or alkenyl groups or with a propano bridge, whether or not further substituted;

(iii) by substitution in the 4-phenyl ring with alkyl, alkoxy, aryloxy, halogeno or haloalkyl groups;

(iv)  by replacement of the 4-ethoxycarbonyl by any other alkoxycarbonyl or any alkoxyalkyl or acyloxy group;

(v)   by formation of an N -oxide or of a quaternary base.][4]

[(f)  any compound (not being benzyl($\alpha$-methyl-3,4-methylenedioxyphenethyl)amine) structurally derived from mescaline, 4-bromo-2,5-dimethoxy-$\alpha$-methylphenethylamine, 2,5-dimethoxy-$\alpha$,4-dimethylphenethylamine, N -hydroxytenamphetamine, or a compound specified in sub-paragraph (ba) or (c) above, by substitution at the nitrogen atom of the amino group with a benzyl substituent, whether or not substituted in the phenyl ring of the benzyl group to any extent.][21]

**Amendments**

1   Inserted by the Misuse of Drugs Act 1971 (Modification) Order 1977, SI 1977/1243, arts 2, 3.
2   Inserted by the Misuse of Drugs Act 1971 (Modification) Order 1984, SI 1984/859, art 2(1), (2).
3   Repealed by the Misuse of Drugs Act 1971 (Modification) (No 2) Order 2003, SI 2003/3201, art 2(1), (2).
4   Inserted by the Misuse of Drugs Act 1971 (Modification) Order 1986, SI 1986/2230, art 2(1), (2).
5   Inserted by the Misuse of Drugs Act 1971 (Modification) Order 1975, SI 1975/421, art 3.
6   Inserted by the Misuse of Drugs Act 1971 (Modification) Order 2003, SI 2003/1243, art 2(1), (2).
7   Inserted by the Misuse of Drugs Act 1971 (Modification) Order 1973, SI 1973/771, art 2(a).
8   Inserted by the Misuse of Drugs Act 1971 (Modification) Order 1998, SI 1998/750 art 2(1), (2).
9   Inserted by the Drugs Act 2005, s 21.
10  Inserted by the Misuse of Drugs Act 1971 (Amendment) Order 2006, SI 2006/3331, art 2(1).
11  Repealed by the Misuse of Drugs Act 1971 (Modification) Order 1973, SI 1973/771, art 2(a).
12  Inserted by the Misuse of Drugs Act 1971 (Modification) Order 1979, SI 1979/299, art 2.
13  Inserted by the Misuse of Drugs Act 1971 (Modification) Order 1983, SI 1983/765, art 2(a).
14  Inserted by the Misuse of Drugs Act 1971 (Amendment) Order 2011, SI 2011/744, art 2.
15  Inserted by the Misuse of Drugs Act 1971 (Amendment) (No 2) Order 2014, SI 2014/3271, arts 2, 3.
16  Inserted by the Misuse of Drugs Act 1971 (Amendment) Order 2015, SI 2015/215, arts 2, 3.
17  Inserted by the Misuse of Drugs Act 1971 (Amendment) Order 2017, SI 2017/634, arts 2, 3.
18  Inserted by the Misuse of Drugs Act 1971 (Modification) Order 1990, SI 1990/2589, art 2(a).

19 Substituted by the Misuse of Drugs Act 1971 (Amendment) (No 2) Order 2014, SI 2014/3271, arts 2, 4.
20 Inserted by the Misuse of Drugs Act 1971 (Modification) Order 2001, SI 2001/3932, art 2(1), (2).
21 Inserted by the Misuse of Drugs Act 1971 (Ketamine etc.) (Amendment) Order 2014, SI 2014/1106, arts 2, 3.

**2**

Any stereoisomeric form of a substance for the time being specified in paragraph 1 above not being dextromethorphan or dextrorphan.

**3**

Any ester or ether of a substance for the time being specified in paragraph 1 or 2 above [not being a substance for the time being specified in Part II of this Schedule][1].

**Amendments**
1  Inserted by the Misuse of Drugs Act 1971 (Modification) Order 1973, SI 1973/771, art 2(b).

**4**

Any salt of a substance for the time being specified in any of paragraphs 1 to 3 above.

**5**

Any preparation or other product containing a substance or product for the time being specified in any of paragraphs 1 to 4 above.

**6**

Any preparation designed for administration by injection which includes a substance or product for the time being specified in any of paragraphs 1 to 3 of Part II of this Schedule.

## *Part II Class B drugs*

**1**

The following substances and products, namely:

[(a)][1]
Acetyldihydrocodeine.
Amphetamine.
[N–Benzyl-ethylphenidate.][2]
[Cannabinol.
Cannabinol derivatives.
Cannabis and cannabis resin.][3]
…[4]
Codeine.
…[5]
Dihydrocodeine.

Ethylmorphine (3-ethylmorphine).
[Ethylnaphthidate.
Ethylphenidate.][2]
[Glutethimide.][6]
[Isopropylphenidate (IPP or IPPD).][2]
[Ketamine.][7]
[Lefetamine.][6]
[Lisdexamphetamine.][7]
[Mecloqualone.][1]
[Methaqualone.][1]
[Methcathinone][8]
[Methylmorphenate.
Methylnaphthidate (HDMP-28).][2]
[...[9]][10]
...[11]
[α-Methylphenethylhydroxylamine.][12]
Methylphenidate.
[Methylphenobarbitone.][1]
Nicocodine.
[Nicodicodine (6-nicotinoyldihydrocodeine).][13]
Norcodeine.
[Pentazocine.][6]
Phenmetrazine.
Pholcodine.
[Propiram.][13]
[Propylphenidate.][2]
[Zipeprol][8]
[3,4-Dichloroethylphenidate.
3,4-Dichloromethylphenidate (3,4-DCMP).][2]
[2-((Dimethylamino)methyl)-1-(3-hydroxyphenyl)cyclohexanol.][14]
[4-Fluoroethylphenidate.
4-Fluoromethylphenidate.
4-Methylmethylphenidate.][2]

[(aa) Any compound (not being bupropion, cathinone, diethylpropion, pyrovalerone or a compound for the time being specified in sub-paragraph (a) above) structurally derived from 2-amino-1-phenyl-1-propanone by modification in any of the following ways, that is to say,

(i) by substitution in the phenyl ring to any extent with alkyl, alkoxy, alkylenedioxy, haloalkyl or halide substituents, whether or not further substituted in the phenyl ring by one or more other univalent substituents;

(ii) by substitution at the 3-position with an alkyl substituent;

(iii) by substitution at the nitrogen atom with alkyl or dialkyl groups, or by inclusion of the nitrogen atom in a cyclic structure.][10]

[(ab) Any compound structurally derived from 2-aminopropan-1-one by substitution at the 1-position with any monocyclic, or fused-polycyclic ring system (not being a phenyl ring or alkylenedioxyphenyl ring system), whether or not the compound is further modified in any of the following ways, that is to say,

    (i)   by substitution in the ring system to any extent with alkyl, alkoxy, haloalkyl or halide substituents, whether or not further substituted in the ring system by one or more other univalent substituents;

    (ii)  by substitution at the 3-position with an alkyl substituent;

    (iii) by substitution at the 2-amino nitrogen atom with alkyl or dialkyl groups, or by inclusion of the 2-amino nitrogen atom in a cyclic structure.][15]

[(ac) Any compound (not being pipradrol) structurally derived from piperidine, pyrrolidine, azepane, morpholine or pyridine by substitution at a ring carbon atom with a diphenylmethyl group, whether or not the compound is further modified in any of the following ways, that is to say,

    (i)   by substitution in any of the phenyl rings to any extent with alkyl, alkoxy, haloalkyl or halide groups;

    (ii)  by substitution at the methyl carbon atom with an alkyl, hydroxyalkyl or hydroxy group;

    (iii) by substitution at the ring nitrogen atom with an alkyl, alkenyl, haloalkyl or hydroxyalkyl group.][16]

[(b)   any 5,5 disubstituted barbituric acid.][1]

[[(c)

    [2,3–Dihydro–5–methyl–3–(4–morpholinylmethyl)pyrrolo[1, 2, 3–de]–1,4–benzoxazin–6–yl]–1–naphthalenylmethanone.

    [9–Hydroxy–6–methyl–3–[5–phenylpentan–2–yl] oxy–5, 6, 6a, 7, 8, 9, 10, 10a–octahydrophenanthridin–1–yl] acetate.

    [9–Hydroxy–6–methyl–3–[5–phenylpentan–2–yl] oxy–5, 6, 6a, 7, 8, 9, 10, 10a–octahydrophenanthridin–1–yl] acetate.

    9-(Hydroxymethyl)–6, 6–dimethyl–3–(2–methyloctan–2–yl)–6a, 7, 10, 10a–tetrahydrobenzo[c]chromen–1–ol.

    Any compound structurally derived from 3–(1–naphthoyl)indole, 3–(2–naphthoyl) indole, 1 H –indol–3–yl–(1–naphthyl) methane or 1 H –indol-3-yl-(2–naphthyl)methane by substitution at the nitrogen atom of the indole ring by alkyl, haloalkyl, alkenyl, cyanoalkyl, hydroxyalkyl, cycloalkylmethyl, cycloalkylethyl, (N -methylpiperidin-2-yl)methyl or 2–(4–morpholinyl)ethyl, whether or not further substituted in the indole ring to any extent and whether or not substituted in the naphthyl ring to any extent.

Any compound structurally derived from 3–(1–naphthoyl) pyrrole or 3-(2-naphthoyl)pyrrole by substitution at the nitrogen atom of the pyrrole ring by alkyl, haloalkyl, alkenyl, cyanoalkyl, hydroxyalkyl, cycloalkylmethyl, cycloalkylethyl, (N -methylpiperidin-2-yl)methyl or 2–(4–morpholinyl)ethyl, whether or not further substituted in the pyrrole ring to any extent and whether or not substituted in the naphthyl ring to any extent.

Any compound structurally derived from 1–(1–naphthylmethylene) indene or 1-(2-naphthylmethylene)indene by substitution at the 3–position of the indene ring by alkyl, haloalkyl, alkenyl, cyanoalkyl, hydroxyalkyl, cycloalkylmethyl, cycloalkylethyl, (N -methylpiperidin-2-yl)methyl or 2–(4–morpholinyl)ethyl, whether or not further substituted in the indene ring to any extent and whether or not substituted in the naphthyl ring to any extent.

Nabilone.

Any compound structurally derived from 3–phenylacetylindole by substitution at the nitrogen atom of the indole ring by alkyl, haloalkyl, alkenyl, cyanoalkyl, hydroxyalkyl, cycloalkylmethyl, cycloalkylethyl, (N -methylpiperidin-2-yl)methyl or 2–(4–morpholinyl)ethyl, whether or not further substituted in the indole ring to any extent and whether or not substituted in the phenyl ring to any extent.

Any compound structurally derived from 2–(3–hydroxycyclohexyl) phenol by substitution at the 5–position of the phenolic ring by alkyl, alkenyl, cycloalkylmethyl, cycloalkylethyl or 2–(4–morpholinyl)ethyl, whether or not further substituted in the cyclohexyl ring to any extent.

Any compound structurally derived from 3-benzoylindole by substitution at the nitrogen atom of the indole ring by alkyl, haloalkyl, alkenyl, cyanoalkyl, hydroxyalkyl, cycloalkylmethyl, cycloalkylethyl, (N -methylpiperidin-2-yl)methyl or 2–(4–morpholinyl)ethyl, whether or not further substituted in the indole ring to any extent and whether or not substituted in the phenyl ring to any extent.

Any compound structurally derived from 3-(1-adamantoyl) indole or 3-(2-adamantoyl)indole by substitution at the nitrogen atom of the indole ring by alkyl, haloalkyl, alkenyl, cyanoalkyl, hydroxyalkyl, cycloalkylmethyl, cycloalkylethyl, (N -methylpiperidin-2-yl)methyl or 2–(4–morpholinyl)ethyl, whether or not further substituted in the indole ring to any extent and whether or not substituted in the adamantyl ring to any extent.

Any compound structurally derived from
3-(2,2,3,3-tetramethylcyclopropylcarbonyl)indole by substitution at the nitrogen atom of the indole ring by alkyl, haloalkyl, alkenyl, cyanoalkyl, hydroxyalkyl, cycloalkylmethyl, cycloalkylethyl, (N -methylpiperidin-2-yl)methyl or 2–(4– morpholinyl)ethyl, whether or not further substituted in the indole ring to any extent.

[(ca) any compound (not being clonitazene, etonitazene, acemetacin, atorvastatin, bazedoxifene, indometacin, losartan, olmesartan, proglumetacin, telmisartan, viminol, zafirlukast or a compound for the time being specified in sub-paragraph (c) above) structurally related to 1-pentyl-3-(1-naphthoyl)indole (JWH-018), in that the four substructures, that is to say the indole ring, the pentyl substituent, the methanone linking group and the naphthyl ring, are linked together in a similar manner, whether or not any of the sub-structures have been modified, and whether or not substituted in any of the linked sub-structures with one or more univalent substituents and, where any of the sub-structures have been modified, the modifications of the sub-structures are limited to any of the following, that is to say—

(i)    replacement of the indole ring with indane, indene, indazole, pyrrole, pyrazole, imidazole, benzimidazole, pyrrolo[2,3-b] pyridine, pyrrolo[3,2-c]pyridine or pyrazolo[3,4-b]pyridine;

(ii)   replacement of the pentyl substituent with alkyl, alkenyl, benzyl, cycloalkylmethyl, cycloalkylethyl, (N -methylpiperidin-2-yl) methyl, 2-(4-morpholinyl)ethyl or (tetrahydropyran-4-yl) methyl;

(iii)  replacement of the methanone linking group with an ethanone, carboxamide, carboxylate, methylene bridge or methine group;

(iv)   replacement of the 1-naphthyl ring with 2-naphthyl, phenyl, benzyl, adamantyl, cycloalkyl, cycloalkylmethyl, cycloalkylethyl, bicyclo[2.2.1]heptanyl, 1,2,3,4-tetrahydronaphthyl, quinolinyl, isoquinolinyl, 1-amino-1-oxopropan-2-yl, 1-hydroxy-1-oxopropan-2-yl, piperidinyl, morpholinyl, pyrrolidinyl, tetrahydropyranyl or piperazinyl;][17]

(d)   1-Phenylcyclohexylamine or any compound (not being ketamine, tiletamine or a compound for the time being specified in paragraph 1(a) of Part 1 of this Schedule) structurally derived from 1-phenylcyclohexylamine or 2-amino-2-phenylcyclohexanone by modification in any of the following ways, that is to say,

(i)     by substitution at the nitrogen atom to any extent by alkyl, alkenyl or hydroxyalkyl groups, or replacement of the amino group with a 1-piperidyl, 1-pyrrolidyl or 1-azepyl group, whether or not the nitrogen containing ring is further substituted by one or more alkyl groups;

(ii)    by substitution in the phenyl ring to any extent by amino, alkyl, hydroxy, alkoxy or halide substituents, whether or not further substituted in the phenyl ring to any extent;

(iii)   by substitution in the cyclohexyl or cyclohexanone ring by one or more alkyl substituents;

(iv)    by replacement of the phenyl ring with a thienyl ring.][18]][19]

[(e)    Any compound (not being a compound for the time being specified in paragraph 1(ba) of Part 1 of this Schedule) structurally derived from 1-benzofuran, 2,3-dihydro-1-benzofuran, 1H-indole, indoline, 1H-indene, or indane by substitution in the 6-membered ring with a 2-ethylamino substituent whether or not further substituted in the ring system to any extent with alkyl, alkoxy, halide or haloalkyl substituents and whether or not substituted in the ethylamino side-chain with one or more alkyl substituents.][7]

---

**Amendments**

1   Inserted by the Misuse of Drugs Act 1971 (Modification) Order 1984, SI 1984/859, art 2(1), (3)
2   Inserted by the Misuse of Drugs Act 1971 (Amendment) Order 2017, SI 2017/634, arts 2, 4(a).
3   Inserted by the Misuse of Drugs Act 1971 (Amendment) Order 2008, SI 2008/3130, art 2(1), (2)(a).
4   Repealed by the Misuse of Drugs Act 1971 (Modification) (No 2) Order 2003, SI 2003/3201, art 2(1), (3).
5   Repealed by the Misuse of Drugs Act 1971 (Modification) Order 1985, SI 1985/1995, art 2(1), (2)(a).
6   Inserted by the Misuse of Drugs Act 1971 (Modification) Order 1985, SI 1985/1995, art 2(1), (2)(b), (c).
7   Inserted by the Misuse of Drugs Act 1971 (Ketamine etc.) (Amendment) Order 2014, SI 2014/1106, arts 2, 4.
8   Inserted by the Misuse of Drugs Act 1971 (Modification) Order 1998, SI 1998/750 art 2(1), (3)(a).
9   Repealed by the Misuse of Drugs Act 1971 (Amendment) Order 2011, SI 2011/744, art 3.
10  Inserted by the Misuse of Drugs Act 1971 (Amendment) Order 2010, SI 2010/1207, art 2.
11  Repealed by the Misuse of Drugs Act 1971 (Amendment) Order 2006, SI 2006/3331, art 2(2).
12  Substituted by the Misuse of Drugs Act 1971 (Modification) Order 2001, SI 2001/3932, art 2(1), (3).
13  Inserted by the Misuse of Drugs Act 1971 (Modification) Order 1973, SI 1973/771, art 2(c).
14  Inserted by the Misuse of Drugs Act 1971 (Amendment) Order 2013, SI 2013/239, arts 2, 3.
15  Inserted by the Misuse of Drugs Act 1971 (Amendment No 2) Order 2010, SI 2010/1833, art 2.
16  Inserted by the Misuse of Drugs Act 1971 (Amendment) Order 2012, SI 2012/1390, art 2(a).
17  Inserted by the Misuse of Drugs Act 1971 (Amendment) Order 2016, SI 2016/1109, arts 2, 3(a).
18  Substituted by the Misuse of Drugs Act 1971 (Amendment) Order 2013, SI 2013/239, arts 2, 4.
19  Inserted by the Misuse of Drugs Act 1971 (Amendment) Order 2009, SI 2009/3209, art 2(1), (2)(a).

**2**

Any stereoisomeric form of a substance for the time being specified in paragraph 1 of this Part of this Schedule.

**[2A**

Any ester or ether of cannabinol or of a cannabinol derivative [or of a substance for the time being specified in [paragraph 1(ac), [(c), (ca)]¹ or (d)]² of this Part of this Schedule]³.]⁴

**Amendments**

1   Substituted by the Misuse of Drugs Act 1971 (Amendment) Order 2016, SI 2016/1109, arts 2, 3(b).
2   Substituted by the Misuse of Drugs Act 1971 (Amendment) Order 2013, SI 2013/239, arts 2, 5.
3   Inserted by the Misuse of Drugs Act 1971 (Amendment) Order 2009, SI 2009/3209, art 2(1), (2)(b).
4   Inserted by the Misuse of Drugs Act 1971 (Amendment) Order 2008, SI 2008/3130, art 2(1), (2)(b).

**3**

Any salt of a substance for the time being specified in paragraph 1, [2 or 2A]¹ of this Part of this Schedule.

**Amendments**

1   Substituted by the Misuse of Drugs Act 1971 (Amendment) Order 2008, SI 2008/3130, art 2(1), (2)(c).

**4**

Any preparation or other product containing a substance or product for the time being specified in any of paragraphs 1 to 3 of this Part of this Schedule, not being a preparation falling within paragraph 6 of Part I of this Schedule.

## Part III Class C drugs

**1**

The following substances, namely:

[(a)]¹

[Adinazolam (1-(8-Chloro-6-phenyl-4 H -[1,2,4]triazolo[4,3-a][1,4]benzodiazepin-1-yl)-N,Ndimethylmethanamine).]²
[Alprazolam.]³
[Amineptine]⁴
[Aminorex]⁵
Benzphetamine.
[Bromazepam.]³
[Bromazolam (8-bromo-1-methyl-6-phenyl-4 H -[1,2,4]triazolo[4,3-a][1,4]benzodiazepine).]²
[7-bromo-5-(2-chlorophenyl)-1,3-dihydro-2 H -1,4-benzodiazepin-2-one.]⁶
[Brotizolam]⁵
Buprenorphine
[Camazepam.]³
...⁷
Cathine.
Cathinone.
[4'-Chlorodiazepam (7-Chloro-5-(4-chlorophenyl)-1-methyl-1,3-dihydro-2 H-1,4-benzodiazepin-2-one).]²

[Chlordiazepoxide.][3]
Chlorphentermine.
[Clobazam.][3]
[Clonazepam.][3]
[Clorazepic acid.][3]
[Clonazolam (6-(2-Chlorophenyl)-1-methyl-8-nitro-4 H -[1,2,4]
    triazolo[4,3-a][1,4] benzodiazepine).][2]
[Clotiazepam.][3]
[Cloxazolam.][3]
[Delorazepam.][3]
[Deschloroetizolam (2-Ethyl-9-methyl-4-
    phenyl-6 H -thieno[3,2-f][1,2,4]triazolo[4,3-a][1,4]
    diazepine).][2]
Dextropropoxyphene.
[Diazepam.][3]
[Diclazepam (7-Chloro-5-(2-chlorophenyl)-1-methyl-1,3-
    dihydro-2 H-1,4-benzodiazepin-2-one).][2]
Diethylpropion.
[Estazolam.][3]
[Ethchlorvynol.][3]
[Ethinamate.][3]
[Ethyl loflazepate.][3]
[Etizolam.][2]
Fencamfamin.
Fenethylline.
Fenproporex.
[Flubromazepam (7-Bromo-5-(2-fluorophenyl)-1,3-
    dihydro-2 H -1,4-benzodiazepin-2-one).][2]
[Flubromazolam (8-Bromo-6-(2-fluorophenyl)-1-
    methyl-4 H -[1,2,4]triazolo[4,3-a][1,4] benzodiazepine).][2]
[Fludiazepam.][3]
[Flunitrazepam.][3]
[Flurazepam.][3]
[Fonazepam (5-(2-Fluorophenyl)-7-nitro-1,3-
    dihydro-2 H -1,4-benzodiazepin-2-one).][2]
[Gamma-butyrolactone.][8]
[Halazepam.][3]
[Haloxazolam.][3]
[4-Hydroxy-n-butyric acid.][9]
[3-Hydroxyphenazepam (7-Bromo-5-(2-chlorophenyl)-3-
    hydroxy-1,3-dihydro-2 H -1,4-benzodiazepin-2-one).][2]
[...][10]
[Ketazolam.][3]
[Khat.][11]
[Loprazolam.][3]
[Lorazepam.][3]

[Lormetazepam.][3]
[Mazindol.][3]
[Meclonazepam (5-(2-Chlorophenyl)-3-methyl-7-nitro-1,3-
dihydro-2 H -1,4-benzodiazepin-2-one).][2]
[Medazepam.][3]
Mefenorex.
Mephentermine.
[Meprobamate.][3]
[Mesocarb][5]
[Methyprylone.][3]
[Metizolam (4-(2-Chlorophenyl)-2-ethyl-6 H -thieno[3,2-f][1,2,4]
triazolo[4,3-a][1,4]diazepine).][2]
Midazolam.
[Nifoxipam (5-(2-Fluorophenyl)-3-hydroxy-7-nitro-1,3-
dihydro-2 H -1,4-benzodiazepin-2-one).][2]
[Nimetazepam.][3]
[Nitrazepam.][3]
[Nitrazolam (1-Methyl-8-nitro-6-phenyl-4 H -[1,2,4]triazolo[4,3-a]
[1,4]benzodiazepine).][2]
[Nordazepam.][3]
[Oxazepam.][3]
[Oxazolam.][3]
Pemoline
Phendimetrazine.
[Phentermine.][3]
[Pinazepam.][3]
... [12]
[Prazepam.][3]
[Pyrazolam (8-Bromo-1-methyl-6-(2-pyridinyl)-4 H -[1,2,4]
triazolo[4,3-a][1,4]benzodiazepine).][2]
Pyrovalerone.
[Temazepam.][3]
[Tetrazepam.][3]
[Tramadol.][13]
[Triazolam.][3]
N-Ethylamphetamine.
[Zaleplon.][13]
[Zolpidem.][9]
[Zopiclone.][13]

[(b)

[5α-Androstane-3,17-diol.][8]
[Androst-4-ene-3,17-diol.][8]
[1-Androstenediol.][8]
[1-Androstenedione.][8]
[4-Androstene-3, 17-dione.][9]

[5-Androstenedione.][8]
[5-Androstene-3, 17-diol.][9]
Atamestane.
Bolandiol.
Bolasterone.
Bolazine.
Boldenone.
[Boldione.][8]
Bolenol.
Bolmantalate.
[1,4-Butanediol.][8]
Calusterone.
4-Chloromethandienone.
Clostebol.
[Danazol.][8]
[Desoxymethyltestosterone.][8]
[Dienedione (estra-4, 9-diene-3,17-dione).][14]
Drostanolone.
Enestebol.
Epitiostanol.
Ethyloestrenol.
Fluoxymesterone.
Formebolone.
Furazabol.
[Gestrinone.][8]
[3-Hydroxy-5$\alpha$-androstan-17-one.][8]
Mebolazine.
Mepitiostane.
Mesabolone.
Mestanolone.
Mesterolone.
Methandienone.
Methandriol.
Methenolone.
Methyltestosterone.
Metribolone.
Mibolerone.
Nandrolone.
[19-Norandrostenedione.][8]
[19-Nor-4-Androstene-3, 17-dione.][9]
[19-Nor-5-Androstene-13, 17-diol.][9]
[19-Norandrosterone.][8]
Norboletone.
Norclostebol.
Norethandrolone.
[19-Noretiocholanolone.][8]

[Oripavine.][8]
Ovandrotone.
Oxabolone.
Oxandrolone.
Oxymesterone.
Oxymetholone.
[Pipradrol.][6]
Prasterone.
Propetandrol.
[Prostanozol.][8]
Quinbolone.
Roxibolone.
Silandrone.
Stanolone.
Stanozolol.
Stenbolone.
Testosterone.
[Tetrahydrogestrinone.][8]
Thiomesterone.
Trenbolone.

(c)   any compound (not being Trilostane or a compound for the time being specified in sub-paragraph (b) above) structurally derived from 17-hydroxyandrostan-3-one or from 17-hydroxyestran-3-one by modification in any of the following ways, that is to say,

  (i)   by further substitution at position 17 by a methyl or ethyl group;

  (ii)   by substitution to any extent at one or more of positions 1, 2, 4, 6, 7, 9, 11 or 16, but at no other position;

  (iii)   by unsaturation in the carbocyclic ring system to any extent, provided that there are no more than two ethylenic bonds in any one carbocyclic ring;

  (iv)   by fusion of ring A with a heterocyclic system;

[(ca)   1-benzylpiperazine or any compound structurally derived from 1-benzylpiperazine or 1-phenylpiperazine by modification in any of the following ways—

  (i)   by substitution at the second nitrogen atom of the piperazine ring with alkyl, benzyl, haloalkyl or phenyl groups;

  (ii)   by substitution in the aromatic ring to any extent with alkyl, alkoxy, alkylenedioxy, halide or haloalkyl groups.][8]

(d)   any substance which is an ester or ether (or, where more than one hydroxyl function is available, both an ester and an ether) of a substance specified in sub-paragraph (b) or described in sub-paragraph (c) above ...[7];

(e)

Chorionic Gonadotrophin (HCG).

Clenbuterol.

Non–human chorionic gonadotrophin.

Somatotropin.

Somatrem.

Somatropin.

[Zeranol.]⁸

[Zilpaterol.]⁸]¹

**Amendments**

1   Inserted by the Misuse of Drugs Act 1971 (Modification) Order 1996, SI 1996/1300, art 2(1), (2).
2   Inserted by the Misuse of Drugs Act 1971 (Amendment) Order 2017, SI 2017/634, arts 2, 5.
3   Inserted by the Misuse of Drugs Act 1971 (Modification) Order 1985, SI 1985/1995, art 2(1), (3).
4   Inserted by the Misuse of Drugs Act 1971 (Amendment) Order 2011, SI 2011/744, art 4.
5   Inserted by the Misuse of Drugs Act 1971 (Modification) Order 1998, SI 1998/750 art 2(1), (4).
6   Inserted by the Misuse of Drugs Act 1971 (Amendment) Order 2012, SI 2012/1390, art 3(a)(ii), (b).
7   Repealed by the Misuse of Drugs Act 1971 (Amendment) Order 2008, SI 2008/3130, art 2(1), (3).
8   Inserted by the Misuse of Drugs Act 1971 (Amendment) Order 2009, SI 2009/3209, art 2(1), (3).
9   Entry inserted by the Misuse of Drugs Act 1971 (Modification) Order 2003, SI 2003/1243, art 2(1), (3), (4).
10  Repealed by the Misuse of Drugs Act 1971 (Ketamine etc.) (Amendment) Order 2014, SI 2014/1106, arts 2, 5(a).
11  Inserted by the Misuse of Drugs Act 1971 (Amendment) Order 2014, SI 2014/1352, arts 2, 3.
12  Repealed by the Misuse of Drugs Act 1971 (Amendment) Order 2012, SI 2012/1390, art 3(a)(i).
13  Inserted by the Misuse of Drugs Act 1971 (Ketamine etc.) (Amendment) Order 2014, SI 2014/1106, arts 2, 5(b), (c), (d).
14  Inserted by the Misuse of Drugs Act 1971 (Amendment) Order 2016, SI 2016/1109, arts 2, 4.

**2**

Any stereoisomeric form of a substance for the time being specified in paragraph 1 of this Part of this Schedule [not being phenylpropanolamine]¹.

**Amendments**

1   Inserted by the Misuse of Drugs Act 1971 (Modification) Order 1986, SI 1986/2230, art 2(1), (4)

**3**

Any salt of a substance for the time being specified in paragraph 1 or 2 of this Part of this Schedule.

**4**

Any preparation or other product containing a substance for the time being specified in any of paragraphs 1 to 3 of this Part of this Schedule.

## Part IV Meaning of certain expressions used in this Schedule

For the purposes of this Schedule the following expressions (which are not among those defined in section 37(1) of this Act) have the meanings hereby assigned to them respectively, that is to say—

'cannabinol derivatives' means the following substances, except where contained in cannabis or cannabis resin, namely tetrahydro derivatives of cannabinol and 3-alkyl homologues of cannabinol or of its tetrahydro derivatives;

'coca leaf' means the leaf of any plant of the genus Erythroxylon from whose leaves cocaine can be extracted either directly or by chemical transformation;

'concentrate of poppy-straw' means the material produced when poppy-straw has entered into a process for the concentration of its alkaloids;

['khat' means the leaves, stems or shoots of the plant of the species 'Catha edulis';][1]

'medicinal opium' means raw opium which has undergone the process necessary to adapt it for medicinal use in accordance with the requirements of the British Pharmacopoeia, whether it is in the form of powder or is granulated or is in any other form, and whether it is or is not mixed with neutral substances;

'opium poppy' means the plant of the species Papaver somniferum L;

'poppy straw' means all parts, except the seeds, of the opium poppy, after mowing;

'raw opium' includes powdered or granulated opium but does not include medicinal opium.

**Amendments**
1   Inserted by the Misuse of Drugs Act 1971 (Amendment) Order 2014, SI 2014/1352, arts 2, 4.

# Appendix B
# Psychoactive Substances Act 2016, sections 4 to 11, 36 to 48

*Offences*

### 4    Producing a psychoactive substance

(1)    A person commits an offence if—

    (a)    the person intentionally produces a psychoactive substance,

    (b)    the person knows or suspects that the substance is a psychoactive substance, and

    (c)    the person—

        (i)    intends to consume the psychoactive substance for its psychoactive effects, or

        (ii)    knows, or is reckless as to whether, the psychoactive substance is likely to be consumed by some other person for its psychoactive effects.

(2)    This section is subject to section 11 (exceptions to offences).

### 5    Supplying, or offering to supply, a psychoactive substance

(1)    A person commits an offence if—

    (a)    the person intentionally supplies a substance to another person,

    (b)    the substance is a psychoactive substance,

    (c)    the person knows or suspects, or ought to know or suspect, that the substance is a psychoactive substance, and

    (d)    the person knows, or is reckless as to whether, the psychoactive substance is likely to be consumed by the person to whom it is supplied, or by some other person, for its psychoactive effects.

(2)    A person ('P') commits an offence if—

    (a)    P offers to supply a psychoactive substance to another person ('R'), and

(b)    P knows or is reckless as to whether R, or some other person, would, if P supplied a substance to R in accordance with the offer, be likely to consume the substance for its psychoactive effects.

(3)    For the purposes of subsection (2)(b), the reference to a substance's psychoactive effects includes a reference to the psychoactive effects which the substance would have if it were the substance which P had offered to supply to R.

(4)    This section is subject to section 11 (exceptions to offences).

**6    Aggravation of offence under section 5**

(1)    This section applies if—

(a)    a court is considering the seriousness of an offence under section 5, and

(b)    at the time the offence was committed the offender was aged 18 or over.

(2)    If condition A, B or C is met the court—

(a)    must treat the fact that the condition is met as an aggravating factor (that is to say, a factor that increases the seriousness of the offence), and

(b)    must state in open court that the offence is so aggravated.

(3)    Condition A is that the offence was committed on or in the vicinity of school premises at a relevant time.

(4)    For the purposes of subsection (3) a 'relevant time' is—

(a)    any time when the school premises are in use by persons under the age of 18;

(b)    one hour before the start and one hour after the end of any such time.

(5)    In this section—

'school premises' means land used for the purposes of a school, other than any land occupied solely as a dwelling by a person employed at the school;

'school' has the same meaning—

(a)    in England and Wales, as in section 4 of the Education Act 1996;

(b)    in Scotland, as in section 135(1) of the Education (Scotland) Act 1980;

(c)    in Northern Ireland, as in Article 2(2) of the Education and Libraries (Northern Ireland) Order 1986 (S.I. 1986/594 (N.I. 3)).

(6)     Condition B is that in connection with the commission of the offence the offender used a courier who, at the time the offence was committed, was under the age of 18.

(7)     For the purposes of subsection (6) a person ('P') uses a courier in connection with an offence under section 5 if P causes or permits another person (the courier)—

    (a)     to deliver a substance to a third person, or

    (b)     to deliver a drug-related consideration to P or a third person.

(8)     A drug-related consideration is a consideration of any description which—

    (a)     is obtained in connection with the supply of a psychoactive substance, or

    (b)     is intended to be used in connection with obtaining a psychoactive substance.

(9)     Condition C is that the offence was committed in a custodial institution.

(10)   In this section—

'custodial institution' means any of the following—

    (a)     a prison;

    (b)     a young offender institution, secure training centre, secure college, young offenders institution, young offenders centre, juvenile justice centre or remand centre;

    (c)     a removal centre, a short-term holding facility or pre-departure accommodation;

    (d)     service custody premises;

'removal centre', 'short-term holding facility' and 'pre-departure accommodation' have the meaning given by section 147 of the Immigration and Asylum Act 1999;

'service custody premises' has the meaning given by section 300(7) of the Armed Forces Act 2006.

## 7     Possession of psychoactive substance with intent to supply

(1)     A person commits an offence if—

    (a)     the person is in possession of a psychoactive substance,

    (b)     the person knows or suspects that the substance is a psychoactive substance, and

    (c)     the person intends to supply the psychoactive substance to another person for its consumption, whether by any person to whom it is supplied or by some other person, for its psychoactive effects.

(2)     This section is subject to section 11 (exceptions to offences).

**8      Importing or exporting a psychoactive substance**

(1)     A person commits an offence if—

    (a)     the person intentionally imports a substance,

    (b)     the substance is a psychoactive substance,

    (c)     the person knows or suspects, or ought to know or suspect, that the substance is a psychoactive substance, and

    (d)     the person—

        (i)      intends to consume the psychoactive substance for its psychoactive effects, or

        (ii)     knows, or is reckless as to whether, the psychoactive substance is likely to be consumed by some other person for its psychoactive effects.

(2)     A person commits an offence if—

    (a)     the person intentionally exports a substance,

    (b)     the substance is a psychoactive substance,

    (c)     the person knows or suspects, or ought to know or suspect, that the substance is a psychoactive substance, and

    (d)     the person—

        (i)      intends to consume the psychoactive substance for its psychoactive effects, or

        (ii)     knows, or is reckless as to whether, the psychoactive substance is likely to be consumed by some other person for its psychoactive effects.

(3)     In a case where a person imports or exports a controlled drug suspecting it to be a psychoactive substance, the person is to be treated for the purposes of this section as if the person had imported or exported a psychoactive substance suspecting it to be such a substance.

       In this subsection 'controlled drug' has the same meaning as in the Misuse of Drugs Act 1971.

(4)     Section 5 of the Customs and Excise Management Act 1979 (time of importation, exportation, etc) applies for the purposes of this section as it applies for the purposes of that Act.

(5)     This section is subject to section 11 (exceptions to offences).

**9      Possession of a psychoactive substance in a custodial institution**

(1)     A person commits an offence if—

(a) the person is in possession of a psychoactive substance in a custodial institution,

(b) the person knows or suspects that the substance is a psychoactive substance, and

(c) the person intends to consume the psychoactive substance for its psychoactive effects.

(2) In this section 'custodial institution' has the same meaning as in section 6.

(3) This section is subject to section 11 (exceptions to offences).

## 10 Penalties

(1) A person guilty of an offence under any of sections 4 to 8 is liable—

    (a) on summary conviction in England and Wales—

        (i) to imprisonment for a term not exceeding 12 months (or 6 months, if the offence was committed before the commencement of section 154(1) of the Criminal Justice Act 2003), or

        (ii) to a fine,

    or both;

    (b) on summary conviction in Scotland—

        (i) to imprisonment for a term not exceeding 12 months, or

        (ii) to a fine not exceeding the statutory maximum,

    or both;

    (c) on summary conviction in Northern Ireland—

        (i) to imprisonment for a term not exceeding 6 months, or

        (ii) to a fine not exceeding the statutory maximum,

    or both;

    (d) on conviction on indictment, to imprisonment for a term not exceeding 7 years or a fine, or both.

(2) A person guilty of an offence under section 9 is liable—

    (a) on summary conviction in England and Wales—

        (i) to imprisonment for a term not exceeding 12 months (or 6 months, if the offence was committed before the commencement of section 154(1) of the Criminal Justice Act 2003), or

        (ii) to a fine,

    or both;

(b)　on summary conviction in Scotland—

    (i)　to imprisonment for a term not exceeding 12 months, or

    (ii)　to a fine not exceeding the statutory maximum,

or both;

(c)　on summary conviction in Northern Ireland—

    (i)　to imprisonment for a term not exceeding 6 months, or

    (ii)　to a fine not exceeding the statutory maximum,

or both;

(d)　on conviction on indictment, to imprisonment for a term not exceeding 2 years or a fine, or both.

## 11　Exceptions to offences

(1)　It is not an offence under this Act for a person to carry on any activity listed in subsection (3) if, in the circumstances in which it is carried on by that person, the activity is an exempted activity.

(2)　In this section 'exempted activity' means an activity listed in Schedule 2.

(3)　The activities referred to in subsection (1) are—

(a)　producing a psychoactive substance;

(b)　supplying such a substance;

(c)　offering to supply such a substance;

(d)　possessing such a substance with intent to supply it;

(e)　importing or exporting such a substance;

(f)　possessing such a substance in a custodial institution (within the meaning of section 9).

(4)　The Secretary of State may by regulations amend Schedule 2 in order to—

(a)　add or vary any description of activity;

(b)　remove any description of activity added under paragraph (a).

(5)　Before making any regulations under this section the Secretary of State must consult—

(a)　the Advisory Council on the Misuse of Drugs, and

(b)　such other persons as the Secretary of State considers appropriate.

(6)　The power to make regulations under this section is exercisable by statutory instrument.

(7)     A statutory instrument containing regulations under this section may not be made unless a draft of the instrument has been laid before, and approved by a resolution of, each House of Parliament.

*Powers of entry, search and seizure*

### 36   Power to stop and search persons

(1)     This section applies where a police or customs officer has reasonable grounds to suspect that a person has committed, or is likely to commit, an offence under any of sections 4 to 9 or section 26.

(2)     The officer may—

   (a)     search the person for relevant evidence, and

   (b)     stop and detain the person for the purposes of the search.

(3)     The powers conferred by this section may be exercised in any place to which the officer lawfully has access (whether or not it is a place to which the public has access).

(4)     In this Act—

'police or customs officer' means—

   (a)     a constable,

   (b)     a general customs official, or

   (c)     a designated NCA officer authorised by the Director General of the National Crime Agency (whether generally or specifically) to exercise the powers of a police or customs officer under this Act;

'relevant evidence' means evidence that an offence has been committed under any of sections 4 to 9 or section 26.

### 37   Power to enter and search vehicles

(1)     This section applies where—

   (a)     a police or customs officer has reasonable grounds to suspect that there is relevant evidence in a vehicle, and

   (b)     the vehicle is not a dwelling.

(2)     The officer may at any time—

   (a)     enter the vehicle and search it for relevant evidence;

   (b)     stop and detain the vehicle for the purposes of entering and searching it.

(3)   Where—

    (a)   a police or customs officer has stopped a vehicle under this section, and

    (b)   the officer considers that it would be impracticable to search the vehicle in the place where it has stopped,

the officer may require the vehicle to be taken to such place as the officer directs to enable the vehicle to be searched.

(4)   A police or customs officer may require—

    (a)   any person travelling in a vehicle, or

    (b)   the registered keeper of a vehicle,

to afford such facilities and assistance with respect to matters under that person's control as the officer considers would facilitate the exercise of any power conferred by this section.

(5)   The powers conferred by this section may be exercised in any place to which the officer lawfully has access (whether or not it is a place to which the public has access).

(6)   In this section 'vehicle' does not include any vessel or aircraft.

(7)   For provision conferring additional powers to enter and search vehicles, see section 39.

**38   Power to board and search vessels or aircraft**

(1)   This section applies where—

    (a)   a police or customs officer has reasonable grounds to believe that there is relevant evidence in or on any vessel or aircraft, and

    (b)   the vessel or aircraft is not a dwelling.

(2)   The officer may at any time—

    (a)   board the vessel or aircraft, and

    (b)   search it for relevant evidence.

(3)   For the purposes of exercising the power conferred by subsection (2), the officer may require a vessel or aircraft—

    (a)   to stop, or

    (b)   to do anything else that will facilitate the boarding of that or any other vessel or aircraft.

(4)   A police or customs officer who has boarded a vessel or aircraft may, for the purposes of disembarking from the vessel or aircraft, require that or any other vessel or aircraft—

(a)    to stop, or

(b)    to do anything else that will enable the officer to disembark from the vessel or aircraft.

(5)    A police or customs officer may require any person on board a vessel or aircraft to afford such facilities and assistance with respect to matters under that person's control as the officer considers would facilitate the exercise of any power conferred by this section.

(6)    For provision conferring additional powers to enter and search vessels and aircraft, see section 39.

### 39    Power to enter and search premises

(1)    Where a justice is satisfied that the requirements in subsection (4) are met in relation to any premises, the justice may issue a warrant (a 'search warrant') authorising a relevant enforcement officer—

(a)    to enter the premises, and

(b)    to search them for relevant evidence.

(2)    A search warrant may be issued only on the application of—

(a)    a relevant enforcement officer, in England and Wales or Northern Ireland;

(b)    a relevant enforcement officer or a procurator fiscal, in Scotland.

(3)    A search warrant may be either—

(a)    a warrant that relates only to premises specified in the warrant (a 'specific-premises warrant'), or

(b)    in the case of a warrant issued in England and Wales or Northern Ireland, a warrant that relates to any premises occupied or controlled by a person specified in the warrant (an 'all-premises warrant').

(4)    The requirements of this subsection are met in relation to premises if there are reasonable grounds to suspect that—

(a)    there are items on the premises that are relevant evidence, and

(b)    in a case where the premises are specified in the application, any of the conditions in subsection (5) is met.

(5)    The conditions referred to in subsection (4)(b) are—

(a)    that it is not practicable to communicate with any person entitled to grant entry to the premises;

(b)    that it is not practicable to communicate with any person entitled to grant access to the items;

(c)   that entry to the premises is unlikely to be granted unless a warrant is produced;

(d)   that the purpose of entry may be frustrated or seriously prejudiced unless a relevant enforcement officer arriving at the premises can secure immediate entry to them.

(6)   In this Act 'relevant enforcement officer' means—

(a)   a police or customs officer (see section 36(4)), or

(b)   an officer of a local authority.

## 40   Further provision about search warrants

(1)   An application for a search warrant may be made without notice being given to persons who might be affected by the warrant.

(2)   The application must be supported—

(a)   in England and Wales, by an information in writing;

(b)   in Scotland, by evidence on oath;

(c)   in Northern Ireland, by a complaint on oath.

(3)   A person applying for a search warrant must answer on oath any question that the justice hearing the application asks the person.

In the case of an application made by a procurator fiscal, that requirement may be met by a relevant enforcement officer.

(4)   A search warrant may be executed by any relevant enforcement officer.

(5)   A search warrant may authorise persons to accompany any relevant enforcement officer who is executing it.

(6)   A person authorised under subsection (5) to accompany a relevant enforcement officer may exercise any power conferred by sections 39 to 45 which the officer may exercise as a result of the warrant.

But the person may exercise such a power only in the company of, and under the supervision of, a relevant enforcement officer.

(7)   Schedule 3 contains further provision about—

(a)   applications for search warrants made in England and Wales or Northern Ireland, and

(b)   search warrants issued in England and Wales or Northern Ireland.

(8)   An entry on or search of premises under a search warrant issued in England and Wales or Northern Ireland is unlawful unless it complies with the provisions of Part 3 of that Schedule (execution of search warrants).

**41  Powers of examination, etc**

(1)  This section applies where a relevant enforcement officer is exercising a power of search conferred by section 37, 38 or 39 in relation to any premises.

(2)  The officer may examine anything that is in or on the premises.

(3)  The officer may carry out any measurement or test of anything which the officer has power under this section to examine.

(4)  The power conferred by subsection (3) includes power to take a sample from any live plant.

(5)  For the purpose of exercising—

(a)  a power of search conferred by section 37, 38 or 39, or

(b)  any power conferred by this section,

the officer may, so far as is reasonably necessary for that purpose, break open any container or other locked thing.

(6)  The officer may require any person in or on the premises to afford such facilities and assistance with respect to matters under that person's control as the officer considers would facilitate the exercise of—

(a)  a power of search conferred by section 37, 38 or 39, or

(b)  any power conferred by this section.

(7)  Nothing in this section confers any power to search a person.

**42  Power to require production of documents, etc**

(1)  This section applies where a relevant enforcement officer is exercising a power of search conferred by section 37, 38 or 39 in relation to any premises.

(2)  The officer may require any person in or on the premises to produce any document or record that is in the person's possession or control.

(3)  A reference in this section to the production of a document includes a reference to the production of—

(a)  a hard copy of information recorded otherwise than in hard copy form, or

(b)  information in a form from which a hard copy can be readily obtained.

(4)  For the purposes of this section—

(a)  information is recorded in hard copy form if it is recorded in a paper copy or similar form capable of being read (and references to hard copy have a corresponding meaning);

(b)    information can be read only if—

    (i)    it can be read with the naked eye, or

    (ii)   to the extent that it consists of images (for example photographs, pictures, maps, plans or drawings), it can be seen with the naked eye.

## 43    Powers of seizure, etc

(1)    A police or customs officer who is exercising the power of search conferred by section 36 may seize and detain anything found in the course of the search.

(2)    This subsection applies where a relevant enforcement officer—

(a)    is exercising a power of search conferred by section 37, 38 or 39 in relation to any premises, or

(b)    is otherwise lawfully on premises.

(3)    Where subsection (2) applies, the officer may—

(a)    seize and detain or remove any item found on the premises;

(b)    take copies of or extracts from any document or record found on the premises.

(4)    A relevant enforcement officer to whom any document or record has been produced in accordance with a requirement imposed under section 42 may—

(a)    seize and detain or remove that document or record;

(b)    take copies of or extracts from that document or record.

In this subsection 'document' includes anything falling within paragraph (a) or (b) of section 42(3).

(5)    The powers under this section may only be exercised—

(a)    for the purposes of determining whether an offence under any of sections 4 to 9 or section 26 has been committed, or

(b)    in relation to an item which a relevant enforcement officer reasonably believes to be—

    (i)    relevant evidence, or

    (ii)   a psychoactive substance (whether or not it is relevant evidence).

(6)    Nothing in this section confers power on a relevant enforcement officer to seize an item which is an excluded item (see section 44).

## 44 Excluded items

(1) This section defines what is meant by 'excluded items' for the purposes of section 43.

(2) In England and Wales 'excluded items' means—

    (a) items subject to legal privilege, within the meaning of the Police and Criminal Evidence Act 1984 (see section 10 of that Act);

    (b) excluded material, within the meaning of that Act (see section 11 of that Act);

    (c) special procedure material, within the meaning of that Act (see section 14 of that Act).

(3) In Scotland 'excluded items' means items in respect of which a claim to confidentiality of communications could be maintained in legal proceedings.

(4) In Northern Ireland 'excluded items' means—

    (a) items subject to legal privilege, within the meaning of the Police and Criminal Evidence (Northern Ireland) Order 1989 (S.I. 1989/1341 (N.I. 12)) (see Article 12 of that Order);

    (b) excluded material, within the meaning of that Order (see Article 13 of that Order);

    (c) special procedure material, within the meaning of that Order (see Article 16 of that Order).

## 45 Further provision about seizure under section 43

(1) Where—

    (a) any items which a relevant enforcement officer wishes to seize and remove are in a container, and

    (b) the officer reasonably considers that it would facilitate the seizure and removal of the items if they remained in the container for that purpose,

any power to seize and remove the items conferred by section 43 includes power to seize and remove the container.

(2) If a container is seized under this section, reasonable efforts must be made to return it to—

    (a) the person from whom it was seized, or

    (b) (if different) a person to whom it belongs.

(3) Subsection (2) does not apply—

    (a) if the container appears to be of negligible value,

(b)    if it is not practicable for the container to be returned, or

(c)    while the container is or may be needed for use as evidence at a trial for an offence.

(4)    If, in the opinion of a relevant enforcement officer, it is not for the time being practicable for the officer to seize and remove any item, the officer may require—

    (a)    the person from whom the item is being seized, or

    (b)    where the officer is exercising a power of search conferred by section 37, 38 or 39 in relation to any premises, any person in or on the premises,

to secure that the item is not removed or otherwise interfered with until such time as the officer may seize and remove it.

## 46    Notices and records in relation to seized items

(1)    This section applies where a relevant enforcement officer, or a person accompanying a relevant enforcement officer, seizes any item under section 43.

(2)    When the item is seized, the officer must make reasonable efforts to give written notice to each of the following persons—

    (a)    in the case of an item seized from a person, the person from whom the item was seized;

    (b)    in the case of an item seized from premises, any person who appears to the officer to be the occupier of the premises or otherwise to be in charge of the premises;

    (c)    if the officer thinks that the item may belong to any person not falling within paragraph (a) or (b), that other person.

A person falling within any of paragraphs (a) to (c) is referred to in this section as an 'affected person'.

(3)    If—

    (a)    the item is seized from premises, and

    (b)    at the time of the seizure it is not reasonably practicable to give a notice to any affected person,

the officer must leave a copy of the notice in a prominent place on the premises.

(4)    The notice must—

    (a)    state what has been seized and the reason for its seizure;

    (b)    specify any offence which the officer believes has been committed;

(c)    explain the effect of sections 49 to 51 and 53.

(5)    The officer must make a record of what has been seized.

(6)    If a person who appears to a relevant enforcement officer to be an affected person asks for a copy of that record, the officer must, within a reasonable time, provide a copy of that record to that person.

## 47    Powers of entry, search and seizure: supplementary provision

(1)    A relevant enforcement officer may use reasonable force, if necessary, for the purpose of exercising any power conferred by sections 36 to 45.

(2)    A person authorised under section 40(5) to accompany a relevant enforcement officer may use reasonable force, if necessary, for the purpose of exercising any power conferred by sections 39 to 45.

(3)    The powers conferred on a relevant enforcement officer by any of sections 36 to 45 do not affect any powers exercisable by the officer apart from that section.

## 48    Offences in relation to enforcement officers

(1)    A person commits an offence if, without reasonable excuse, the person intentionally obstructs a relevant enforcement officer in the performance of any of the officer's functions under sections 36 to 45.

(2)    A person commits an offence if—

(a)    the person fails without reasonable excuse to comply with a requirement reasonably made, or a direction reasonably given, by a relevant enforcement officer in the exercise of any power conferred by sections 37 to 45, or

(b)    the person prevents any other person from complying with any such requirement or direction.

(3)    In this section any reference to a relevant enforcement officer includes a reference to a person authorised under section 40(5) to accompany a relevant enforcement officer.

(4)    A person who is guilty of an offence under this section is liable—

(a)    on summary conviction in England and Wales, to either or both of the following—

(i)    imprisonment for a term not exceeding 51 weeks (or 6 months, if the offence was committed before the commencement of section 281(5) of the Criminal Justice Act 2003);

(ii)    a fine;

(b)    on summary conviction in Scotland, to either or both of the following—

303

        (i)    imprisonment for a term not exceeding 12 months;

        (ii)   a fine not exceeding level 5 on the standard scale;

(c)   on summary conviction in Northern Ireland, to either or both of the following—

        (i)    imprisonment for a term not exceeding 6 months;

        (ii)   a fine not exceeding level 5 on the standard scale.

# Appendix C
# Police and Criminal Evidence Act 1984, sections 1 to 23

## Part I Powers to stop and search

**1 Power of constable to stop and search persons, vehicles etc.**

(1) A constable may exercise any power conferred by this section—

    (a) in any place to which at the time when he proposes to exercise the power the public or any section of the public has access, on payment or otherwise, as of right or by virtue of express or implied permission; or

    (b) in any other place to which people have ready access at the time when he proposes to exercise the power but which is not a dwelling.

(2) Subject to subsection (3) to (5) below, a constable—

    (a) may search—

        (i) any person or vehicle;

        (ii) anything which is in or on a vehicle,

    for stolen or prohibited articles[[, any article to which subsection (8A) below applies or any firework to which subsection (8B) below applies]¹]²; and

    (b) may detain a person or vehicle for the purpose of such a search.

(3) This section does not give a constable power to search a person or vehicle or anything in or on a vehicle unless he has reasonable grounds for suspecting that he will find stolen or prohibited articles[[, any article to which subsection (8A) below applies or any firework to which subsection (8B) below applies]¹]².

(4) If a person is in a garden or yard occupied with and used for the purposes of a dwelling or on other land so occupied and used, a constable may not search him in the exercise of the power conferred by this section unless the constable has reasonable grounds for believing—

    (a) that he does not reside in the dwelling; and

(b)    that he is not in the place in question with the express or implied permission of a person who resides in the dwelling.

(5)    If a vehicle is in a garden or yard occupied with and used for the purposes of a dwelling or on other land so occupied and used, a constable may not search the vehicle or anything in or on it in the exercise of the power conferred by this section unless he has reasonable grounds for believing—

(a)    that the person in charge of the vehicle does not reside in the dwelling; and

(b)    that the vehicle is not in the place in question with the express or implied permission of a person who resides in the dwelling.

(6)    If in the course of such a search a constable discovers an article which he has reasonable grounds for suspecting to be a stolen or prohibited article[[, an article to which subsection (8A) below applies or a firework to which subsection (8B) below applies]¹]², he may seize it.

(7)    An article is prohibited for the purposes of this Part of this Act if it is—

(a)    an offensive weapon; or

(b)    an article—

    (i)    made or adapted for use in the course of or in connection with an offence to which this sub-paragraph applies; or

    (ii)    intended by the person having it with him for such use by him or by some other person.

(8)    The offences to which subsection (7)(b)(i) above applies are—

(a)    burglary;

(b)    theft;

(c)    offences under section 12 of the Theft Act 1968 (taking motor vehicle or other conveyance without authority); ...³

[(d)    fraud (contrary to section 1 of the Fraud Act 2006);]⁴ and

[(e)    offences under section 1 of the Criminal Damage Act 1971 (destroying or damaging property).]⁵

[(8A)    This subsection applies to any article in relation to which a person has committed, or is committing or is going to commit an offence under section 139 [or 139AA]⁶ of the Criminal Justice Act 1988.]²

[(8B)    This subsection applies to any firework which a person possesses in contravention of a prohibition imposed by fireworks regulations.

(8C)    In this section—

(a)    'firework' shall be construed in accordance with the definition of 'fireworks' in section 1(1) of the Fireworks Act 2003; and

    (b)    'fireworks regulations' has the same meaning as in that Act.][7]

(9)    In this Part of this Act 'offensive weapon' means any article—

    (a)    made or adapted for use for causing injury to persons; or

    (b)    intended by the person having it with him for such use by him or by some other person.

**Amendments**

1   Substituted by the Serious Organised Crime and Police Act 2005, s 115(1)-(4).
2   Inserted by the Criminal Justice Act 1988, s 140(1).
3   Repealed by the Criminal Justice Act 2003, s 332, Sch 37, Pt 1.
4   Substituted by the Fraud Act 2006, s 14(1), Sch 1, para 21.
5   Inserted by the Criminal Justice Act 2003, s 1(2).
6   Inserted by the Legal Aid, Sentencing and Punishment of Offenders Act 2012, s 142(3), Sch 26, para 3.
7   Inserted by the Serious Organised Crime and Police Act 2005, s 115(1), (5).

## 2    Provisions relating to search under section 1 and other powers.

(1)    A constable who detains a person or vehicle in the exercise—

    (a)    of the power conferred by section 1 above; or

    (b)    of any other power—

        (i)    to search a person without first arresting him; or

        (ii)    to search a vehicle without making an arrest,

need not conduct a search if it appears to him subsequently—

        (i)    that no search is required; or

        (ii)    that a search is impracticable.

(2)    If a constable contemplates a search, other than a search of an unattended vehicle, in the exercise—

    (a)    of the power conferred by section 1 above; or

    (b)    of any other power, except the power conferred by section 6 below and the power conferred by section 27(2) of the Aviation Security Act 1982—

        (i)    to search a person without first arresting him; or

        (ii)    to search a vehicle without making an arrest,

it shall be his duty, subject to subsection (4) below, to take reasonable steps before he commences the search to bring to the attention of the appropriate person—

        (i)    if the constable is not in uniform, documentary evidence that he is a constable; and

        (ii)    whether he is in uniform or not, the matters specified in subsection (3) below;

and the constable shall not commence the search until he has performed that duty.

(3) The matters referred to in subsection (2)(ii) above are—

    (a) the constable's name and the name of the police station to which he is attached;

    (b) the object of the proposed search;

    (c) the constable's grounds for proposing to make it; and

    (d) the effect of section 3(7) or (8) below, as may be appropriate.

(4) A constable need not bring the effect of section 3(7) or (8) below to the attention of the appropriate person if it appears to the constable that it will not be practicable to make the record in section 3(1) below.

(5) In this section 'the appropriate person' means —

    (a) if the constable proposes to search a person, that person; and

    (b) if he proposes to search a vehicle, or anything in or on a vehicle, the person in charge of the vehicle.

(6) On completing a search of an unattended vehicle or anything in or on such a vehicle in the exercise of any such power as is mentioned in subsection (2) above a constable shall leave a notice—

    (a) stating that he has searched it;

    (b) giving the name of the police station to which he is attached;

    (c) stating that an application for compensation for any damage caused by the search may be made to that police station; and

    (d) stating the effect of section 3(8) below.

(7) The constable shall leave the notice inside the vehicle unless it is not reasonably practicable to do so without damaging the vehicle.

(8) The time for which a person or vehicle may be detained for the purposes of such a search is such time as is reasonably required to permit a search to be carried out either at the place where the person or vehicle was first detained or nearby.

(9) Neither the power conferred by section 1 above nor any other power to detain and search a person without first arresting him or to detain and search a vehicle without making an arrest is to be construed—

    (a) as authorising a constable to require a person to remove any of his clothing in public other than an outer coat, jacket or gloves; or

    (b) as authorising a constable not in uniform to stop a vehicle.

(10) This section and section 1 above apply to vessels, aircraft and hovercraft as they apply to vehicles.

**3    Duty to make records concerning searches.**

(1)    Where a constable has carried out a search in the exercise of any such power as is mentioned in section 2(1) above, other than a search—

    (a)    under section 6 below; or

    (b)    under section 27(2) of the Aviation Security Act 1982,

[a record of the search shall be made][1] in writing unless it is not practicable to do so.

[(2)    If a record of a search is required to be made by subsection (1) above—

    (a)    in a case where the search results in a person being arrested and taken to a police station, the constable shall secure that the record is made as part of the person's custody record;

    (b)    in any other case, the constable shall make the record on the spot, or, if that is not practicable, as soon as practicable after the completion of the search.][1]

(3)    …[2]

(4)    …[2]

(5)    …[2]

(6)    The record of a search of a person or a vehicle—

    (a)    shall state—

        (i)    the object of the search;

        (ii)    the grounds for making it;

        (iii)    the date and time when it was made;

        (iv)    the place where it was made;

        [(v)    except in the case of a search of an unattended vehicle, the ethnic origins of the person searched or the person in charge of the vehicle searched (as the case may be); and][1]

    (b)    shall identify the constable [who carried out the search][1].

[(6A) The requirement in subsection (6)(a)(v) above for a record to state a person's ethnic origins is a requirement to state—

    (a)    the ethnic origins of the person as described by the person, and

    (b)    if different, the ethnic origins of the person as perceived by the constable.][3]

(7)    [If a record of a search of a person has been made under this section,][1] the person who was searched shall be entitled to a copy of the record if he asks for one before the end of the period specified in subsection (9) below.

(8)  If—

    (a)  the owner of a vehicle which has been searched or the person who was in charge of the vehicle at the time when it was searched asks for a copy of the record of the search before the end of the period specified in subsection (9) below; and

    [(b)  a record of the search of the vehicle has been made under this section,]¹

the person who made the request shall be entitled to a copy.

(9)  The period mentioned in subsections (7) and (8) above is the period of [3 months]¹ beginning with the date on which the search was made.

(10)  The requirements imposed by this section with regard to records of searches of vehicles shall apply also to records of searches of vessels, aircraft and hovercraft.

**Amendments**
1  Substituted by the Crime and Security Act 2010, s 1(1)-(3), (5), (7)-(9).
2  Repealed by the Crime and Security Act 2010, s 1(1), (4).
3  Inserted by the Crime and Security Act 2010, s 1(1), (6).

## 4   Road checks.

(1)  This section shall have effect in relation to the conduct of road checks by police officers for the purpose of ascertaining whether a vehicle is carrying—

    (a)  a person who has committed an offence other than a road traffic offence or a [vehicle]¹ excise offence;

    (b)  a person who is a witness to such an offence;

    (c)  a person intending to commit such an offence; or

    (d)  a person who is unlawfully at large.

(2)  For the purposes of this section a road check consists of the exercise in a locality of the power conferred by [section 163 of the Road Traffic Act 1988]² in such a way as to stop during the period for which its exercise in that way in that locality continues all vehicles or vehicles selected by any criterion.

(3)  Subject to subsection (5) below, there may only be such a road check if a police officer of the rank of superintendent or above authorises it in writing.

(4)  An officer may only authorise a road check under subsection (3) above—

    (a)  for the purpose specified in subsection (1)(a) above, if he has reasonable grounds—

        (i)  for believing that the offence is [an indictable offence]³; and

(ii)    for suspecting that the person is, or is about to be, in the locality in which vehicles would be stopped if the road check were authorised;

(b)    for the purpose specified in subsection (1)(b) above, if he has reasonable grounds for believing that the offence is [an indictable offence]³;

(c)    for the purpose specified in subsection (1)(c) above, if he has reasonable grounds—

(i)    for believing that the offence would be [an indictable offence]³; and

(ii)    for suspecting that the person is, or is about to be, in the locality in which vehicles would be stopped if the road check were authorised;

(d)    for the purpose specified in subsection (1)(d) above, if he has reasonable grounds for suspecting that the person is, or is about to be, in that locality.

(5)    An officer below the rank of superintendent may authorise such a road check if it appears to him that it is required as a matter of urgency for one of the purposes specified in subsection (1) above.

(6)    If an authorisation is given under subsection (5) above, it shall be the duty of the officer who gives it—

(a)    to make a written record of the time at which he gives it; and

(b)    to cause an officer of the rank of superintendent or above to be informed that it has been given.

(7)    The duties imposed by subsection (6) above shall be performed as soon as it is practicable to do so.

(8)    An officer to whom a report is made under subsection (6) above may, in writing, authorise the road check to continue.

(9)    If such an officer considers that the road check should not continue, he shall record in writing—

(a)    the fact that it took place; and

(b)    the purpose for which it took place.

(10)  An officer giving an authorisation under this section shall specify the locality in which vehicles are to be stopped.

(11)  An officer giving an authorisation under this section, other than an authorisation under subsection (5) above—

(a)    shall specify a period, not exceeding seven days, during which the road check may continue; and

(b)    may direct that the road check—

   (i)    shall be continuous; or

   (ii)    shall be conducted at specified times,

during that period.

(12)  If it appears to an officer of the rank of superintendent or above that a road check ought to continue beyond the period for which it has been authorised he may, from time to time, in writing specify a further period, not exceeding seven days, during which it may continue.

(13)  Every written authorisation shall specify—

(a)    the name of the officer giving it;

(b)    the purpose of the road check; and

(c)    the locality in which vehicles are to be stopped.

(14)  The duties to specify the purposes of a road check imposed by subsections (9) and (13) above include duties to specify any relevant [indictable offence][3].

(15)  Where a vehicle is stopped in a road check, the person in charge of the vehicle at the time when it is stopped shall be entitled to obtain a written statement of the purpose of the road check if he applies for such a statement not later than the end of the period of twelve months from the day on which the vehicle was stopped.

(16)  Nothing in this section affects the exercise by police officers of any power to stop vehicles for purposes other than those specified in subsection (1) above.

**Amendments**

1    Substituted by the Vehicle Excise and Registration Act 1994, s 63, Sch 3, para 19.
2    Substituted by the Road Traffic (Consequential Provisions) Act 1988, s 4, Sch 3, para 27(1).
3    Substituted by the Serious Organised Crime and Police Act 2005, s 111, Sch 7, para 43(1), (2).

## 5    Reports of recorded searches and of road checks.

(1)    Every annual report—

[(a)    under section 22 of the Police Act 1996; or][1]

(b)    made by the Commissioner of Police of the Metropolis,

shall contain information—

   (i)    about searches recorded under section 3 above which have been carried out in the area to which the report relates during the period to which it relates; and

   (ii)    about road checks authorised in that area during that period under section 4 above.

[(1A)...²]³

(2) The information about searches shall not include information about specific searches but shall include—

    (a) the total numbers of searches in each month during the period to which the report relates—

        (i) for stolen articles;

        (ii) for offensive weapons [or articles to which section 1(8A) above applies]⁴; and

        (iii) for other prohibited articles;

    (b) the total number of persons arrested in each such month in consequence of searches of each of the descriptions specified in paragraph (a)(i) to (iii) above.

(3) The information about road checks shall include information—

    (a) about the reason for authorising each road check; and

    (b) about the result of each of them.

**Amendments**
1 Substituted by the Police Act 1996, s 103(1), Sch 7, para 34.
2 Repealed by the Serious Organised Crime and Police Act 2005, s 174(2), Sch 17, Pt 2.
3 Inserted by the Police Act 1997, s 134(1), Sch 9, para 46.
4 Inserted by the Criminal Justice Act 1988, s 140(2).

## 6    Statutory undertakers etc.

(1) A constable employed by statutory undertakers may stop, detain and search any vehicle before it leaves a goods area included in the premises of the statutory undertakers.

[(1A) Without prejudice to any powers under subsection (1) above, a constable employed [by the [British Transport Police Authority]¹]² may stop, detain and search any vehicle before it leaves a goods area which is included in the premises of any successor of the British Railways Board and is used wholly or mainly for the purposes of a relevant undertaking.]³

(2) In this section 'goods area' means any area used wholly or mainly for the storage or handling of goods[, and 'successor of the British Railways Board' and 'relevant undertaking' have the same meaning as in the Railways Act 1993 (Consequential Modifications) Order 1999]³.

(3)    ...⁴

(4)    ...⁴

**Amendments**
1 Substituted by the British Transport Police (Transitional and Consequential Provisions) Order 2004, SI 2004/1573, art 12(1)(e).
2 Substituted by the Transport Act 2000, s 217(1), Sch 18, para 5.

3  Inserted by the Railways Act 1993 (Consequential Modifications) (No 2) Order 1999, SI 1999/1998, art 5.
4  Repealed by the Energy Act 2004, s 197(9), Sch 23, Pt 1.

**7    Part I—supplementary.**

(1)    The following enactments shall cease to have effect—

(a)    section 8 of the Vagrancy Act 1824;

(b)    section 66 of the Metropolitan Police Act 1839;

(c)    section 11 of the Canals (Offences) Act 1840;

(d)    section 19 of the Pedlars Act 1871;

(e)    section 33 of the County of Merseyside Act 1980; and

(f)    section 42 of the West Midlands County Council Act 1980.

(2)    There shall also cease to have effect—

(a)    so much of any enactment contained in an Act passed before 1974, other than—

(i)    an enactment contained in a public general Act; or

(ii)    an enactment relating to statutory undertakers,

as confers power on a constable to search for stolen or unlawfully obtained goods; and

(b)    so much of any enactment relating to statutory undertakers as provides that such a power shall not be exercisable after the end of a specified period.

(3)    In this Part of this Act 'statutory undertakers' means persons authorised by any enactment to carry on any railway, light railway, road transport, water transport, canal, inland navigation, dock or harbour undertaking.

## Part II Powers of entry, search and seizure

*Search warrants*

**8    Power of justice of the peace to authorise entry and search of premises.**

(1)    If on an application made by a constable a justice of the peace is satisfied that there are reasonable grounds for believing—

(a)    that [an indictable offence][1] has been committed; and

(b)    that there is material on premises [mentioned in subsection (1A) below][2] which is likely to be of substantial value (whether by itself or together with other material) to the investigation of the offence; and

(c)   that the material is likely to be relevant evidence; and

(d)   that it does not consist of or include items subject to legal privilege, excluded material or special procedure material; and

(e)   that any of the conditions specified in subsection (3) below applies [in relation to each set of premises specified in the application]², 

he may issue a warrant authorising a constable to enter and search the premises.

[(1A) The premises referred to in subsection (1)(b) above are—

(a)   one or more sets of premises specified in the application (in which case the application is for a 'specific premises warrant'); or

(b)   any premises occupied or controlled by a person specified in the application, including such sets of premises as are so specified (in which case the application is for an 'all premises warrant').

(1B)  If the application is for an all premises warrant, the justice of the peace must also be satisfied—

(a)   that because of the particulars of the offence referred to in paragraph (a) of subsection (1) above, there are reasonable grounds for believing that it is necessary to search premises occupied or controlled by the person in question which are not specified in the application in order to find the material referred to in paragraph (b) of that subsection; and

(b)   that it is not reasonably practicable to specify in the application all the premises which he occupies or controls and which might need to be searched.]²

[(1C) The warrant may authorise entry to and search of premises on more than one occasion if, on the application, the justice of the peace is satisfied that it is necessary to authorise multiple entries in order to achieve the purpose for which he issues the warrant.

(1D)  If it authorises multiple entries, the number of entries authorised may be unlimited, or limited to a maximum.]³

(2)   A constable may seize and retain anything for which a search has been authorised under subsection (1) above.

(3)   The conditions mentioned in subsection (1)(e) above are—

(a)   that it is not practicable to communicate with any person entitled to grant entry to the premises;

(b)   that it is practicable to communicate with a person entitled to grant entry to the premises but it is not practicable to communicate with any person entitled to grant access to the evidence;

(c)    that entry to the premises will not be granted unless a warrant is produced;

(d)    that the purpose of a search may be frustrated or seriously prejudiced unless a constable arriving at the premises can secure immediate entry to them.

(4)    In this Act 'relevant evidence', in relation to an offence, means anything that would be admissible in evidence at a trial for the offence.

(5)    The power to issue a warrant conferred by this section is in addition to any such power otherwise conferred.

[(6)    This section applies in relation to a relevant offence (as defined in section 28D(4) of the Immigration Act 1971) as it applies in relation to [an indictable offence]¹.]⁴

[(7)    Section 4 of the Summary Jurisdiction (Process) Act 1881 (execution of process of English courts in Scotland) shall apply to a warrant issued on the application of an officer of Revenue and Customs under this section by virtue of section 114 below.]⁵

**Amendments**

1    Substituted by the Serious Organised Crime and Police Act 2005, s 111, Sch 7, para 43(1), (3).
2    Substituted by the Serious Organised Crime and Police Act 2005, s 113(1)-(3).
3    Inserted by the Serious Organised Crime and Police Act 2005, s 114(1), (2).
4    Inserted by the Immigration and Asylum Act 1999, s 169(1), Sch 14, para 80(1), (2).
5    Inserted by the Finance Act 2007, s 86.

## 9    Special provisions as to access.

(1)    A constable may obtain access to excluded material or special procedure material for the purposes of a criminal investigation by making an application under Schedule 1 below and in accordance with that Schedule.

(2)    Any Act (including a local Act) passed before this Act under which a search of premises for the purposes of a criminal investigation could be authorised by the issue of a warrant to a constable shall cease to have effect so far as it relates to the authorisation of searches—

(a)    for items subject to legal privilege; or

(b)    for excluded material; or

(c)    for special procedure material consisting of documents or records other than documents.

[(2A) Section 4 of the Summary Jurisdiction (Process) Act 1881 (c. 24) (which includes provision for the execution of process of English courts in Scotland) and section 29 of the Petty Sessions (Ireland) Act 1851 (c. 93) (which makes equivalent provision for execution in Northern Ireland) shall each apply to any process issued by a [judge]¹ under Schedule 1 to this Act as it applies to process issued by a magistrates' court under the Magistrates' Courts Act 1980 (c. 43).]²

**Amendments**
1 Substituted by the Courts Act 2003, s 65(2), Sch 4, para 5.
2 Inserted by the Criminal Justice and Police Act 2001, s 86(1).

## 10 Meaning of 'items subject to legal privilege'.

(1) Subject to subsection (2) below, in this Act 'items subject to legal privilege' means—

    (a) communications between a professional legal adviser and his client or any person representing his client made in connection with the giving of legal advice to the client;

    (b) communications between a professional legal adviser and his client or any person representing his client or between such an adviser or his client or any such representative and any other person made in connection with or in contemplation of legal proceedings and for the purposes of such proceedings; and

    (c) items enclosed with or referred to in such communications and made—

        (i) in connection with the giving of legal advice; or

        (ii) in connection with or in contemplation of legal proceedings and for the purposes of such proceedings,

when they are in the possession of a person who is entitled to possession of them.

(2) Items held with the intention of furthering a criminal purpose are not items subject to legal privilege.

## 11 Meaning of 'excluded material'.

(1) Subject to the following provisions of this section, in this Act 'excluded material' means—

    (a) personal records which a person has acquired or created in the course of any trade, business, profession or other occupation or for the purposes of any paid or unpaid office and which he holds in confidence;

    (b) human tissue or tissue fluid which has been taken for the purposes of diagnosis or medical treatment and which a person holds in confidence;

    (c) journalistic material which a person holds in confidence and which consists—

        (i) of documents; or

        (ii) of records other than documents.

(2)  A person holds material other than journalistic material in confidence for the purposes of this section if he holds it subject—

(a)  to an express or implied undertaking to hold it in confidence; or

(b)  to a restriction on disclosure or an obligation of secrecy contained in any enactment, including an enactment contained in an Act passed after this Act.

(3)  A person holds journalistic material in confidence for the purposes of this section if—

(a)  he holds it subject to such an undertaking, restriction or obligation; and

(b)  it has been continuously held (by one or more persons) subject to such an undertaking, restriction or obligation since it was first acquired or created for the purposes of journalism.

## 12  Meaning of 'personal records'.

In this Part of this Act 'personal records' means documentary and other records concerning an individual (whether living or dead) who can be identified from them and relating—

(a)  to his physical or mental health;

(b)  to spiritual counselling or assistance given or to be given to him; or

(c)  to counselling or assistance given or to be given to him, for the purposes of his personal welfare, by any voluntary organisation or by any individual who—

(i)  by reason of his office or occupation has responsibilities for his personal welfare; or

(ii)  by reason of an order of a court has responsibilities for his supervision.

## 13  Meaning of 'journalistic material'.

(1)  Subject to subsection (2) below, in this Act 'journalistic material' means material acquired or created for the purposes of journalism.

(2)  Material is only journalistic material for the purposes of this Act if it is in the possession of a person who acquired or created it for the purposes of journalism.

(3)  A person who receives material from someone who intends that the recipient shall use it for the purposes of journalism is to be taken to have acquired it for those purposes.

## 14 Meaning of 'special procedure material'.

(1) In this Act 'special procedure material' means —

    (a) material to which subsection (2) below applies; and

    (b) journalistic material, other than excluded material.

(2) Subject to the following provisions of this section, this subsection applies to material, other than items subject to legal privilege and excluded material, in the possession of a person who—

    (a) acquired or created it in the course of any trade, business, profession or other occupation or for the purpose of any paid or unpaid office; and

    (b) holds it subject—

        (i) to an express or implied undertaking to hold it in confidence; or

        (ii) to a restriction or obligation such as is mentioned in section 11(2)(b) above.

(3) Where material is acquired—

    (a) by an employee from his employer and in the course of his employment; or

    (b) by a company from an associated company,

it is only special procedure material if it was special procedure material immediately before the acquisition.

(4) Where material is created by an employee in the course of his employment, it is only special procedure material if it would have been special procedure material had his employer created it.

(5) Where material is created by a company on behalf of an associated company, it is only special procedure material if it would have been special procedure material had the associated company created it.

(6) A company is to be treated as another's associated company for the purposes of this section if it would be so treated under [section 449 of the Corporation Tax Act 2010][1].

**Amendments**
1 Substituted by the Corporation Tax Act 2010, s 1177, Sch 1, para 193.

## 15 Search warrants—safeguards.

(1) This section and section 16 below have effect in relation to the issue to constables under any enactment, including an enactment contained in an Act passed after this Act, of warrants to enter and search premises; and an entry on or search of premises under a warrant is unlawful unless it complies with this section and section 16 below.

(2)   Where a constable applies for any such warrant, it shall be his duty—

   (a)   to state—

      (i)   the ground on which he makes the application; ...[1]

      (ii)   the enactment under which the warrant would be issued; [and][2]

      [(iii)   if the application is for a warrant authorising entry and search on more than one occasion, the ground on which he applies for such a warrant, and whether he seeks a warrant authorising an unlimited number of entries, or (if not) the maximum number of entries desired;][2]

   [(b)   to specify the matters set out in subsection (2A) below; and][3]

   (c)   to identify, so far as is practicable, the articles or persons to be sought.

[(2A) The matters which must be specified pursuant to subsection (2)(b) above are—

   [(a)   if the application relates to one or more sets of premises specified in the application, each set of premises which it is desired to enter and search;][4]

   (b)   [if the application relates to any premises occupied or controlled by a person specified in the application–][4]

      (i)   as many sets of premises which it is desired to enter and search as it is reasonably practicable to specify;

      (ii)   the person who is in occupation or control of those premises and any others which it is desired to enter and search;

      (iii)   why it is necessary to search more premises than those specified under sub-paragraph (i); and

      (iv)   why it is not reasonably practicable to specify all the premises which it is desired to enter and search.][5]

(3)   An application for such a warrant shall be made ex parte and supported by an information in writing.

(4)   The constable shall answer on oath any question that the justice of the peace or judge hearing the application asks him.

(5)   A warrant shall authorise an entry on one occasion only [unless it specifies that it authorises multiple entries][2].

[(5A) If it specifies that it authorises multiple entries, it must also specify whether the number of entries authorised is unlimited, or limited to a specified maximum.][2]

(6)  A warrant—

    (a)  shall specify—

        (i)  the name of the person who applies for it;

        (ii)  the date on which it is issued;

        (iii)  the enactment under which it is issued; and

        [(iv)  each set of premises to be searched, or (in the case of an all premises warrant) the person who is in occupation or control of premises to be searched, together with any premises under his occupation or control which can be specified and which are to be searched; and][3]

    (b)  shall identify, so far as is practicable, the articles or persons to be sought.

[(7)  Two copies shall be made of a [warrant][4] which specifies only one set of premises and does not authorise multiple entries; and as many copies as are reasonably required may be made of any other kind of warrant.][6]

(8)  The copies shall be clearly certified as copies.

**Amendments**

1  Repealed by the Serious Organised Crime and Police Act 2005, ss 114(1), (3), (4)(a), 174(2), Sch 17, Pt 2.
2  Inserted by the Serious Organised Crime and Police Act 2005, s 114(1), (3), (4)(b), (c), (5), (6).
3  Substituted by the Serious Organised Crime and Police Act 2005, s 113(1), (5), (6), (8).
4  Substituted by the Serious Organised Crime and Police Act 2005 (Amendment) Order 2005, SI 2005/3496, art 7.
5  Inserted by the Serious Organised Crime and Police Act 2005, s 113(1), (5), (7).
6  Substituted by the Serious Organised Crime and Police Act 2005, s 114(1), (3), (7).

## 16  Execution of warrants.

(1)  A warrant to enter and search premises may be executed by any constable.

(2)  Such a warrant may authorise persons to accompany any constable who is executing it.

[(2A) A person so authorised has the same powers as the constable whom he accompanies in respect of—

    (a)  the execution of the warrant, and

    (b)  the seizure of anything to which the warrant relates.

(2B)  But he may exercise those powers only in the company, and under the supervision, of a constable.][1]

(3)  Entry and search under a warrant must be within [three months][2] from the date of its issue.

[(3A) If the warrant is an all premises warrant, no premises which are not specified in it may be entered or searched unless a police officer of at least the rank of inspector has in writing authorised them to be entered.][3]

[(3B) No premises may be entered or searched for the second or any subsequent time under a warrant which authorises multiple entries unless a police officer of at least the rank of inspector has in writing authorised that entry to those premises.][4]

(4)   Entry and search under a warrant must be at a reasonable hour unless it appears to the constable executing it that the purpose of a search may be frustrated on an entry at a reasonable hour.

(5)   Where the occupier of premises which are to be entered and searched is present at the time when a constable seeks to execute a warrant to enter and search them, the constable—

   (a)   shall identify himself to the occupier and, if not in uniform, shall produce to him documentary evidence that he is a constable;

   (b)   shall produce the warrant to him; and

   (c)   shall supply him with a copy of it.

(6)   Where—

   (a)   the occupier of such premises is not present at the time when a constable seeks to execute such a warrant; but

   (b)   some other person who appears to the constable to be in charge of the premises is present,

   subsection (5) above shall have effect as if any reference to the occupier were a reference to that other person.

(7)   If there is no person present who appears to the constable to be in charge of the premises, he shall leave a copy of the warrant in a prominent place on the premises.

(8)   A search under a warrant may only be a search to the extent required for the purpose for which the warrant was issued.

(9)   A constable executing a warrant shall make an endorsement on it stating—

   (a)   whether the articles or persons sought were found; and

   (b)   whether any articles were seized, other than articles which were sought;

   [and, unless the warrant is a …[5] warrant specifying one set of premises only, he shall do so separately in respect of each set of premises entered and searched, which he shall in each case state in the endorsement.][3]

[(10) A warrant shall be returned to the appropriate person mentioned in subsection (10A) below—

   (a)   when it has been executed; or

   (b)   in the case of a specific premises warrant which has not been executed, or an all premises warrant, or any warrant authorising multiple entries, upon the expiry of the period of three months referred to in subsection (3) above or sooner.

(10A)   The appropriate person is—

(a)   if the warrant was issued by a justice of the peace, the designated officer for the local justice area in which the justice was acting when he issued the warrant;

(b)   if it was issued by a judge, the appropriate officer of the court from which he issued it.][2]

(11)   A warrant which is returned under subsection (10) above shall be retained for 12 months from its return—

(a)   by the [designated officer for the local justice area][6], if it was returned under paragraph (i) of that subsection; and

(b)   by the appropriate officer, if it was returned under paragraph (ii).

(12)   If during the period for which a warrant is to be retained the occupier of [premises][7] to which it relates asks to inspect it, he shall be allowed to do so.

**Amendments**

1   Inserted by the Criminal Justice Act 2003, s 2.
2   Substituted by the Serious Organised Crime and Police Act 2005, s 114(1), (8)(a), (c).
3   Inserted by the Serious Organised Crime and Police Act 2005, s 113(1), (9)(a), (b).
4   Inserted by the Serious Organised Crime and Police Act 2005, s 114(8)(b).
5   Repealed by the Serious Organised Crime and Police Act 2005 (Amendment) Order 2005, SI 2005/3496, art 8.
6   Substituted by the Courts Act 2003, s 109(1), Sch 8, para 281(1), (3).
7   Substituted by the Serious Organised Crime and Police Act 2005, s 113(9)(c).

*Entry and search without search warrant*

## 17   Entry for purpose of arrest etc.

(1)   Subject to the following provisions of this section, and without prejudice to any other enactment, a constable may enter and search any premises for the purpose—

(a)   of executing—

(i)   a warrant of arrest issued in connection with or arising out of criminal proceedings; or

(ii)   a warrant of commitment issued under section 76 of the Magistrates' Courts Act 1980;

(b)   of arresting a person for an [indictable][1] offence;

(c)   of arresting a person for an offence under—

(i)   section 1 (prohibition of uniforms in connection with political objects) ...[2] of the Public Order Act 1936;

(ii) any enactment contained in sections 6 to 8 or 10 of the Criminal Law Act 1977 (offences relating to entering and remaining on property);

[(iii) section 4 of the Public Order Act 1986 (fear or provocation of violence);]³

[[(iiia) section 4 (driving etc. when under influence of drink or drugs) or 163 (failure to stop when required to do so by constable in uniform) of the Road Traffic Act 1988;

(iiib) section 27 of the Transport and Works Act 1992 (which relates to offences involving drink or drugs);]⁴]⁵

[(iv) section 76 of the Criminal Justice and Public Order Act 1994 (failure to comply with interim possession order);]⁶

[(v) any of sections 4, 5, 6(1) and (2), 7 and 8(1) and (2) of the Animal Welfare Act 2006 (offences relating to the prevention of harm to animals);]⁷

[(vi) section 144 of the Legal Aid, Sentencing and Punishment of Offenders Act 2012 (squatting in a residential building);]⁸

[(ca) of arresting, in pursuance of section 32(1A) of the Children and Young Persons Act 1969 , any child or young person who has been remanded [to local authority accommodation or youth detention accommodation under section 91 of the Legal Aid, Sentencing and Punishment of Offenders Act 2012]⁹;

[(caa) of arresting a person for an offence to which section 61 of the Animal Health Act 1981 applies;]¹⁰

[(cab) of arresting a person under any of the following provisions—

(i) section 30D(1) or (2A);

(ii) section 46A(1) or (1A);

(iii) section 5B(7) of the Bail Act 1976 (arrest where a person fails to surrender to custody in accordance with a court order);

(iv) section 7(3) of the Bail Act 1976 (arrest where a person is not likely to surrender to custody etc);

(v) section 97(1) of the Legal Aid, Sentencing and Punishment of Offenders Act 2012 (arrest where a child is suspected of breaking conditions of remand);]¹¹

(cb) of recapturing any person who is, or is deemed for any purpose to be, unlawfully at large while liable to be detained—

(i) in a prison, [young offender institution, secure training centre or secure college]¹², or

      (ii)    in pursuance of [section 92 of the Powers of Criminal Courts (Sentencing) Act 2000][13] (dealing with children and young persons guilty of grave crimes), in any other place;][14]

  (d)    of recapturing [any person whatever][15] who is unlawfully at large and whom he is pursuing; or

  (e)    of saving life or limb or preventing serious damage to property.

(2)    Except for the purpose specified in paragraph (e) of subsection (1) above, the powers of entry and search conferred by this section—

  (a)    are only exercisable if the constable has reasonable grounds for believing that the person whom he is seeking is on the premises; and

  (b)    are limited, in relation to premises consisting of two or more separate dwellings, to powers to enter and search—

      (i)    any parts of the premises which the occupiers of any dwelling comprised in the premises use in common with the occupiers of any other such dwelling; and

      (ii)    any such dwelling in which the constable has reasonable grounds for believing that the person whom he is seeking may be.

(3)    The powers of entry and search conferred by this section are only exercisable for the purposes specified in subsection (1)(c)(ii)[, (iv) or (vi)][16] above by a constable in uniform.

(4)    The power of search conferred by this section is only a power to search to the extent that is reasonably required for the purpose for which the power of entry is exercised.

(5)    Subject to subsection (6) below, all the rules of common law under which a constable has power to enter premises without a warrant are hereby abolished.

(6)    Nothing in subsection (5) above affects any power of entry to deal with or prevent a breach of the peace.

**Amendments**

1    Substituted by the Serious Organised Crime and Police Act 2005, s 111, Sch 7, para 43(1), (4).
2    Repealed by the Public Order Act 1986, s 40(2), (3), Sch 2, para 7, Sch 3.
3    Inserted by the Public Order Act 1986, s 40(2), Sch 2, para 7.
4    Substituted by the Serious Organised Crime and Police Act 2005, s 111, Sch 7, para 58(a).
5    Inserted by the Police Reform Act 2002, s 49(2)
6    Inserted by the Criminal Justice and Public Order Act 1994, s 168(2), Sch 10, para 53(a).
7    Inserted by the Animal Welfare Act 2006, s 24.
8    Inserted by the Legal Aid, Sentencing and Punishment of Offenders Act 2012, s 144(8)(a).
9    Substituted by the Legal Aid, Sentencing and Punishment of Offenders Act 2012, s 105, Sch 12, para 21.
10  Inserted by the Serious Organised Crime and Police Act 2005, s 111, Sch 7, para 58(b).
11  Inserted by the Policing and Crime Act 2017, s 72.
12  Substituted by the Criminal Justice and Courts Act 2015, s 38(3), Sch 9, para 9.
13  Substituted by the Powers of Criminal Courts (Sentencing) Act 2000, s 165(1), Sch 9, para 95.

14 Inserted by the Prisoners (Return to Custody) Act 1995, s 2(1).
15 Substituted by the Prisoners (Return to Custody) Act 1995, s 2(1).
16 Substituted by the Legal Aid, Sentencing and Punishment of Offenders Act 2012, s 144(8)(b).

## 18 Entry and search after arrest.

(1) Subject to the following provisions of this section, a constable may enter and search any premises occupied or controlled by a person who is under arrest for an [indictable][1] offence, if he has reasonable grounds for suspecting that there is on the premises evidence, other than items subject to legal privilege, that relates—

   (a) to that offence; or

   (b) to some other [indictable][1] offence which is connected with or similar to that offence.

(2) A constable may seize and retain anything for which he may search under subsection (1) above.

(3) The power to search conferred by subsection (1) above is only a power to search to the extent that is reasonably required for the purpose of discovering such evidence.

(4) Subject to subsection (5) below, the powers conferred by this section may not be exercised unless an officer of the rank of inspector or above has authorised them in writing.

[(5) A constable may conduct a search under subsection (1)—

   (a) before the person is taken to a police station or released ...[2] under section 30A, and

   (b) without obtaining an authorisation under subsection (4),

   if the condition in subsection (5A) is satisfied.

(5A) The condition is that the presence of the person at a place (other than a police station) is necessary for the effective investigation of the offence.][3]

(6) If a constable conducts a search by virtue of subsection (5) above, he shall inform an officer of the rank of inspector or above that he has made the search as soon as practicable after he has made it.

(7) An officer who—

   (a) authorises a search; or

   (b) is informed of a search under subsection (6) above, shall make a record in writing—

      (i) of the grounds for the search; and

      (ii) of the nature of the evidence that was sought.

(8)   If the person who was in occupation or control of the premises at the time of the search is in police detention at the time the record is to be made, the officer shall make the record as part of his custody record.

**Amendments**

1   Substituted by the Serious Organised Crime and Police Act 2005, s 111, Sch 7, para 43(1), (5).
2   Repealed by the Policing and Crime Act 2017, s 53(1), (2).
3   Substituted by the Criminal Justice Act 2003, s 12, Sch 1, paras 1, 2.

*Seizure etc.*

## 19   General power of seizure etc.

(1)   The powers conferred by subsections (2), (3) and (4) below are exercisable by a constable who is lawfully on any premises.

(2)   The constable may seize anything which is on the premises if he has reasonable grounds for believing—

(a)   that it has been obtained in consequence of the commission of an offence; and

(b)   that it is necessary to seize it in order to prevent it being concealed, lost, damaged, altered or destroyed.

(3)   The constable may seize anything which is on the premises if he has reasonable grounds for believing—

(a)   that it is evidence in relation to an offence which he is investigating or any other offence; and

(b)   that it is necessary to seize it in order to prevent the evidence being concealed, lost, altered or destroyed.

(4)   The constable may require any information which is [stored in any electronic form]¹ and is accessible from the premises to be produced in a form in which it can be taken away and in which it is visible and legible [or from which it can readily be produced in a visible and legible form]² if he has reasonable grounds for believing—

(a)   that—

(i)   it is evidence in relation to an offence which he is investigating or any other offence; or

(ii)   it has been obtained in consequence of the commission of an offence; and

(b)   that it is necessary to do so in order to prevent it being concealed, lost, tampered with or destroyed.

(5)   The powers conferred by this section are in addition to any power otherwise conferred.

(6)     No power of seizure conferred on a constable under any enactment (including an enactment contained in an Act passed after this Act) is to be taken to authorise the seizure of an item which the constable exercising the power has reasonable grounds for believing to be subject to legal privilege.

**Amendments**
1   Substituted by the Criminal Justice and Police Act 2001, s 70, Sch 2, para 13(1)(a), (2)(a).
2   Inserted by the Criminal Justice and Police Act 2001, s 70, Sch 2, para 13(1)(b), (2)(a).

## 20    Extension of powers of seizure to computerised information.

(1)     Every power of seizure which is conferred by an enactment to which this section applies on a constable who has entered premises in the exercise of a power conferred by an enactment shall be construed as including a power to require any information [stored in any electronic form][1] and accessible from the premises to be produced in a form in which it can be taken away and in which it is visible and legible [or from which it can readily be produced in a visible and legible form][2].

(2)     This section applies—

  (a)     to any enactment contained in an Act passed before this Act;

  (b)     to sections 8 and 18 above;

  (c)     to paragraph 13 of Schedule 1 to this Act; and

  (d)     to any enactment contained in an Act passed after this Act.

**Amendments**
1   Substituted by the Criminal Justice and Police Act 2001, s 70, Sch 2, para 13(1)(a), (2)(a).
2   Inserted by the Criminal Justice and Police Act 2001, s 70, Sch 2, para 13(1)(b), (2)(a).

## 21    Access and copying.

(1)     A constable who seizes anything in the exercise of a power conferred by any enactment, including an enactment contained in an Act passed after this Act, shall, if so requested by a person showing himself—

  (a)     to be the occupier of premises on which it was seized; or

  (b)     to have had custody or control of it immediately before the seizure,

provide that person with a record of what he seized.

(2)     The officer shall provide the record within a reasonable time from the making of the request for it.

(3)     Subject to subsection (8) below, if a request for permission to be granted access to anything which—

  (a)     has been seized by a constable; and

  (b)     is retained by the police for the purpose of investigating an offence, is made to the officer in charge of the investigation by a person who had custody or control of the thing immediately before it was so seized or by someone acting on behalf of such a person, the officer shall allow the person who made the request access to it under the supervision of a constable.

(4) Subject to subsection (8) below, if a request for a photograph or copy of any such thing is made to the officer in charge of the investigation by a person who had custody or control of the thing immediately before it was so seized, or by someone acting on behalf of such a person, the officer shall—

(a) allow the person who made the request access to it under the supervision of a constable for the purpose of photographing or copying it; or

(b) photograph or copy it, or cause it to be photographed or copied.

(5) A constable may also photograph or copy, or have photographed or copied, anything which he has power to seize, without a request being made under subsection (4) above.

(6) Where anything is photographed or copied under subsection (4)(b) above, the photograph or copy shall be supplied to the person who made the request.

(7) The photograph or copy shall be so supplied within a reasonable time from the making of the request.

(8) There is no duty under this section to grant access to, or to supply a photograph or copy of, anything if the officer in charge of the investigation for the purposes of which it was seized has reasonable grounds for believing that to do so would prejudice—

(a) that investigation;

(b) the investigation of an offence other than the offence for the purposes of investigating which the thing was seized; or

(c) any criminal proceedings which may be brought as a result of—

(i) the investigation of which he is in charge; or

(ii) any such investigation as is mentioned in paragraph (b) above.

[(9) The references to a constable in subsections (1), (2), (3)(a) and (5) include a person authorised under section 16(2) to accompany a constable executing a warrant.]¹

**Amendments**
1    Inserted by the Criminal Justice Act 2003, s 12, Sch 1, paras 1, 3.

## 22    Retention.

(1) Subject to subsection (4) below, anything which has been seized by a constable or taken away by a constable following a requirement made by

virtue of section 19 or 20 above may be retained so long as is necessary in all the circumstances.

(2)     Without prejudice to the generality of subsection (1) above—

(a)     anything seized for the purposes of a criminal investigation may be retained, except as provided by subsection (4) below—

    (i)     for use as evidence at a trial for an offence; or

    (ii)    for forensic examination or for investigation in connection with an offence; and

(b)     anything may be retained in order to establish its lawful owner, where there are reasonable grounds for believing that it has been obtained in consequence of the commission of an offence.

(3)     Nothing seized on the ground that it may be used—

(a)     to cause physical injury to any person;

(b)     to damage property;

(c)     to interfere with evidence; or

(d)     to assist in escape from police detention or lawful custody,

may be retained when the person from whom it was seized is no longer in police detention or the custody of a court or is in the custody of a court but has been released on bail.

(4)     Nothing may be retained for either of the purposes mentioned in subsection (2)(a) above if a photograph or copy would be sufficient for that purpose.

(5)     Nothing in this section affects any power of a court to make an order under section 1 of the Police (Property) Act 1897.

[(6)    This section also applies to anything retained by the police under section 28H(5) of the Immigration Act 1971.]¹

[(7)    The reference in subsection (1) to anything seized by a constable includes anything seized by a person authorised under section 16(2) to accompany a constable executing a warrant.]²

**Amendments**

1   Inserted by the Immigration and Asylum Act 1999, s 169(1), Sch 14, para 80(1), (3).

2   Inserted by the Criminal Justice Act 2003, s 12, Sch 1, paras 1, 4.

*Supplementary*

## 23     Meaning of 'premises' etc.

In this Act—

'premises' includes any place and, in particular, includes—

(a)    any vehicle, vessel, aircraft or hovercraft;

(b)    any offshore installation;

[(ba)  any renewable energy installation;]¹

(c)    any tent or movable structure; ...²

'offshore installation' has the meaning given to it by section 1 of the Mineral Workings (Offshore Installations) Act 1971;

['renewable energy installation' has the same meaning as in Chapter 2 of Part 2 of the Energy Act 2004.]¹

**Amendments**
1   Inserted by the Energy Act 2004, s 103(2).
2   Repealed by the Energy Act 2004, s 197(9), Sch 23, Pt 1.

# Appendix D
# Drug Offences: Definitive Guideline

## Applicability of guideline

In accordance with section 120 of the Coroners and Justice Act 2009, the Sentencing Council issues this definitive guideline. It applies to all offenders aged 18 and older, who are sentenced on or after 27 February 2012, regardless of the date of the offence.

Section 125(1) of the Coroners and Justice Act 2009 provides that when sentencing offences committed after 6 April 2010:

'Every court –

(a) must, in sentencing an offender, follow any sentencing guideline which is relevant to the offender's case, and

(b) must, in exercising any other function relating to the sentencing of offenders, follow any sentencing guidelines which are relevant to the exercise of the function,

unless the court is satisfied that it would be contrary to the interests of justice to do so.'

This guideline applies only to offenders aged 18 and older. General principles to be considered in the sentencing of youths are in the Sentencing Guidelines Council's definitive guideline, Overarching Principles – Sentencing Youths.

### Structure, ranges and starting points

For the purposes of section 125(3) – (4) of the Coroners and Justice Act 2009, the guideline specifies offence ranges – the range of sentences appropriate for each type of offence. Within each offence, the Council has specified three categories which reflect varying degrees of seriousness. The offence range is split into category ranges – sentences appropriate for each level of seriousness. The Council has also identified a starting point within each category.

Starting points define the position within a category range from which to start calculating the provisional sentence. Starting points apply to all offences within the corresponding category and are applicable to all offenders, in all cases. Once the starting point is established, the court should consider further aggravating and mitigating factors and previous convictions so as to adjust the sentence within the range. Starting points and ranges apply to all offenders, whether they have pleaded guilty or been convicted after trial. Credit for a guilty plea is taken into consideration only at step four in the decision making process, after the appropriate sentence has been identified.

Information on community orders and fine bands is set out in the annex at page 33.

## Fraudulent evasion of a prohibition by bringing into or taking out of the UK a controlled drug

### *Misuse of Drugs Act 1971 (section 3) Customs and Excise Management Act 1979 (section 170(2))*

Triable either way unless the defendant could receive the minimum sentence of seven years for a third drug trafficking offence under section 110 Powers of Criminal Courts (Sentencing) Act 2000 in which case the offence is triable only on indictment.

### *Class A*

Maximum: Life imprisonment

Offence range: 3 years 6 months' – 16 years' custody

A class A offence is a drug trafficking offence for the purpose of imposing a minimum sentence under section 110 Powers of Criminal Courts (Sentencing) Act 2000

### *Class B*

Maximum: 14 years' custody and/or unlimited fine

Offence range: 12 weeks' – 10 years' custody

### *Class C*

Maximum: 14 years' custody and/or unlimited fine

Offence range: Community order – 8 years' custody

### *STEP ONE*
*Determining the offence category*

The court should determine the offender's culpability (role) and the harm caused (quantity) with reference to the tables below.

> In assessing culpability, the sentencer should weigh up all the factors of the case to determine role. Where there are characteristics present which fall under different role categories, the court should balance these characteristics to reach a fair assessment of the offender's culpability.

> In assessing harm, quantity is determined by the weight of the product. Purity is not taken into account at step 1 but is dealt with at step 2.

Where the operation is on the most serious and commercial scale, involving a quantity of drugs significantly higher than category 1, sentences of 20 years and above may be appropriate, depending on the role of the offender.

| Culpability demonstrated by offender's role | Category of harm |
|---|---|
| One or more of these characteristics may demonstrate the offender's role. These lists are not exhaustive. | Indicative quantity of drug concerned (upon which the starting point is based): |
| **LEADING role:**<br><br>• directing or organising buying and selling on a commercial scale;<br><br>• substantial links to, and influence on, others in a chain;<br><br>• close links to original source;<br><br>• expectation of substantial financial gain;<br><br>• uses business as cover;<br><br>• abuses a position of trust or responsibility.<br><br>**SIGNIFICANT role:**<br><br>• operational or management function within a chain;<br><br>• involves others in the operation whether by pressure, influence, intimidation or reward;<br><br>• motivated by financial or other advantage, whether or not operating alone;<br><br>• some awareness and understanding of scale of operation.<br><br>**LESSER role:**<br><br>• performs a limited function under direction;<br><br>• engaged by pressure, coercion, intimidation;<br><br>• involvement through naivety/exploitation;<br><br>• no influence on those above in a chain;<br><br>• very little, if any, awareness or understanding of the scale of operation;<br><br>• if own operation, solely for own use (considering reasonableness of account in all the circumstances). | **Category 1**<br><br>• heroin, cocaine – 5kg;<br><br>• ecstasy – 10,000 tablets;<br><br>• LSD – 250,000 squares;<br><br>• amphetamine – 20kg;<br><br>• cannabis – 200kg;<br><br>• ketamine – 5kg.<br><br>**Category 2**<br><br>• heroin, cocaine – 1kg;<br><br>• ecstasy – 2,000 tablets;<br><br>• LSD – 25,000 squares;<br><br>• amphetamine – 4kg;<br><br>• cannabis – 40kg;<br><br>• ketamine – 1kg.<br><br>**Category 3**<br><br>• heroin, cocaine – 150g;<br><br>• ecstasy – 300 tablets;<br><br>• LSD – 2,500 squares;<br><br>• amphetamine – 750g;<br><br>• cannabis – 6kg;<br><br>• ketamine – 150g.<br><br>**Category 4**<br><br>• heroin, cocaine – 5g;<br><br>• ecstasy – 20 tablets;<br><br>• LSD – 170 squares;<br><br>• amphetamine – 20g;<br><br>• cannabis – 100g;<br><br>• ketamine – 5g. |

## STEP TWO
*Starting point and category range*

Having determined the category, the court should use the corresponding starting point to reach a sentence within the category range below. The starting point applies to all offenders irrespective of plea or previous convictions. The court should then consider further adjustment within the category range for aggravating or mitigating features, set out over the page. In cases where the offender is regarded as being at the very top of the 'leading' role it may be justifiable for the court to depart from the guideline.

Where the defendant is dependent on or has a propensity to misuse drugs and there is sufficient prospect of success, a community order with a drug rehabilitation requirement under section 209 of the Criminal Justice Act 2003 can be a proper alternative to a short or moderate length custodial sentence.

For class A cases, section 110 of the Powers of Criminal Courts (Sentencing) Act 2000 provides that a court should impose a minimum sentence of at least seven years' imprisonment for a third class A trafficking offence except where the court is of the opinion that there are particular circumstances which (a) relate to any of the offences or to the offender; and (b) would make it unjust to do so in all the circumstances.

| CLASS A | Leading role | Significant role | Lesser role |
|---|---|---|---|
| Category 1 | Starting point | Starting point | Starting point |
|  | 14 years' custody | 10 years' custody | 8 years' custody |
|  | Category range | Category range | Category range |
|  | 12 – 16 years' custody | 9 – 12 years' custody | 6 – 9 years' custody |
| Category 2 | Starting point | Starting point | Starting point |
|  | 11 years' custody | 8 years' custody | 6 years' custody |
|  | Category range | Category range | Category range |
|  | 9 – 13 years' custody | 6 years 6 months' – 10 years' custody | 5 – 7 years' custody |
| Category 3 | Starting point | Starting point | Starting point |
|  | 8 years 6 months' custody | 6 years' custody | 4 years 6 months' custody |
|  | Category range | Category range | Category range |
|  | 6 years 6 months' – 10 years' custody | 5 – 7 years' custody | 3 years 6 months' – 5 years' custody |

| CLASS A | Leading role | Significant role | Lesser role |
|---|---|---|---|
| Category 4 | Where the quantity falls below the indicative amount set out for category 4 on the previous page, first identify the role for the importation offence, then refer to the Starting point and ranges for possession or supply offences, depending on intent.<br><br>Where the quantity is significantly larger than the indicative amounts for category 4 but below category 3 amounts, refer to the category 3 ranges above. | | |

| CLASS B | Leading role | Significant role | Lesser role |
|---|---|---|---|
| Category 1 | Starting point<br><br>8 years' custody | Starting point<br><br>5 years 6 months' custody | Starting point<br><br>4 years' custody |
| | Category range<br><br>7 – 10 years' custody | Category range<br><br>5 – 7 years' custody | Category range<br><br>2 years 6 months' – 5 years' custody |
| Category 2 | Starting point<br><br>6 years' custody | Starting point<br><br>4 years' custody | Starting point<br><br>2 years' custody |
| | Category range<br><br>4 years 6 months' – 8 years' custody | Category range<br><br>2 years 6 months' – 5 years' custody | Category range<br><br>18 months' – 3 years' custody |
| Category 3 | Starting point<br><br>4 years' custody | Starting point<br><br>2 years' custody | Starting point<br><br>1 year's custody |
| | Category range<br><br>2 years 6 months' – 5 years' custody | Category range<br><br>18 months' – 3 years' custody | Category range<br><br>12 weeks' – 18 months' custody |
| Category 4 | Where the quantity falls below the indicative amount set out for category 4 on the previous page, first identify the role for the importation offence, then refer to the Starting point and ranges for possession or supply offences, depending on intent.<br><br>Where the quantity is significantly larger than the indicative amounts for category 4 but below category 3 amounts, refer to the category 3 ranges above. | | |

| CLASS C | Leading role | Significant role | Lesser role |
|---|---|---|---|
| Category 1 | Starting point<br><br>5 years' custody | Starting point<br><br>3 years' custody | Starting point<br><br>18 months' custody |
| | Category range<br><br>4 – 8 years' custody | Category range<br><br>2 – 5 years' custody | Category range<br><br>1 – 3 years' custody |
| Category 2 | Starting point<br><br>3 years 6 months' custody | Starting point<br><br>18 months' custody | Starting point<br><br>26 weeks' custody |
| | Category range<br><br>2 – 5 years' custody | Category range<br><br>1 – 3 years' custody | Category range<br><br>12 weeks' – 18 months' custody |
| Category 3 | Starting point<br><br>18 months' custody | Starting point<br><br>26 weeks' custody | Starting point<br><br>High level community order |
| | Category range<br><br>1 – 3 years' custody | Category range<br><br>12 weeks' – 18 months' custody | Category range<br><br>Medium level community order – 12 weeks' custody |
| Category 4 | Where the quantity falls below the indicative amount set out for category 4 on the previous page, first identify the role for the importation offence, then refer to the Starting point and ranges for possession or supply offences, depending on intent.<br><br>Where the quantity is significantly larger than the indicative amounts for category 4 but below category 3 amounts, refer to the category 3 ranges above. | | |

The table below contains a non-exhaustive list of additional factual elements providing the context of the offence and factors relating to the offender. Identify whether any combination of these, or other relevant factors, should result in an upward or downward adjustment from the starting point. In some cases, having considered these factors, it may be appropriate to move outside the identified category range.

For appropriate class C ranges, consider the custody threshold as follows:

- has the custody threshold been passed?
- if so, is it unavoidable that a custodial sentence be imposed?
- if so, can that sentence be suspended?

| Factors increasing seriousness | Factors reducing seriousness or reflecting personal mitigation |
|---|---|
| **Statutory aggravating factors:** Previous convictions, having regard to a) nature of the offence to which conviction relates and relevance to current offence; and b) time elapsed since conviction (see box at page 5 if third drug trafficking conviction) Offender used or permitted a person under 18 to deliver a controlled drug to a third person Offence committed on bail **Other aggravating factors include:** Sophisticated nature of concealment and/or attempts to avoid detection Attempts to conceal or dispose of evidence, where not charged separately Exposure of others to more than usual danger, for example drugs cut with harmful substances Presence of weapon, where not charged separately High purity Failure to comply with current court orders Offence committed on licence | Lack of sophistication as to nature of concealment Involvement due to pressure, intimidation or coercion falling short of duress, except where already taken into account at step 1 Mistaken belief of the offender regarding the type of drug, taking into account the reasonableness of such belief in all the circumstances Isolated incident Low purity No previous convictions or no relevant or recent convictions Offender's vulnerability was exploited Remorse Good character and/or exemplary conduct Determination and/or demonstration of steps having been taken to address addiction or offending behaviour Serious medical conditions requiring urgent, intensive or long-term treatment Age and/or lack of maturity where it affects the responsibility of the offender Mental disorder or learning disability Sole or primary carer for dependent relatives |

## STEP THREE
### Consider any factors which indicate a reduction, such as assistance to the prosecution

The court should take into account sections 73 and 74 of the Serious Organised Crime and Police Act 2005 (assistance by defendants: reduction or review of sentence) and any other rule of law by virtue of which an offender may receive a discounted sentence in consequence of assistance given (or offered) to the prosecutor or investigator.

## STEP FOUR
### Reduction for guilty pleas

The court should take account of any potential reduction for a guilty plea in accordance with section 144 of the Criminal Justice Act 2003 and the Guilty Plea guideline.

For class A offences, where a minimum mandatory sentence is imposed under section 110 Powers of Criminal Courts (Sentencing) Act, the discount for an early guilty plea must not exceed 20 per cent.

## STEP FIVE
### Totality principle

If sentencing an offender for more than one offence, or where the offender is already serving a sentence, consider whether the total sentence is just and proportionate to the offending behaviour.

## STEP SIX
### Confiscation and ancillary orders

In all cases, the court is required to consider confiscation where the Crown invokes the process or where the court considers it appropriate. It should also consider whether to make ancillary orders.

## STEP SEVEN
### Reasons

Section 174 of the Criminal Justice Act 2003 imposes a duty to give reasons for, and explain the effect of, the sentence.

## STEP EIGHT
### Consideration for remand time

Sentencers should take into consideration any remand time served in relation to the final sentence at this final step. The court should consider whether to give credit for time spent on remand in custody or on bail in accordance with sections 240 and 240A of the Criminal Justice Act 2003.

# Supplying or offering to supply a controlled drug

*Misuse of Drugs Act 1971 (section 4(3))*

# Possession of a controlled drug with intent to supply it to another

*Misuse of Drugs Act 1971 (section 5(3))*

Triable either way unless the defendant could receive the minimum sentence of seven years for a third drug trafficking offence under section 110 Powers of Criminal Courts (Sentencing) Act 2000 in which case the offence is triable only on indictment.

*Class A*

Maximum: Life imprisonment

Offence range: Community order – 16 years' custody

A class A offence is a drug trafficking offence for the purpose of imposing a minimum sentence under section 110 Powers of Criminal Courts (Sentencing) Act 2000

*Class B*

Maximum: 14 years' custody and/or unlimited fine

Offence range: Fine – 10 years' custody

*Class C*

Maximum: 14 years' custody and/or unlimited fine

Offence range: Fine – 8 years' custody

*STEP ONE*
*Determining the offence category*

The court should determine the offender's culpability (role) and the harm caused (quantity/type of offender) with reference to the tables below.

> In assessing culpability, the sentencer should weigh up all the factors of the case to determine role. Where there are characteristics present which fall under different role categories, the court should balance these characteristics to reach a fair assessment of the offender's culpability.

341

In assessing harm, quantity is determined by the weight of the product. Purity is not taken into account at step 1 but is dealt with at step 2. Where the offence is street dealing or supply of drugs in prison by a prison employee, the quantity of the product is less indicative of the harm caused and therefore the starting point is not based on quantity.

Where the operation is on the most serious and commercial scale, involving a quantity of drugs significantly higher than category 1, sentences of 20 years and above may be appropriate, depending on the role of the offender.

| Culpability demonstrated by offender's role<br><br>One or more of these characteristics may demonstrate the offender's role. These lists are not exhaustive. | Category of harm<br>Indicative quantity of drug concerned (upon which the starting point is based): |
|---|---|
| **LEADING role:**<br>• directing or organising buying and selling on a commercial scale;<br>• substantial links to, and influence on, others in a chain;<br>• close links to original source;<br>• expectation of substantial financial gain;<br>• uses business as cover;<br>• abuses a position of trust or responsibility, for example prison employee, medical professional.<br><br>**SIGNIFICANT role:**<br>• operational or management function within a chain;<br>• involves others in the operation whether by pressure, influence, intimidation or reward;<br>• motivated by financial or other advantage, whether or not operating alone;<br>• some awareness and understanding of scale of operation;<br>• supply, other than by a person in a position of responsibility, to a prisoner for gain without coercion. | **Category 1**<br>• heroin, cocaine – 5kg;<br>• ecstasy – 10,000 tablets;<br>• LSD – 250,000 squares;<br>• amphetamine – 20kg;<br>• cannabis – 200kg;<br>• ketamine – 5kg.<br><br>**Category 2**<br>• heroin, cocaine – 1kg;<br>• ecstasy – 2,000 tablets;<br>• LSD – 25,000 squares;<br>• amphetamine – 4kg;<br>• cannabis – 40kg;<br>• ketamine – 1kg.<br><br>**Category 3**<br>Where the offence is selling directly to users★ ('street dealing'), the starting point is not based on a quantity,<br><br>OR<br><br>where the offence is supply of drugs in prison by a prison employee, the starting point is not based on a quantity – see [above], |

| Culpability demonstrated by offender's role | Category of harm |
|---|---|
| One or more of these characteristics may demonstrate the offender's role. These lists are not exhaustive. | Indicative quantity of drug concerned (upon which the starting point is based): |
| **LESSER role:**<br><br>• performs a limited function under direction;<br><br>• engaged by pressure, coercion, intimidation;<br><br>• involvement through naivety/exploitation;<br><br>• no influence on those above in a chain;<br><br>• very little, if any, awareness or understanding of the scale of operation;<br><br>• if own operation, absence of any financial gain, for example joint purchase for no profit, or sharing minimal quantity between peers on non-commercial basis. | OR<br><br>• heroin, cocaine – 150g;<br><br>• ecstasy – 300 tablets;<br><br>• LSD – 2,500 squares;<br><br>• amphetamine – 750g;<br><br>• cannabis – 6kg;<br><br>• ketamine – 150g.<br><br>**Category 4**<br><br>• heroin, cocaine – 5g;<br><br>• ecstasy – 20 tablets;<br><br>• LSD – 170 squares;<br><br>• amphetamine – 20g;<br><br>•     cannabis – 100g;<br><br>•     ketamine – 5g;<br><br>OR<br><br>where the offence is selling directly to users★ ('street dealing') the starting point is not based on quantity – go to category 3. |

★    Including test purchase officers

## STEP TWO
### Starting point and category range

Having determined the category, the court should use the corresponding starting point to reach a sentence within the category range below. The starting point applies to all offenders irrespective of plea or previous convictions. The court should then consider further adjustment within the category range for aggravating or mitigating features, set out on page 14. In cases where the offender is regarded as being at the very top of the 'leading' role it may be justifiable for the court to depart from the guideline.

Where the defendant is dependent on or has a propensity to misuse drugs and there is sufficient prospect of success, a community order with a drug rehabilitation requirement under section 209 of the Criminal Justice Act 2003 can be a proper alternative to a short or moderate length custodial sentence.

For class A cases, section 110 of the Powers of Criminal Courts (Sentencing) Act 2000 provides that a court should impose a minimum sentence of at least seven years' imprisonment for a third class A trafficking offence except where the court is of the opinion that there are particular circumstances which (a) relate to any of the offences or to the offender; and (b) would make it unjust to do so in all the circumstances.

| CLASS A | Leading role | Significant role | Lesser role |
|---|---|---|---|
| Category 1 | Starting point<br>14 years' custody | Starting point<br>10 years' custody | Starting point<br>7 years' custody |
| | Category range<br>12 – 16 years' custody | Category range<br>9 – 12 years' custody | Category range<br>6 – 9 years' custody |
| Category 2 | Starting point<br>11 years' custody | Starting point<br>8 years' custody | Starting point<br>5 years' custody |
| | Category range<br>9 – 13 years' custody | Category range<br>6 years 6 months' – 10 years' custody | Category range<br>3 years 6 months' – 7 years' custody |
| Category 3 | Starting point<br>8 years 6 months' custody | Starting point<br>4 years 6 months' custody | Starting point<br>3 years' custody |
| | Category range<br>6 years 6 months' – 10 years' custody | Category range<br>3 years 6 months' – 7 years' custody | Category range<br>2 – 4 years 6 months' custody |
| Category 4 | Starting point<br>5 years 6 months' custody | Starting point<br>3 years 6 months' custody | Starting point<br>18 months' custody |
| | Category range<br>4 years 6 months' – 7 years 6 months' custody | Category range<br>2 – 5 years' custody | Category range<br>High level community order – 3 years' custody |

| CLASS B | Leading role | Significant role | Lesser role |
|---|---|---|---|
| Category 1 | Starting point<br><br>8 years' custody | Starting point<br><br>5 years 6 months' custody | Starting point<br><br>3 years' custody |
| | Category range<br><br>7 – 10 years' custody | Category range<br><br>5 – 7 years' custody | Category range<br><br>2 years 6 months' – 5 years' custody |
| Category 2 | Starting point<br><br>6 years' custody | Starting point<br><br>4 years' custody | Starting point<br><br>1 year's custody |
| | Category range<br><br>4 years 6 months' – 8 years' custody | Category range<br><br>2 years 6 months' – 5 years' custody | Category range<br><br>26 weeks' – 3 years' custody |
| Category 3 | Starting point<br><br>4 years' custody | Starting point<br><br>1 year's custody | Starting point<br><br>High level community order |
| | Category range<br><br>2 years 6 months' – 5 years' custody | Category range<br><br>26 weeks' – 3 years' custody | Category range<br><br>Low level community order – 26 weeks' custody |
| Category 4 | Starting point<br><br>18 months' custody | Starting point<br><br>High level community order | Starting point<br><br>Low level community order |
| | Category range<br><br>26 weeks' – 3 years' custody | Category range<br><br>Medium level community order – 26 weeks' custody | Category range<br><br>Band B fine – medium level community order |

| CLASS C | Leading role | Significant role | Lesser role |
|---|---|---|---|
| Category 1 | Starting point<br><br>5 years' custody | Starting point<br><br>3 years' custody | Starting point<br><br>18 months' custody |
| | Category range<br><br>4 – 8 years' custody | Category range<br><br>2 – 5 years' custody | Category range<br><br>1 – 3 years' custody |

| CLASS C | Leading role | Significant role | Lesser role |
|---|---|---|---|
| Category 2 | Starting point<br><br>3 years 6 months' custody | Starting point<br><br>18 months' custody | Starting point<br><br>26 weeks' custody |
| | Category range<br><br>2 – 5 years' custody | Category range<br><br>1 – 3 years' custody | Category range<br><br>12 weeks' – 18 months' custody |
| Category 3 | Starting point<br><br>18 months' custody | Starting point<br><br>26 weeks' custody | Starting point<br><br>High level community order |
| | Category range<br><br>1 – 3 years' custody | Category range<br><br>12 weeks' – 18 months' custody | Category range<br><br>Low level community order – 12 weeks' custody |
| Category 4 | Starting point<br><br>26 weeks' custody | Starting point<br><br>High level community order | Starting point<br><br>Low level community order |
| | Category range<br><br>High level community order – 18 months' custody | Category range<br><br>Low level community order – 12 weeks' custody | Category range<br><br>Band A fine – medium level community order |

The table below contains a non-exhaustive list of additional factual elements providing the context of the offence and factors relating to the offender. Identify whether any combination of these, or other relevant factors, should result in an upward or downward adjustment from the starting point. In some cases, having considered these factors, it may be appropriate to move outside the identified category range.

For appropriate class B and C ranges, consider the custody threshold as follows:

- has the custody threshold been passed?
- if so, is it unavoidable that a custodial sentence be imposed?
- if so, can that sentence be suspended?

For appropriate class B and C ranges, the court should also consider the community threshold as follows:

- has the community threshold been passed?

| Factors increasing seriousness | Factors reducing seriousness or reflecting personal mitigation |
|---|---|
| **Statutory aggravating factors:** | Involvement due to pressure, intimidation or coercion falling short of duress, except where already taken into account at step 1 |
| Previous convictions, having regard to a) nature of the offence to which conviction relates and relevance to current offence; and b) time elapsed since conviction (see shaded box at page 12 if third drug trafficking conviction) | |
| | Supply only of drug to which offender addicted |
| Offender used or permitted a person under 18 to deliver a controlled drug to a third person | Mistaken belief of the offender regarding the type of drug, taking into account the reasonableness of such belief in all the circumstances |
| Offender 18 or over supplies or offers to supply a drug on, or in the vicinity of, school premises either when school in use as such or at a time between one hour before and one hour after they are to be used | |
| | Isolated incident |
| Offence committed on bail | Low purity |
| **Other aggravating factors include:** | No previous convictions or no relevant or recent convictions |
| Targeting of any premises intended to locate vulnerable individuals or supply to such individuals and/or supply to those under 18 | Offender's vulnerability was exploited |
| Exposure of others to more than usual danger, for example drugs cut with harmful substances | Remorse |
| | Good character and/or exemplary conduct |
| Attempts to conceal or dispose of evidence, where not charged separately | Determination and/or demonstration of steps having been taken to address addiction or offending behaviour |
| Presence of others, especially children and/or non-users | |
| Presence of weapon, where not charged separately | Serious medical conditions requiring urgent, intensive or long-term treatment |
| Charged as importation of a very small amount | Age and/or lack of maturity where it affects the responsibility of the offender |
| High purity | |
| Failure to comply with current court orders | Mental disorder or learning disability |
| Offence committed on licence | |
| Established evidence of community impact | Sole or primary carer for dependent relatives |

## STEP THREE
*Consider any factors which indicate a reduction, such as assistance to the prosecution*

The court should take into account sections 73 and 74 of the Serious Organised Crime and Police Act 2005 (assistance by defendants: reduction or review of sentence) and any other rule of law by virtue of which an offender may receive a discounted sentence in consequence of assistance given (or offered) to the prosecutor or investigator.

## STEP FOUR
*Reduction for guilty pleas*

The court should take account of any potential reduction for a guilty plea in accordance with section 144 of the Criminal Justice Act 2003 and the Guilty Plea guideline.

For class A offences, where a minimum mandatory sentence is imposed under section 110 Powers of Criminal Courts (Sentencing) Act, the discount for an early guilty plea must not exceed 20 per cent.

## STEP FIVE
*Totality principle*

If sentencing an offender for more than one offence, or where the offender is already serving a sentence, consider whether the total sentence is just and proportionate to the offending behaviour.

## STEP SIX
*Confiscation and ancillary orders*

In all cases, the court is required to consider confiscation where the Crown invokes the process or where the court considers it appropriate. It should also consider whether to make ancillary orders.

## STEP SEVEN
*Reasons*

Section 174 of the Criminal Justice Act 2003 imposes a duty to give reasons for, and explain the effect of, the sentence.

## STEP EIGHT
*Consideration for remand time*

Sentencers should take into consideration any remand time served in relation to the final sentence at this final step. The court should consider whether to

give credit for time spent on remand in custody or on bail in accordance with sections 240 and 240A of the Criminal Justice Act 2003.

# Production of a controlled drug

## *Misuse of Drugs Act 1971 (section 4(2)(a) or (b))*

Triable either way unless the defendant could receive the minimum sentence of seven years for a third drug trafficking offence under section 110 Powers of Criminal Courts (Sentencing) Act 2000 in which case the offence is triable only on indictment.

### *Class A*

Maximum: Life imprisonment

Offence range: Community order – 16 years' custody

A class A offence is a drug trafficking offence for the purpose of imposing a minimum sentence under section 110 Powers of Criminal Courts (Sentencing) Act 2000

### *Class B*

Maximum: 14 years' custody

Offence range: Discharge – 10 years' custody

### *Class C*

Maximum: 14 years' custody

Offence range: Discharge – 8 years' custody

# Cultivation of cannabis plant

## *Misuse of Drugs Act 1971 (section 6(2))*

Maximum: 14 years' custody

Offence range: Discharge – 10 years' custody

*STEP ONE*
*Determining the offence category*

The court should determine the offender's culpability (role) and the harm caused (output or potential output) with reference to the tables below.

In assessing culpability, the sentencer should weigh up all of the factors of the case to determine role. Where there are characteristics present which fall under different role categories, the court should balance these characteristics to reach a fair assessment of the offender's culpability.

In assessing harm, output or potential output is determined by the weight of the product or number of plants/scale of operation. For production offences, purity is not taken into account at step 1 but is dealt with at step 2.

Where the operation is on the most serious and commercial scale, involving a quantity of drugs significantly higher than category 1, sentences of 20 years and above may be appropriate, depending on the role of the offender.

| Culpability demonstrated by offender's role<br><br>One or more of these characteristics may demonstrate the offender's role. These lists are not exhaustive. | Category of harm<br><br>Indicative output or potential output (upon which the starting point is based): |
| --- | --- |
| **LEADING role:**<br><br>• directing or organising production on a commercial scale;<br><br>• substantial links to, and influence on, others in a chain;<br><br>• expectation of substantial financial gain;<br><br>• uses business as cover;<br><br>• abuses a position of trust or responsibility.<br><br>**SIGNIFICANT role:**<br><br>• operational or management function within a chain;<br><br>• involves others in the operation whether by pressure, influence, intimidation or reward;<br><br>• motivated by financial or other advantage, whether or not operating alone;<br><br>• some awareness and understanding of scale of operation. | **Category 1**<br><br>• heroin, cocaine – 5kg;<br><br>• ecstasy – 10,000 tablets;<br><br>• LSD – 250,000 tablets;<br><br>• amphetamine – 20kg;<br><br>• cannabis – operation capable of producing industrial quantities for commercial use;<br><br>• ketamine – 5kg.<br><br>**Category 2**<br><br>• heroin, cocaine – 1kg;<br><br>• ecstasy – 2,000 tablets;<br><br>• LSD – 25,000 squares;<br><br>• amphetamine – 4kg;<br><br>• cannabis – operation capable of producing significant quantities for commercial use;<br><br>• ketamine – 1kg. |

| Culpability demonstrated by offender's role | Category of harm |
|---|---|
| One or more of these characteristics may demonstrate the offender's role. These lists are not exhaustive. | Indicative output or potential output (upon which the starting point is based): |
| **LESSER role:**<br><br>• performs a limited function under direction;<br><br>• engaged by pressure, coercion, intimidation;<br><br>• involvement through naivety/ exploitation; • no influence on those above in a chain;<br><br>• very little, if any, awareness or understanding of the scale of operation;<br><br>• if own operation, solely for own use (considering reasonableness of account in all the circumstances). | **Category 3**<br>• heroin, cocaine – 150g;<br>• ecstasy – 300 tablets;<br>• LSD – 2,500 squares;<br>• amphetamine – 750g;<br>• cannabis – 28 plants;★<br>• ketamine – 150g.<br><br>**Category 4**<br>• heroin, cocaine – 5g;<br>• ecstasy – 20 tablets;<br>• LSD – 170 squares;<br>• amphetamine – 20g;<br>• cannabis – 9 plants (domestic operation);★<br>• ketamine – 5g. |

★     With assumed yield of 40g per plant


## STEP TWO
*Starting point and category range*

Having determined the category, the court should use the corresponding starting point to reach a sentence within the category range below. The starting point applies to all offenders irrespective of plea or previous convictions. The court should then consider further adjustment within the category range for aggravating or mitigating features, set out on page 21. In cases where the offender is regarded as being at the very top of the 'leading' role it may be justifiable for the court to depart from the guideline.

Where the defendant is dependent on or has a propensity to misuse drugs and there is sufficient prospect of success, a community order with a drug rehabilitation requirement under section 209 of the Criminal Justice Act 2003 can be a proper alternative to a short or moderate length custodial sentence.

For class A cases, section 110 of the Powers of Criminal Courts (Sentencing) Act 2000 provides that a court should impose a minimum sentence of at least seven years' imprisonment for a third class A trafficking offence except where the court is of the opinion that there are particular circumstances which (a) relate to any of the offences or to the offender; and (b) would make it unjust to do so in all the circumstances.

| CLASS A | Leading role | Significant role | Lesser role |
|---|---|---|---|
| Category 1 | Starting point<br><br>14 years' custody | Starting point<br><br>10 years' custody | Starting point<br><br>7 years' custody |
| | Category range<br><br>12 – 16 years' custody | Category range<br><br>9 – 12 years' custody | Category range<br><br>6 – 9 years' custody |
| Category 2 | Starting point<br><br>11 years' custody | Starting point<br><br>8 years' custody | Starting point<br><br>5 years' custody |
| | Category range<br><br>9 – 13 years' custody | Category range<br><br>6 years 6 months' – 10 years' custody | Category range<br><br>3 years 6 months' – 7 years' custody |
| Category 3 | Starting point<br><br>8 years 6 months' custody | Starting point<br><br>5 years' custody | Starting point<br><br>3 years 6 months' custody |
| | Category range<br><br>6 years 6 months' – 10 years' custody | Category range<br><br>3 years 6 months' – 7 years' custody | Category range<br><br>2 – 5 years' custody |
| Category 4 | Starting point<br><br>5 years 6 months' custody | Starting point<br><br>3 years 6 months' custody | Starting point<br><br>18 months' custody |
| | Category range<br><br>4 years 6 months' – 7 years 6 months' custody | Category range<br><br>2 – 5 years' custody | Category range<br><br>High level community order – 3 years' custody |

| CLASS B | Leading role | Significant role | Lesser role |
|---|---|---|---|
| Category 1 | Starting point<br><br>8 years' custody | Starting point<br><br>5 years 6 months' custody | Starting point<br><br>3 years' custody |
| | Category range<br><br>7 – 10 years' custody | Category range<br><br>5 – 7 years' custody | Category range<br><br>2 years 6 months' – 5 years' custody |

| CLASS B | Leading role | Significant role | Lesser role |
|---|---|---|---|
| Category 2 | Starting point<br><br>6 years' custody | Starting point<br><br>4 years' custody | Starting point<br><br>1 year's custody |
| | Category range<br><br>4 years 6 months' – 8 years' custody | Category range<br><br>2 years 6 months' – 5 years' custody | Category range<br><br>26 weeks' – 3 years' custody |
| Category 3 | Starting point<br><br>4 years' custody | Starting point<br><br>1 year's custody | Starting point<br><br>High level community order |
| | Category range<br><br>2 years 6 months' – 5 years' custody | Category range<br><br>26 weeks' – 3 years' custody | Category range<br><br>Low level community order – 26 weeks' custody |
| Category 4 | Starting point<br><br>1 year's custody | Starting point<br><br>High level community order | Starting point<br><br>Band C fine |
| | Category range<br><br>High level community order – 3 years' custody | Category range<br><br>Medium level community order – 26 weeks' custody | Category range<br><br>Discharge – medium level community order |

| CLASS C | Leading role | Significant role | Lesser role |
|---|---|---|---|
| Category 1 | Starting point<br><br>5 years' custody | Starting point<br><br>3 years' custody | Starting point<br><br>18 months' custody |
| | Category range<br><br>4 – 8 years' custody | Category range<br><br>2 – 5 years' custody | Category range<br><br>1 – 3 years' custody |
| Category 2 | Starting point<br><br>3 years 6 months' custody | Starting point<br><br>18 months' custody | Starting point<br><br>26 weeks' custody |
| | Category range<br><br>2 – 5 years' custody | Category range<br><br>1 – 3 years' custody | Category range<br><br>High level community order – 18 months' custody |

| CLASS C | Leading role | Significant role | Lesser role |
|---|---|---|---|
| Category 3 | Starting point<br><br>18 months' custody | Starting point<br><br>26 weeks' custody | Starting point<br><br>High level community order |
|  | Category range<br><br>1 – 3 years' custody | Category range<br><br>High level community order – 18 months' custody | Category range<br><br>Low level community order – 12 weeks' custody |
| Category 4 | Starting point<br><br>26 weeks' custody | Starting point<br><br>High level community order | Starting point<br><br>Band C fine |
|  | Category range<br><br>High level community order – 18 months' custody | Category range<br><br>Low level community order – 12 weeks' custody | Category range<br><br>Discharge – medium level community order |

The table below contains a non-exhaustive list of additional factual elements providing the context of the offence and factors relating to the offender. Identify whether any combination of these, or other relevant factors, should result in an upward or downward adjustment from the starting point. In some cases, having considered these factors, it may be appropriate to move outside the identified category range.

Where appropriate, consider the custody threshold as follows:

- has the custody threshold been passed?
- if so, is it unavoidable that a custodial sentence be imposed?
- if so, can that sentence be suspended?

Where appropriate, the court should also consider the community threshold as follows:

- has the community threshold been passed?

| Factors increasing seriousness | Factors reducing seriousness or reflecting personal mitigation |
|---|---|
| **Statutory aggravating factors:** Previous convictions, having regard to a) nature of the offence to which conviction relates and relevance to current offence; and b) time elapsed since conviction (see shaded box at page 19 if third drug trafficking conviction) Offence committed on bail **Other aggravating factors include:** Nature of any likely supply Level of any profit element Use of premises accompanied by unlawful access to electricity/other utility supply of others Ongoing/large scale operation as evidenced by presence and nature of specialist equipment Exposure of others to more than usual danger, for example drugs cut with harmful substances Attempts to conceal or dispose of evidence, where not charged separately Presence of others, especially children and/or non-users Presence of weapon, where not charged separately High purity or high potential yield Failure to comply with current court orders Offence committed on licence Established evidence of community impact | Involvement due to pressure, intimidation or coercion falling short of duress, except where already taken into account at step 1 Isolated incident Low purity No previous convictions or no relevant or recent convictions Offender's vulnerability was exploited Remorse Good character and/or exemplary conduct Determination and/or demonstration of steps having been taken to address addiction or offending behaviour Serious medical conditions requiring urgent, intensive or long-term treatment Age and/or lack of maturity where it affects the responsibility of the offender Mental disorder or learning disability Sole or primary carer for dependent relatives |

## STEP THREE
*Consider any factors which indicate a reduction, such as assistance to the prosecution*

The court should take into account sections 73 and 74 of the Serious Organised Crime and Police Act 2005 (assistance by defendants: reduction or review of sentence) and any other rule of law by virtue of which an offender may receive a discounted sentence in consequence of assistance given (or offered) to the prosecutor or investigator.

## STEP FOUR
*Reduction for guilty pleas*

The court should take account of any potential reduction for a guilty plea in accordance with section 144 of the Criminal Justice Act 2003 and the Guilty Plea guideline.

For class A offences, where a minimum mandatory sentence is imposed under section 110 Powers of Criminal Courts (Sentencing) Act, the discount for an early guilty plea must not exceed 20 per cent.

## STEP FIVE
*Totality principle*

If sentencing an offender for more than one offence, or where the offender is already serving a sentence, consider whether the total sentence is just and proportionate to the offending behaviour.

## STEP SIX
*Confiscation and ancillary orders*

In all cases, the court is required to consider confiscation where the Crown invokes the process or where the court considers it appropriate. It should also consider whether to make ancillary orders.

## STEP SEVEN
*Reasons*

Section 174 of the Criminal Justice Act 2003 imposes a duty to give reasons for, and explain the effect of, the sentence.

## STEP EIGHT
*Consideration for remand time*

Sentencers should take into consideration any remand time served in relation to the final sentence at this final step. The court should consider whether to

give credit for time spent on remand in custody or on bail in accordance with sections 240 and 240A of the Criminal Justice Act 2003.

## Permitting premises to be used

### *Misuse of Drugs Act 1971 (section 8)*

Triable either way unless the defendant could receive the minimum sentence of seven years for a third drug trafficking offence under section 110 Powers of Criminal Courts (Sentencing) Act 2000 in which case the offence is triable only on indictment.

### *Class A*

Maximum: 14 years' custody

Offence range: Community order – 4 years' custody

A class A offence is a drug trafficking offence for the purpose of imposing a minimum sentence under section 110 Powers of Criminal Courts (Sentencing) Act 2000

### *Class B*

Maximum: 14 years' custody

Offence range: Fine – 18 months' custody

### *Class C*

Maximum: 14 years' custody

Offence range: Discharge – 26 weeks' custody

### *STEP ONE*
*Determining the offence category*

The court should determine the offender's culpability and the harm caused (extent of the activity and/or the quantity of drugs) with reference to the table below.

In assessing harm, quantity is determined by the weight of the product. Purity is not taken into account at step 1 but is dealt with at step 2.

| Category 1 | Higher culpability and greater harm |
| --- | --- |
| Category 2 | Lower culpability and greater harm; or higher culpability and lesser harm |
| Category 3 | Lower culpability and lesser harm |

| Factors indicating culpability (non-exhaustive) | Factors indicating harm (non-exhaustive) |
|---|---|
| Higher culpability: | Greater harm: |
| Permits premises to be used primarily for drug activity, for example crack house | Regular drug-related activity |
| Permits use in expectation of substantial financial gain | Higher quantity of drugs, for example: |
| Uses legitimate business premises to aid and/or conceal illegal activity, for example public house or club | • heroin, cocaine – more than 5g; <br> • cannabis – more than 50g. <br> Lesser harm: |
| | Infrequent drug-related activity |
| Lower culpability: | Lower quantity of drugs, for example: |
| Permits use for limited or no financial gain | • heroin, cocaine – up to 5g; |
| No active role in any supply taking place | • cannabis – up to 50g. |
| Involvement through naivety | |

## STEP TWO
### Starting point and category range

Having determined the category, the court should use the table below to identify the corresponding starting point to reach a sentence within the category range. The starting point applies to all offenders irrespective of plea or previous convictions. The court should then consider further adjustment within the category range for aggravating or mitigating features, set out over the page.

Where the defendant is dependent on or has a propensity to misuse drugs and there is sufficient prospect of success, a community order with a drug rehabilitation requirement under section 209 of the Criminal Justice Act 2003 can be a proper alternative to a short or moderate length custodial sentence.

> For class A cases, section 110 of the Powers of Criminal Courts (Sentencing) Act 2000 provides that a court should impose a minimum sentence of at least seven years' imprisonment for a third class A trafficking offence except where the court is of the opinion that there are particular circumstances which (a) relate to any of the offences or to the offender; and (b) would make it unjust to do so in all the circumstances.

## Class A

| Offence category | Starting point (applicable to all offenders) | Category range (applicable to all offenders) |
|---|---|---|
| Category 1 | 2 years 6 months' custody | 18 months' – 4 years' custody |
| Category 2 | 36 weeks' custody | High level community order – 18 months' custody |
| Category 3 | Medium level community order | Low level community order – high level community order |

## Class B

| Offence category | Starting point (applicable to all offenders) | Category range (applicable to all offenders) |
|---|---|---|
| Category 1 | 1 year's custody | 26 weeks' – 18 months' custody |
| Category 2 | High level community order | Low level community order – 26 weeks' custody |
| Category 3 | Band C fine | Band A fine – low level community order |

## Class C

| Offence category | Starting point (applicable to all offenders) | Category range (applicable to all offenders) |
|---|---|---|
| Category 1 | 12 weeks' custody | High level community order – 26 weeks' custody★ |
| Category 2 | Low level community order | Band C fine – high level community order |
| Category 3 | Band A fine | Discharge – band C fine |

★    When tried summarily, the maximum penalty is 12 weeks' custody.

The table below contains a non-exhaustive list of additional factual elements providing the context of the offence and factors relating to the offender. Identify whether any combination of these, or other relevant factors, should result in an upward or downward adjustment from the starting point. In some cases, having considered these factors, it may be appropriate to move outside the identified category range.

Where appropriate, consider the custody threshold as follows:

- has the custody threshold been passed?

- if so, is it unavoidable that a custodial sentence be imposed?

- if so, can that sentence be suspended?

Where appropriate, the court should also consider the community threshold as follows:

- has the community threshold been passed?

| Factors increasing seriousness | Factors reducing seriousness or reflecting personal mitigation |
|---|---|
| **Statutory aggravating factors:**<br><br>Previous convictions, having regard to a) nature of the offence to which conviction relates and relevance to current offence; and b) time elapsed since conviction (see shaded box at page 25 if third drug trafficking conviction)<br><br>Offence committed on bail | Involvement due to pressure, intimidation or coercion falling short of duress |
| | Isolated incident |
| | Low purity |
| | No previous convictions or no relevant or recent convictions |
| **Other aggravating factors include:**<br><br>Length of time over which premises used for drug activity | Offender's vulnerability was exploited |
| Volume of drug activity permitted | Remorse |
| Premises adapted to facilitate drug activity | Good character and/or exemplary conduct |
| Location of premises, for example proximity to school | Determination and/or demonstration of steps having been taken to address addiction or offending behaviour |
| Attempts to conceal or dispose of evidence, where not charged separately | |
| Presence of others, especially children and/or non-users | Serious medical conditions requiring urgent, intensive or long-term treatment |
| High purity | |
| Presence of weapons, where not charged separately | Age and/or lack of maturity where it affects the responsibility of the offender |
| Failure to comply with current court orders | Mental disorder or learning disability |
| Offence committed on licence | |
| Established evidence of community impact | Sole or primary carer for dependent relatives |

## STEP THREE
*Consider any factors which indicate a reduction, such as assistance to the prosecution*

The court should take into account sections 73 and 74 of the Serious Organised Crime and Police Act 2005 (assistance by defendants: reduction or review of sentence) and any other rule of law by virtue of which an offender may receive a discounted sentence in consequence of assistance given (or offered) to the prosecutor or investigator.

## STEP FOUR
*Reduction for guilty pleas*

The court should take account of any potential reduction for a guilty plea in accordance with section 144 of the Criminal Justice Act 2003 and the Guilty Plea guideline.

For class A offences, where a minimum mandatory sentence is imposed under section 110 Powers of Criminal Courts (Sentencing) Act, the discount for an early guilty plea must not exceed 20 per cent.

## STEP FIVE
*Totality principle*

If sentencing an offender for more than one offence or where the offender is already serving a sentence, consider whether the total sentence is just and proportionate to the offending behaviour.

## STEP SIX
*Confiscation and ancillary orders*

In all cases, the court is required to consider confiscation where the Crown invokes the process or where the court considers it appropriate. It should also consider whether to make ancillary orders.

## STEP SEVEN
*Reasons*

Section 174 of the Criminal Justice Act 2003 imposes a duty to give reasons for, and explain the effect of, the sentence.

## STEP EIGHT
*Consideration for remand time*

Sentencers should take into consideration any remand time served in relation to the final sentence at this final step. The court should consider whether to

give credit for time spent on remand in custody or on bail in accordance with sections 240 and 240A of the Criminal Justice Act 2003.

# Possession of a controlled drug

## *Misuse of Drugs Act 1971 (section 5(2))*

Triable either way

### Class A

Maximum: 7 years' custody

Offence range: Fine – 51 weeks' custody

### Class B

Maximum: 5 years' custody

Offence range: Discharge – 26 weeks' custody

### Class C

Maximum: 2 years' custody

Offence range: Discharge – Community order

## STEP ONE
*Determining the offence category*

The court should identify the offence category based on the class of drug involved.

| Category 1 | Class A drug |
|------------|--------------|
| Category 2 | Class B drug |
| Category 3 | Class C drug |

## STEP TWO
*Starting point and category range*

The court should use the table below to identify the corresponding starting point. The starting point applies to all offenders irrespective of plea or previous convictions. The court should then consider further adjustment within the category range for aggravating or mitigating features, set out on the opposite page.

Where the defendant is dependent on or has a propensity to misuse drugs and there is sufficient prospect of success, a community order with a drug rehabilitation requirement under section 209 of the Criminal Justice Act 2003 can be a proper alternative to a short or moderate length custodial sentence.

| Offence category | Starting point (applicable to all offenders) | Category range (applicable to all offenders) |
|---|---|---|
| Category 1 (class A) | Band C fine | Band A fine – 51 weeks' custody |
| Category 2 (class B) | Band B fine | Discharge – 26 weeks' custody |
| Category 3 (class C) | Band A fine | Discharge – medium level community order |

The table below contains a non-exhaustive list of additional factual elements providing the context of the offence and factors relating to the offender. Identify whether any combination of these, or other relevant factors, should result in an upward or downward adjustment from the starting point. In particular, possession of drugs in prison is likely to result in an upward adjustment. In some cases, having considered these factors, it may be appropriate to move outside the identified category range.

Where appropriate, consider the custody threshold as follows:

- has the custody threshold been passed?

- if so, is it unavoidable that a custodial sentence be imposed?

- if so, can that sentence be suspended?

Where appropriate, the court should also consider the community threshold as follows:

- has the community threshold been passed?

| Factors increasing seriousness | Factors reducing seriousness or reflecting personal mitigation |
|---|---|
| **Statutory aggravating factors:** | No previous convictions or no relevant or recent convictions |
| Previous convictions, having regard to a) nature of the offence to which conviction relates and relevance to current offence; and b) time elapsed since conviction | Remorse |
| | Good character and/or exemplary conduct |
| Offence committed on bail | Offender is using cannabis to help with a diagnosed medical condition |
| **Other aggravating factors include:** | Determination and/or demonstration of steps having been taken to address addiction or offending behaviour |
| Possession of drug in prison | |
| Presence of others, especially children and/or non-users | Serious medical conditions requiring urgent, intensive or long-term treatment |
| Possession of drug in a school or licensed premises | |
| Failure to comply with current court orders | Isolated incident |
| Offence committed on licence | Age and/or lack of maturity where it affects the responsibility of the offender |
| Attempts to conceal or dispose of evidence, where not charged separately | |
| Charged as importation of a very small amount | Mental disorder or learning disability |
| Established evidence of community impact | Sole or primary carer for dependent relatives |

## STEP THREE

*Consider any factors which indicate a reduction, such as assistance to the prosecution*

The court should take into account sections 73 and 74 of the Serious Organised Crime and Police Act 2005 (assistance by defendants: reduction or review of sentence) and any other rule of law by virtue of which an offender may receive a discounted sentence in consequence of assistance given (or offered) to the prosecutor or investigator.

## STEP FOUR

*Reduction for guilty pleas*

The court should take account of any potential reduction for a guilty plea in accordance with section 144 of the Criminal Justice Act 2003 and the Guilty Plea guideline.

*STEP FIVE*
*Totality principle*

If sentencing an offender for more than one offence, or where the offender is already serving a sentence, consider whether the total sentence is just and proportionate to the offending behaviour.

*STEP SIX*
*Ancillary orders*

In all cases, the court should consider whether to make ancillary orders.

*STEP SEVEN*
*Reasons*

Section 174 of the Criminal Justice Act 2003 imposes a duty to give reasons for, and explain the effect of, the sentence.

*STEP EIGHT*
*Consideration for remand time*

Sentencers should take into consideration any remand time served in relation to the final sentence at this final step. The court should consider whether to give credit for time spent on remand in custody or on bail in accordance with sections 240 and 240A of the Criminal Justice Act 2003.

## Annex:
## Fine bands and community orders

### *FINE BANDS*

In this guideline, fines are expressed as one of three fine bands (A, B or C).

| Fine Band | Starting point (applicable to all offenders) | Category range (applicable to all offenders) |
|-----------|----------------------------------------------|----------------------------------------------|
| Band A | 50% of relevant weekly income | 25–75% of relevant weekly income |
| Band B | 100% of relevant weekly income | 75–125% of relevant weekly income |
| Band C | 150% of relevant weekly income | 125–175% of relevant weekly income |

# COMMUNITY ORDERS

In this guideline, community sentences are expressed as one of three levels (low, medium and high).

An illustrative description of examples of requirements that might be appropriate for each level is provided below. Where two or more requirements are ordered, they must be compatible with each other.

| LOW | MEDIUM | HIGH |
|---|---|---|
| In general, only one requirement will be appropriate and the length may be curtailed if additional requirements are necessary | | More intensive sentences which combine two or more requirements may be appropriate |
| Suitable requirements might include:<br><br>• 40 – 80 hours unpaid work;<br><br>• curfew requirement within the lowest range (for example, up to 12 hours per day for a few weeks);<br><br>• exclusion requirement, without electronic monitoring, for a few months;<br><br>• prohibited activity requirement;<br><br>• attendance centre requirement (where available). | Suitable requirements might include:<br><br>• greater number of hours of unpaid work (for example, 80 – 150 hours);<br><br>• an activity requirement in the middle range (20 to 30 days);<br><br>• curfew requirement within the middle range (for example, up to 12 hours for two to three months);<br><br>• exclusion requirement, lasting in the region of six months;<br><br>• prohibited activity requirement. | Suitable requirements might include:<br><br>• 150 – 300 hours unpaid work;<br><br>• activity requirement up to the maximum of 60 days;<br><br>• curfew requirement up to 12 hours per day for four to six months;<br><br>• exclusion order lasting in the region of 12 months. |

The tables above are also set out in the Magistrates' Court Sentencing Guidelines which includes further guidance on fines and community orders.

www.sentencingcouncil.org.uk

# Index

[*All references are to paragraph number*]

**Actus reus**
import and export of controlled goods, 2.27–2.44
possession of controlled goods, 3.14–3.35

**Administering drugs**
supply of controlled drugs, and, 5.85–5.87

**Admissibility of evidence**
covert evidence, 10.34–10.37
import and export of controlled goods, 2.60–2.70

**Admissions**
prohibited drugs, 4.41–4.47

**Advisory Council on the Misuse of Drugs (ACMD)**
classification of drugs, 4.3

**Agents provocateurs**
covert evidence, 10.38–10.44

**Aggravated supply**
possession with intent, and, 6.71–6.88

**Anti-social behaviour orders**
occupiers of premises, 7.50–7.53

**'Any other method'**
manufacture of controlled drugs, 1.11

**Authorisation of activities**
manufacture of controlled drugs, 1.4

**Being concerned in management of premises**
occupiers of premises, 7.4–7.10

**Being 'concerned' in offer or making offer to supply**
construction, 5.118–5.129
generally, 5.114–5.117
Hughes definition, 5.122–5.129
introduction, 5.3

**Benefit of recipient**
supply of controlled drugs, 5.24–5.33

**Bogus offer**
supply of controlled drugs, 5.98–5.110

**Burden of proof**
lack of knowledge, 4.72–4.79

**Burden of proof** – *contd*
prohibited drugs
cocaine cases, 4.29–4.35
evidence not always required, 4.36–4.40
generally, 4.20–4.28

**Cannabis**
defences to possession offences
lack of knowledge, 4.75
lawful intention, 4.53
medical necessity, 4.108–4.120
manufacture of controlled drugs, 1.12
prohibited drugs
forensic analysis, 4.37–4.40
generally, 4.4

**'Certain drug precursors'**
manufacture of controlled drugs, 1.16

**Channel Tunnel**
import and export of controlled goods, 2.9

**Charges**
import and export of controlled goods, 2.10–2.11

**Cocaine**
prohibited drugs, 4.29–4.35

**Concerned in management of premises**
occupiers of premises, 7.4–7.10

**Concerned in offer or making offer to supply**
construction, 5.118–5.129
generally, 5.114–5.117
Hughes definition, 5.122–5.129
introduction, 5.3

**Confiscation orders**
assumptions, 12.99–12.108
available amount, 12.118–12.123
benefit, 12.78–12.82
'corporate veil', 12.89–12.92
courtiers, 12.83–12.88
criminal conduct, 12.70–12.77
criminal lifestyle, 12.61–12.69
custodians, 12.83–12.88

**Confiscation orders** – *contd*
defendant's response to statement of
information, 12.55–12.59
determinations to be made by court
assumptions, 12.99–12.108
available amount, 12.118–12.123
benefit, 12.78–12.82
'corporate veil', 12.89–12.92
courtiers, 12.83–12.88
criminal conduct, 12.70–12.77
criminal lifestyle, 12.61–12.69
custodians, 12.83–12.88
extent of defendant's interest in
property, 12.124–12.137
introduction, 12.60
joint benefit, 12.93–12.96
legal aid contributions from capital,
12.138–12.142
recoverable amount, 12.109–12.117
value, 12.97–12.98
enforcement, 12.165–12.168
extent of defendant's interest in property,
12.124–12.137
instigation of proceedings, 12.34–12.41
interest on unpaid sums, 12.152
introduction, 12.1–12.5
joint benefit, 12.93–12.96
legal aid contributions from capital,
12.138–12.142
making of, 12.143–12.145
overview, 11.99
period in default, 12.153–12.158
procedure, 12.42–12.43
prosecutor's statement of information,
12.49–12.54
provision of information by defendant,
12.44–12.48
public funds for proceedings, 12.169–
12.173
recoverable amount, 12.109–12.117
summary, 12.174
time to pay
generally, 12.146–12.151
interest on unpaid sums, 12.152
period in default, 12.153–12.158
value, 12.97–12.98
variation
defendant application, 12.159–12.161
prosecution application, 12.162–
12.164

**Conspiracy**
acquittal of co-conspirator, 8.79–8.84
agreement
generally, 8.17–8.25
parties, 8.30–8.39
proof, 8.77–8.78
qualified, 8.26–8.29
co-conspirator based around, 8.86
commit crime abroad, to
generally, 8.1
jurisdiction, 8.87–8.90
commit offence under CLA 1977, under,
8.1
common law, at, 8.1–8.2
consent of DPP, 8.5
corrupt public morals, to, 8.2
criminal conduct, 8.40–8.52
definition, 8.4
defraud, to, 8.2
either/or conspiracies, 8.8
elements, 8.3
impossibility, 8.72–8.76
indictment, 8.5–8.16
introduction, 8.1–8.3
jurisdiction
co-conspirator based around, 8.86
domestic conspiracy to commit offence
abroad, 8.87–8.90
foreign conspiracy to commit offence
abroad, 8.98–8.99
foreign conspiracy to commit offence
in England and Wales, 8.91–8.97
introduction, 8.85
lack of knowledge, and, 4.95–4.96
meaning, 8.3
mens rea, 8.53–8.71
outrage public decency, to, 8.2
parties to agreement, 8.30–8.39
proof of agreement
acquittal of co-conspirator, 8.79–
8.84
generally, 8.77–8.78
qualified agreements, 8.26–8.29
sentencing, 11.13–11.20
statutory provision, 8.4
summary, 8.100
types, 8.1
**Consumption**
permitting premises to be used for drug
offending, 7.14

**Consumption** – *contd*
  possession of controlled goods, 3.84–3.88
  possession with intent to supply, 6.45–6.57
  supply of controlled drugs, 5.117–5.119
**Control**
  possession of controlled goods, 3.14–3.35
**Controlled drugs**
  being concerned in supply, 5.1–5.143
  cultivation, 1.1–1.68
  exportation, 2.1–2.79
  importation, 2.1–2.79
  manufacture, 1.1–1.68
  medicinal uses, 1.18–1.22
  possession
    defences, 4.48–4.123
    general provisions, 3.1–3.89
    prohibited drugs, 4.1–4.47
    psychoactive substances, 4.124–4.151
    summary, 4.152
  possession with intent to supply, 6.1–6.91
  supply, 5.1–5.143
**Co-tenants**
  permitting premises to be used for drug
    offending, 7.11
**Covert evidence**
  admissibility, 10.34–10.37
  agents provocateurs, 10.38–10.44
  'directed surveillance', 10.19–10.23
  entrapment, 10.38–10.44
  generally, 10.18–10.28
  human intelligence sources, 10.25–10.28
  human rights, 10.22
  'intrusive surveillance', 10.19–10.23
  legal professional privilege, 10.21
  non-compliance with requirements,
    10.29–10.33
  statutory framework, 10.18
  summary, 10.45
  'surveillance', 10.24
  test purchases, 10.40
  undercover police, 10.38–10.44
**Criminal conduct**
  occupiers of premises, 7.1
**Cuckooing**
  sentencing, 11.57–11.63
**Culpability of offender**
  import and export of controlled goods
    Class A drugs, 2.18
    generally, 2.17
  sentencing, 11.6–11.7

**Cultivation of controlled drugs**
  *See also* **Manufacture of controlled
    drugs**
  defences available, 1.44–1.61
  extradition, and, 1.62–1.67
  generally, 1.40–1.43
  introduction, 1.1–1.17
  medicinal products, and, 1.18–1.22
  'preparation', 1.24–1.39
  'product', 1.23–1.39
  sentencing, 11.64–11.82
  summary, 1.68
**Cultural practices**
  manufacture of controlled drugs, 1.61
**Custody**
  possession of controlled goods, 3.14–3.35
**Customs and Excise offences**
  import and export of controlled goods,
    2.4–2.6

**Defences**
  lack of knowledge
    burden of proof, 4.72–4.79
    conspiracy offences, and, 4.95–4.96
    evidential burden, 4.80–4.88
    generally, 4.56–4.57
    parameters, 4.58–4.71
    self-induced intoxication, 4.89–4.94
    statutory provision, 4.57
  lawful intention, 4.50–4.55
  lawful possession
    controls, 4.121–4.123
    generally, 4.97–4.102
    medical necessity, 4.107–4.120
    psychoactive substances, 4.124–4.151
    self-treatment, 4.103–4.106
    statutory provision, 4.97–4.102
  manufacture of controlled drugs, 1.44–1.61
  medical necessity, 4.107–4.120
  possession of controlled drugs
    generally, 4.48–4.49
    lack of knowledge, 4.56–4.96
    lawful intention, 4.50–4.55
    lawful possession, 4.97–4.151
    medical necessity, 4.107–4.120
    summary, 4.152
**Distribution of controlled drugs**
  generally, 5.71–5.72
  introduction, 5.9
  joint possession, 5.73–5.84

**Double jeopardy**
import and export of controlled goods,
2.13
**Drugs paraphernalia**
possession with intent to supply, 6.58

**Enhancement of penalty**
import and export of controlled goods
Class A drugs, 2.15
Class B drugs, 2.15
Class C drugs, 2.16
**Enter and search powers**
*See also* **Search and seizure powers**
occupiers of premises
generally, 7.26–7.27
permitting premises to be used for
drug offending, 7.16
**Entrapment**
covert evidence, 10.38–10.44
**European Arrest Warrant**
manufacture of controlled drugs, 1.63
**Expert evidence**
forensic analysis
drugs and drug traces, 10.5–10.17
introduction, 10.1–10.4
possession with intent to supply, 6.45–
6.57
**Exportation of controlled drugs**
actus reus, 2.27–2.44
admissibility of evidence, 2.60–2.70
Channel Tunnel, through, 2.9
charges, 2.10–2.11
Customs and Excise offences, 2.4–2.6
double jeopardy, 2.13
elements of offence
actus reus, 2.27–2.44
introduction, 2.22–2.23
mens rea, 2.45–2.59
s 170(1) and 170(2), 2.24–2.26
enhancement
Class A drugs, 2.15
Class B drugs, 2.15
Class C drugs, 2.16
fraudulent evasion of prohibition, 2.4–2.5
general prohibition, 2.4
harm and culpability
Class A drugs, 2.18
generally, 2.17
improper export of goods, 2.4–2.5
introduction, 2.1–2.9

**Exportation of controlled drugs** – *contd*
'lifestyle offence', 2.21
mens rea, 2.45–2.59
offences, 2.4–2.6
penalty
enhancement, 2.15–2.16
fraudulent evasion of duty, 2.6
generally, 2.14
harm and culpability, 2.17–2.18
'lifestyle offence', 2.21
non-exhaustive factors, 2.19–2.20
'serious offence', 2.21
pipeline, by, 2.8
procedure, 2.12–2.21
prohibition, 2.4
psychoactive substances, 2.71–2.78
s 170(1) and 170(2), 2.24–2.26
sentencing, 2.12–2.21
'serious offence', 2.21
statutory framework, 2.1–2.6
summary, 2.79
terms of licence issued by Secretary of
State, 2.2–2.3
time limits, 2.12
**Extradition**
manufacture of controlled drugs, 1.62–
1.67
**Extravagant lifestyle**
possession with intent to supply, 6.58–
6.73

**Financial gain**
possession with intent to supply, 6.9–6.14
**Forensic analysis**
CPS guidance, 10.5
drugs, 10.5–10.17
introduction, 10.1–10.4
prohibited drugs
cocaine cases, 4.29–4.35
evidence not always required, 4.36–
4.40
generally, 4.20–4.28
traces of drugs, 10.5–10.17
**Forfeiture orders**
sentencing, 11.100–11.111
**'Forgetting'**
possession of controlled goods, 3.69–3.73
**Fraudulent evasion**
import and export of controlled good,
2.4–2.5

**Guilty plea**
  possession with intent to supply, 6.74–
    6.80

**Harm**
  import and export of controlled goods
    Class A drugs, 2.18
    generally, 2.17
  sentencing, 11.8–11.12
**Human rights**
  covert evidence, 10.22
  manufacture of controlled drugs, 1.56

**Importation of controlled drugs**
  actus reus, 2.27–2.44
  admissibility of evidence, 2.60–2.70
  Channel Tunnel, through, 2.9
  charges, 2.10–2.11
  Customs and Excise offences, 2.4–2.6
  double jeopardy, 2.13
  elements of offence
    actus reus, 2.27–2.44
    introduction, 2.22–2.23
    mens rea, 2.45–2.59
    s 170(1) and 170(2), 2.24–2.26
  enhancement
    Class A drugs, 2.15
    Class B drugs, 2.15
    Class C drugs, 2.16
  fraudulent evasion of prohibition, 2.4–2.5
  general prohibition, 2.4
  harm and culpability
    Class A drugs, 2.18
    generally, 2.17
  improper import of goods, 2.4–2.5
  introduction, 2.1–2.9
  'lifestyle offence', 2.21
  mens rea, 2.45–2.59
  offences, 2.4–2.6
  penalty
    enhancement, 2.15–2.16
    fraudulent evasion of duty, 2.6
    generally, 2.14
    harm and culpability, 2.17–2.18
    'lifestyle offence', 2.21
    non-exhaustive factors, 2.19–2.20
    'serious offence', 2.21
  pipeline, by, 2.8
  procedure, 2.12–2.21
  prohibition, 2.4

**Importation of controlled drugs** – *contd*
  psychoactive substances, 2.71–2.78
  s 170(1) and 170(2), 2.24–2.26
  sentencing
    generally, 11.21–11.38
    introduction, 2.14
  'serious offence', 2.21
  statutory framework, 2.1–2.6
  summary, 2.79
  terms of licence issued by Secretary of
    State, 2.2–2.3
  time limits, 2.12
**Intoxication**
  lack of knowledge, 4.89–4.94
**Investigatory powers**
  occupiers of premises
    enter and search, 7.26–7.27
    introduction, 7.25
    psychoactive substances, 7.32–7.46
    search and seizure, 7.28–7.31
**Involuntary possession**
  supply of controlled drugs, 5.59–5.62

**Joint possession**
  supply of controlled drugs, 5.73–5.84

**Knowledge**
  defences, and
    burden of proof, 4.72–4.79
    conspiracy offences, and, 4.95–4.96
    evidential burden, 4.80–4.88
    generally, 4.56–4.57
    parameters, 4.58–4.71
    self-induced intoxication, 4.89–4.94
    statutory provision, 4.57
  possession of controlled goods, 3.36–3.49

**Lack of knowledge**
  burden of proof, 4.72–4.79
  conspiracy offences, and, 4.95–4.96
  evidential burden, 4.80–4.88
  generally, 4.56–4.57
  parameters, 4.58–4.71
  self-induced intoxication, 4.89–4.94
  statutory provision, 4.57
**Lawful intention**
  generally, 4.50–4.55
**Lawful possession**
  controls, 4.121–4.123
  generally, 4.97–4.102

**Lawful possession** – *contd*
medical necessity, 4.107–4.120
psychoactive substances, 4.124–4.151
self-treatment, 4.103–4.106
statutory provision, 4.97–4.102
**Lawful supply**
possession with intent to supply, 6.89–
6.90
**'Legal highs'**
prohibited drugs, 4.6
**Legal professional privilege**
covert evidence, 10.21
**Licence issued by Secretary of State**
import and export of controlled goods,
2.2–2.3
**Lifestyle evidence**
possession with intent to supply
direction to jury, 6.71–6.73
generally, 6.58–6.70
**'Lifestyle offence'**
import and export of controlled goods,
2.21
possession with intent to supply, 6.2

**'Magic mushrooms'**
manufacture of controlled drugs, 1.23–
1.28
**Making an offer**
being 'concerned' in
construction, 5.118–5.129
generally, 5.114–5.117
Hughes definition, 5.122–5.129
introduction, 5.3
bogus offer to supply drug, 5.98–5.110
consumption, and, 5.117–5.119
generally, 5.88–5.91
introduction, 5.3
offer to supply drug believing it to be
controlled but supplies uncontrolled
substance, 5.94–5.97
offer to supply one drug but supplies
another, 5.92–5.93
proof of actual supply, 5.130–5.141
remains until either resiled form or been
completed, 5.111–5.116
**Manufacture of controlled drugs**
'any other method', 1.11
authorisation of activities otherwise
unlawful, 1.4
basis of restriction, 1.2

**Manufacture of controlled drugs** – *contd*
'certain drug precursors', 1.16
cultivation, 1.40–1.43
cultural practices, and, 1.61
defences available, 1.44–1.61
European Arrest Warrant, and, 1.63
extradition, and, 1.62–1.67
handling substances useful for, 1.10
human rights, and, 1.56
introduction, 1.1–1.17
'magic mushrooms', 1.23–1.28
medical necessity, 1.45–1.55
medicinal products, and, 1.18–1.22
observance of religious or cultural
practices, 1.61
policy, and, 1.8
possessing substances useful for, 1.10
'preparation', 1.24–1.39
'product', 1.23–1.39
'production', 1.9–1.14
purposive interpretation, 1.7
religious observance, and, 1.61
stripping cannabis plants, 1.12
summary, 1.68
temporary class drugs, 1.5–1.6
'to be concerned in', 1.3
**Medical necessity**
manufacture of controlled drugs, 1.45–
1.55
possession of controlled goods, 4.107–
4.120
**Medicinal products**
manufacture of controlled drugs, and,
1.18–1.22
**Memory**
possession of controlled goods, 3.69–3.73
**Mens rea**
conspiracy, 8.53–8.71
import and export of controlled goods,
2.45–2.59
possession of controlled goods, 3.36–3.49
**Mistake**
possession of controlled goods, 3.66–3.68
**Motive**
possession with intent to supply, 6.32–
6.36

**Observance of religious or cultural
practices**
manufacture of controlled drugs, 1.61

**Occupiers of premises**
anti-social behaviour orders, 7.50–7.53
being the occupier or concerned in
management of premises, 7.4–7.10
consumption of controlled drugs, 7.14
co-tenants, 7.11
criminal conduct, 7.1
definition, 7.1–7.2
degree of control, 7.3
enter and search powers
generally, 7.26–7.27
permitting premises to be used for
drug offending, 7.16
investigatory powers
enter and search, 7.26–7.27
introduction, 7.25
psychoactive substances, 7.32–7.46
search and seizure, 7.28–7.31
meaning, 7.1–7.2
overview, 7.1–7.3
permitting premises to be used for drug
offending
consumption of controlled drugs, 7.14
enter and search powers, 7.16
generally, 7.11–7.13
knowledge, 7.23–7.24
liability, 7.14–7.19
'permit', 7.23
'premises', 7.21–7.22
psychoactive substances, 7.15–7.16
production of controlled drugs, 7.14
psychoactive substances, 7.15–7.16
squatters, 7.12
stop and search powers, 7.1
'suffer', 7.24
supply of controlled drugs, 7.14
trespassers, 7.12
production of controlled drugs, 7.14
prohibition orders, 7.47–7.49
psychoactive substances
generally, 7.15–7.16
investigatory powers, 7.32–7.46
prohibition orders, 7.47–7.49
search and seizure powers
generally, 7.28–7.31
permitting premises to be used for
drug offending, 7.16
squatters, 7.12
stop and search powers, 7.16
summary, 7.54

**Occupiers of premises** – *contd*
supply of controlled drugs, 7.14
trespassers, 7.12
**Offer to consume**
supply of controlled drugs, 5.117–5.119
**Offering to supply**
being 'concerned' in
construction, 5.118–5.129
generally, 5.114–5.117
Hughes definition, 5.122–5.129
introduction, 5.3
bogus offer to supply drug, 5.98–5.110
consumption, and, 5.117–5.119
generally, 5.88–5.91
introduction, 5.3
offer to supply drug believing it to be
controlled but supplies uncontrolled
substance, 5.94–5.97
offer to supply one drug but supplies
another, 5.92–5.93
proof of actual supply, 5.130–5.141
remains until either resiled form or been
completed, 5.111–5.116
sentencing
Class A drugs, 11.39–11.46
Class B drugs, 11.47–11.49
Class C drugs, 11.50
cuckooing, 11.57–11.63
prevalence of supply, 11.51–11.56

**Penalties**
*See also* **Sentencing**
import and export of controlled goods
enhancement, 2.15–2.16
fraudulent evasion of duty, 2.6
generally, 11.21–11.38
harm and culpability, 2.17–2.18
introduction, 2.14
'lifestyle offence', 2.21
non-exhaustive factors, 2.19–2.20
'serious offence', 2.21
**Permitting premises to be used for
drug offending**
consumption of controlled drugs, 7.14
enter and search powers, 7.16
generally, 7.11–7.13
knowledge, 7.23–7.24
liability, 7.14–7.19
'permit', 7.23
'premises', 7.21–7.22

**Permitting premises to be used for drug offending** – *contd*
psychoactive substances, 7.15–7.16
production of controlled drugs, 7.14
psychoactive substances, 7.15–7.16
sentencing, 11.83–11.86
squatters, 7.12
stop and search powers, 7.16
'suffer', 7.24
supply of controlled drugs, 7.14
trespassers, 7.12

**Pharmaceutical description**
prohibited drugs, 4.4

**Physical transfer of control**
supply of controlled drugs
generally, 5.14–5.18
issue of prescription, 5.19–5.23

**Physical element**
import and export of controlled goods, 2.27–2.44
possession of controlled goods, 3.14–3.35

**Pipelines**
import and export of controlled goods, 2.8

**Possessing substances useful for manufacture**
controlled drugs, 1.10

**Possession of controlled drugs**
consumed drugs, 3.84–3.88
custody and/or control, 3.14–3.35
defences
generally, 4.48–4.49
lack of knowledge, 4.56–4.96
lawful intention, 4.50–4.55
lawful possession, 4.97–4.151
medical necessity, 4.107–4.120
summary, 4.152
elements of offence, 3.12–3.13
'forgetting' excuse, 3.69–3.73
generally, 3.6–3.11
imputing an intention, 3.53–3.62
intent to supply, with
*See also* **Possession with intent to supply**
aggravated supply, 6.71–6.88
different drug to that charged, 6.15–6.18
drugs not ready for harvest, 6.23–6.31
expert evidence on consumption patterns, 6.45–6.57
financial gain, 6.9–6.14

**Possession of controlled drugs** – *contd*
intent to supply, with – *contd*
generally, 6.1–6.2
guilty plea to possession, 6.74–6.80
lawful supply, 6.89–6.90
lifestyle evidence, 6.58–6.73
motive, 6.32–6.36
overview, 6.3–6.8
proof, 6.37
quantity of drug, 6.38–6.44
summary, 6.91
timing, 6.19–6.22
introduction, 3.1–3.5
knowledge, 3.36–3.49
lack of knowledge
burden of proof, 4.72–4.79
conspiracy offences, and, 4.95–4.96
evidential burden, 4.80–4.88
generally, 4.56–4.57
parameters, 4.58–4.71
self-induced intoxication, 4.89–4.94
statutory provision, 4.57
Lambert decision, 3.63–3.65
lawful intention, 4.50–4.55
lawful possession
controls, 4.121–4.123
generally, 4.97–4.102
medical necessity, 4.107–4.120
psychoactive substances, 4.124–4.151
lawful possession
self-treatment, 4.103–4.106
statutory provision, 4.97–4.102
McNamara decision, 3.50–3.52
mental element, 3.36–3.49
memory, and, 3.69–3.73
mistake as to drug possessed, 3.66–3.68
physical element, 3.14–3.35
prohibited drugs
admissions, 4.41–4.47
burden of proof, 4.20–4.40
categories, 4.3–4.5
cocaine cases, 4.29–4.35
'controlled drug', 4.2
forensic analysis, 4.20–4.40
introduction, 4.1
'legal highs', 4.6
pharmaceutical description, 4.4
psychoactive substances, 4.6
statutory framework, 4.2–4.5
temporary class drugs orders, 4.6–4.19

**Possession of controlled drugs** – *contd*
psychoactive substances, 4.124–4.151
quantity of drug, 3.74–3.83
sentencing, 11.87–11.89
statutory framework, 3.6–3.11
summary, 3.89
supply of controlled drugs, and, 5.4
temporary class drugs orders
commencement, 4.10
conditions, 4.8
criteria, 4.9
duration, 4.11
generally, 4.6–4.7
possession offences, and, 4.12–4.19
procedure, 4.8–4.11
search and detention powers, and,
4.14
Warner decision, 3.42–3.49
**Possession with intent to supply**
aggravated supply, 6.71–6.88
consumption patterns, 6.45–6.57
different drug to that charged, 6.15–
6.18
drugs not ready for harvest, 6.23–6.31
drugs paraphernalia, and, 6.58
elements, 6.3–6.8
expert evidence on consumption
patterns, 6.45–6.57
extravagant lifestyle, 6.58–6.73
financial gain, 6.9–6.14
future requirement, 6.5–6.6
generally, 6.1–6.2
guilty plea to possession, 6.74–6.80
identity of intended recipient, 6.7
introduction, 5.4
lawful supply, 6.89–6.90
lifestyle evidence
direction to jury, 6.71–6.73
generally, 6.58–6.70
lifestyle offence, as, 6.2
motive, 6.32–6.36
overview, 6.3–6.8
'possession', 6.4
proceeds of crime, 6.2
proof, 6.37
quantity of drug, 6.38–6.44
'social' supply, 6.8
statutory framework, 6.1–6.2
summary, 6.91
timing of supply, 6.19–6.22

**Premises**
*See also* **Occupiers of premises**
overview, 7.1–7.3
permitting to be used for drug offending
consumption of controlled drugs, 7.14
enter and search powers, 7.16
generally, 7.11–7.13
knowledge, 7.23–7.24
liability, 7.14–7.19
'permit', 7.23
'premises', 7.21–7.22
psychoactive substances, 7.15–7.16
production of controlled drugs, 7.14
psychoactive substances, 7.15–7.16
squatters, 7.12
stop and search powers, 7.1
'suffer', 7.24
supply of controlled drugs, 7.14
trespassers, 7.12
summary, 7.54
**'Preparation'**
manufacture of controlled drugs, 1.24–
1.39
**Prescriptions**
supply of controlled drugs, 5.19–5.23
**Proceeds of crime**
import and export of controlled goods,
2.21
possession with intent to supply, 6.2
**'Product'**
manufacture of controlled drugs, 1.23–
1.39
**Production of controlled drugs**
*See also* **Manufacture of controlled
drugs**
generally, 1.9–1.14
permitting premises to be used for drug
offending, 7.14
sentencing, 11.64–11.82
**Prohibited drugs**
admissions, 4.41–4.47
burden of proof, 4.20–4.40
categories, 4.3–4.5
cocaine cases, 4.29–4.35
'controlled drug', 4.2
forensic analysis, 4.20–4.40
introduction, 4.1
'legal highs', 4.6
pharmaceutical description, 4.4
psychoactive substances, 4.6

**Prohibited drugs** – *contd*
statutory framework, 4.2–4.5
temporary class drugs orders
commencement, 4.10
conditions, 4.8
criteria, 4.9
duration, 4.11
generally, 4.6–4.7
possession offences, and, 4.12–4.19
procedure, 4.8–4.11
search and detention powers, and, 4.14
**Prohibition orders**
occupiers of premises, 7.47–7.49
**Psychoactive substances**
import and export of controlled goods,
2.71–2.78
occupiers of premises
generally, 7.15–7.16
investigatory powers, 7.32–7.46
prohibition orders, 7.47–7.49
prohibited drugs, 4.6
sentencing, 11.95–11.98

**Quantity of drug**
possession of controlled goods, 3.74–3.83
possession with intent to supply, 6.38–
6.44
supply of controlled drugs, 5.7

**Religious observance**
manufacture of controlled drugs, 1.61
**Restraint orders**
application, 12.17
before charge, 12.8
conditions, 12.7
effect, 12.29
format, 12.16
generally, 12.6
human rights, 12.27
legal aid, and, 12.21–12.33
legal expenses, 12.20
living expenses,. 12.18–12.19
post charge, 12.9–12.10
post conviction, 12.11–12.15
purpose, 12.6
risk of dissipation of assets, 12.28
terms, 12.18
timing, 12.7
**Return of drugs by custodian**
supply of controlled drugs, 5.43–5.50

**Search and detention**
temporary class drugs orders, and, 4.14
**Search and seizure**
CJPA 2001, under, 9.1
conduct of search, 9.17–9.18
detention of person, 9.20–9.21
drugs offences, and, 9.7–9.15
forfeiture of seized property, 9.36–9.40
lawfulness, 9.3
obstruction of searches, 9.22–9.27
occupiers of premises
generally, 7.28–7.31
permitting premises to be used for
drug offending, 7.16
PACE Code, 9.4
powers, 9.1–9.21
'reasonable suspicion', 9.4
return of seized property, 9.28–9.35
statutory provision, 9.1–9.2
stop and search persons and vehicles, 9.1
summary, 9.41
temporary class drugs, and, 4.14, 9.8
unlawful searches, 9.16–9.19
**Self-induced intoxication**
lack of knowledge, 4.89–4.94
**Sentencing**
ancillary orders
confiscation, 11.99
forfeiture, 11.100–11.111
class of controlled drug, 11.12
confiscation orders, 11.99
conspiracy offences, 11.13–11.20
cuckooing, 11.57–11.63
culpability of offender, 11.6–11.7
cultivation of controlled goods, 11.64–
11.82
factors
class of controlled drug, 11.12
culpability of offender, 11.6–11.7
introduction, 11.5
harm caused, 11.8–11.12
forfeiture orders, 11.100–11.111
Guideline
application, 11.4–11.20
class of controlled drug, 11.5
coverage, 11.3
culpability of offender, 11.6–11.7
factors, 11.5–11.12
harm caused, 11.8–11.12
introduction, 11.1–11.3

**Sentencing** – *contd*
  Guideline – *contd*
    status, 11.2
  harm caused, 11.8–11.12
  import and export of controlled goods
    enhancement, 2.15–2.16
    fraudulent evasion of duty, 2.6
    generally, 11.21–11.38
    harm and culpability, 2.17–2.18
    introduction, 2.14
    'lifestyle offence', 2.21
    non-exhaustive factors, 2.19–2.20
    'serious offence', 2.21
  possession of controlled goods, 11.87–
    11.89
  production of controlled goods, 11.64–
    11.82
  psychoactive substances, 11.95–11.98
  putting premises to be used for
    consumption of drugs, 11.83–11.86
  service personnel, 11.90–11.94
  summary, 11.112
  supply of controlled goods
    Class A drugs, 11.39–11.46
    Class B drugs, 11.47–11.49
    Class C drugs, 11.50
    cuckooing, 11.57–11.63
    prevalence of supply, 11.51–11.56
**'Serious offence'**
  import and export of controlled goods,
    2.21
**Service personnel**
  sentencing, 11.90–11.94
**'Social' situations**
  possession with intent to supply, 6.8
  supply of controlled drugs, 5.8
**Squatters**
  permitting premises to be used for drug
    offending, 7.12
**Stop and search powers**
  permitting premises to be used for drug
    offending, 7.16
**Stripping cannabis plants**
  manufacture of controlled drugs, 1.12
**Supply of controlled drugs**
  administering drugs, 5.85–5.87
  another, to, 5.142
  being 'concerned' in making offer to
    supply
    construction, 5.118–5.129

**Supply of controlled drugs** – *contd*
  being 'concerned' in making offer to
      supply – *contd*
    generally, 5.114–5.117
    Hughes definition, 5.122–5.129
    introduction, 5.3
  being 'concerned' in supply
    construction, 5.118–5.129
    generally, 5.114–5.117
    Hughes definition, 5.122–5.129
    introduction, 5.3
  benefit of recipient, 5.24–5.33
  bogus offer to supply drug, 5.98–5.110
  consumption, and, 5.117–5.119
  'distributing'
    generally, 5.71–5.72
    introduction, 5.9
    joint possession, 5.73–5.84
  for purposes of recipient, 5.24–5.33
  generally, 5.1–5.6
  involuntary possession, 5.59–5.62
  issue of prescription, 5.19–5.23
  joint possession, 5.73–5.84
  making an offer
    being 'concerned' in, 5.114–5.129
    bogus offer to supply drug, 5.98–5.110
    consumption, and, 5.117–5.119
    generally, 5.88–5.91
    introduction, 5.3
    offer to supply drug believing it
        to be controlled but supplies
        uncontrolled substance, 5.94–5.97
    offer to supply one drug but supplies
        another, 5.92–5.93
    proof of actual supply, 5.130–5.141
    remains until either resiled form or
        been completed, 5.111–5.116
  meaning
    benefit of recipient, 5.24–5.33
    for purposes of recipient, 5.24–5.33
    Maginnis decision, 5.51–5.58
    physical transfer of control, 5.14–5.23
    return of drugs by custodian, 5.43–5.50
    transfer to custodian or courier,
        5.34–5.42
  offences, 5.3–5.5
  offer to consume, 5.117–5.119
  offering to supply
    bogus offer to supply drug, 5.98–5.110
    consumption, and, 5.117–5.119

**Supply of controlled drugs** – *contd*
  offering to supply – *contd*
    generally, 5.88–5.91
    introduction, 5.3
    offer to supply drug believing it
      to be controlled but supplies
      uncontrolled substance, 5.94–5.97
    offer to supply one drug but supplies
      another, 5.92–5.93
    proof of actual supply, 5.130–5.141
    remains until either resiled form or
      been completed, 5.111–5.116
  overview, 5.7–5.13
  permitting premises to be used for drug
    offending, 7.14
  physical transfer of control
    generally, 5.14–5.18
    issue of prescription, 5.19–5.23
  possession with 'an intention' of supply
    *See also* **Possession with intent to
      supply**
    aggravated supply, 6.71–6.88
    different drug to that charged, 6.15–
      6.18
    drugs not ready for harvest, 6.23–
      6.31
    expert evidence on consumption
      patterns, 6.45–6.57
    financial gain, 6.9–6.14
    generally, 6.1–6.2
    guilty plea to possession, 6.74–6.80
    introduction, 5.4
    lawful supply, 6.89–6.90
    lifestyle evidence, 6.58–6.73
    motive, 6.32–6.36
    overview, 6.3–6.8
    proof, 6.37
    quantity of drug, 6.38–6.44
    summary, 6.91
    timing, 6.19–6.22
  prescriptions, 5.19–5.23
  proof of actual supply, 5.130–5.141
  quantity of drugs, 5.7
  return of drugs by custodian, 5.43–5.50
  sentencing
    Class A drugs, 11.39–11.46
    Class B drugs, 11.47–11.49
    Class C drugs, 11.50
    cuckooing, 11.57–11.63
    prevalence of supply, 11.51–11.56

**Supply of controlled drugs** – *contd*
  'social' supply, 5.8
  statutory framework, 5.1–5.4
  summary, 5.143
  temporary safekeeping, 5.34–5.35
  territorial restrictions, 5.63–5.70
  transfer to custodian or courier, 5.34–
    5.42

**Temporary class drugs orders**
  commencement, 4.10
  conditions, 4.8
  criteria, 4.9
  duration, 4.11
  generally, 4.6–4.7
  manufacture of controlled drugs, and,
    1.5–1.6
  possession offences, and, 4.12–4.19
  procedure, 4.8–4.11
  search and detention powers, and, 4.14,
    9.8
**Temporary safekeeping**
  supply of controlled drugs, 5.34–5.35
**Terms of licence issued by Secretary
  of State**
  import and export of controlled goods,
    2.2–2.3
**Test purchases**
  covert evidence, 10.40
**Time limits**
  import and export of controlled goods,
    2.12
**'To be concerned in'**
  manufacture of controlled drugs, 1.3
**Transfer to custodian or courier**
  supply of controlled drugs, 5.34–5.42
**Trespassers**
  permitting premises to be used for drug
    offending, 7.12

**Undercover police**
  covert evidence, 10.38–10.44
**Unlawful possession of controlled
  drugs**
  consumed drugs, 3.84–3.88
  custody and/or control, 3.14–3.35
  elements of offence, 3.12–3.13
  'forgetting' excuse, 3.69–3.73
  generally, 3.6–3.11
  imputing an intention, 3.53–3.62

**Unlawful possession of controlled drugs** – *contd*
introduction, 3.1–3.5
knowledge, 3.36–3.49
Lambert decision, 3.63–3.65
McNamara decision, 3.50–3.52
mental element, 3.36–3.49
memory, and, 3.69–3.73

**Unlawful possession of controlled drugs** – *contd*
mistake as to drug possessed, 3.66–3.68
physical element, 3.14–3.35
quantity of drug, 3.74–3.83
statutory framework, 3.6–3.11
summary, 3.89
Warner decision, 3.42–3.49

# DOUGHTY STREET CHAMBERS

doughty street chambers

Since its foundation in 1990, Doughty Street Chambers and its barristers have taken as their guiding principle the use of the law for the advancement of the protection of human rights and civil liberties. It is now amongst the very largest and most wide-ranging civil liberties practices in the world, providing specialist advice, advocacy and training in the UK and around the world. Their practice areas include crime and criminal appeals, international crime (such as war crimes), fraud and financial services regulation, extradition, prisoners' rights, actions against the police, immigration, media law, professional regulation, social welfare and housing, clinical negligence and more.

The Criminal Team is the largest practice group at Doughty Street Chambers, comprising almost half the total number of barristers at the set. Its members have long-standing experience of defending in many of the most serious and complex criminal trials, appeals and extradition cases to come before the UK Supreme Court, Privy Council, Court of Appeal, and High Court, as well as their daily work in the Crown and Magistrates' Courts. Abroad they appear in the courts of Northern Ireland, Hong Kong, Singapore, the Caribbean, South America, the International Criminal Court and the European Court of Human Rights.

Authors from Doughty Street:

### Tim Moloney QC

Tim has consistently acted in high profile cases involving allegations of homicide, fraud, terrorism and general crime including sexual offences. He also has extensive experience of all levels of appellate advocacy including in both the House of Lords and the Supreme Court. He has acted in a number of criminal law related judicial reviews and has substantial experience in extradition proceedings. Tim also advises high profile organisations on their exposure to involvement with acts of terrorism and is regularly involved in training of lawyers overseas in the law and practice relating to terrorism.

### Tom Stevens

Tom is a specialist criminal defence barrister with extensive experience of both Crown Court and appellate advocacy, instructed in cases ranging from homicide and complex fraud to serious sexual offences and high-level drug conspiracies. Tom also has particular expertise within the field of professional discipline and regulatory law, frequently appearing before a wide range of healthcare tribunals including the GDC, NMC and HCPC.

## Paul Mason

Paul specialises in defending serious criminal offences. His practice encompasses media law and public law also. Before coming to the Bar, Paul worked in the Public Law team at the Law Commission and was previously a Senior Lecturer at Cardiff University where he published extensively in law, criminology and politics.

## Abigail Bright

Abigail has a significant profile in fraud, financial crime, and extradition. She has expertise in statutory and non-statutory public inquiries, having been appointed counsel to the Inquiry to both kinds of inquiry. In 2016, Abigail was appointed counsel to the Inquiry, Undercover Policing Inquiry, a statutory public inquiry, instructed by Government Legal Service. Also in 2016, she was appointed counsel to the Inquiry, Independent Inquiry into Child Sexual Abuse, re the investigation into the late Baron Janner of Braunstone QC, a statutory public inquiry, instructed by Fieldfisher. In 2011, Abigail was appointed noting counsel to the Inquiry, the Mid Staffordshire NHS Foundation Trust Public Inquiry, a non-statutory public inquiry, instructed by the Department of Health.

## Harriet Johnson

Harriet is a specialist defence barrister who practices exclusively in cases featuring the most serious criminal allegations. She has particular experience in complex cases, including murder, and multi-handed drugs and fraud conspiracies.

# BIRDS SOLICITORS

Since its formation in 2000, Birds Solicitors has established itself as one of the foremost criminal defence firms in the country, undertaking a mixture of criminal defence work ranging from minor offences to the most serious allegations that an individual can face.

The firm represents clients from the police station to the Magistrates Court, the Crown Court and into the Appellate Courts. A large proportion of the work is carried out under the various legal aid schemes.

Birds Solicitors has expertise stretching back three decades and is regularly instructed in serious drugs cases, murder, serious fraud, money laundering and Proceeds of Crime cases. The firm has a specialist appeals department advising clients on appealing convictions out of time, on applications to the Criminal Cases Review Commission and on compensation for miscarriages of justice claims.

In addition, Birds Solicitors is known specifically for its work with victims of human trafficking and challenging the convictions of those let down by the criminal justice system and not identified as trafficking victims at the time of their criminal proceedings at first instance.

The firm also has expertise in regulatory matters and has been involved in a number of the largest fraud and regulatory cases and enquiries of the last decade including LIBOR, Operation Elveden, the MPs expenses enquiry and the two largest insider FCA prosecuted dealing cases: Operations Saturn and Tabernula.

Birds Solicitors is highly recommended in both the Legal 500 and Chambers & Partners directories as one of the top firms in London for criminal and fraud work. Both Steven Bird and Tim Greene are highly recommended in Chambers & Partners as individuals and Steven Bird is also listed as a leading individual in the Legal 500.

Steven Bird has been involved in drugs cases since 1988 and was a volunteer adviser on the Release advice line for many years. He regularly deals with confiscation cases under the Proceeds of Crime Act 2002 in matters where he did not act at trial whether the index offences be drugs offences, frauds or other serious offences attracting possible confiscation of assets. He has lectured on confiscation in drugs cases.